CAMERA OBTRUSA

THE ACTION DOCUMENTARIES OF HARA KAZUO

CAMERA OBTRUSA

THE ACTION DOCUMENTARIES OF HARA KAZUO

Foreword by **Abé Mark Nornes**
Translated by **Pat Noonan** and **Takuo Yasuda**

KAYA PRESS
NEW YORK, NY

CAMERA OBTRUSA: THE ACTION DOCUMENTARIES OF HARA KAZUO

Originally published in Japan as:
Fumikoeru Kamera: Waga Hōhō, Akushon Dokyumentarii by Film Art

Yukiyukite Shingun: Seisaku Nōto+Sairoku Shinario by Hanashi no Tokushu Henshushitsu

13 12 11 10 09 5 4 3 2 1

Kaya Press (Muae Publishing, Inc.)
www.kaya.com

Cover design and artwork by spoon+fork

Manufactured in the United States of America

Distributed by D.A.P./Distributed Art Publishers
155 Avenue of the Americas, 2nd Floor
New York, NY 10013
800.338.BOOK, www.artbook.com

ISBN: 978 - 1 - 885030 - 44 - 3
Library of Congress Control Number: 2009925441

This publication is made possible by support from the National Endowment for the Arts and public funds from the New York State Council on the Arts, a state agency. Additional funding was provided by the Department of East Asian Languages & Cultures at the University of California, Berkeley, and the generous contributions of Jim K. Chu, Qing Lan Huang, Keesoo & Jisun Huh, ICEC, Bill Lee & Corey Ohama, Whakyung & Hong Yung Lee, Min Song, Duncan Williams, and others.

Kaya Press would also like to thank Kyung Hyun Kim and Akira Lippit for introducing us to Hara Kazuo and Kobayashi Sachiko; Pat Noonan for his hard work on and Takuo Yasuda for his intrepid dedication to this difficult translation; Abé Mark Nornes for his essay; our talented and patient designers, Chez Bryan Ong and Jennifer Chou at spoon+fork, for their brilliant work; Zach Braun for his generous technical expertise; Alan Tansman for his support of this project; Matt Fargo, for his title suggestion; Jane Kim for her keen editorial eye; Claire Light for her encouragement; and Patricia Wakida for her willingness to step in when necessary and make things happen.

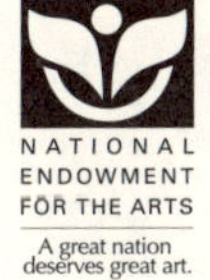

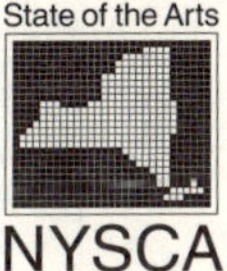

Note: Throughout the book, Japanese names appear according to Japanese custom, with last names first.

TABLE OF CONTENTS

03 The Healthy vs. The Disabled: *Goodbye CP*

04 Man vs. Woman: *Extreme Private Eros: Love Song 1974*

05 The Film that Summoned God: *The Emperor's Naked Army Marches On*

06 A Fictional Person, A Fictional Era: *A Dedicated Life*

The Emperor's Naked Army Marches On: Production Notes

The Obtrusive and Bewildering Cinema of Hara Kazuo[1]

ABÉ MARK NORNES

As is the case with most non-Japanese viewers, my introduction to Hara Kazuo's work was the explosive *Emperor's Naked Army Marches On,* which I caught at a festival in Los Angeles. I was already an admirer of Japanese cinema, and this was my first Japanese documentary—an initial step into a world that would soon become a passion.

A short but notorious article in *American Film* had brought the film to my attention.[2] The author memorably wrote that the film "swathes the gradual disclosure of a wartime atrocity in the mysteries of Japanese social decorum." This was enough to pique my interest. Unfortunately, the critic followed this provocative description with the cardinal sin of criticism—he gave away the film's dreadful secret (jump to the next paragraph if you have yet to see this remarkable film): "Three weeks after the Japanese surrender," he wrote, "one unit of the 36th Corps executed several privates for their officers to eat."

Needless to say, the screening was one of those riveting experiences of cinema where the film leaves its audience thoroughly stunned. *Speed Racer* had been my first Japanese TV show, *Godzilla* my first Japanese movie, and *The Emperor's Naked Army Marches On* my first Japanese documentary. All had made an impression, but the last was the experience that changed the course of my life.

I met Hara Kazuo and his wife and producer Kobayashi Sachiko, in the dead of an Iowa winter in 1992. The University of Iowa was holding a conference on Japanese film, and Hara was the honored guest. I was living in Japan, and Hara was on a year-long fellowship in New York. After covering that much ground, our conversation took a somber turn. Documentary filmmaker Ogawa Shinsuke had just passed away, and I had come to the conference directly from the tsuya or wake, an alcohol-fueled Japanese tradition where friends and family stay up all night with the corpse before its cremation. Hara was curious how it had gone, who had come, and especially who had stayed up all night. What a shock, what a pity, we agreed. And we turned to happier topics.

Hara was very much the center of attention at this gathering, and I don't

---

1 Having said my piece on the matter of Hara Kazuo elsewhere, I would like to introduce this director from a more personal perspective. [Nornes, Abé Mark. "Private Reality," in *Identity Replays: Realism and Cinema,* ed. Ivonne Margulies (Duke University Press, 2003), 145-163; also "The Postwar Documentary Trace: *Groping in the Dark,*" in *Open to the Public: Studies in Japan's Recent Past,* ed. Leslie Pincus, a special issue of *Positions* 10.1 (Spring 2002): 39-78.]

2 Hoberman, J. "*The Emperor's Naked Army Marches On,*" *American Film: A Journal of the Film and Television Arts* (March 13, 1988): 11.

know if he gave Ogawa's death another thought. In contrast, I was reeling. I had arrived hoping to escape my grief with the distractions of academia; instead, my encounter with Hara turned my grief academic. It got me thinking about the history of Japanese documentary. Ogawa's sudden death at age 56 had sent a shockwave through the Japanese film community, catching everyone by surprise. The independent documentarians who had achieved prominence in the 1960s were forced to confront mortality, while their fans were abruptly faced with generational difference. Ogawa's generation was passing; indeed, they were making fewer and fewer films. Who would be coming up behind them? Who would be leading the charge?

Hara Kazuo, no doubt. This was what I found myself thinking as he took the stage in Iowa. The landscape of Japanese documentary had experienced something of a convulsion, and I was looking at its new center—or at least its hopeful future.

Needless to say, I kept a close eye on Hara Kazuo after this. We would bump into each other at festivals, or try to catch up over occasional beers in Shinjuku. He made new films, and worked hard to nurture the generation of documentary filmmakers emerging behind him (perhaps a dig at the legacy of Ogawa Shinsuke, who only gave lip service to mentorship).

Yet Hara always expressed great frustration with his students. As one gathers from *Camera Obtrusa*, he forged his own approach to documentary in reaction to Ogawa's generation; but they still deeply informed his values. I think he saw himself as a bridge between past and future generations, pouring enormous energy into his "Cinema Cram School [Cinema Juku]." Much to his chagrin, his pupils just didn't seem to get it.

As a historian, I always found it fruitful to explore the differences between these successive generations in order to learn about the nature and possibilities of documentary—whether in Japan or elsewhere. Indeed, the example of Hara proved useful for my approach to postwar Japanese documentary in *Forest of Pressure*.[3]

However, I learned more about Hara himself by comparing him to a U.S. compatriot. This was around the time *Fahrenheit 911* arrived in Japan, making quite a splash. During one of our Shinjuku reunions, Hara and I chatted about the film, our respective memories of the attacks, and our very different experiences of the world that had been left in its wake. Starting with his initial election, every move George W. Bush made had left me feeling bruised and battered. *Fahrenheit 911* was energizing; it pumped me up for the 2004 election (at which point I felt bashed down once again). Hara, typically, was somewhat bemused, and the film had left him with many questions. Good ones at that.

3 Nornes, Abé Mark. *Forest of Pressure: Ogawa Shinsuke and Postwar Japanese Documentary* (Minneapolis: University of Minnesota Press, 2007).

He mentioned an intriguing rumor, something he had picked up at a film festival. It seemed Michael Moore admired his work.

Somehow this was no surprise. Both filmmakers pull the swirling chaos of history into orbit around their peculiar points of view. They step into—obtrude into—history, cameras a-whirring, to see what happens. Their films are records of meetings, interventions by personalities that easily engage or enrage people—both of which responses are always revelatory. Moore may have a stronger onscreen persona, but the presence of both Moore and Hara in the texture of their films is equally palpable. And both have a knack for uncovering things that would otherwise have remained lost to history. Or for provoking things that disclose the past and present world in all its complexity. At the same time, the two seem so utterly different.

Our discussion made Hara want to meet his American colleague, and I suggested that this was something I might be able to arrange. After all, Moore is a proud native of Michigan, and had shown his work to my film students at the University of Michigan. I contacted Moore, and was pleasantly surprised at his response. Although horribly busy with post-production on *Sicko*, he was ready to drop everything for a chance to meet Hara Kazuo.

When they finally appeared on-stage at the Michigan Theater, Ann Arbor's stunning silent movie palace, we found out why Moore had been so quick to accept our invitation. This is how Moore described his discovery of Hara's work:

> I was two-thirds of the way through post-production for *Roger and Me*, editing the film just four blocks from the White House and five blocks from the Kennedy Center. They were playing a film that night called *The Emperor's Naked Army Marches On*. I thought that was such a bizarre title for a film. Not that I had an interest in naked armies or anything—I just really wanted to get out of the editing room.
>
> So I walked over there and sat down, and I was riveted for two hours. First, as a lover of movies, but also it was like I had this soul brother in Japan. I don't know if I'd say he was doing a similar thing, but certainly he was using this documentary art form in a way that was very different from Discovery Channel-type fare. I remember walking back that night: I was inspired, I was exhilarated. I had never seen anything like this. I had truly never seen this… I mean it's lonely out there being a regular feature on Fox News, and

> anytime I can be made to feel like the conservative one, I'll take it...
>
> Hara was grappling with how to do a documentary in an unconventional way that didn't numb people... To have a kindred spirit, to have someone who has inspired me very early on, and did that completely unbeknownst to himself. I felt after watching that film that I had permission—I gave myself permission—to make *Roger and Me* the way I was making it.[4]

For the next couple of hours, Moore and Hara hashed it out. Exploring each other's work, they simultaneously revealed volumes about themselves. Their many points of convergence clearly made them kindred spirits. At the same time, they were quite different. The following exchange was particularly illuminating:

> Hara: For any filmmaker, on top of money, you need a certain energy that sustains you through the arduous process of making a film. I've read in various interviews and books by you that you're often sustained by the anger you have. But I believe you need something underneath that. In my case, what sustains me is the question mark I have about myself. There is something unknown within me that leads me to unfamiliar places, and perhaps I'm afraid of that. But I do have a very strong desire to find out what that is, and when I make a documentary film, I'm not doing it for social justice, or to organize the masses, or to expound some theme, or anything except finding out that question mark within me. Therefore, although I use my camera to shoot my subjects, I'm also carrying the camera toward the inside of myself, and going further and deeper within. Do you do anything like that?
>
> Moore: I actually disagree with you in terms of the anger. I worry that my anger is actually disruptive to myself, to me personally. You said that anger sustains me, but I think it's

4 The entire discussion was published in "Dokyumentarii to wa Nani na no ka: Maikeru Mōa X Hara Kazuo," *Tsukuru* (September/October 2007): the subsequent text is a revision of my "X-Treme Private Documentary: Michael Moore and Kazuo Hara," *International Institute* (Fall 2007): 9.

> really my optimistic, hopeful belief that people are good to the core. And to keep one's sense of humor in dark times is a very important thing to do. To keep your soul from collapsing from the anger and the despair that exists... as a filmmaker, I set out to make these films, first and foremost, to express myself artistically, and I always put the art before the politics. Because if you put politics first, you end up, at least in film, with a pretty crappy movie that nobody wants to see.

As this short dialogue suggests, the audience at the Michigan Theater witnessed two of the world's best documentary filmmakers trying to figure each other out. Part of that process involved comparing what they thought about the other with what they understood about themselves. It seemed as though they felt like kindred spirits because of their inclination to interfere with the reality before the camera, and also from their formative experiences in the turbulent 1960s and 1970s.

However, this seeming historical simultaneity is in fact more likely a point of departure, as the situations in Japan and America from that era differed in some very fundamental ways. Moore essentially picked up on the political spirit of the era and forged ahead with a cinematic path that paired the first person point-of-view with his now signature use of humor and irony. In contrast, Hara began making films at a time when the student movement in Japan had devolved into shocking violence and feelings of despair and failure. This helps explain why he prefers not to see himself connected to social movements, even while making profoundly political films.

This difference was palpable when an audience member asked about the representation of bodies in documentaries, an interesting question considering Hara's innovative films about cerebral palsy, sex, and war, and Moore's new film on the healthcare crisis. Moore prefaced his answer with a joke—"*Sicko* has the first nudity I have ever put in a film, and I just got my rating back from the ratings board, and it's my first PG-13. And it's male nudity, too!" Then he struggled to answer the question. He seemed much more comfortable discussing the challenges of creatively rendering recent history, politics, and the struggles of everyday life.

On the other hand, Hara used the question to think about his relationship to Moore, stating:

> This gets to the major difference, as I see it, between Michael's works and mine. What I try to do in documentary

> films is really to work towards the emotions of the people in the audience, to energize them. Michael does this through his words, and I think I do it through bodies. I like to leave people in the audience aching and itching in their desire to do something with their bodies after seeing my films. I would like to kidnap their bodies in that way.

On this note, both directors left the stage, and the bodies in the audience were then "kidnapped," just as I had been snatched away fifteen years before, by a screening of *The Emperor's Naked Army Marches On*.

This sense of abduction is predicated on a bewildered spectatorship. One can see this effect in the dazed faces revealed when the theater lights turn back on. Hara's films have always inspired a strong desire to learn more, to figure out what exactly is going on in these films, and the puzzling ways they work on one's body and soul. The publication of *Camera Obtrusa* will go far in sating this hunger to know more, helping Hara's bewildered spectators understand what they are to do next.

Notes on Translation

Hara Kazuo stands among the most controversial directors in the history of documentary filmmaking. Best known for the award-winning *The Emperor's Naked Army Marches On*, a film about repressed guilt and war responsibility in Japan, Hara is notorious for methods that are as provocative as the content of his films. His passion lies in transgressing the limits of the medium of documentary film, and in a forthright, often painfully intense examination of guilt, responsibility, and taboos. In pioneering this method, he has attracted the acclaim of artists and critics from around the world.

Documentary filmmaking, for Hara Kazuo, is an act of communication between himself and his subjects. As audiences of his films have come to see, Hara's filmmaking—his means of interacting with those he films—involves, and even requires, conflict. With his camera, Hara confronts his subjects to reveal what he calls the "shameful parts" that they (and he) hide from themselves and the world.

In *Goodbye CP*, we see Hara force Yokotoa Hiroshi, the leader of an association of people with cerebral palsy, to confront the humiliation he feels for his crippled body. In *Extreme Private Eros: Love Song 1974*, Hara exposes the pain and jealousy that underlie his relationship with his ex-wife, Takeda Miyuki. And in *The Emperor's Naked Army Marches On*, through his protagonist Okuzaki Kenzō, Hara forces ex-soldiers to admit to their role in shocking atrocities.

In this book, the first full-length English-language translation of Hara's writings about his work, Hara does to himself what he has done to the people he has filmed: he transcends the conventional boundaries separating personal from public life and "steps into" the realm of private thoughts and experiences. Hara explains how he uses his camera to create a type of "action" that entertains while forcing his subjects to expose societal and historical truths they would rather ignore. Similarly, in this book, he uses language to reveal to us what documentary filmmaking has taught him about himself.

The present volume actually comprises two books, which were originally published separately in Japan: *Camera Obtrusa* [originally *Fumikoeru Kamera*] and *The Emperor's Naked Army Marches On: Production Notes*. The first selection, *Camera Obtrusa*, is an autobiography of sorts, a lengthy monologue formed by transcribed and edited interviews conducted by Ishizaka Kenji and Izuchi Kishū. The original transcriptions retain the pauses, repetitions, and digressions that characterize Hara's speech when he searches for the details of particular events, or recalls emotionally troubling incidents. In this translation, we have attempted to render into English the candid tone of the original, and the moments when

Hara himself struggles to find language to express the thoughts, emotions, and events that define his private life.

Following a short introductory chapter and an account of Hara's childhood, *Camera Obtrusa* continues through four more chapters, each titled according to the four major films he produced between 1972 and 1994 (the original Japanese book was published in 1995). As Hara describes his method for producing each of these films, he also reveals the personal delights and traumas that he experienced while creating them. Each film constitutes a stage in his artistic and personal development.

In *The Emperor's Naked Army: Production Notes,* Hara goes into a more detailed candid recounting of the internal struggles and discoveries he experienced making that particular film. As he explains in his introduction, he intended these notes to document what he was unable to capture during production, or could not include in the film. Here, Hara narrates in detail nearly every event in the filmmaking process, from the moment he first became interested in shooting the film, until its eventual, harrowing completion. Interspersed throughout are shorthand notes kept during this process that display his technical and personal difficulties working with the film's protagonist, Okuzaki Kenzō. Throughout, we have tried to remain true to Hara's informal tone, rendering any shorthand notes in their closest English equivalent. Of particular interest to those familiar with this film will be Part 2 of this book, where Hara describes the crew's ill-fated venture to New Guinea, which never made it into the final cut.

Production Notes and *Camera Obtrusa* present Hara's private experiences, but they also bespeak collective, social ones. Through Hara's childhood with his mother, we see the struggles of working-class single mothers of that era. His experiences working with and filming people with cerebral palsy expose society's attempts to marginalize the disabled. In his account of his life with his ex-wife Takeda Miyuki, he explores the conflicts between personal sentiment and the ideological commitments that Hara believes defined his generation, the 1970s. His time in the film and television industries shows us what many have described as a decline in the political potential of the documentary form from the 1960s to the present.

Hara has spent his career exploring through film the private lives of individuals. His book explores his own private life and convictions, a process that exposes and documents the social and institutional structures that lurk out of sight yet define us all. *Camera Obtrusa: The Action Documentaries of Hara Kazuo* chronicles Hara's own account of coming to recognize and overcome those structures within himself.

—Pat Noonan

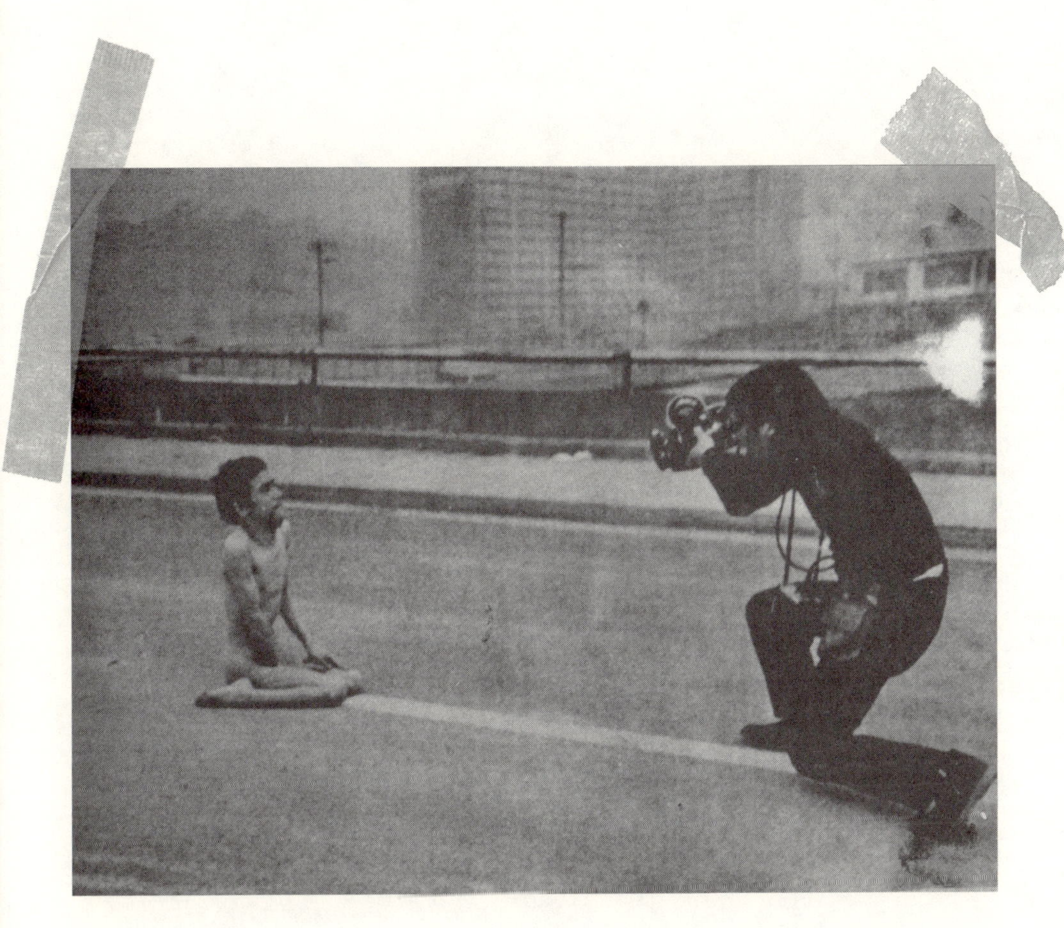

01 My Method

INVADING THE REALM OF PRIVACY

We all have this notion of privacy: privacy as something that protects us from society and state power. I don't object in any way to the idea of privacy being protected by law; it's something I accept. But I think a significant contradiction lies somewhere in the common notion of privacy that we carry within ourselves. We are fundamentally aware of this contradiction, so whenever we try to express ourselves, we feel that we have no choice but to push past it, to confront it.

What I mean is this: even though we might speak about privacy in terms of an individual's values or sensibilities, if I look more closely at the way each individual experiences the world—their feelings—I'm led to believe that those very values, those different ways of sensing the world, contain an institutionalized, and thus self-contradictory, element. So when I take up my camera to try to challenge those institutionalized elements, I must aim it at the world of feelings within individuals. As a result—or as a necessary consequence—I have no choice but to cross into the realm of privacy.

While working with Okuzaki Kenzō on *The Emperor's Naked Army Marches On,* I asked, just in case, if he wanted me to contact the soldiers we were about to visit.[1] When he told me not to—saying dismissively that the soldiers would just try to avoid us if I did—I at least tried to think about how to prepare. And I'm not saying this to blame everything on Mr. Okuzaki; it wasn't hard to guess that we'd be criticized for the way we were going to do those shoots.

So you could say that we filmed knowing what the consequences would be, and were determined to accept them. I thought that no matter how often Okuzaki, the crew, and I quarreled over our

1 Throughout *The Emperor's Naked Army Marches On*, Okuzaki, a former soldier who fought in the Pacific theater in World War II, barges in unannounced on his former army commanders and comrades, demanding that they admit to and take responsibility for various actions they took during the war.

differences regarding the progress of the film, we would appear to our subjects—and also to our viewers—as just a single entity. So criticism was inevitable. It couldn't be helped; I just had to accept it. I had a sort of a "so-what" attitude at the time, as if we weren't doing anything wrong. It was what some may call an "even-a-tiny-insect-has-a-big-soul" kind of stance. But it's not as if I really believed in it.

I didn't shoot *The Emperor's Naked Army Marches On* thinking that justice was on our side; actually, I felt apologetic. I went so far as to think that I would totally agree with anyone who thought that what had driven me to film those scenes with the soldiers the way I did was egoism. I didn't want to excuse myself on the basis of "justice." That's how I felt while shooting. Call it egoism if you like. Any attempt at rebuttal would only be self-justification.

If, for example, I were asked in a public forum why I shot those scenes of Okuzaki invading the homes of the former soldiers and fighting with them, I would defend myself: it's a public forum, after all. It's not that I would want to start a fight, but when it comes to artistic expression and film, I believe I must make a point of saying what I need to say. In other words, in a situation where it's difficult to communicate one-on-one—a question-and-answer session at a public venue, for example—I would prepare to defend myself. But any words I might say on such an occasion would, in the end, feel dishonest, even as I uttered them.

What, then, is the truth? The truth is the logic I use when I get inside other people. But how do I, the person behind that logic, establish it? That's been the same from the very beginning until now....

Perhaps there is in fact no guiding logic at the core of what I am. And there's no way I can establish any. Or, to be more precise, perhaps I don't care if I don't have any. I *do* think about it from time to time, though. It's not as though I don't think about it at all.

It's like that idea in *Lone Wolf and Cub*: the idea of "entering the realm of the damned," to put it hyperbolically. A part of me thinks that it's OK to think this way, that we'll always be entering the realm

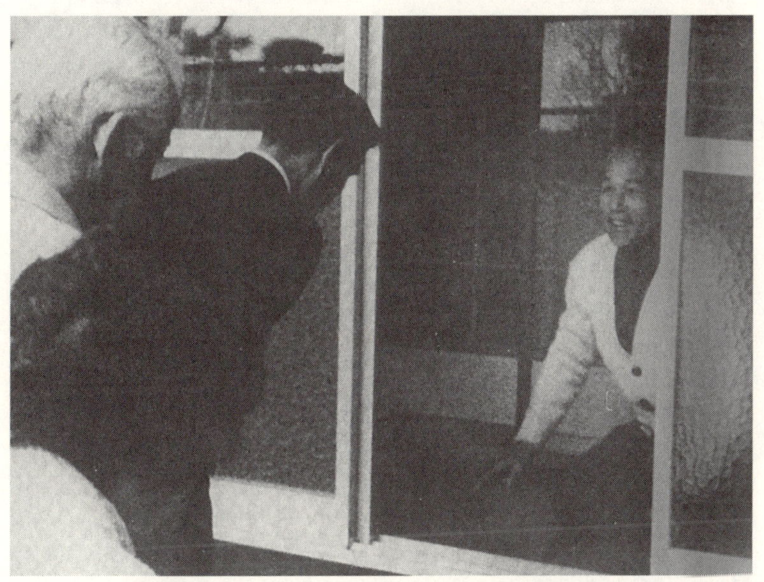

The Emperor's Naked Army Marches On. Okuzaki says,
"They'll just try to avoid us if you contact them, so don't bother."

of the damned, regardless of whether or not we're criticized for it.[2] No—it's not "we." I don't force others. This is *my* way of interpreting the work I do. I ask, "Do you really want to do this? Those who do will probably burn in the fires of hell. OK? Well, if you insist." That's how I feel. Otherwise I couldn't do it. Is it possible to talk openly, in a public forum, about the logic behind entering the realm of the damned? Entering the realm of the damned is something I have to do precisely *because* I'm unable to talk openly about it.

Part of me also believes that this way of thinking can't be helped. But I often wonder if I can really follow through with it. To tell you the truth, it scares me. It sounds cool to say, "entering the realm of the damned," but if I were really serious about it, I think I'd be making far more cult-like, underground-type films. Such films—films that are formally quite extreme and made at the margins—do in fact get made.

Ultimately, though, we want our films to be screened in movie theaters. We may turn off half of our viewers, but we harbor a secret desire to be understood by at least 20 to 30 percent of them. So I'm fully aware that while I might say I "enter the realm of damned," I also know that I actually don't quite get there. How do I bridge this gap? Only by concluding that blame is inevitable, and that I have to accept whatever accusations may be directed at me.

So, speaking at the level of the body, I can only begin this work by lifting myself off of my own heavy ass; that is, by forcibly prodding myself into action. I prod myself because I want to step into other people's worlds and drag things out, exposing them to broad daylight. Which is a far cry from feeling obliged to have a thorough discussion with my subjects and obtaining their consent before I start filming.

In sum, I can only say, "I hear you. I'm sorry."

---

2 *Lone Wolf and Cub*: A 28-volume manga, first created in 1970 by writer Kazuo Koike and artist Goseki Kojima, that tells the story of a samurai-turned-assassin and his young son, who embark on a journey of violence and revenge. Made into seven films.

HOW I DIFFER FROM OGAWA SHINSUKE

Let's look at an example. If I were Ogawa Shinsuke, I would go to a farming village and establish a relationship with the elders there over a period of two or three years.[3] I would help them grow rice, then eventually enter their living room from the back door and say, "OK, I'm going to film you now." With me, it's like: "In the beginning was the camera." I try to forcibly generate action with the camera. I try to wrench it into existence. With deliberate force.

Ultimately, I think that the difference between Ogawa and myself lies in what each of us wants to see.

What, then, do I want to see? In Inoue Mitsuharu's words, "the embarrassing things that human beings keep hidden inside themselves."[4] Those "embarrassing things" are what I want to see: the things people want to hide, the parts they find shameful. *Because* people hide them, I want to see them. This idea runs through everything I do.

Of course, underpinning such feelings of embarrassment are social conventions. I want to completely break down the institutionalized ideologies that cause us to feel embarrassment. Things that people believe to be embarrassing don't readily surface. Even people who recognize that their embarrassment results from social conditioning might still consider it to be negative, a personal weakness. However, people try to find something positive in their lives precisely because something negative exists. This contradiction could be considered the source or the structure of an individual's will to live. The only way I can depict an individual is by seeing the raw entirety of that will to live.

---

3 Ogawa Shinsuke (1936–1992): Documentary filmmaker. Began his career in 1960 directing PR films. In the middle of the '60s, he began producing politically charged, independent films such as *Sea of Youth* (1966) and *The Oppressed Students* (1967), which documented the Japanese student protest movement. He is best known for his *Sanrizuka* series, which documents the often violent struggles waged by the people of Sanrizuka against the Japanese government, which was trying to force them to relocate in order to build Narita Airport.

4 Inoue Mitsuharu (1926–1992): Renowned Japanese writer who is the subject of Hara Kazuo's film *A Dedicated Life*. See Chapter 6, note 1.

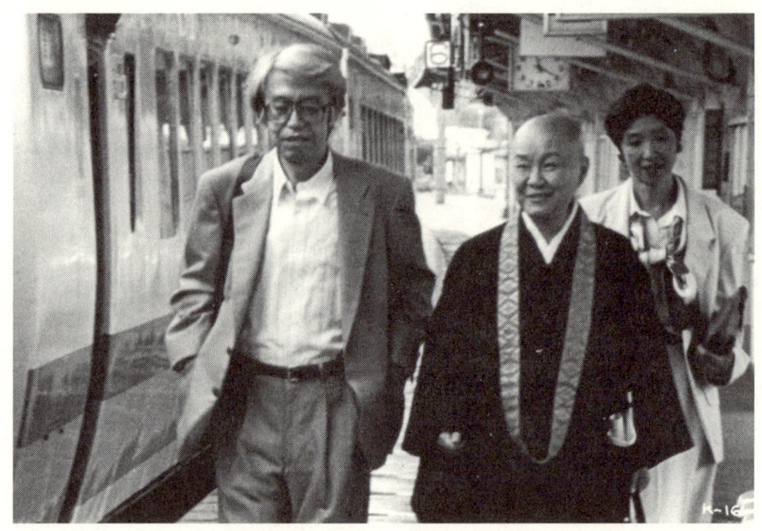

A Dedicated Life. Inoue Mitsuharu says that there are "embarrassing things that human keep hidden inside themselves."

I want to find what is buried inside live people, not actors, and to drag it to the surface. So I'm not satisfied when people only reveal what they allow me to film. The parts they allow me to film are actually just the tip of the iceberg; if people don't reveal what they don't want to show, I can't be sure how the parts they do reveal fit into the entirety of their lives.

So I can't help but wonder how far I can delve into the things that people are embarrassed by, using my camera as a weapon. I want to dig deeper and deeper and try to see the entirety of that person's existence.

For a time in the 1960s, there was this idea that the camera should be used as a weapon. However, it was thought of as something anti-national, anti-institutional.

That's not for me. I want to turn my camera on the places where, within each individual, institutions operate. Even the farmers Ogawa filmed must have had things that they were embarrassed by. I see it in the scenes of the fields. Then again, every filmmaker has his or her own image of utopia. That expression "utopia" might be misleading: Ogawa certainly had his own image of freedom. I think that Ogawa's image of freedom was drinking saké with the farmers—singing with them and having friendly conversations about this and that. Of course, Ogawa must have known the embarrassing things that lay beneath the surface of all that, but he didn't depict them when making his films.

The fact that Ogawa doesn't show the embarrassing bits is, I think, his romanticism at work. As for me, I believe that we all have embarrassing things that we keep inside ourselves, so I want us to get to know them better. Mutual understanding is very painful, but since we are all full of things that embarrass us, we might as well be more open about them with one another. So I apologize and force my way in.

My romanticism is that I think these negative parts—the painful parts, the sad parts, the parts you don't want to remember—*do* in fact exist, and that we're so full of them that we might as well be in hell. But since that's what it means to be human, we should accept things as they are. So I think Ogawa and I differ in how we look at people after all.

PEOPLE DON'T CHANGE THAT EASILY

When taking a camera and stepping into someone else's private inner realm, something might emerge that even that person might not expect. At such times—when facing the darkest recesses of oneself—the peace we've constructed around having ignored the things we're embarrassed by might collapse.

Regrettably, that kind of collapse doesn't happen that easily. I've realized this from making films. For example, you might think that something in the daily lives of the former soldiers that Okuzaki Kenzō and I stepped into with our camera would have changed. But unfortunately, that didn't happen. Things still haven't changed. Perhaps we made a few ripples; in fact, I know we did. But did any of the former soldiers kill themselves as a result? Was it such a big shock to them? No. What's been built up over the years is inevitably going to be heavy and difficult to overcome.

This makes me even more impatient. I have to wonder what it is, exactly, that we're doing? We're only making these tiny little waves. That's all we can do.

At the end of *Goodbye CP*, Yokota Hiroshi says, "I've been emptied out." However, after making the film, he became a senior member of the Kanagawa Green Grasses group. And whether he's living happily with his wife or not, he did go back to his peaceful daily life. After he went through that film, some part of Yokota should have changed. But unfortunately, even the general framework of his life didn't change. Not only did it not change, it didn't even budge. The same is true of the former soldiers. We've made a number of tiny ripples. But did the film significantly changed their lives? Unfortunately, films have no such absolute power.

So I've got a long way to go. At some level, I'm still soft.

I should be prepared to be locked up in a solitary cell, like Okuzaki, or to even risk death. But creative expression is not quite like that...

Having spent the entire *Emperor's Naked Army* shoot in close proximity to Okuzaki Kenzō, a convicted criminal, I, as a director, came dangerously close to becoming a criminal myself. I don't know if I would have actually gone so far as to do something criminal: I'm incredibly timid, so when I think something's trouble, I instinctually avoid it. But somewhere inside me, I'm always wondering how far I'm determined to go for the sake of creative expression.

Fortunately—or should I say, fortunately or unfortunately—I won't go to prison in present-day Japan for making a film, regardless of what I do. Whether this is fortunate or not, I don't know. But to tell you the truth, when it comes to creative expression, the sharper the blade your work has, the less likely you'll be able to live peacefully. As it stands, though, I find myself living at ease, with my works receiving rather high praise and so on.

Would I be able to live like Okuzaki, who thought that being imprisoned by the state was like being decorated with a medal? I must say that going all the way like that is definitely one way to live one's life. Such a path would basically require an element of criminality. In theory, at least...

But wanting to change something doesn't necessarily require going immediately into solitary confinement like Okuzaki did. Many issues still exist in the very private inner realm of each individual. So that's the direction in which I feel I should pursue those issues, at least for the time being.

Ultimately, in answer to the question why I make films, it's because I want to express myself. What causes me to want to make a documentary is an encounter: I feel like shooting a film because I encounter a fascinating character. That is, without a doubt, why I make films. But while filming—while capturing my subject on film—I'm inevitably forced into situations from which there's no turning back.

There are aspects of myself that I can only see if I create such situations. In everyday circumstances, I'll question who I am according to any number of preconceived notions, but this only leads back to those preconceptions in an endless loop. To get through that, a camera is, for me, absolutely necessary. At the same time, I'm frightened by the part of myself that, rolling camera, gets through to the other side.

In *The Emperor's Naked Army Marches On,* I shot a scene in which Okuzaki goes to Yamada Kichitarō's house and gets into a fistfight with him.[5] Before they start fighting, Okuzaki and Yamada get into a heated argument. At that moment, I positioned the camera right between the two, where their lines of sight met. I hadn't planned on setting up my camera that way; it was just an impulse. That part of myself only rears up on impulse.

In the shot, Yamada was on one side of me and Okuzaki was on the other. It would have been easiest to set up the camera at a distance from both, in a triangulated position. But at that moment, I felt I had to take up a position right in the midst of their argument, panning an entire 180 degrees between the two. Objectively, the way I shot that scene looks completely unnatural; it would normally be an inconceivable position. Physically, too: I had to twist my body an entire 180 degrees.

It looks quite odd. But it was impossible for me to resist the impulse to take that position in that situation. I was determined to get the shot. The moment I thought, "That's it. Get the shot," I had to get right in the middle of the fight and pan back and forth between the two of them.

I wanted to see how I—that impulse—would react in the middle of that scene. I can trust that impulsive part of myself as one aspect of my total being. I might even venture to say that by examining my own reactions at such moments, it's possible for me to gain insight into my own true self.

Describing things in this way might lead to some misunderstanding: I might seem either extremely sadistic, or very masochistic. Moreover, the way that my self is revealed in such situations is inconsistent. I myself get frightened that I don't know how I'm going to react. In fact,

5 Yamada Kichitarō: Okuzaki's war buddy and the only other member from their platoon to have survived the war.

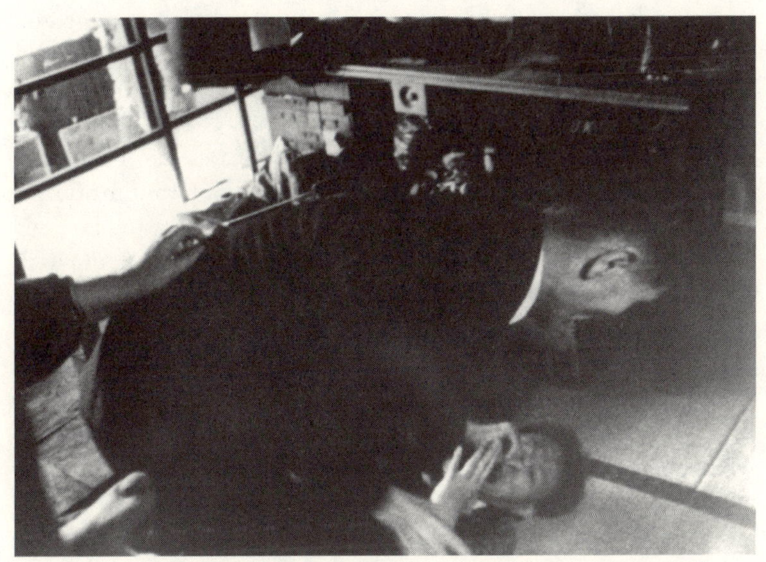

The Emperor's Naked Army Marches On. The camera stepped right in the middle of Okuzaki and Yamada just before they started fighting.

I don't even understand that fear, that inner world.

But I'm driven into such situations when holding my camera.

Perhaps this comes from a part of me that is beyond self-control. Or a part of me that is as-yet unknown to myself. But I'll encounter it once or twice per film.

CONSCIOUSLY GOING CRAZY

What eventually happens if such experiences accumulate? That part of myself that I'm encountering inevitably becomes more and more extreme. The potential outcome of this terrifies me. It could lead to my going crazy—as described at the very end of the *Production Notes* for *The Emperor's Naked Army Marches On*.[6] I say I'm frightened, but if I don't step right into the very thing that scares me, I can't get anywhere near the level of creative expression that I want to attain.

I've thus begun to feel lately that I've been going too far. But the more I feel that way, the more determined I become not to back away. This way of thinking is, in a sense, characteristic of the '70s generation: the more one thinks about something, the more one gets pulled in. So when people ask me how I decide what my next subject will be, I find myself choosing one that I can't pull away from. I make films through this kind of back and forth. I inevitably think about what I would like to do next, and about the project after that. So making one film becomes preparation for the next one.

Perhaps people think of me as a person who would walk right into someone else's personal space, dirty shoes and all.[7]

But it's not like that. When I invade someone else's personal space, I apologize in my mind. I don't apologize in order to justify myself. Rather, I want to develop within myself the toughness to step into someone else's world with my shoes still on. This kind of toughness is easier said than done, however. At least for me.

---

6 A translation of the *Production Notes* can be found in the second part of this book.

7 According to Japanese custom, shoes are always taken off when entering a home.

Okuzaki Kenzō has, in a way, already broken through. To touch upon something I wrote about in the afterword to one of his books, Okuzaki is able to invoke God as part of his logic for invading other people's privacy. Because he's invoked God, he can step right in with his shoes on.

When I wonder what I, someone who isn't able to invoke God, should do, I figure that I have to conjure up something close to God in order to develop my own toughness, making it possible for me to step right in with my shoes on.

That's what I mean by consciously going crazy. Being crazy means that I can step right in with my shoes on, without making a conscious effort. To go crazy "consciously" is an oxymoron. But if I'm repeatedly making myself go crazy consciously, won't I one day enter the world of insanity for real? That part of myself really frightens me. Then again, should I stop and hold my ground? No. What else can I do but go forward, and as far as I can? I have to keep at it for however long it takes.

Since I've already referred to Mr. Okuzaki as an extraordinary hero, you might think that he's a special person. But I don't think he is. I'm a coward, so I tend to think that, in theory at least, one must do one's best to live like him. But there are in fact many people in this world who are able to get through to what's real. There are those who up and die, and those who up and commit crimes. This has nothing to do with the abstractions of art. Just think of your neighbors. They go about their lives without thinking. So what I'd most like to do is to look at the internal universe of each individual, at the internal mechanisms each individual possesses.

Take Takeda Miyuki, the heroine of *Extreme Private Eros*, for example. I'm sure she's had a breakthrough moment somewhere along the way; Inoue Mitsuharu from *A Dedicated Life* also must have had his own such experience; and ditto for the women in his class. I believe that fundamentally, everyone has the potential to get through to what's real.

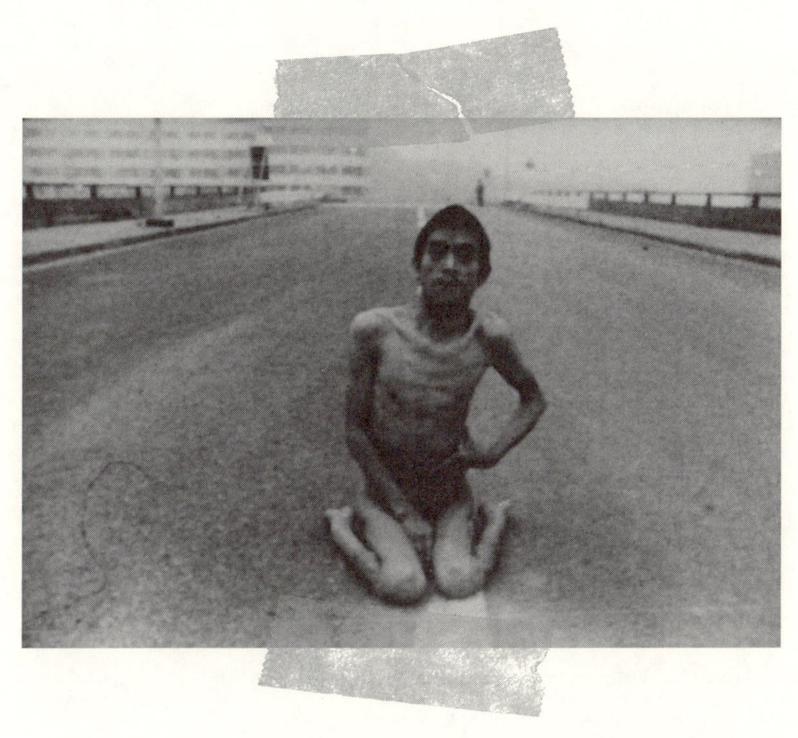

02 Childhood

I DON'T KNOW WHERE MY FATHER IS

My mother tells me that when she was young, she worked in a kind of cabaret in Osaka. She says I was the child of a patron of hers and that she, my mother, had been his mistress. According to her, the person who fathered me was the owner of a small general store. She later told me—and I don't know whether this is true or not—"Out of all the men I've been with, your father was the man I liked the most."

I've wanted to get the story of my childhood straight, once and for all, from my mother, but I feel that I still haven't fully done that. I've been wanting to capture my mother's personal history, as related by herself, whether on video or on film, but here I am, not having done so. I've heard fragments of her story, but she never seems to want to talk about it much. Inoue Mitsuharu once said, "There's a lot a person can't talk about." That's probably because there are some things people are just embarrassed about.

It seems as though my father went to war and, in the end, went missing. I was born on June 8, 1945. That means that my father was sent to the front while I was still in utero. After he was conscripted, the air raids on Osaka grew increasingly destructive, and my mother could no longer stay in the city. Since she was from rural Yamaguchi City, she went home, and it seems she gave birth to me there. She took refuge in a shelter during an air raid, protecting me, her newly born infant, by spreading herself over me. She told me that I once stopped breathing when in that position, so she had to quickly shake me, trying various things to get me to breathe again.

The war eventually ended, but my mother said she never heard from the person who'd fathered me, so she doesn't know whether or not he came home alive. After that, she took care of me by herself. Since raising me alone was difficult, she followed the advice of those around her and remarried. The man she married was a coal miner who worked at the Nishiokinoyama Mine in Ube. After they were married, I spent my entire childhood there.

The two of them also had a child, my sister, who was two years younger than me. That dad also ended up getting killed—in a mining accident. It wasn't something dramatic, like a mine collapsing in on him or anything. He was apparently electrocuted to death when he touched a bare wire with an iron rod or something like that. So I have no memory of this person.

My mother was left raising two kids. Life was hard, so she married again, for the third time. This third husband's name was Hara Tokio. I have some memories of this one. He had a child by a former marriage who was older than I was. My mother and Hara had two children together. The first, my younger brother, was named Hara Yūji, and the second, my youngest sister, was named Hara Midori. I no longer remember what characters were used to write "Midori," whether it was in hiragana or kanji.[1] At that point, my family was at its largest, with five children.

If I might borrow my mother's expression, she would often say that my stepbrother had a "warped" personality. When I think back on that time now, I have a few vague memories of him being mean to me. But I still remember one time when neighborhood bullies pushed me around and my step-brother, hearing about it, went to beat them up for me. He was a strong fighter; that must have been why my mother called him a "delinquent." I don't think he actually was a delinquent, but our mother's generation would call anyone who caused even the slightest trouble "delinquent." He may have bullied me, but I don't remember becoming despondent because of it; rather, I have this fond memory of him taking my side that one time.

We weren't together for all that long. The two kids were born. I was six years older than my younger brother, the older of the two, and I stayed with him until he was one or two years old before going to elementary school. I guess that means that I was with this man Hara till my younger brother was four or five.

1 *Hiragana* refers to Japanese written script, while *kanji* refers to a written script that utilizes Chinese characters.

I think we had a so-so life while Hara worked. Since we lived in housing provided by the mining company, we paid practically no rent. It wasn't easy, but we didn't starve. I suspect that our life wasn't easy because Hara was sending money to his parents. My mother had remarried, and so had he. He had a complicated family life. I think I heard he was sending money somewhere.

When my mother was young, she wasn't a beauty, but there was something alluring about her. She was kind and generous. I wouldn't say she was flirtatious, but she was the type that attracted men, and she liked having fun. Men liked her. For her, "fun" meant nothing more than going to a pachinko parlor with me on her back. The only way we could get to a city or town from the Nishiokinoyama Mine was by train. It took about ten to twenty minutes by train to get to the town of Ube from the mine.

A game called bingo was popular then. She wouldn't buy just one ticket, or should I say card, she'd buy ten. They would throw a ball, and if the numbers lined up vertically or horizontally, you'd win. So she'd buy ten cards, and since she couldn't keep track of them by herself, she'd sit me next to her and say, "Watch carefully," and line up the cards. Then she'd place the marker over the numbers. She'd often take me to such things.

On the way home, she'd sometimes take me to the movies. My memories of loving to watch movies begins from around that time. My experiences with film started with movies like Tōei's *Beni Kujaku* [Red Peacock], *Fuefuki Dōji* [The Flute-Playing Boy] and Azuma Chiyonosuke's *Hyakumen Dōji* [The Boy with a Hundred Faces]. It was the golden age of Japanese cinema.

MY STEPFATHER "HARA"

This man Hara was extremely high-strung. He was apparently a violent man and would beat my mom. Such scenes didn't leave a lasting impression on me, but I do faintly remember him slapping my mother's head. His neurotic nature would come out when he brushed his teeth. Normal people usually take about a minute or two to quickly run a toothbrush over their teeth, but Hara would take close to ten minutes, vigorously scraping and grinding with his toothbrush. I still remember this manifestation of his neuroticism.

When my mother couldn't bear his beatings any longer, she left him. One memory from that time is more vivid than the others.

One day, my mother said that we were going to go to town as always. She told me to go ahead. "Okay," I replied. I left the house, walked for a while, then stopped. It was about a twenty-minute walk from the housing to the station, so I decided to wait for her. I still clearly remember what she said to me when she arrived. It was a bit of a shock.

"That Hara guy"—I think that's what she called him—"just mounted me." I don't remember the exact words she used, but she implied that it had been awful, and that he had forced himself on her. She said something implying that she had said he had not, but that in fact he had forced himself on her. She said this to me, a third- or fourth-grader. She was talking about sex, no beating around the bush. I'm not saying that this repulsed or disgusted me. I was just shocked at hearing her speak in such a straightforward manner about sex.

It was summer. I remember this because the miner's union was hosting the obon festival dance, and loudspeakers had been set up around the company housing units so we could hear music from the record *The Moon Is Out*.[2] I vividly remember hearing that record wafting over that scene.

So there was this incident. In any case, I often heard her complain about that Hara guy. I'm not sure if that was why they separated. Or maybe the mine fell on hard times around then, so perhaps they separated because the mine was downsizing. It's not quite clear to me.

It was the late '50s, a time when strikes were breaking out in Miike and a number of other mines around the country. But I don't

2 *obon*: Annual summer festival to honor the dead.

remember any strikes at our mine, or if there were any Koreans working there. I faintly remember there being some Koreans among the miners because I have this feeling that a few of my classmates were Korean. But in those days, there was absolutely none of the awareness about the problem of forced labor and so on that there is today. And I was only in the third or fourth grade—too young to know about such things.

Moving on to the next stage of my story, my mother ended up divorcing Hara. She was still young, so she got a divorce. Then the mine went out of business, so she left company housing and started working as a construction laborer. In the process, there were some messy, complicated issues, such as my mother taking care of Hara's children, sending them away, then adopting them back again out of pity. So, for a time, we lived with my younger brother. By then, we had left the mine in Ube and were renting a room in someone's house in an adjacent city, an industrial town called Onoda where Onoda Cement was located. There, at her job, my mother met a man slightly younger than she was with whom we eventually lived.

My mother and this man worked in manual labor, so whenever it rained, there was no work. They were day laborers, paid by the day. As a result, we would have no money to buy even rice when the rain lasted for two or three days. During the day, when they went to work, there was no one around to look after my younger sister. So, given the circumstances, they put her up for adoption. By this time, I was in fourth or fifth grade, and would take my younger brother to school. We had nothing to eat. No lunchbox. So, during afternoon recess, I would head out to the playground where my brother would be waiting for me, and we'd drink water together. It may seem like I'm just re-telling something out of Kawakami Hajime's *Tale of Poverty*, but there was a time like that.[3]

Once, when he couldn't bear the hunger pangs any longer, my

3 Kawakami Hajime (1879–1946): Japanese Marxist who wrote essays, novels (including *Tale of Poverty*, published in 1917), poetry, and a well-known autobiography. In 1937, he translated *Das Kapital* from German into Japanese.

brother stole some food from a grocer. This made my mother furious, bringing her to tears. We have such sad memories. He was such a humble boy. Really. Even now, my mother sometimes tells me she thinks about him. My poor brother.

Eventually, she couldn't take care of him any longer, so it was decided that he should be sent to live with Hara's mother. My mother must have thought that since she was unable to care for him, his father should take him back. Hara's mother lived in the company housing of another mine. Back then, even the homes the mine provided for its employees were getting worse and worse.

So my mother told me to drop him off—that is, to drop my brother off at Hara's mother's place. I had no choice, so I took him. We got on the bus. As soon as we crossed a small river, we arrived at the housing for the miners. These homes were actually rows of tenements. Hara's mother lived in the first one. I told my brother, "It's the one over there." I told him to be a good boy and go. "Go and call her 'Gran' ma. Don't even think about coming back this way," I said. Then, after a moment, I told him, "Now go." I made sure he went into the house, then ran as fast as I could and jumped onto the bus, which had just arrived. The bus passed by his house once more, so I rode in the very back. Looking out the rear window, I didn't see anyone. At the thought of my brother meeting Hara's mother, I started bawling helplessly.

That was the last I saw of my brother. I haven't heard a word from him since then, so I know nothing of what became of him. If he didn't die from some disease or accident, he must be living well somewhere, but I have no idea what kind of life he might be leading.

Rather than think I was forced to do this painful job, I'd like to think my mother entrusted it to me. One man replaced another, but to me, none were my father; they were just men my mother cycled through. I never felt that she was dirty, though. Nor did I feel disgusted with her or become a delinquent. Even at my tender young age, I understood that she trusted and depended on me. I think it gave me a sense of satisfaction.

I also tried to help her make ends meet. There was a coal mine near Onoda where I would go to pick up low-grade coal that had been discarded in piles as unfit for sale. If you went through each pile carefully, you'd often find a few usable coals. I would stuff these into a wooden box and take them back to sell to the family of a friend of mine, a cute girl classmate from elementary school. Her family would buy the pieces of coal from me. Since we lived in the same neighborhood and were still in elementary school, we could somehow understand each other. I think that's why I went to the girl's house to sell the coal.

As for this young man we were living with, he was, despite his youth, at least making a living as a construction laborer. I mean, I don't mean to discriminate against construction laborers, but he was lazy. He loved to gamble, and, in the end, never worked much. Because he never worked, and because my mother grew tired of trying to coax him into working, she eventually left him, and we moved to Yamaguchi City.

"HOME" AS AN IDEA

My mother went to Yamaguchi City by herself and started working as a live-in waitress at a restaurant. Some time elapsed before she had me brought over to join her. My mother's older sister lived in Ube near where the coal mine was located. Her husband was more or less dependable, and they had five children. I was entrusted to them for a while.

One of the children was the same age as me. The kids there were all good, but for some reason, there was a kind of conscious sibling rivalry at work between the one my age and myself. He was mean to me at times. But no matter how mean he was, I could never openly fight with him. I knew that he and his family were taking care of me; I knew what my situation was. When we see each other now, I don't hold any grudges for what he did to me then. But at the time...

Once, he told me to go into an extremely hot Goemon bath, saying that the temperature of the water was perfect.[4] In a Goemon bath, you sit on a wooden board that's sunken into the bathtub. He'd say, "Let's go in together," so I'd go into the bathtub with him. It would get crowded, and he'd deliberately push me so I'd touch the hot iron bottom. He'd do these little nasty things to me. There was another reason for this, perhaps. I did pretty well in school, so when we brought our report cards home, he might have felt a sense of rivalry.

My mother's older sister had a different father. It's really complicated, you know. She pitied my mother very much, and I was my mother's son, so she took very good care of me. The boy my age didn't like that so much; it just added to his spite for me. I had to put up with his bullying because I appreciated how his mother was taking good care of me. That made my life pretty hard.

Then my mother had me brought over to live with her in Yamaguchi City. At that time, my sister, who was two years younger than me, was in the care of a completely unrelated family. My mother also had her brought over to Yamaguchi, and the three of us started living together. Around that time, my mother again found a new man. He was twelve years younger than she was, from Kagoshima, and a member of the Self-Defense Force. To put food on the table, he quit the Force and took a job as a bus driver for a private railroad company. My mother is still with him. And so the four of us started living like that in Yamaguchi City, renting a room. And here we are today.

So when people ask me where I spent my childhood, I tell them "I was raised in a mining town," but I was only at a mine up until around the fourth grade. For a year or a year and a half after that, I went to school in Onoda City. When I was in the third trimester of fifth grade, I moved to Yamaguchi City and spent the rest of my childhood there. Yamaguchi City is situated in a basin, and even

4 Goemon bath: A bath with a bottom made of iron that is heated directly from beneath. Named after a famous thief, Ishikawa Goemon, who was punished by being boiled to death.

though it's the capital of the prefecture, it's off the main Sanyō train line. Anyway, it was a tiny town of twenty to thirty thousand people. But it was immaculate—quiet and peaceful, a place where nothing much happened. It was also completely closed to outsiders.

While living there, all I wanted to do was to get out as quickly as I could and work on my own. I was just full of this desire to work on my own.

Home, for me, was not an actual dwelling. It was more like an idea—and in my case, it was practically non-existent. Issues related to a home—being attached to it, for example, or wanting to destroy it—were somehow foreign to me.

For that reason, when speaking of home, I can only remember the company housing at the mine and the tenement houses and how many times we drifted from one place to the next. After splitting from that man named Hara, we rented rooms. Then I was put in the care of other people. I stayed in that situation for several months while my mother worked as a live-in waitress at a restaurant. Then we began our lives as renters again, living with the former Self-Defense Force member. After that, we won the housing lottery and lived in municipal housing. That's pretty much what growing up was like for me.

Every time we changed homes, my father would also change with it. Even within company housing, we wouldn't stay in one house, but would move three or four times. Our house would change, the man would change. Then our lives as a whole would change. It wasn't as if these fathers had been transferred for work; their whole way of making a living would change.

However, I was never a delinquent. Under the circumstances, I felt my mother was the only person I could connect directly with. I wasn't aware of this at the time, but when looking back on myself then, I never harbored any negative feelings against her. It wasn't until I was perhaps over 20 that things soured.

I eventually became conscious of the fact that I felt the men who perpetually came in and out of my life were not my fathers, but my "mother's men."

I was asked several times to call each and every one of these men "father." As for my younger sister's father, the one who died in the mining accident... I don't remember much about that guy. I don't remember if I called him "father" or not. I may have called Hara, the one who came after him, "father," but I don't remember doing so. I recall being asked several times to call the young guy who came along after Hara "father." But I don't think I did in the end. It wasn't easy to do. I think I was somehow aware that I thought of them as my "mother's men."

They weren't my father, but because they put food on the table, my mother told me I had to call them "father." So I felt I had to. With that in mind, I tried, but in the end, I couldn't.

I've also been asked to call the man my mother is still living with "father," so I've rather jokingly done so a few times. We started living together when I was in the sixth grade, and I've called him "father" only a handful of times since then. Most of the time, I call him by his name, "Mr. Yamamoto."

Not having a father has recently become an issue for me. I never had a father, so when I became a father, I felt completely lost. I never had someone who could serve as a model for me. I really feel that I was at a total loss about how to be a father, how to be a parent to a child, how to act towards my own children.

I WAS A "GOOD BOY" FOR MY MOTHER

The most heartbreaking time in my childhood was when we lived with the young man who worked in construction.

A generations-old pawn shop in that area owned a big house that had been divided up and rented out to several households. They split up the rooms amongst who knows how many generations and rented them out. The room we rented was on the top floor in the attic. The space was so small that when we stood up to walk, we would hit our heads on the beams. So we had to squat to move about the apartment. Even the windows weren't your normal windows. They were covered with the kind of iron bars used on warehouse windows. It was a fun space to be in for a child, but it wasn't much of a room. That's the place we rented.

There were five of us living there, I think: that man, my mother, my younger sister, my brother, and me. My mother had already put my youngest sister up for adoption.

Sometimes, in the middle of the night, I would have this sense that something was happening, and I'd wake up. That something happening was people having sex, my mother and the young man. It was a problem. I couldn't sleep as a result, so I'd cough or do something. Then they would realize that I'd woken up and stop.

I found myself in that situation several times. What exactly was going on? That young man hated working, but my mother wanted him to go work. This created conflict. They would fight, and my mother would be brought to tears. Then, at night, they would usually have sex. In other words, she would use sex to mitigate his bad mood and get him to work. Even then I understood the situation. Such scenes between the two of them broke my heart.

For that reason, I don't have many fond memories of home. The sex was one reason. Of course, for the man, the sex was purely physical desire, but for my mother, it inevitably had another aspect to it—making a living.

Back then, my mother would sometimes tell me, "I married a man I didn't like so I could raise you kids and live with you." Not in so many words, perhaps, but I could sense the sadness in what she said. On my part, I wouldn't then reply, "I don't remember asking you to give birth to me." Not back then at least. Only much later did I use that retort. In those days, I truly sympathized with my mother. I took pity on her.

I think that's why I was a good boy to my mother, working hard in order to help her, collecting low-grade coal and so forth.

Was I then filled with hostility or something of the sort for that young man? No. He would sometimes take me to play at his parent's home. For him, I was the child of the woman he was with, so he took me there as though he were my father. On those occasions, I tried to be a good kid to him, too. That's how I got by.

The person I think I held feelings of hatred for was the man named Hara. Why was that? Perhaps it was because I knew my mother didn't love him. Even when she said she'd only married so she could raise us, I could tell she had a decent amount of love for the construction laborer and guy from the Self-Defense Force. I probably thought it wasn't all that horrible or unbearable for her to be with them, and so I did her a favor by acting like a good kid in their company. As such, I never hated them.

All these years later, because of the kind of films I've made, people might think that I'm an incredibly warped character, or have an aggressive side somewhere. But as far as my childhood is concerned, I never hated anyone or bore a grudge against anyone. I was a genuinely good kid. I never rebelled.

One often hears of kids in junior high school starting to rebel against their teachers, but my homeroom teacher was quite fond of me. When he was on night watch, he would invite me to hang out with him, so I would go stay in the night-duty room. During summer vacation, I invited him to go camping with me and four or five of my classmates. I was a good boy to him as well.

Kobayashi Sachiko tells me she was unbelievably rebellious when she was young, but it never crossed my mind to be rebellious or disobedient, incredible though it might sound now.[5]

WORKING AT THE JAPANESE RED CROSS

My junior high school was the Ōtono Junior High School in Yamaguchi City. Since we were poor, I would deliver newspapers. Hearing this, you might think that I was working to help out with household expenses. But that wasn't the case. Ever since junior

5 Kobayashi Sachiko: Hara Kazuo's longtime partner, producer, and co-founder of Shissō Productions.

high, I've felt that I needed to work for my own necessities. In the end, though, I may have helped out a little.

When I graduated from junior high, I wanted to move to Osaka. Why Osaka? Simply because it was closer than Tokyo. When I graduated, I checked out the classifieds for a job as a live-in delivery boy. Consulting no one, I wrote a letter and received a reply inviting me to move to Osaka for the job.

When my mother saw the letter, she said, "I don't object to you wanting to work, but why don't you at least finish high school first?" She was convincing: and since we were poor, and I really didn't like studying much, we compromised. "I'll work afternoons," I said. "Then night school should be enough." And so I went to high school in the evenings.

During the day, I started working at the Yamaguchi Prefecture branch of the Japanese Red Cross. They had just decided on a brand-new project: developing Red Cross workers by recruiting youngsters fresh out of junior high. I went to take the test, and—God knows why—I passed it. Their idea was probably to develop me into a Red Cross man slowly, over 10, 20, 30 years. But after a year, I'd had enough.

Basically, the Red Cross is what they call a quasi-governmental agency. It's quite bureaucratic as an institution, and like any institution, it has its hierarchy: a bureau director, clerical staff, departmental managers, and section managers. It's not like they were doing anything important, either. When there was a disaster, they would send blankets and collect donations. I had just graduated from junior high school and was full of life, so I wanted to do something interesting.

When I thought about what it would be like to work for the Red Cross for 10 or 20 years, I realized there was just no way I could do it. After a year, I was fed up, so I quit.

I quit and, for some reason, I wanted to work in business. I was quite serious about wanting to make money. I wanted to succeed—to make my name—by making money. So I discussed my desire to work in business with a teacher in charge of evening classes at Yamaguchi

High School. And I landed a job at a cutlery store. I went there to get business experience, but I ended up sharpening knives and scissors with a whetting stone. I can still sharpen anything masterfully. I worked there for about half a year.

I went there intending to study the ins and outs of the business world, but it was just a mom-and-pop store, so it wasn't very interesting. So I quit. I worked at a bookstore next. I served primarily high schools, delivering periodical subscriptions and books that teachers had ordered. I often visited the teachers in charge of books, asking if they wanted to order any of the newly published titles. Then I'd take their orders. The store I worked at was the third largest in the city, but I still had very few orders. After about a year and a half, I couldn't stand working there any longer, so I quit.

Of course, my teacher was finding jobs that she thought were appropriate for me. She'd introduced me to these businesses because I'd told her that I wanted to work hard and earn money. If I had worked long enough, whether at the cutlery store or the bookstore, I would probably have been able to get a store or something. Then, in my teacher's mind, I'd be able to save up some money and earn a steady living in my hometown... But that wasn't my plan.

I went from one job to the next. Every time this happened, my teacher would look incredulous and say, "Well, that's that." Still, I think she treated me very well. Night-school teachers generally also have day jobs: the teacher who took care of me was a doctor's wife, and she also worked as a doctor herself. A middle-aged woman, she would practice medicine in the afternoons and teach in the evenings. She took good care of me without ever getting annoyed.

Since Yamaguchi City had a Self-Defense Force base, a number of the students in the evening classes were members of the Force. Some assistant nurses attended the school as well because Yamaguchi had a Red Cross Hospital. Both the assistant nurses and the soldiers had gone straight into their respective professions right after junior high, so they were taking classes in order to earn high-school diplomas that would make them eligible for promotion. Such students made up just over half the population in the evening classes. The school had two evening classes of about twenty students each. Probably less than half were there because they had no other choice, because they were poor.

But evening classes are, in the end, dull and uninspiring. In a film like Yamada Yōji's *A Class to Remember* series, you get the impression that all night-school students have unsolvable problems, that something dramatic happens every day.[6] But it's not like that at all. A sense of decay hung over the place. Nobody felt like studying.

As for the teachers, not a single one had the energy and vitality of Nishida Toshiyuki, who played the teacher in Yamada's film.[7] Most were near retirement, or taught as though they were working a part-time job that required no commitment. None of the classes were very stimulating. And since I worked during the day, I usually slept through classes. And I often played hooky.

We were supposed to fail if we missed more than one third of our classes, but I always exceeded that limit. Still, my teachers kindly allowed me to advance to the higher grades. Basically, I didn't go to school much because I didn't find it interesting.

However, when skipping school, I wasn't off getting into trouble. Right near the school was a mountain, halfway up which was an Inari shrine.[8] The wooden boards of the floor there felt nice and cool during the summer. It felt great. I'd finish work and tell everyone I was going to school, then head up the mountain to the shrine and lie down. I could see the school directly below me. I'd skip school, lie down, and let my thoughts wander.

I'd think about how I had to do something interesting soon. When school got out, I'd head home.

I hardly went to school, so my grades were horrible. You'll see if you get a hold of my report cards. Those high school grades were really the worst.

---

6 Yamada Yōji (1931–): Filmmaker. Best known for directing the *Tora-san* series.

7 Nishida Toshiyuki (1947–): Actor. Won the Japanese equivalent of the Academy Award for best actor in 1993 for his role in the *A Class to Remember* series.

8 Inari shrine: Shrine to the popular Shinto god of harvests, fertility, and industry, who typically takes on the shape of a fox.

I WANT TO BE A PHOTOJOURNALIST

After the bookstore job, I was introduced to and hired by the Yamaguchi regional office of the *Asahi Shimbun*.[9]

That was a blast. Newspaper companies would give an exam to hire fresh college graduates in Tokyo, then send these reporters out to regional branches around the country. So the Yamaguchi regional office received one or two fresh recruits every year.

These newspaper reporters were proud of having gotten merit scholarships from Waseda University's School of Political Sciences and Economics; or of graduating from the University of Tokyo; or of having been a star student at Hitotsubashi University. Naturally, they were all smart. And some of them were really nice to me. For example, they would take me drinking with them after work, even though I was a minor. One guy was from Tokyo, and for the New Year's holiday, he brought me with him to Tokyo for fun. It's not as though these guys taught me anything concrete, but they all lived with optimism and purpose, which had a profound influence on me.

At the newspaper, I would develop the photographs taken by the journalists, then make prints and transmit them to the main office. That was the sequence of my work. Since the reporters were all young, they would take me along with them on photo shoots. They couldn't take me to crime scenes, but they would take me with them when shooting the seasonal photographs that were always expected from regional offices. In spring, they shot rape blossoms, cherry blossoms, and school entrance ceremonies. In summer, they shot the summer festivals. Yamaguchi has a famous lantern festival.

They would say, "Let's see who can get the best shot," and would let me try as well. I took better photos than they did, and these were often published in the paper. The pictures I took looked pretty decent. I was delighted. Back then, the last page of the newspaper would

9 *Asahi Shimbun*: The *Asahi Daily News*, one of Japan's leading newspapers.

be devoted to local events; the second to the last page was called the second social page. That's where my photos would sometimes be printed. Quite a lot of space—three or four columns—would be allocated to the regional photos. Seeing my photographs in the newspaper, I couldn't help but feel elated.

Even though the reporters didn't know what they were doing at first, they naturally got better at writing articles after a year or two. I also got to read the pieces they wrote. I didn't understand them perfectly, but it seemed like a fun thing to do.

With all this, the time came for me to graduate from high school. And when I thought about what I was going to do with my life, I realized that I wanted to be a photojournalist. To do that, I had to go to school. But I didn't have enough money. So it was suggested that I work another year and go to Tokyo after saving up some more. Which is why I worked at the Yamaguchi regional branch of the *Asahi Shimbun* for another year.

I was, as a result, already 20 years old when I arrived in Tokyo. People usually leave home when they're 18, but it took me a year longer than most because it takes four years to graduate from an evening school. After graduating, I continued to work for another year, so I ended up going to Tokyo two years later than kids my age normally would. I enrolled in the Tokyo College of Photography to study photojournalism. I wanted to be a photojournalist.

When I was in junior high, my school wouldn't allow us to go see movies—that is, ones other than those sanctioned by the school or recommended by the Ministry of Education. But I would always play hooky and go to the movies. So my teachers would always call me to their offices and chew me out.

"You went to the movies didn't you?" they would ask. "Yes, I did," I would reply. "You need to write up an explanation and an apology," they would demand. "OK." Then I'd go see a movie again.

I would also go to the movies quite frequently when I was in high school—all the more so because we had quite a number of holidays. It was the heyday of Japanese cinema, so I saw all the major studio releases: Tōei period films, Nikkatsu action films. And then Shintōhō films—which, if you watched them now, would probably be nothing special.[10] But back then, I thought they were really erotic and mysterious.

So I saw Shintōhō films, as well as Daiei films and Shochiku films.[11] I'd even go see a soft, fuzzy film like Tōhō's *The Path Under the Plane Trees*. I saw almost everything.

It felt as if downtown were full of theaters. Even a tiny town would have five or six of them. And there was a period when they would play quadruple features that started at 9 o'clock in the morning and lasted until 10:30 or 11 o'clock at night. Did we like movies so much, or was it just that there were no other sources of entertainment? In any case, my sister and I would go see movies together. We would go to the theater at 9 and stay until 11 at night, watching all four movies. The two of us saw every film from start to finish. We really did—all four. I think my sister could endure more than I could. I would often leave after the second movie; she would stay until the end. In the countryside, a stupid thing like that was all there was in the way of fun.

THE "ONE-METER" ASSIGNMENT

I was 19 when I graduated from high school. To tell you the truth, the Yamaguchi branch of the *Asahi Shimbun* would basically hire kids who were in school in order to help them pay tuition. But for some reason, they made an exception for me and allowed me to stay on for an extra year. When I left for Tokyo at the end of that year, the head guy at the Yamaguchi regional office told me he would ask the Tokyo office to find me a job. So he introduced me to the *Asahi*

---

10 Tōei period films: Genre films, produced by Tōei studios, set during the Edo period (1603–1868). Nikkatsu action films: Various genre films such as *Plains Wanderer* and *Crimson Pistol* that were produced by Nikkatsu Studios, primarily during the 1960s. Shintōhō films: Films produced by Shintōhō Studios, known for its exploitation cinema.

11 Daiei and Shochiku: Major film studios.

Shimbun in Tokyo, saying I could work part-time there while going to photography school during the day. The school offered both day and evening classes, but I was usually tired in the evening, so going to school at night just wasn't very appealing. I told my boss this, received his letter of introduction, and left for Tokyo.

The idea was that I would join the *Asahi Shimbun* and this time around, work in the evening. But I couldn't get to work in time for the beginning of my shift. The photography school was in Hiyoshi, and the main *Asahi Shimbun* offices back then were in Yurakucho, where the Marion Building is now. So even if I rushed over after school ended, I still wouldn't make it to work in time. I had come to Tokyo on the assumption that I'd be able to work at *Asahi*, but in the end, things didn't work out. It just wasn't possible.

Since, as it turned out, there was no other choice, I was sent to the delivery office again. It was suggested that I make money by delivering papers while going to school. The first place I lived as a live-in delivery boy was in Myōrenji, off the Tōyoko train line.

I roomed there and started going to photography school while at the same time delivering newspapers. The residence was awful. People worked on the first floor, and some of the live-in delivery boys lived on the second floor. At that time, no one lived in private rooms. We would go up the stairs, down the hall, and to the tatami rooms.[12] We didn't treat the tatami in those rooms the way they should be treated, and would go in with our shoes on. There were three rooms, about four and a half to six mats in size. Two or three beds would be lined up in a row in each room. Those beds were the only private space we had. We were each given some space in the closet, where we could keep our stuff, so we kept everything in our suitcases.

When I began going to school and delivering newspapers, my most significant problem was not being able to do my homework, which was to develop photographs at home.

Developing photographs requires a space that's pitch black, but with my residence as I've described it, I was in a bit of a bind. Once,

12 *tatami*: Traditional Japanese straw mats used for flooring.

apologizing to my roommates, I put up a black cloth like a curtain around the room. But the room wasn't well built to begin with, and light seeped in from somewhere. Worse than that, my delivery-boy roommates didn't want me using our room as a darkroom. I tried, but since I wasn't able to work where I was living, I went to the house of one of my schoolmates, who let me develop my pictures there.

The first trimester ended, and, with the start of the summer vacation approaching, my teacher gave us our first longer project. The school offered a variety of classes, and each class had its own assignments. For example, we'd be given an assignment to capture the texture of an object.

The assignment I found most challenging—the one most worth going to school for—was the "one-meter" assignment. For it, we had to shoot a person from a meter or less away—and not from behind, but from the front. I learned a lot from this. We couldn't shoot someone we knew, but had to get a surprise shot of someone's face. You'd normally be too scared to do something like that. We were told not to use a telephoto lens; so, equipped with a standard or wider-angle lens, we would suddenly get in front of a person only one meter away and shoot. Since I'm skittish, I'd be momentarily frightened, thinking I might get hit or something. Something as frightening as that is really worthwhile. That was the only fruit of my study at that school.

MEETING MENTALLY AND PHYSICALLY DISABLED CHILDREN

I cheated my way through that exercise and shot what I could; then, when summer vacation came, our teacher asked us to work on an even longer project. I wondered what to shoot. One day, I saw a touching newspaper article about some girls from Akita who'd been hired by a facility for severely mentally and physically disabled children, and who were coming to Tokyo. I went to the place where these girls had been hired so I could take pictures of them.

I walked from the Akitsu Station on the Seibu Ikebukuro Line, which was not far from the Akitsu Rehabilitation Center. I went alone. This was the first I'd known of the existence of mentally and physically disabled children. The children there were intellectually impaired, and on top of that, they were severely physically disabled. Severely. I couldn't help feeling quite shocked when I learned of their existence.

I asked the directors if I could photograph the center, and they let me. My eyes were naturally drawn to the children, rather than the young girls taking care of them, so that's whom I ended up taking pictures of. As for establishing a relationship with the children, fortunately or unfortunately, their condition made it impossible for them to protest or object to my photographing them. I had the consent of the institution, and that was enough.

I submitted the photos of the children to my school when summer vacation was over, but I began to wonder if it should just end there. Having taken their pictures, there was no way I could stop. I felt compelled to continue visiting them—or to be more exact, to continue taking photographs of them. In the meantime, I was given one school assignment after another that somehow had to get done. I'm not that good at juggling things, so more and more assignments were being left undone. I was delivering newspapers, too. It was just physically impossible to deliver newspapers in the morning and in the evening, go to school during the day, and frequent the facility on top of that. So I quit school. I enjoyed going to the facility and spending time with the children—and taking their photographs—more than going to school. So I stopped going to school as a matter of course. In the end, I only went to school for a few months.

When I first visited the facility, I was filled with sugar-coated notions about the young girls from Akita who were working there. However, such notions flew out the window when I saw the reality of their situation. These girls thought about the children and about helping them day and night. They allowed me to sit in on their workshops with the children, and little by little, they influenced my own thinking. So when I finished taking my pictures, I didn't think it was over.

The girls never asked me what I was going to do with the pictures I had taken, but there was one female employee there with cerebral palsy who was a little older than them. She asked me several times, with some bitterness, what I was going to do with the photos, what I was trying to achieve. That had something to do with it as well.

I continued to go, and she eventually introduced me to other groups of people with disabilities. A number of facilities for varying degrees of disabilities exist in what one might call the "world of the disabled." Some are for adults; others are for children.

At the time, there was this guy who was putting up a fight at the Second National Hospital. He had somehow cut his leg off in an attempted suicide or something, and needed an operation to use a prosthetic leg. He had started a political movement demanding that the operation be paid for with public funds. A group of activists that included people both with and without disabilities supported him. Members of a group of people with cerebral palsy called "Green Grasses" took the lead in this new movement. I was introduced to and began hanging out with them. I came to understand the meaning of political movements from participating in their activities. This particular protest had been going on for some time. At its most intense, it culminated in such actions as a sit-in at the Ministry of Health and Welfare.

When these groups of people with disabilities said they were going to stage a sit-in, they clearly intended that only those with disabilities should participate. I innocently tagged along and came to know about such things. I had come to Tokyo knowing really nothing about the world, and, bit by bit, I was learning how society functioned, how people lived their lives.

THE REVOLUTION IN MAHARABA VILLAGE

While I was hanging out with these people with cerebral palsy, they introduced me to another facility. My circle expanded. I went here and there, making more and more connections. It was thus that I began to go to Maharaba Village.

Maharaba Village was in Niihari County in Ibaraki Prefecture.[13] To get there, you had to get off at Ishioka Station and take a bus from Ishioka City all the way out to Chiyoda. I think Chiyoda Village is now a city, but back then, it was a village.

At the base of a mountain there called Mt. Kankyo was a temple. The head monk of the temple was actually a revolutionary. His name was Osaragi Akira. He was a revolutionary and a philosopher, a monk and a radical. He brought people with cerebral palsy together and started a commune he called Maharaba Village. My friends introduced me to the place, so I went to see it. I returned a number of times.

Going to this place was a powerful experience for me. Osaragi would scold and teach me, telling me that I knew nothing about the world.

I went there sometime in the mid-'60s, when the student movement hadn't yet gained momentum, just before the street demonstrations in Shinjuku grew to their full force. I can recall the sequence of what happened in that period because, first of all, I began frequenting Mt. Kankyo, and after that, I began visiting the Kyōmyō School for Handicapped Children, where I met a woman called Takeda Miyuki with whom I eventually started living. It was around that time that massive street demonstrations—huge folk music gatherings, for example—were taking place in Shinjuku, and we jumped into the foray and protested together.

Maharaba Village didn't bring people with cerebral palsy together in order to sequester them away from the townspeople. In fact, Osaragi let them use property that was part of the temple. But since it was in the mountains, the people with cerebral palsy wouldn't run into the townspeople on a daily basis.

Since Osaragi was a monk whose family had been priests in the region for ages, he didn't have any conflicts with the locals. I don't know much about his life, but he was a member of the Socialist Party.

13 Niihara County: Now Omitama City.

He was fascinating: a communist member of the Socialist Party of Japan and also a Buddhist.

In those days, people with mild cerebral palsy could enter a school for the disabled, but those whose conditions were more severe weren't allowed to do so. Not being able to go to school, many such people stayed at home until they passed away, as if left to die from utter uselessness.

One of the revolutionary steps Rev. Osaragi took was to find people with serious cases of cerebral palsy and to marry them to each other. He was hoping that such marriages would make Maharaba Village a stronghold for people with disabilities.

He'd tell me about the buraku villages[14]—that is, villages populated by people who were discriminated against as social outcasts—and say that they served as the very foundation of the emperor system.[15] He would then say that he wasn't setting out to eliminate such areas. Instead, he was going to establish a multitude of them all over the country. He believed that this would in effect make them as good as irrelevant. So he gathered together people with cerebral palsy to establish an area for social outcasts. It was all part of his plan to establish a number of such areas.

"Hmm, that's one way to think about things," I thought. It opened my eyes. Instead of eliminating such areas, let's make a lot of them.

Osaragi once said that it was interesting how we humans can't help discriminating against even parts of our own bodies. We can't help thinking of our butts, our legs, or our hands as dirty. The beautiful parts of the body are segregated from the sordid parts. Humans are creatures who discriminate, so by creating a lot of discrimination everywhere, it would become meaningless. That's

---

14 *buraku* (Lit. "village"): Refers to a social minority group descended from outcast communities whose members worked in occupations that often related to death and so carried the social stigma of being "tainted" or "defiled" (e.g. executioners, undertakers, leatherworkers, etc.).

15 "emperor system": Ideology that emerged in Japan with the Meiji Restoration (circa 1868) that asserts the emperor's centrality to the Japanese nation and polity. In this system, all Japanese subjects must revere and fight for the emperor as a way of showing their loyalty to their country.

the way Osaragi thought.

He said, "Think about education. Education requires discrimination." He had a point.

That was his philosophy. But interestingly enough, Maharaba Village could not, in the end, keep from falling apart.

Marrying together people with cerebral palsy was, obviously, a revolutionary act. I thought so at the time. Those with cerebral palsy had never even dreamed of being able to get married, but they were brought to Maharaba Village anyway. There they could meet a member of the opposite sex and fall in love. True, the meetings were arranged, but they could get married and become a couple. And they would be given a house—really just a small barrack—in the expanse at the base of the mountain. They could then have a home. Since they were married, they would have children. Cerebral palsy is not genetically inherited, so they could have healthy kids.

Trouble soon followed, though. It was at this point that the women, more so than the men, began to have second thoughts. From their perspective, they'd been kicked out of society because they had a disability. But now they'd been able to get married and have a husband. They'd been able to have kids. In short, they'd been able to have a home, a family. But their children were healthy. These women began to wonder if they shouldn't raise their healthy children in the society of healthy people—and if not amongst healthy people, then at least not in a village where only people with cerebral palsy lived.

Rev. Osaragi would say that by giving birth to healthy children, they had earned a banner made of diapers instead of brocade. And so people began to think about leaving the village. That's when the philosophy of Maharaba Village started to unravel. Some couples expressed their wish to leave, and they did in fact leave. And so, as an idea, Maharaba Village was destined to perish. And it did.

The Green Grasses group in Kanagawa had been formed by one of the groups that had left Maharaba Village. The person who'd most wanted to go out into the society of healthy people was the wife of Yokota Hiroshi, one of the protagonists of *Goodbye CP*. That's the history of Maharaba Village. Those who left would say that the greatest misfortune for a person with disabilities would be to have a healthy child. Outcast parents have outcast children. Black parents have black children. In other words, their children are no different from them. But it's not the same for people with disabilities. Parents with disabilities can have healthy children, children on the other side of the fence. According to them, that was their misfortune.

So I would visit the group from time to time, watching with interest how things were going.

BECOMING A FULL-TIME HELPER AT THE KŌMYŌ SCHOOL FOR HANDICAPPED CHILDREN.

While Maharaba Village was disintegrating, I started visiting the Kōmyō Municipal School for Handicapped Children in Tokyo. Until I visited, I had no idea how things there worked. Basically, the children's daily needs were provided for by their parents. When the parents couldn't come, they would hire young men and women part-time to provide that service. These part-time workers would come to the classroom and take the kids to the bathroom or open their notebooks for them, tending to their daily needs. Among these helpers was a woman named Takeda Miyuki.

I started visiting the school from time to time. A kind of union had been formed by those part-time employees who believed in the ideas of the Japanese Communist Party. They presented their situation to the governor of Tokyo at that time, Governor Minobe.[16] These employees believed that parents of children with disabilities had a basic right to not have to pay for the care of their children, and that the government should create a system that would do so for them. They started a movement based on these beliefs, and the government responded.

16 Governor Minobe: Governor of Tokyo from 1967 to 1979. Formerly a Marxist economist. Supported by the Socialist Party of Japan.

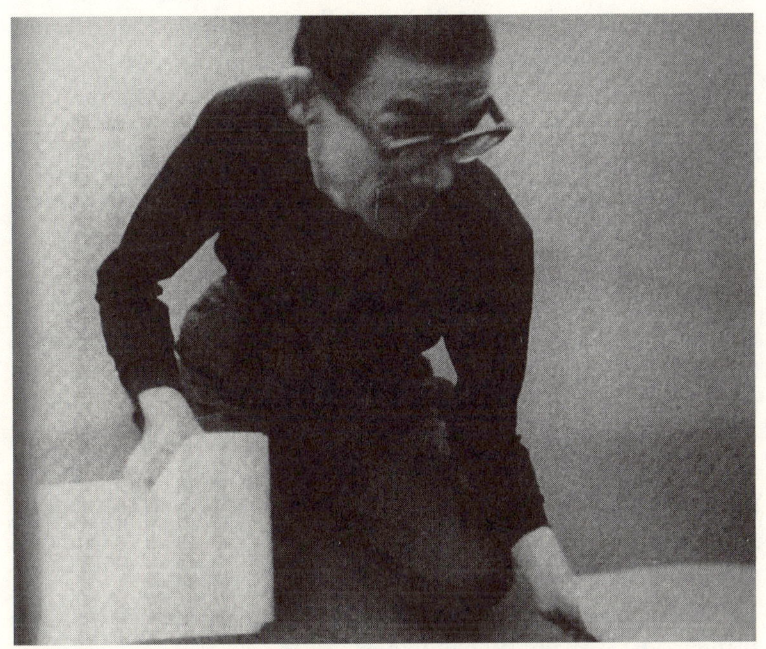

Goodbye CP. I met and began to spend time with "Green Grasses," a group of activists with cerebral palsy in Kanagawa Prefecture.

Out of this was born the full-time helper system. Those who worked part-time were re-hired as full-time employees. Takeda Miyuki was in this first generation of full-time helpers. I started visiting around that time, and thought I should try working there. So I started as a full-time helper in the second year of the program. That was about the time when the street protests began to escalate.

Sometime around then, I was invited to join the Japan Communist Party (JCP). In order to join, you had to have an interview of some kind. I made it past the interview, then went as far as the trial period. Because I was working as a full-time helper at the school during Minobe's governorship, I was automatically part of union activities. I was functioning more or less like a union director, and the idea of becoming a photographer had pretty much left my mind. I was beginning to think that life as an activist might suit me better.

I aided students in the fourth grade as a full-time helper. Taking care of the children in my class, I was resigned to quitting photography, but I continued to take pictures of them anyway.

Union activities were pretty interesting. The JCP had the most influence at the school. I guess this was the case with most schools back then. Young people associated with the party surrounded me, so I was naturally invited to join. The party itself urged me to join. They said, "Why don't you at least take an interview?" So I took one. I went that far. On the other hand, street conflicts were taking place. Those who participated in them were, of course, anti-JCP, and I found myself drawn to them as well. Since my union denounced those fighting in the streets, I found myself torn. I wondered what to do.

Takeda Miyuki and I started living together while I was working at the school. Cohabitation didn't go over so well at the JCP, so they criticized our situation.

Takeda Miyuki was from Gifu Prefecture. After graduating from high school, she moved to Tokyo. Her high school had been a fine-arts school, so her desire to express herself was much stronger than mine. After moving to Tokyo, she naturally wanted to do something creative. At first, she tried painting; then she started wanting to paint in three dimensions, not two. In other words, she wanted to use her body for self-expression. Her desire for expression grew, or rather, assumed manifold forms. With the struggles going on in Shinjuku, the streets were in an uproar, and she was drawn to them as well. Takeda Miyuki was like a ball of energy back then. It seemed as though she herself had no idea where her energy was going to lead her. She went this way, hit a wall that way, then got bashed over this way again.

We got to know each other, and she began to consult me whenever she hit a wall. "Let's see what this is..." We would put our heads together, and I would try to affirm her energy through words—or, to put it another way, to sort things out. As a result of what I said, she would realize that her energy was fundamentally on the right track, despite being bashed about, and this would strengthen her self-confidence another notch. She gradually became more self-assured, but Takeda Miyuki's energy, which went banging about every which way, was incompatible with the sensibility of the JCP. So they criticized her even more, for things beyond the fact that we were living together.

I learned this later, but Takeda Miyuki had been invited by someone else to join the JCP, and had deferred her answer. Then she'd gotten together with me, so the criticisms from the party and those around the party had grown even harsher. Our relationship with JCP members at work grew worse.

For that reason, she quit the school before I did. Having quit first, she tried to find her own mode of expression while doing part-time work.

That was a time when new genre-defying experimental movements were taking place in areas such as the theater and cinema. But we weren't a part of those scenes. The most significant thing for us at the time was, inevitably, the street conflicts. Since we lived in Umegaoka, we'd often go to Shinjuku, where we would find the streets in a tumult. For example, if we went to town, we'd hook up with our colleagues—the guys in the JCP, I mean—for a drink. We'd go to a sushi restaurant, and there'd be an uproar on the other side of the street. The JCP members would then criticize the demonstrators, saying, "They're idiots. They're Trotskyites." Listening to them, we realized that we didn't really share those views. I think that's why I became increasingly more interested in the street conflicts than I was in consorting with the JCP. Did I get involved with the demonstrations as a result? Not really.

I didn't really associate with the student movement, with the exception of one group: the Okinawa Joint Struggle Committee. I participated in a number of their demonstrations. The majority of the Committee was made up of members of the Japan Revolutionary Communist League, National Committee (Middle Core Faction). A few members of the Marxist Revolutionary Faction came to the rallies. I think that's basically how the Committee was made up. Of course, most of the members were students from Okinawa; there were also a few sympathetic students from the mainland. Once you hung out with the Okinawan students, they were all nice people. Smart, too.

To us, Okinawa was at the cutting edge of the era. I had the impression that it was a leading contestant for the term "Third World," which was being tossed around at the time. I don't mean that as something the movement represented, but as a general impression.

I visited and chatted with them a few times, but I only saw the "feud" between the Japan Revolutionary Communist League, National Committee (Middle Core Faction) and the Marxist Revolutionary Faction from the outside.[17] As for the All-Campus Joint Struggle Committee, all I did was join their demonstrations, so I know very little of what it was really like. In other words, precisely *because* I know so little, I think I can look back on that era at my age. If I had been a central member of an organization, deep inside a movement,

17 The Japanese Revolutionary Communist League (JRCL): A far-left revolutionary group originally formed in 1957. In 1963, members split off from the JRCL to form the JRCL Marxist Revolutionary Faction. Loyalists to the JRCL were referred to as the Middle Core Faction. During the 1970s, the two factions were engaged in a bloody rivalry.

I would have been left with a different feeling. But because I was on the fringes of the fringe, it felt as if I only absorbed the atmosphere of those times. That is to say, I organically absorbed my own version of the culture of that era.

THE IMPORTANCE OF FOCUSING ON URBAN "INDIVIDUALS"

At the Kōmyō School for Handicapped Children, I worked with members of the JCP, but I never got along with them fully. I was personally close to some of those in the student movement, but they were all from Okinawa, so when I hung out with them, I was inevitably made self-conscious about the fact that I was from the mainland. Being in such a compromised position, I think I had no choice but to seek out my own arena for self-representation. Somewhere, at my very core, I probably wanted to express myself. In other words, when it came to the labor movement, I was neither a laborer nor, of course, a student—which is why, I guess, I ended up aspiring to make movies. As such, I'm not critical of the student movement: I wasn't in a position to critique it.

Intellectuals were at the vanguard of the student movement, so it wasn't as though I got involved with them. The Japan Communist Party was pretty influential on the fringes of the labor movement, but I didn't think about getting involved in any part of the labor movement, either. I didn't get directly involved in art—in theater or cinema, for example—so all my stimulus came from being in contact with something like the atmosphere of the era.

Ogawa Productions' *Sanrizuka* series had already started playing by then, so I made a point of seeing every single film whenever it came out. I was dying to see each one. They would play at places like Toshima Public Hall in Ikebukuro, not regular movie theaters. The lines would go around the block. Inside, the theater would be full of energy. Though I didn't throw myself into the hubbub right away, I did soon thereafter.

Speaking of the documentary film movement at that time: filmmakers like Ogawa and Tsuchimoto Noriaki began their careers out of a sympathetic association with the student movement.[18]

Around that time, I became infatuated by Ogawa Productions.[19] I thought that Ogawa's company seemed like fun, so, for a while, I thought about joining. But that feeling only lasted for a moment: I couldn't think of anything I'd be able to contribute if I did join. By this I mean that my character prevents me from being a team player. I think that was why I couldn't just dive into it.

At the time, Ogawa Productions was promoting the idea that documentary filmmaking required taking sides, that there was no such thing as a neutral camera position. For me, the most significant dilemma raised by the *Sanrizuka* films was whether or not to shoot the struggle against state power from one side or the other. Even television documentaries were intensively pursuing such questions at the time. When I would read books by or meet people like Tahara Sōichirō, I would learn that they were discussing and developing strategies to address similar kinds of problems.[20] This was an era when the question of how expression should take place on television was being grappled with from within the gigantic, state-run system called television, right at the frontlines, by the likes of Tahara and

---

18 Tsuchimoto Noriaki (1928 – 2008): Documentary filmmaker and social activist. His "Minamata series" is well-known for its stark portrayal of people with Minamata disease, a neurological syndrome caused by the release of mercury into the water around Minamata city by local industries.

19 Ogawa Productions: Ogawa Productions is closely identified with collective modes of production. Although director Ogawa was at it's undisputed center, the collective worked as a group photographing—and deeply identifying with—other groups. Their first films on the political activism of 1960s established their reputation with the student movement, which recognized the radicality of their practice. The New Left continued to support their filmmaking through loans and donations for two major series of films. For the *Sanrizuka* series, they lived with the farmers who were fighting the construction of Narita Airport, and filmed their struggle. After that, the collective moved to a farmhouse deep in the northern mountains and made another series on village life. Ogawa's commitment to the politics of collective modes of production stand in stark contrast to Hara's individual approach. Where their conception of documentary intersects is the absolute importance placed on the relationship between the filming subject and filmed object. [Nornes]

20 Tahara Sōichirō (1934 -): Prolific writer, translator, and documentary filmmaker.

Muraki Yoshihiko.[21]

During that period, I was taking pictures of subjects other than children. For example, I thought it was important to be *in* a demonstration first rather than trying to capture it objectively from the outside. So I would be in the rank and file in the middle of a demonstration, snapping shots while marching. But no matter how I tried, there was no way I could get a shot of the demonstration in its entirety if I were in the middle of it. But there I was, like a fool, taking pictures from the midst of a demonstration.

When I went to Okinawa with my friends from the Okinawa Joint Struggle Committee, we traveled together by boat all the way from Tokyo to Naha. When the Port of Naha refused the group permission to dock, I naturally took shots from the perspective of my friends.

Later, after I started making films, a cameraman for Ogawa Productions was arrested. An article published in the *Asahi Shimbun* covered the event in detail. Printed along with it was a famous image of a riot trooper putting his hand over the lens of a camera. This took place during the production of *Summer in Narita*.[22]

I must admit that when I saw that image, I realized that filming with a camera required taking a position against authority—or rather, that it was impossible to make a film without having the kind of determination necessary to take such a position.

The films made by Ogawa Productions left an indelible mark on me in that they represented the era in the way I just described. But in truth, the films that I enjoyed watching the most were television documentaries: works by Tahara, or serialized pieces by Muraki such as *My Volcano*, which used the camera from a first-person perspective.

I remember a 30-minute program from Muraki's series, *The Rising Sun* or something, which showed a soccer game in which Kamamoto or someone played, and the only sound used was that of the spectators watching the game. Muraki had a number of pieces like that. I

21 Muraki Yoshihiko (1936 – 2008): Director and television producer.
22 *Summer in Narita* (1968): The first film in Ogawa's *Sanrizuka* series.

watched the works of these television directors thinking that they were doing something truly interesting. To sum up: when thinking of that era's influence on me, I can't disregard Ogawa Productions, of course, but what really excited me back then, what I really loved, were television documentaries.

There's something else I've realized after the fact. When you think of Ogawa Productions, you think of the *Sanrizuka* series. The subjects of their films were farmers who lived communally. After making *Goodbye CP*, I thought that Ogawa Productions focused on communities, I would focus on individuals. In other words, if they shot documentaries of the "village type," I would opt for documentaries that dealt with the "urban." This was all very theoretical, though.

After all, they were from the '60s; they belonged to a previous generation. What was it about the '70s that had influenced us the most? It wasn't just the struggles: it was the act of questioning oneself. That was why we'd gotten involved in such struggles. We'd look at ourselves, at our own individuality, and keep questioning who we were. Who are you, the you who wants to express yourself? How are you going to do so? Who is this individual driven to self-expression? As such, I think I would have focused on myself, even if I had joined Ogawa Productions. Creating something as a group was an attractive idea, but the people in Ogawa Productions were already doing that. So I decided to concentrate on individuals. I think that was my reasoning process.

It's not that I was vehemently against Ogawa Productions. But there's no question that I somehow didn't completely accept their methods.

THE OPENING OF MY ONE-MAN SHOW AT THE NIKON SALON

I'd been working for a year as a full-time helper at the Kōmyō School for Handicapped Children when I started thinking that I didn't want to be there for much longer. So I quit. After I quit, I submitted my photographs of children to the Nikon Salon photo gallery in Ginza.

I was given a one-man show that ran there for a week in 1969 from July 14th to the 20th. It didn't attract many people. At the time, the Nikon Salon would put on socially relevant exhibitions, then approach TV stations with them. One TV station had apparently liked my exhibit, and planned to invite me to their studio, but something else came up, and my TV appearance was canceled.

In terms of the print media, two magazines saw my exhibit and bought my photos. As for photography magazine reviews, I don't think they were anything extraordinary, given the nature of my photos. They just touched upon the exhibit, without any fanfare.

However, I was the first of my photography school classmates to have a solo exhibition. I beat everyone who hadn't dropped out of school. So almost everyone I knew from school came to see my show when it opened. The teacher who'd been in charge of my class when I'd entered school recommended what music to play and lent me a tape. His name was Kajiwara Takao; he was the person who shot the stills for *Woman in the Dunes*.[23]

Two stories from the exhibition left an impression on me.

The first: Takeda Miyuki was sitting in the midst of that solemn atmosphere in the exhibit space downstairs where all the photos were on display. She'd just been sitting on the floor, leaning against a wall. A photographer who was also a juror for the Nikon Salon saw her and said that she shouldn't be allowed to sit like that. He didn't tell her directly, but told the manager.

When I heard this and told Takeda Miyuki about it, she went ballistic, demanding to know why she couldn't sit however she wanted. She said that this showed how conservative and authoritarian the photographer was, despite his importance.

I remember trying to console by her by saying, "Well, that's just how it is..."

23 *Woman in the Dunes*: 1964 film by Teshigahara Hiroshi that was based on the 1962 novel by Abe Kobo.

The second: Kobayashi Sachiko, who had just moved to Tokyo, came to see my exhibition. She saw my pictures and spoke to me, not the other way around. So we started to talk. She was wearing braids, and I remember asking her if she were a junior-high-school student.

After the show, I began playing with the idea of becoming a photographer again. Somehow, I'd already forgotten that I'd wanted to be an activist, and had decided instead to become a photographer. It wasn't so much that I wanted to take photographs as that I wanted to become a photographer.

Having quit the Kōmyō School for Handicapped Children, I think I was inclined once again toward expressing myself. As before, Takeda Miyuki was groping about for her own mode of self-expression. As she went from one part-time job to the next, her paintings gradually became more three-dimensional. For example, instead of simply applying paint, she would embed or overlay various objects....

I myself wavered between becoming an activist and an artist.

The most decisive factor was that Takeda Miyuki had such a strong desire for expression—much stronger than mine. It was truly amazing. She was aggressive all the time, not knowing where to direct her energy. To put it kindly, she was, for a while, in a magma-like state. While we lived together, she would plow into me every so often. Every time she did so, she'd be hung up on something or other. In response, I would say things like, "What do you mean by that?" I had a tendency to rationalize back then.

As I dealt with her in this way—giving advice, thinking along with her about her desires and her demands—it seemed as though she were teaching me to accept her desires as something positive. On the one hand, perhaps I gave her energy some direction; on the other hand, it was undeniable that her energy stimulated me. I think that's why, when she told me she was going to devote herself to three-dimensional expression, I felt inclined to try photography once more.

At first, I moved into Takeda Miyuki's apartment; then I just stayed on. Those on the periphery of the Japan Communist Party directed quite a bit of negative criticism at us, calling us slackers and so on. Takeda Miyuki was rather defensive about such comments. She didn't want people to criticize what we were doing behind our backs, so we rented an apartment and lived there together. She said she didn't want her parents to say things about us either, so she wanted to register our marriage officially. So we did. In that sense, it was a proper marriage. We didn't scoff at marriage registration. Instead, we were focused at the time on taking proper measures so that we wouldn't be criticized.

When she said she wanted to register our marriage, I agreed. It was her idea. I quit working at the school at around that time, and we talked about living together and renting a room. The mothers of the children in my class insisted on giving us a present, so we got a dining table from them. I'm still using it in my house today. And that's how we began our life together.

Since Takeda Miyuki was painting and working with objects at the time, she wanted to have a studio in the house. Of course, renting a place big enough for a studio would have been incredibly expensive. We ended up renting a place in Ikenoue, but it was too small, so we didn't stay there long.

She wanted a place more like a loft, so we looked for a bigger space. We moved into a house in Yamato City in Kanagawa Prefecture. It was more spacious, so after we moved in, she went and bought a large piece of plywood the size of a tatami mat and painted on it for some time as though it were a canvas.

There were about three or four other one-story houses on our block. Our house was the only one with an unkempt front garden. All the others were beautifully groomed; ours was wild and overgrown, with weeds happily growing everywhere. When I asked if we should get rid of the weeds, Takeda Miyuki said she wanted to leave the front garden natural, so we let them grow as they wanted. Even our landlord asked us to weed the front yard.

In that sense, people in the neighborhood might have thought we were strange, but Takeda Miyuki didn't care one bit. Probably because we didn't spend much time at home.

THE FIRST TIME I SHOT ON 8-MM FILM

I liked watching television, so I would watch a lot of it. I once saw a program about a young woman from Okinawa. I think the director was Arai Kazuko of the Tokyo Broadcasting System.

Some Okinawan students had organized themselves into a group called the Okinawa Joint Struggle Committee. This group had caused an accident, or rather an incident. They had sailed from Okinawa to the Harumi wharf in Tokyo and, without disembarking, had barricaded themselves in their boat and burned their passports. This was before Okinawa was reincorporated into Japan in 1972. They weren't arrested or anything, it was just reported that they had been. A number of these students eventually left the boat and started living in Tokyo. The program followed the lives of these people, focusing on one of the girls in the group. She was incredibly endearing, and this compelled Takeda Miyuki to want to meet her.

Takeda Miyuki asked me if I would go with her to meet the girl, so I went. We met her a few times and talked at a bar, chatting over drinks. I'm saying she was a girl, but she was about 19 or 20. Through our conversations, I became interested in Okinawa—though not in the same way as Takeda Miyuki.

The following year, I thought of visiting Okinawa. Just before Okinawa's reincorporation, I went there with a group of students but without Takeda Miyuki. That was when my association with Okinawa genuinely began.

The year after that, Takeda Miyuki said that she now wanted to go to Okinawa without me, so she went. It was March or April 1970, right when the Japanese Red Army hijacked Japan Airlines Flight 351 and flew it to North Korea.

All of the guys in the Okinawa group were good-looking. None of them went to Ryūkyū University or one of the other schools in Okinawa; they all received money from Tokyo to attend university there. In other words, because Okinawa had yet to be returned to Japan, they were students studying abroad. They were all smart and

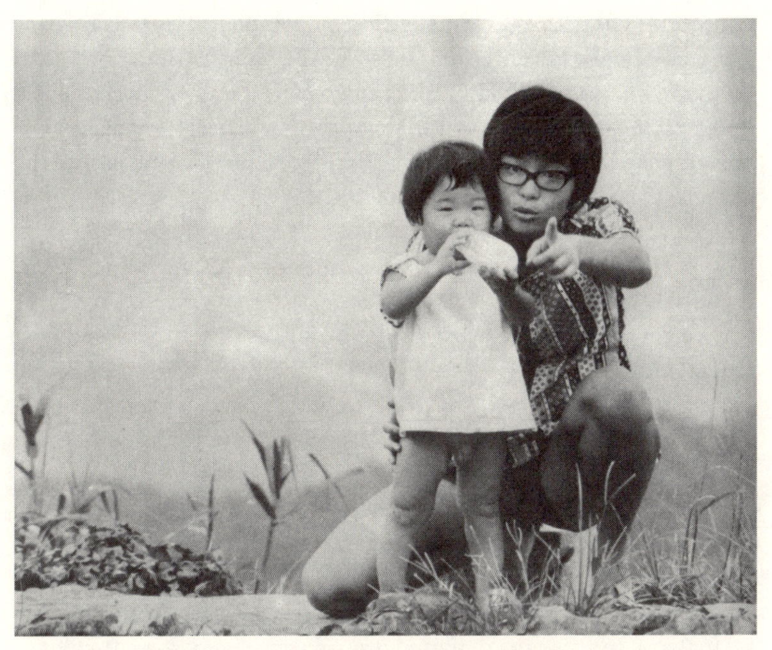

Extreme Private Eros: Love Song 1974. I lived with Takeda Miyuki, on the right. At the time, she was like a ball of energy.

very conscientious.

Takeda Miyuki had a crush on one of the guys. Then she went to Okinawa. And she didn't return on the day she was supposed to. It was strange. I kept wondering what was going on. I got worried and called her a few times, imploring her to come home. Eventually, she did. When she came home, she told me she had fallen for one of the guys in the group. She had seduced him and slept with him.

I was shocked. That was the kind of intense woman she was.

I clearly remember the hijacking of JAL Flight 351 because it happened when Takeda Miyuki didn't come home from Okinawa. I waited alone, worrying myself sick. We were living together in Yamato City, and she hadn't come come back. I was paralyzed. Every image on television was of the hijacking. That era of extreme political movements was an extremely turbulent time for me personally because of my relationship with a woman.

The affair between Takeda Miyuki and the guy from Okinawa didn't continue after that. It was nothing worth noting, and as such, it ended.

To get to the point, while living in Yamato City, we had our first child. Our first son, Takeda Rei, was born in 1970. A weekly magazine picked up our story. However, this wouldn't have happened if we'd simply been living a normal life. There were other events that had led up to our being featured in the magazine article.

First, I'd met Kobayashi Sachiko, who'd told me that she wanted to make a film. She was looking for a partner to make it with, so she asked me.

Kobayashi had graduated from Niigata University. Wanting to make a movie, she'd moved to Tokyo, where she attended a screenwriting institute where the teachers taught their students not to give a damn about screenplays. They believed that a new form of cinematic expression would emerge from subverting old screenwriting methods—from destroying or "deconstructing" the screenplay.

Her teachers were the screenwriter Ishidō Toshirō,[24] the

24 Ishidō Toshirō (1932–): Screenwriter of *The Sun's Burial* and others.

director Urayama Kiriro,[25] and the director Yoshida Kijū.[26] They told their students that they shouldn't be writing scripts, and refused teach them anything. So Kobayashi immediately switched to documentaries. She says she found herself taking a camera and going out into the streets.

It so happened that she met me at such a time and in such an era. "Let's make a film, whatever it may turn out to be," she said, and I said, "It's a deal." I was still living with Takeda Miyuki at the time, so the three of us decided to make a movie together.

We had no money, so we initially thought that each of us would shoot something we were interested in on 8-mm film, and that we'd then put the results together into a single movie.

Takeda Miyuki said that she wanted to do something about seemingly meaningless acts—going in and out of a bathroom, for example. I forget what else she proposed. It was the era for that kind of thing, and I think she was under the influence of that kind of art at the time.

Kobayashi Sachiko wanted to make a film called *Document Okinawa* and handed out flyers in Meiji Park. Why Okinawa? Because it was trendy. [Laughs.] More stuff seemed to be happening in Okinawa than anywhere else. In addition, she wanted to make the movie in Tokyo, without going to Okinawa. Somehow, the two of them were just totally idealistic.

As for me, for some reason, I wanted to meet Nakazawa Keiji, the creator of the manga about the atomic bomb.[27] So we went and interviewed him on 8-mm. Then we interviewed a foreign student from Vietnam, Chua Swee-Lin, the protagonist of Tsuchimoto Noriaki's film *Exchange Student, Chua Swee-Lin*. We borrowed an 8-mm camera from Kawanaka Nobuhiro. I think I operated the camera

25 Urayama Kiriro (1930–1985): Filmmaker and writer. Directed and wrote films such as *Foundry Town*, *Gate of Youth*, and *Taro the Dragon Boy*. Hara discusses his experiences working with Urayama in Chapter 4.

26 Yoshida Kijū (1933–): Filmmaker associated with the so-called Japanese New Wave. Famous for *Good-for-Nothing*, *Eros Plus Massacre*, and other films.

27 Nakazawa Keiji (1939–): Manga artist best known for his *Barefoot Gen* series, which depicts the bombing of Hiroshima and its aftermath.

while Kobayashi Sachiko conducted the interview.

I did the interview with Nakazawa Keiji, and decided to visit and talk to Muraki Yoshihiko, a director, as part of the film. At the time, Muraki was making remarks reminiscent of the All-Campus Joint Struggle Committee on the Tokyo Broadcasting System. He had published a book called *Television! You are Nothing But The Present Moment*. By then, Tahara Sōichirō's serialized *Documentary Youth* had also been made into a book—his first or second—and had been published by San-ichi Publishing under the tile *Youth, This Delirious Thing*. I'd bought and read these books. I think that's why I thought about meeting with Muraki as part of our 8-mm project. We met and chatted, but it didn't go further than that. I didn't film him.

Bit by bit, I was shooting my 8-mm film, with no clear goal in sight.

Some time after meeting with Muraki, I received a phone call from Tahara Sōichirō. He said he was going to film Fuji Keiko for *Documentary Youth*. The song "Dreams Blossom at Night" was a huge hit at the time, and Fuji Keiko was a big star.[28] He'd hired Muraki Yoshihiko as the writer for the piece. Now he was looking for someone to intervew Fuji Keiko—someone young and suitable for the job.

Kobayashi, Takeda Miyuki, and I had gone to see Muraki. He'd remembered Takeda Miyuki, and had in fact contacted her directly. So Takeda Miyuki took on the role of interviewer in the show about Fuji Keiko. The two of them chatted in Hibiya Park while a cameraman named Miyauchi filmed them on 16-mm. During the shoot, I simply watched Miayauchi, thinking to myself, "Hmmm. So that's how you shoot a film."

I think the episode was called "Fuji Keiko Sings Scenes of June." Tahara was the man who'd made *Documentary Youth*; he didn't want to simply give a behind-the-scenes look at Fuji Keiko, he wanted to present the current state of things—the atmosphere of the times—through this meeting between Fuji Keiko and a girl her own age. It was clearly not

28 Fuji Keiko (1951–): Popular female singer of the time; mother of contemporary pop singer Utada Hikaru.

his intention to go deep inside Fuji Keiko the human being.

At that time, it seemed as if popular songs were ubiquitous. I couldn't stand them. Every image, every picture would always be coupled with a tune. The two would be talking in the midst of some June scenery; then a picture of a street demonstration would be inserted, over which "Dreams Blossom at Night" would play. There you have it: "Fuji Keiko Sings Scenes of June." It was that sort of show. Needless to say, it didn't make much of an impact. But that was the first time I'd seen someone shooting a film from up close.

So Takeda Miyuki appeared on the show with Fuji Keiko. In it, if I remember correctly, she revealed that she was pregnant. As a result, a writer for a weekly magazine who'd seen the show and wanted to interview her came to our house. I'd been taking pictures of Takeda Miyuki—of her huge stomach—throughout her pregnancy. We decided to include these photos with the article, and they were published.

APPEARING ON TAHARA SŌICHIRŌ'S TELEVISION SHOW

This would eventually lead to *Extreme Private Eros: Love Song 1974*. When Takeda Miyuki was pregnant with her first-born child, I photographed the progress of her pregnancy, her increasingly expanding stomach. Before the child was born, she asked me to photograph her giving birth. I promised her I would. Then the due date came. She must have been nervous because it was her first child, so she decided to have the baby at the Citizens' Hospital in Yamato City. When she went into labor, I asked the nurses if I could photograph the birth, but they flat-out refused. "No way," they said. Since they wouldn't allow me to photograph her that time, I promised her I would shoot the next one. This promise carried over into *Extreme Private Eros: Love Song 1974*. The phrase "according to a previous promise" that comes up in the opening sequence of the film refers to the one I'd made then.

About three months after the baby was born, we received a

phone call from Tahara again. He said that a program for a one-hour slot called *Friday Special* was being created, and that he was going to direct the first episode. At the time, Hashida Norihiko's song "Bride" was all the rage, so Tahara wanted to name his episode, "Japanese Brides." He proposed that the show be about Takeda Miyuki, myself, and our child as we visited wedding ceremonies or places where young couples were leading their lives all over Japan. In short, he wanted to make a show that depicted an aspect of the lives of young people of the time. He asked if we would play the role of interviewers. We agreed.

We filmed a variety of scenes: people who had once been involved with the student movement but who had gone on to run a farm in Hokkaido, or a wedding ceremony for two members of the Self-Defense Force. We filmed a range of couples, not only iconoclastic ones. We had planned to visit and interview couples all over the country, from the north end to the south, but in the end, we ran out of money and only covered the area between the Tōhoku region and Hokkaido.

Needless to say, Tahara accompanied us and directed the scenes. So back then, I was on the other side of the camera, being filmed along with Takeda Miyuki. But that experience also inspired me to go behind the camera. Since the show was supposed to be one hour long, its actual duration was about 40-odd minutes, I think. I recently asked Tahara what happened to the film, and he said that it's disappeared.

Tahara Sōichirō is mostly known now as the MC of *Live TV Till the Morning*, but back then, we had this image of him as someone who was doing experimental stuff in the medium of television. Four or five directors took turns making episodes for the *Documentary Youth* series, but Tahara's shows were the most radical, the most provocative. It was really fascinating. I loved that series. Before I even met the man himself, I loved his shows. If I had to say what stimulated or influenced me the most, I'd say it was either the *Documentary Youth* series or Tahara's methodology. Those were what fit my feelings best. Replace the word "television" with "cinema" in the title *Television! You Are Nothing But the Present Moment*, and you get a pretty good representation of my films.

Some time after we had our child, Takeda Miyuki decided she couldn't stand living under the aegis of a man. She said she wanted to live on her own and left me. Just like that. She joined a commune of women who were at the forefront of the women's liberation movement.

There's still more to discuss about the drama of Takeda Miyuki. I've talked about the very first bit: the birth of our child and our marriage. But in fact, there's still more.

If a woman has sex, she'll usually have a child. We were young, so we didn't think about using contraception. When she became pregnant, she said she didn't want to have the child, she wanted an abortion. *She* said that, not me. So I told her, "Okay." In my life, women always initiate the action... [Laughs.]

"I see. If you want to have an abortion, then you should have one," I agreed.

Then she got pregnant again. She said that she'd chosen not to have the child before, but she didn't want to do the same thing twice. In other words, she'd decided of her own free will not to have the first baby, so she wanted to have the freedom to decide to have the child this second time.

When it comes to such things, I really learned a lot from this woman Takeda Miyuki.

"I'm going to have this baby," she declared. "Oh. OK. If you say so, then go ahead," was all I could say. [Laughs.] It's always like that with me.

So we had our first child. After everything that had happened, we were a family of three. It's only natural that the three of us would have some blissful moments. In the opening sequence of photographs in *Extreme Private Eros*, there's a picture of the baby and me in the bathtub together. There was a time when the three of us were really close to one another.

But Takeda Miyuki came to loathe that very happiness after a while. Because we were living a peaceful life. She wanted to live with

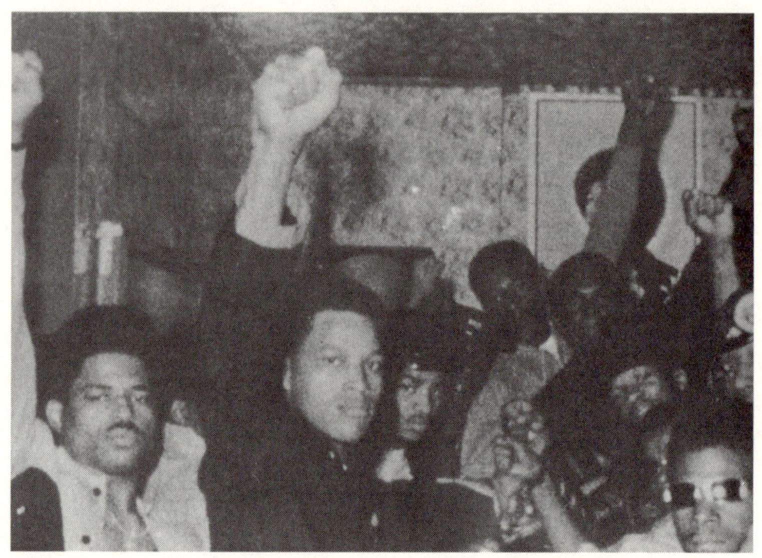

Extreme Private Eros: Love Song 1974. At the time, Okinawa was the most happening place.

intensity, so she left and joined the women's commune.

Earlier, I said that the notion of family is foreign to me. When Takeda Miyuki left, I didn't try to stop her. In theory, what she was saying made a lot of sense. She'd always announce that she was leaving. She'd say, "I'm leaving," and I'd completely understand her reasoning. After all, reasoning was something I'd engaged in all along. Her desire to live on her own was a natural extension of her way of thinking. So I was in no position to stop her, even if I had some lingering feelings for her. However, that's not to say that I was completely emotionless.

Around the time Takeda Miyuki left me, I started having an affair with Kobayashi Sachiko. So there was a period when we had a sort of love triangle.

At the same time, we were trying to make an 8-mm film. However, it was unclear what direction that was going in. Each of us had something we wanted to do, but when it came to putting everything together, we had no idea how to do so. In the meantime, my relationship with Takeda Miyuki was beginning to change, and it eventually fell apart. So, unconsciously perhaps, our motivation to make the 8-mm film began to lessen. That's what was going on during that period.

My house in Yamato City suddenly seemed big and empty. I realized that the place no longer had any significance for me, so I moved. I left Yamato and rented a room in Umegaoka. After Miyuki and I had quit working at the school, I'd taken a number of part-time jobs to make ends meet. Mostly at a printing company—Dai Nippon Printing in Ichigaya. Freshly printed materials would be collated and run through a bundling machine, then sent to the binding shop. Back then, I managed to get by doing part-time work such as that. I also worked as a waiter, but that didn't last for more than three days. I had a number of jobs, but my longest was at the printing company. In the midst of all that—all the situations in my life that were whirling about and melting into a single mass—I wandered this way and that, gradually moving toward my first film.

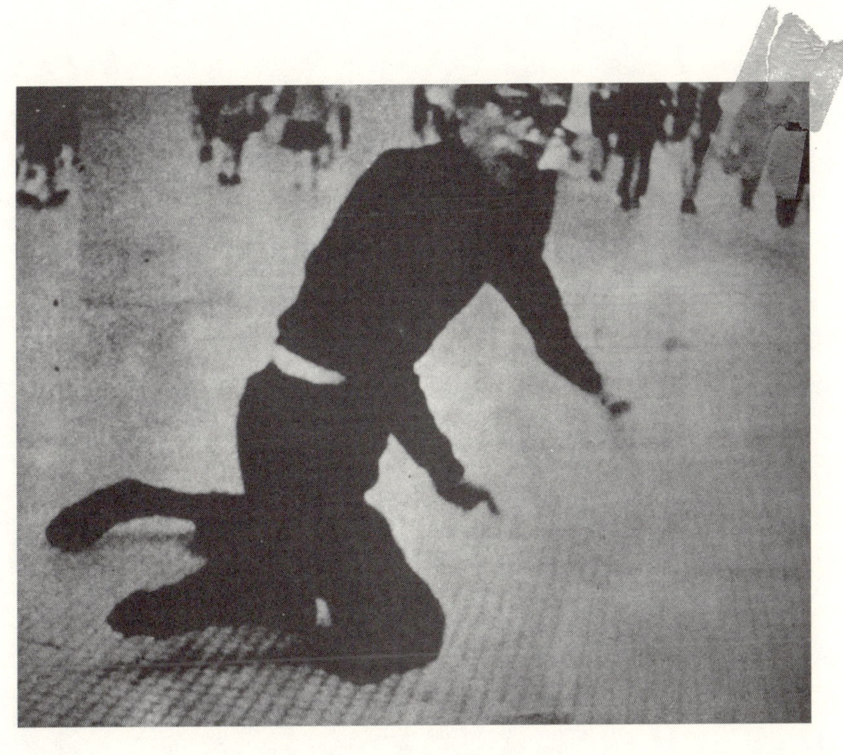

03 The Healthy vs. The Disabled

Goodbye CP

THROW OUT YOUR WHEELCHAIR AND HEAD FOR THE STREETS

So, finally, we've arrived at *Goodbye CP*.

In the end, our project to make a film with an 8-mm camera never got off the ground. At the same time, my photo exhibition had ended, and I had no concrete ideas about what to do next. Takeda Miyuki wanted to live on her own, so she'd left, and our personal relationship had come to an end. In the midst of this, Kobayashi and I continued to discuss making a film.

I think the idea of reuniting with and making a movie about people with cerebral palsy just surfaced naturally. I'd been living in the world of people with disabilities for five years, after all.

I'd been in charge of the fourth-grade class at the Kōmyō School for Handicapped Children, but classes also went all the way up to high school. So something I did while working there was to incite the high-school students into going into town with me. I would get a student in a wheelchair worked up by saying, "Let's take to the streets!" then bring him to Umegaoka Station on the Odakyu Line near the school. Terayama Shūji's book, *Throw Out Your Books and Head for the Streets,* was popular at the time.[1]

I'd tell him, "I'm not going to help you, so ask someone going by if they'd lift you to the top of the stairs in your wheelchair, even though it might be an imposition."

"OK," he'd say innocently.

Then he'd ask some passer-by to carry him upstairs. And they would. But wheelchairs don't fit through the ticket gate, so I'd tell him, "Ask the station staff to help you through."

"OK," he'd say. He'd ask, and we'd get on the train, go to Shinjuku Station, and get off again. And it isn't like this anymore, but as soon as we got out onto the platform, everyone would shoot these awful looks at the student.

---

1 *Throw Out Your Books and Head for the Streets*: 1967 book and play by the poet, playwright, and novelist Terayama Shūji (1935–1983), which he adapted to the screen in 1971.

The train would stop, the student in the wheelchair would exit, and people would just stare. And that was so provocative: it reeked so much of danger, it was so fascinating. Then we'd go out into the streets.

Nowadays, you can tell that there's some awareness of the issues surrounding people with disabilities from headlines about wheelchairs not being accommodated by city infrastructure. But we did all this before any of that had become a part of public discourse. By stirring up the high-school students, we wanted to *make* it an issue. People's reactions at the time were incredible. I took photographs of all of it.

We did this kind of thing a number of times. That's when I realized that, when thinking about the issues surrounding the disabled, you couldn't just build on existing awareness: you had to change something. The street battles and student movements of the time were clearly a direct influence. I thought we somehow had to fundamentally upset people's basic perceptions, their values regarding people with disabilities. Armed with this realization, I took the kids in wheelchairs to the streets in my own attempt to upset the existing order. Thus, after my photo exhibition ended, I began thinking about doing that kind of thing again, consciously, in the medium of film.

By then, Maharaba Village had completely dissolved, and most of its members, including Yokota Hiroshi and Yokotsuka Kōichi, were living in or around Kanagawa. Yokota and Yokotsuka were both smart and had assumed positions of leadership within the group, so I visited them several times. Over a period of half a year, I succeeded in persuading them to make a film with me.

When thinking about the problems of people with disabilities, I realized that what it all came down to in the end was that they were confined indoors for the entirety of their lives. "What about going to school? We have schools for the handicapped," they would reply. I'd tell them they were in effect being sealed up inside these schools, which were fenced in. The school buses that were provided for their transportation were for them alone, so even between their homes and their schools, they were being shut away from the rest of society. They'd finish school and simply transfer to a facility for adults. I'd ask them: "In sum, aren't you spending your entire lives in confinement? In order to change that, wouldn't you have to go out into the streets and change the way your bodies are perceived?"

Perhaps this is a bit abstract, but "disabled" means "deprived of bodily freedom, especially of the limbs." That is, it's an issue of the body, an issue regarding the freedom and restraint of the limbs. That's where society draws the line. In other words, the line dividing "freedom" from "non-freedom" is whether or not you have a body that can contribute labor to society. The prevailing social order is built on this way of thinking.

The disability certificate, which designates the degree of one's disability, exemplifies this hierarchy more clearly than anything else. It says that you have a first-degree disability, a second-degree disability, etc. These grades are based on how much labor you are capable of. This is, in a sense, the essence of the problem being faced by people with disabilities.

How, then, can this problem of standards for the body that are then imposed upon people with disabilities be destroyed? My answer was that people with disabilities had to redefine the way that their bodies were perceived—that they had to overthrow the image of what it meant to have disabilities.

A wheelchair might be necessary for them in their daily lives, but in order for them to confront their own bodies, they had to reject their wheelchairs. I argued with them like this for half a year. I told them to throw out their wheelchairs and take to the streets. The example of the students from the Kōmyo School for Handicapped Children already existed as a precedent. I tried to convince them that by taking to the streets, they could not fail to destroy conventional perceptions. "Let's do it. Let's try and see what happens," I kept saying. In the end, they said, "Why not?" and got on board.

At that point, I talked it over with Kobayashi, and we decided to make a film out of it. Inspired by our encounter with Mr. Tahara, we

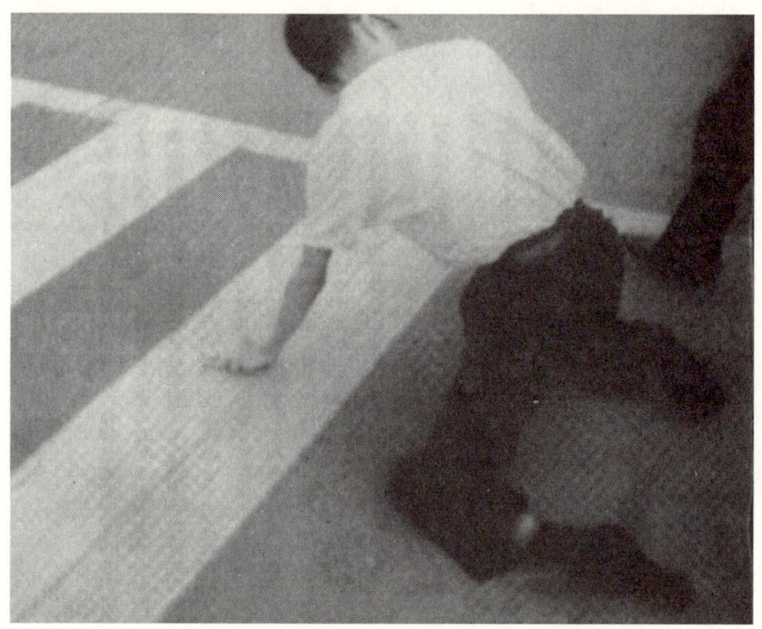

Goodbye CP. The social order is bound to collapse when a disabled person throws away their wheelchair and takes to the street.

decided to shoot on 16-mm film. The decision was set: we were going to shoot on 16-mm, come what may.

When Kobayashi was a child, she'd contracted polio, so her left leg was slightly impaired. She said that in order to come into her own as an artist, she wanted to start by creating a philosophy of the body. She was very idealistic and inspiring.

Even though the Green Grasses group had left Maharaba Village to start their own individual families in Kanagawa, the ideology that had been planted in them by Rev. Osaragi was still strongly rooted. They'd started a group called "Kanagawa Green Grasses." The fundamental difference between the Tokyo Green Grasses and the Kanagawa Green Grasses was that the Tokyo group fought against those in power. Their idea was to seize their rights from the authorities, whereas the Kanagawa group had inherited Osaragi Akira's ideology. They were slightly different in this way.

They told me that they called themselves public servants. Why? Because they received welfare. Since welfare was money provided by the state for them to live on, they were public servants. As public servants, they rebelled against the government from which they received their livelihood. Their very existence raised a fundamental question. Their slogan at the time was: "How can we make society accept our existence?" They didn't aim for easy resolutions, either. They simply persisted in raising the question of whether or not their existence was essentially acceptable.

At around this time, an incident occurred in which a mother who was disabled killed her own disabled child. The mother gained quite a bit of public sympathy, and when her case went to court, newspapers reported on a signature-collecting campaign advocating her innocence. The Kanagawa Green Grasses group organized against this movement, appealing to people to examine the issue from *their* perspective. They asked if they were then disposable; if finding the mother innocent would not then mean that people with disabilities could be justifiably eliminated. They had publicized their movement in various places, so they were already involved in these kinds of activities. We merely persuaded them to do something on a more fundamental level.

The reason this process took half a year was, for one thing, because Yokota Hiroshi had some domestic problems. As I said before, Yokota Hiroshi had more or less left Maharaba Village because of pressure from his wife. Since he was pretty smart, he seemed to have some sense of guilt about what he'd done.

Our plan for the film was to reject wheelchairs—to go out into town on hands and knees. The image of people with cerebral palsy crawling through the streets was probably intolerable to Yokota's wife. Imagining her husband doing such a thing must have caused her anguish. In short, she was against it for a long time. I think it took Yokota a while to convince her. This back-and-forth took close to half a year.

Nevertheless, both Yokota and his wife had been trained ideologically at Maharaba Village, and because I'd gone there many times myself, I had some understanding of their way of thinking. So they eventually said, "Let's do it."

NO SUBTITLES IN *GOODBYE CP*

When I think about *Goodbye* CP now, I realize that it's full of contradictory ideas.

First, it has no subtitles.

If the protagonists of the film had not been Japanese, there's no question that I would have added subtitles. I also might have used subtitles if they had been from far-off areas with strong regional accents—for example, if people living in Tokyo would have had a hard time understanding their local dialect. But the difficulty an audience is confronted with when people with cerebral palsy talk doesn't have to do with dialect. I think an audience has to become accustomed to how people with cerebral palsy speak. That is, if the audience gets used to this, if they spend some time with them, they'll come to understand them. This is completely different from understanding a regional dialect. Then again, would adding subtitles be any kind of a solution? Isn't it necessary for people to first acknowledge that they can't understand the disabled protagonists, and then to think about what this means? To stress this point, we thought it right not to add subtitles.

On top of that, I wanted the film to focus on the actions of the film's protagonists, so I thought that the audience didn't need to understand what they were saying; that as long as the audience was watching their facial expressions, it wouldn't be a problem if they couldn't quite make out the words that were coming from their mouths. If anyone really wanted to understand what the film's protagonists were saying, they could, after watching the film, read the transcript we'd put together. At least that's what I thought at the time.

We've never failed to include transcripts in the pamphlets for every one of my films. If you want to understand *Goodbye CP* in print, through language, please take a look at the transcript. But I thought that as a film, it couldn't have subtitles.

The premise of the film was the dichotomy between "the healthy vs. the disabled." Our starting point was this antagonism between the two—or rather, that we, the healthy, and they, the disabled, were being placed in an antagonistic relationship with one another. I strongly felt that without this premise, anything I might depict would simply turn out to be a lie.

I thought that since I, a healthy person, would be operating the camera, the camera would necessarily assume a position that was hostile to them. This was different from Ogawa Productions' contention that the camera was on the side of the farmers and in opposition to state power. In this film, the conflict we were involved with was not the kind you see when state power assumes the form of riot police: we were part of the very framework according to which the healthy and the disabled are situated in opposition to one another.

Therefore, the premise at the start of the film was the conflict between the healthy and the disabled. As the camera operator, and as a person who wanted to express himself, I stood on the side of the healthy, opposite the disabled subjects of my film. This was extremely clear when I aimed the camera at them; there was no question about it. The real problem was thus how to contradict or negate this dichotomy.

I wanted to start from the recognition that we were in adversarial positions, and to think together with the film's subjects about what commonalities there might be between us. If we were to pursue the problem theoretically, we would inevitably arrive at the question of how to subvert—how to reinvent—the very idea of the body, or prevailing attitudes about it. So I focused all of my attention on the body. Of course, we had to make an issue of the gaze upon the body as well. That's what I thought at the time.

For that reason, I had no choice but to start from an antagonistic position. My camera would persistently and relentlessly gaze upon Yokota Hiroshi's body. All we had to do was to create situations that would occasion such a gaze. More precisely, the question now became one of how profound my gaze could be.

Yokotsuka Kōichi's role in the film also has a further significance: he provides a "reverse gaze." When I spoke to Yokotsuka and the others at the time, that's the term I used. Films about people with disabilities that were made for the purposes of social welfare always showed them in the position of being looked at. But what we were about to do was different. In our film, they would return the gaze—that is, reverse it. In practice, this meant that Yokotsuka held his own camera, which constantly operated in opposition to mine. It was actually quite literal and somewhat schematic. I'd had the scheme precisely figured out even before we'd started filming, so I spent half a year convincing them to agree to it.

As a result, Yokotsuka held a camera the whole time. I asked him how the scene he saw—which included me—appeared to him. He said, "To tell you the truth, it's quite frightening." So I came up with this scheme: he would observe his own act of looking through a camera by internalizing it as an issue he was trying to work through, and we would watch him as he tried to liberate himself from it.

WHATEVER HAPPENS, KEEP THE CAMERA ROLLING

For people with disabilities, wheelchairs are indispensable for daily life. I have no reason to disagree with disabled people who agitate for the right to a wheelchair as a form of resistance against authority and society. It's just that whenever we look at their bodies, their wheelchairs inevitably come to mean something that protects or shelters them. Therefore, I spent half a year telling Yokota, Yokotsuka, and the others that I intended to start the film at the point when their wheelchairs—and anything else that shielded their bodies from society—were discarded.

I didn't know what to expect, but I wanted to see what would happen after they threw out their wheelchairs and took to the streets. It was my form of activism, directed at them. Yokota and Yokotsuka accepted.

At that time, it didn't occur to me to shoot the film with synchronized sound. That was because even Tokyo Channel 12, on whose shows I was basing my film, was still shooting only a tiny portion of each show with synchronized sound. *Goodbye CP* was my first film, and as I was preparing to shoot, I was so preoccupied with just capturing images that it didn't even occur to me to get sync sound. I was using a camera—the Arri ST made by Arriflex—that could shoot a hundred feet at a time. One hundred feet recorded about two minutes and 46 to 47 seconds of footage. So my idea was this: we'd take to the streets; Yokota and the others would start an action; and I'd hit the record button. Once the camera started rolling, it would tie us together. What kind of action would Yokota Hiroshi take, and what would ensue? What would happen and what reaction would follow?

In short, I would keep the camera rolling no matter what. I

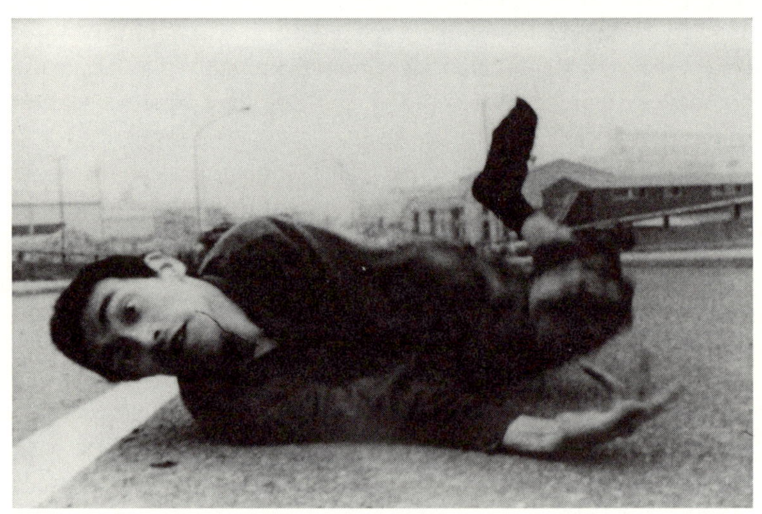

I would keep rolling camera until the film ran out.

wanted to know how I would feel, what my reactions would be. In that way, even though the camera would indeed be pointed at Yokota and the others, the binding power of the camera would also affect me, the person behind the camera, for as long as the camera was rolling. That was how I understood the significance of the camera back then.

I don't think I ever told them to act. I never even used the expression, "acting." For example, in that scene on the train: Yokota was on his way to Yokohama to raise some money, so I told him I was going to film him on the train. We got on at Isogo; our destination was Yokohama Station, two stops away. When we passed the first station, I told Yokota I was going to start rolling camera. I didn't calculate how long it would take for the train to arrive in Yokohama. I just rolled camera, intent on keeping it rolling until the film ran out.

I began in the car next to his, and moved along until I got him sitting in the seat. At first, I held the camera in a low position and shot without using the viewfinder. I moved the camera along parallel to the floor for a while. In the middle of the shot, I looked at last through the viewfinder. When we arrived at the first station, I thought, "OK," and kept filming. When the train started moving again, the camera was still rolling.

The train moved for a while, and I thought to myself, "Hey, there's the announcement saying, 'Yokohama, Yokohama!' We've pulled into the station." Then Yokota Hiroshi turned toward me—that is, toward the camera—and gave me a look that said, "What should I do now?" As soon as I understood, I said, "Get off!" without thinking. I really hadn't calculated anything in advance. He then hopped off the seat. He probably hadn't expected this at all. In fact, at that moment, the bell was screaming, indicating that the doors were about to close. In haste, he tried to crawl off on his knees. It was a narrow escape. I myself had just managed to get off the train, and he was now trying to crawl off. I had gotten off first and was on the platform as he tried desperately to exit. Just then, I heard the clicking of the film roll coming to an end. I continued filming. Right as he tumbled off the train, the doors slid shut. I hadn't expected the film to last so long.

Where did that "Get off!" come from? Later, Yokota said to me, "You completely fooled me, Hara, or else flattered me into doing that; I bet you wanted to film that from the beginning." [Laughs.] But it hadn't been planned at all. Absolutely not. When the camera is rolling, a certain action occurs in a certain situation. I'm looking at the action through the viewfinder, so I have no clue as to how I'm going to react to a given situation until the moment arrives. That's how I shot that scene; basically, I just kept rolling the camera.

After that scene comes the hell that ensued at Yokota's house. That sequence—Yokota falling off the train, then fade to white with a woman's voice over it, then Yokota and his wife yelling at each other—that was all was put together in the order it was shot. The film had no editor; we put it together ourselves, so it's basically in chronological order.

Unfortunately, the film ran out right as Yokota tumbled off the train. We got the sound of the doors closing, but I couldn't get a shot of the image. So the way we edited it was we kept the sound without the picture—what else could we do?

I should give more background on the fight scene between Yokota and his wife. Yokota had probably told his wife that we'd filmed him tumbling off a train. So his wife wanted him to stop doing such things—she wanted no part of it. After all, she probably thought it was dangerous and pathetic. She probably just couldn't tolerate the image of a disabled person crawling through the streets on his knees.

Actually, the fight had already started during my visit to Yokota and his wife on the first day of filming. I'd gone there thinking, "Now the filming is going to start." Filming began as she was threatening to leave if he participated in the film. We were able to record the sound of that scene without the camera rolling because sound equipment is quicker to set up. By the time I got my camera up and running, I was only able to catch the shot of her leaving the house. That's why the first shot of that scene is of her figure from behind.

That unceasing discussion between the two of them had thus continued. After the train scene, the situation probably reached a crisis. When, soon thereafter, Yokota said he was going to quit the film, we thought we couldn't let him quit just then: it would have been a disaster. So we contacted the other people in Green Grasses and decided that we would all visit him. The fight between Yokota and his wife broke out when we arrived. We didn't go to their house in order to film them fighting; the fight just happened while we were there. I thought I had no other choice but to film it.

I wasn't using the Arriflex then. Since we didn't have money for a camera at the time, we used a Filmo. Filmos use a spring-wound mechanism that can run for about 36 to 38 seconds at most. So that's what I had to live with; I managed to shoot the scene by winding up the spring once every 38 seconds.

Yokota himself was having a pretty difficult time then, I think. He was the leader of the Kanagawa Green Grasses group, so he must have been torn between his wife's wishes and those of the group. He was the kind of guy who'd think that he was no longer a man if he quit the film. Still, when his wife begged him to quit, he leaned towards quitting.

During their fight, one of the members said, "Well, I hate to bring this up, but if you quit now, we'll have to talk about money again." What this meant was that when we'd first decided to make *Goodbye CP*, I'd asked Green Grasses to donate a part of the production costs. I negotiated with them, and they'd agreed. The entire cost of the film was around one million yen. Kanagawa Green Grasses covered one hundred thousand of it. That's what that member was referring to. After this discussion, Yokota ended up deciding that he couldn't quit and went on with the film.

On a side note, we basically borrowed all the money that we used to cover the rest of the production costs. We borrowed about 20,000 yen from each of our friends. We didn't raise funds; we simply took out loans.

CREATE ACTION WITH YOUR LIVING, BREATHING BODY!

You might ask, why did I focus on their bodies? Because by throwing their bodies onto the streets, by putting their very existence out there, they were able to cause ripples in the order of things. Of course, I don't mean to say that these acts were purely personal. In a sense, they brought the streets squealing to a halt. I knew that this would happen from my numerous experiences with taking out the high-school students when I worked at the school for handicapped children. Just bringing disabled students to the streets in their wheelchairs had caused the gears to grind. So by rejecting wheelchairs and creating action with their live bodies, they were bound to generate friction. And my intention was to observe this process to the very end.

At first, I didn't actually care what they did to stir things up. What I most wanted to know was how they would experience creating that kind of action. After all, I couldn't walk on my knees. It wasn't part of my world. But I wondered what walking like that must have been like for Yokota.

Going further back in time, long before Yokota and I discussed making a film, we had had an argument. It started with some small thing. He couldn't stand, so he was naturally sitting on the floor. I just happened to be standing. While we were arguing, he just stopped talking, and I went on the offensive.

Afterwards, I asked him why he'd gone quiet like that. He said that he'd refused to answer me because I'd been standing and looking down on him. I was a bit shocked. The only reason I'd been standing was because it was natural for me. When he told me I'd been looking down on him, I couldn't help feeling astonished.

But this made me wonder if that situation mirrored our

relationship. That's why it seemed inevitable that our relationship with one another would be antagonistic.

I wondered how the city, or the spaces in which we lived, would look from a perspective much lower than mine, basically from their knees. This might be getting a bit abstract again, but I wanted to know how they perceived the world. So every time I went out to the streets with Yokota, I asked him what it was like, what he saw, how he felt.

It was the same with Yokotsuka. I told Yokota and Yokotsuka about the "one-meter" assignment I'd been given in photography school. I told them how frightening it had been to take a picture of someone from just one meter away and told them to try it.

Yokotsuka took his camera and did exactly that. He went out into the streets, going right up to so-called healthy people and snapping shots of them. It must have been frightening for him. But it was also the first time he'd ever done anything like that. By taking these photographs, he'd had to concretely confront what it meant to be a disabled person. It must have been the first time any of them had ever aggressively stepped up to a healthy person, camera in hand.

The fundraising scene in the film is the one scene where it's possible to say that the camera takes on the point of view of the disabled protagonists. In that sense, its significance is, cinematically speaking, different. I think this has to do with my impatience behind the camera. I myself am a healthy person, but I couldn't help but wonder what the healthy people making donations were thinking. I mean, I already knew the answer theoretically, but cinematically, I felt the urge to move around with a handheld camera, to go one step further, to express my own impatience on the spot. That's why I shot that scene the way I did. I thought at the time that some meaning might emerge through persistent repetition.

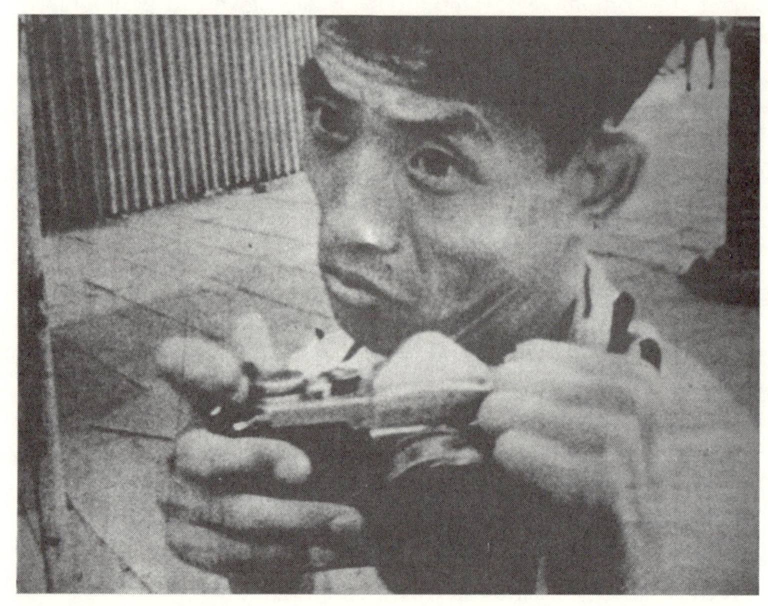

What I wanted most to know was how creating action would feel to them.

I'M EMPTY!

It took half a year to film *Goodbye CP*, but we actually only filmed for fourteen or fifteen days, which isn't that long.

One time we would cross a crosswalk; the next time, we'd go out to Yokohama; then we'd take a train; and then... one day, we got off at Shinjuku and went to Pedestrian Paradise.[2]

Yokota Hiroshi was a poet. He wrote poetry. It was his dream to read his poetry out loud in the streets. He used to tell me that poetry was "the act of sacrificing one's body in order to appeal to others." We said, "Let's give it a try," and took him to Shinjuku. And so the events unfolded as you see in the film.

In that scene, the screen goes to black once. That happened when I stepped away from Yokota for a second after finishing a 100-foot roll of film. By the time I'd finished the first roll, people had gathered around. No one paid attention to us initially, but once people realized I had a camera, they formed a crowd around us. The same thing had happened when Tsuchimoto Noriaki was shooting *Exchange Student: Chua Swee-Lin*. People had formed a crowd around him just because he had a camera.

I'd asked a young man on the street to help me with the shoot, so he was recording the sound. After the first hundred feet had been shot, I was reloading the camera when the young man came over to me and said that Yokota had just been taken away by the police. "What?!" I replied, rushing straight to where he had been. He wasn't there. I asked the young man where they had taken him. There," he said, pointing his finger. A dark tunnel ran from the east to the west side of Shinjuku Station, and above it was a temporary police station that looked like a barracks. That's where Yokota had been taken. Kobayashi Sachiko and I ran in and told the cops that we were shooting such and such a film, so please give Mr. Yokota back to us. But they said Yokata wasn't allowed to do such things in

2 Pedestrian Paradise: A section of a street near Shinjuku that was turned into a shopping area for pedestrians.

the middle of the pedestrian mall. This was back when the city had first blocked off the area from cars. I said, "But isn't he allowed to do whatever he wants to in Pedestrian Paradise? Isn't it supposed to be a Paradise?" They said, "That's not what Paradise is for. You have to keep walking." I said, "Oh yeah? So Pedestrian Paradise is a place where you're not allowed to do anything?" That's exactly what the reasoning of the police was: that you had to keep walking.

Anyway, after arguing like that and getting nowhere, they eventually said they would release Yokota if we agreed to be his guarantors. We consented, and they let Yokota go.

On the train home, Yokota talked about many things with us. He was really elated. The experience had been great fun for him. He said that because of the action he had performed, he had created a situation that required police intervention; that the whole thing had been a form of self-expression. He seemed so pleased saying such things that, as I listened to him, I began to disagree. I said rather coldly, "Mr. Yokota, you say these things, but you couldn't even come to the streets of Shinjuku by yourself. We had to carry you on our backs. You say so excitedly that so many people gathered to see you when you started reading poetry—but in fact, they gathered because of the movie camera."

He was shocked and crushed. A while later—or to be more precise, pretty soon thereafter—we got a call from Yokota. He said he really wanted to quit the film again. This was yet another potential disaster, so we all went to his place again and said, "Why? Stop joking!" and so on. He was determined. He wouldn't budge.

He said we wouldn't get anywhere talking at his house with his wife around, so we went out and started talking outside. He said he'd truly lost all motivation to continue. But we thought we still had a lot to do. We eventually became quite emotional, giving each other tit for tat. Then Kobayashi Sachiko said, "There's no way we can stop filming like this. If you really want to quit, then do a headstand first. Do a striptease." I wasn't the one who said that; she said it.

Yokota said he understood and agreed. Hence the strip and

the headstand in the last scene. Tit for tat. In other words, we said that if he showed us in a convincing way that he couldn't possibly participate in the film any more, we would withdraw our request; and he said he'd do precisely that, and started the striptease and headstand.

So things unfolded as you see in the film. Later, I asked Yokota in a sort of one-on-one interview to tell me the truth. He said that he had thought of the film as an opportunity to positively express the "uselessness" of his own disabled body; he'd thought it would be a positive opportunity. However, he'd been made all too aware of the fact that he couldn't do anything, let alone express himself, without being aided by healthy people in one way or another. This made him feel empty inside. On the other hand, he felt as though he'd been liberated from this illusion. Hence the line, "I've become completely empty." He said something to the effect that he'd utterly lost his drive to do anything.

The remark I had made to him on the train—that the healthy had carried him on their backs to Shinjuku—was pretty cruel, and had obviously had a debilitating effect on him. But it was undoubtedly true. After all, the philosophy he had acquired or built up over the years had also been strongly influenced by Osaragi Akira's way of thinking.

When living with disabilities, what does it mean to face oneself as a disabled person in the true sense of the word? We might use the phrase, "the illusion of being healthy"—but how much of this "illusion of being healthy" can one discern in oneself? In order for Yokota to pursue his identity as a disabled person, it had been necessary for him to rid himself of as much of this "illusion of being healthy" as possible. And as he'd worked on the film, he'd inevitably been cornered into the realization that there was no such thing as one's self. He had been driven into a tighter and tighter spot, until he found that he had no self.

Only when one goes so far as to become empty can the power structure be subverted. Thoroughly examining one's own "illusion of being healthy"—that alone is enough to reverse the power structure. Only by descending to the very depths is it possible to truly strike back at the mechanisms of society with one's own body. I think that that's precisely what we were engaged in. But we could only theorize this after the fact.

Kobayashi had her own reasons for telling Yokota to do a handstand or strip naked for us if he intended to quit.

When we first met Yokota, he'd said that he'd spent his whole life concealing his body, but that now he wanted to expose it, to completely bare himself. It was like when Takeda Miyuki had told me that she wanted me to film her giving birth. That's what made Kobayashi think that we could make the film. Since Yokota had said he wanted to get naked, she thought that that could be the film's highlight; that a whole film could be made around it.

Kobayashi also has a disability with her leg. People used to say that the disabled should conceal their disability, that it was unsightly. So when Yokota had said that he wanted to expose his disability in front of the camera, that he wanted to exhibit his body completely naked, it had apparently had quite an effect on her. Since she was the film's producer, she probably thought that the film wouldn't be complete until that promise had been fulfilled. That's what was behind that remark of hers.

At first, Yokota had romanticized the idea of getting naked in front of the camera. But the reality was that he could only get naked after he was backed into a corner and had nowhere else to go. That's ultimately what it takes to liberate oneself.

I myself—the person who filmed the movie—also experienced change. Changing myself is only possible if the people I film change. In theory, at least. In other words, by going through the process of making *Goodbye CP*, we had reached a point in our relationship where we'd broken down the walls between us; we had arrived at a point where we could say anything we wanted to each other. Establishing such a relationship is normally inconceivable. But because we'd gone through such hell together, we were able to become equals.

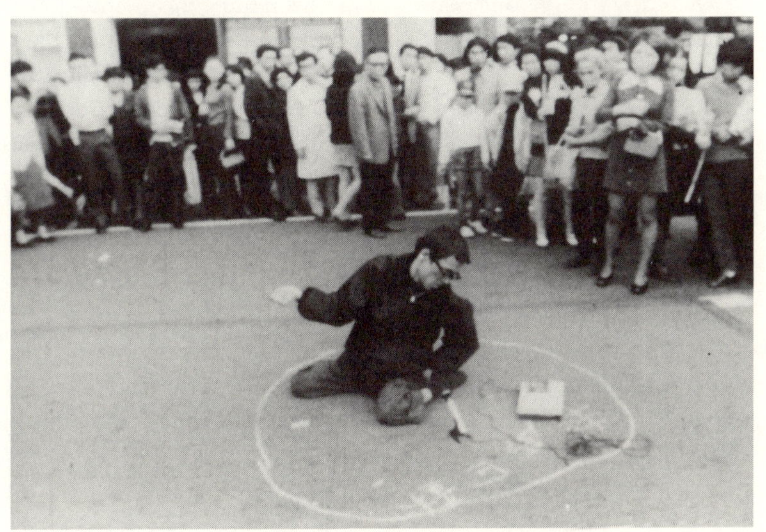

A crowd gathered around us because we had a camera.

In *Goodbye CP*, we explored themes such as reversing viewpoints and recasting the relationship between the healthy and the disabled. We have yet to find another theme that could surpass this creatively or that would be more meaningful to both collaborating parties. With this film, we set out to explore the philosophical issues at the core of the lives of people with disabilities and of the situations they found themselves in. And I think we more or less achieved that. Anything else we might try to do could only be a variation on that. If there had been anything else to pursue, I wouldn't have minded making another film with them. But there could be no better theme.

Actually, there's one issue that I've been hung up on, and that's the issue of the children of people with disabilities. I want to make a film that explores how children understand their disabled parents. As I mentioned earlier, I've been told that "the greatest misfortune for a disabled person is to have a healthy child." I think that issues exist around how the dynamic of the healthy vs. the disabled influences each specific home, each parent-child relationship. Since I've been working on other films all this time, I can't suddenly start working on this idea, but it does interest me. Maybe I'll make a film about it one day. Maybe I won't.

A child does appear in *Goodbye CP*. A child smiling in a hellish scene, the only innocent being there. I'd like to tell his story, how he turned out 20 years later. When I think about it, that's a film I'd like to make.

TRYING TO CHANGE THE PERCEPTION OF THE "PEOPLE WITH DISABILITIES" MOVEMENT

We completed *Goodbye CP* in 1972. We had filmed for about half a year, and spent half a year before that just persuading people to participate in the film. Before that, I had spent close to two years going to Maharaba Village. After we finished the film, we screened it for about a year or two. Most of the screenings were self-financed, so they were often attended by the people with cerebral palsy who'd been the film's subjects. As such, we were working together for a long time.

Then, before the film was even screened, the *Asahi Shimbun* ran a big, scathing article about it. We actually had no idea this article was going to be published. It wasn't for the film review section, but for the so-called third-page section, the one covering social issues.

It said that we had made a public spectacle of people with cerebral palsy. Kobayashi had just gotten the advance tickets ready for sale, but nobody anywhere would buy them. Amazingly, the article said that we were humiliating people with disabilities in the film. One morning I woke up, opened the paper, and there it was. I was shocked. As a result, all the so-called welfare organizations refused to buy tickets.

The headline used the term "public spectacle." We had deliberately used the same phrase as a way of raising exposure for the film, but their use of the phrase had negative connotations. The fact that we'd even made such a film was in itself impermissible. That was how the newspaper article presented the film.

In other words, the article had been written—without a trace of self-awareness—from the precise perspective I had set out to repudiate in the first place. At least the headline had been written that way. The content of the article wasn't so bad, actually; it showed that the writer had given the film some serious thought.

The article also called the film "an uncensored screening" because it included the fight scene between Yokota and his wife. For a time, Yokota's wife had disapproved of that scene. The very person in it... I mean, she's in the scene, and it wasn't like she was claiming that we didn't have her permission to use it; she just disapproved of it. It was as simple as that.

Speaking of which: one might think that the issue of someone not wanting to be filmed is a perpetual problem for me in my films. But no such problem occurred in *Extreme Private Eros*. No one asked me to edit out a scene because they disapproved of it. Nor did anyone demand such a thing in *The Emperor's Naked Army Marches On*. In my film *A Dedicated Life*... the women in Inoue Mitsuharu's classroom, they were quite... Those women published an article in the magazine *Film Art*... The article that Ms. Suzuki wrote in *Film Art* apparently makes the point that the problem with the film was simply procedural.[3]

I first screened *Goodbye CP* at the University of Tokyo in one of Saishu Satoru's independent lectures.[4] The place was enormous, and about 200 people came. The attendance was pretty good, but the moment the film ended, we were subjected to a kangaroo court. The audience rallied against us. "You've made fools out of people with disabilities. What right do you have to humiliate them like that?"

Hearing this, Yokotsuka and the others defended the film as best they could. "We made this film based on an equal balance of power between Hara and his team and ourselves. How can you see it and think that Hara and his team treated us cruelly? That was totally not the case; the film is the result of a collaboration. It's the way *you* look at the film that's old-fashioned and condescending." After hearing Yokotsuka and others defend us, people who'd been criticizing us realized what was actually going on in the film. For about a year, we found ourselves in this situation every time the film was screened.

Yokota and Yokotsuka continued to defend the film. They said that it was different from those social welfare films about the disabled that directed a sympathetic gaze upon them from a distance, looking at them from a privileged position. After a year, everything changed. People began to recognize that the film was about something else. From then on, people would invite Yokota and Yokotsuka to do screenings of the film.

By the way, when people with cerebral palsy saw the film, they could understand what everyone in the film was saying, so they could watch it laughing. They thought we were doing something

---

3 Hara further discusses people's reactions to *A Dedicated Life* in Chapter 6.

4 Saishu Satoru (1936–): Scientist, sociologist, and social critic. When he was an assistant professor at Tokyo University, he famously supported the students in their struggles against the university in the 1960s.

interesting. So they felt like doing something themselves. People who had never before taken to the street felt this way and were inspired. They'd say they wanted to do something. Then people would say, "If you want to do something..." and a support group would be formed. As a result, such-and-such chapters of Green Grasses sprang up all around the country.

Among people with cerebral palsy, Yokota Hiroshi was a hero. "He's so cool!" they'd say. Especially when he took off his clothes in the end.

When screening activities began, they generated a good deal of backlash, but we continued to attend all the screenings as a matter of principle. The criticism lasted for about a year; then it turned into praise. It was as though we had definitively turned a page in the history of the movement for people with disabilities.

Specifically, as mentioned earlier, people with disabilities—those with cerebral palsy—enjoyed the film the most. They thought the people on screen were doing something interesting, and they also wanted to participate. Someone in the audience would raise a hand and say that he or she wanted to do something for their cause, and supporters would gather around the raised hand and form a support group, which in turn would begin a movement. And such groups popped up all over the country. In this way, I think the film truly contributed to the movement for people with disabilities. If I might use a self-aggrandizing expression, it became something like a bible for the movement.

For example, this film is shown every year to students who are going to be involved with education, welfare, and activism on behalf of people with disabilities. The film is screened, then there's an audience discussion. In that sense, I don't think any other film quite like it has yet been made. I think it has more or less influenced the genre of films about people with disabilities to this day.

And it didn't just influence filmmaking. Movements like "the disabled taking to the streets" gained such recognition that newspapers no longer hesitated printing articles about them. And, after the film, people began examining how towns had been designed to exclude people with disabilities. Therefore, I think I can say with confidence that I did my part in raising awareness.

To this day, *Goodbye CP* has been rented more often than any of our other films. Of course, each screening is small. Probably less than a hundred people see the film at a given screening, but in terms of rentals, I think it tops the others.

For some reason, people gradually stopped inviting the very creator of the film—*me*—to the screenings. It no longer mattered who'd made it.

About ten years after we made the film, Yokotsuka passed away. I hear that Yokota has grown old, becoming a senior member of Green Grasses; and that the younger generation is trying to keep the movement alive these days. They have tried to maintain the movement in their own way, and it's endured.

Recently, I've been having this urge to go see Yokota for some reason, so I'm thinking of going to see him at the beginning of the year.

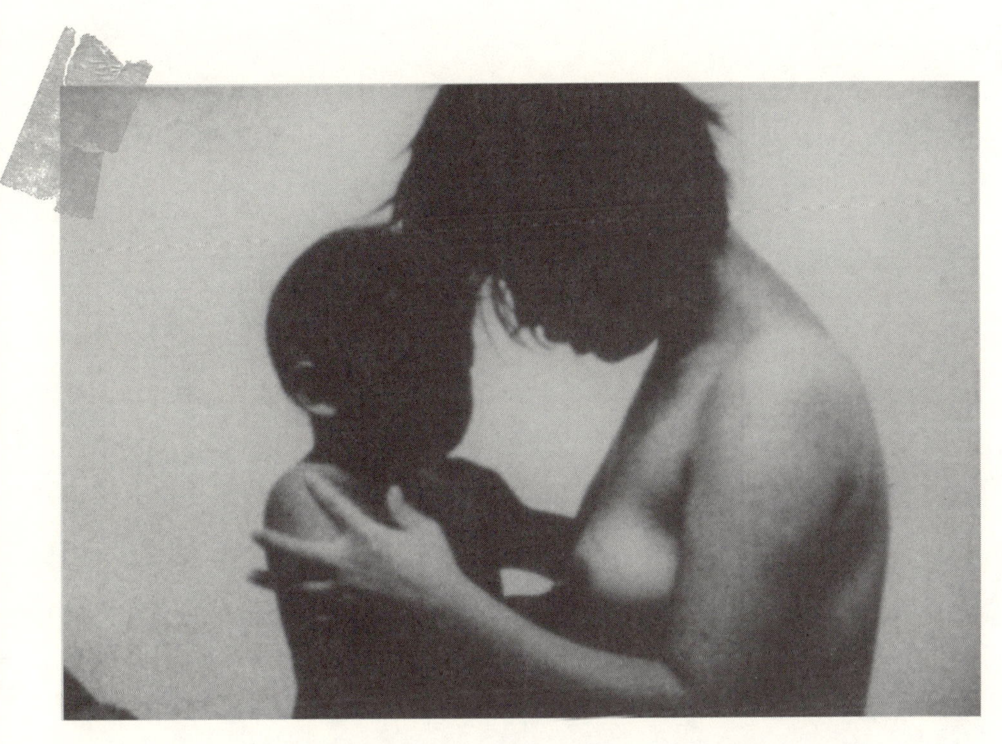

04 Man vs. Woman

Extreme Private Eros: Love Song 1974

LOOKING INTO MYSELF THROUGH A RELATIONSHIP

Within a month or two of finishing *Goodbye CP*, Takeda Miyuki informed me she was going to Okinawa. She asked if I would make a movie about her. This wasn't a surprise, since she'd learned that we'd made *Goodbye CP*; I think that's why she proposed that we make a movie about her next.

Around that time, she and women like Tanaka Mitsu were part of an all-female commune called "Fighting Women."[1] She was living at the time with our child and another woman, Sugako, a pal of hers whom she liked. Sugako was pregnant at the time. Takeda Miyuki said, "I'm going to Okinawa regardless, but why don't you come along to film me?" She also wanted to go to Okinawa to give birth unassisted, which she wanted me to film. So when I refer in the film to "that previous promise," I'm referring to the promise that started it all.

It's hard to connect her very abstract desire to "meet women in Okinawa" with her request that I film her giving birth, but thinking of these two disparate things as one was a reflection of how she truly felt. I definitely think that her asking me to make a movie about her was a testament to the extraordinary intensity of her desire for self-expression. Also, making a movie about her meant that I would be going to Okinawa with her—which meant that the love between us had not yet completely faded away.

In my narration at the beginning the film, I say that the only way I could stay in touch with Takeda Miyuki was by making a film about her. But I think the fact that it was *her* proposal meant that she also had such feelings about me. I believe that she asked me to make a film about her because she was still in love with me. So there was this love affair between a man and a woman; and then there was Okinawa, which had quite a bit of significance at the time. We thought of it as intense, as cutting-edge.

1 Tanaka Mitsu: Women's Liberation activist and writer. Founded the Shinjuku Women's Liberation Center in 1971.

Okinawa seemed like the closest Third World country to Japan. Takeda Miyuki had joined Tanaka Mitsu's group when the women's liberation movement had just started, so it was natural for her to want to meet the women in Okinawa. It wasn't necessarily as if there were some underlying meaning unifying her reasoning regarding Okinawa and her demand that I film her.

At that time, I'd seen films about Okinawa such as Higashi Yōichi's *Okinawan Archipelago* and Ōshima Nagisa's *Dear Summer Sister*. I don't think Nunokawa Tetsurō had made *An Unofficial Story of Eros in Okinawa, Motoshinkakarann* yet.[2] So when I embarked on *Extreme Private Eros: Love Song 1974*, I decided not to portray the political climate of Okinawa at the time. Even though I was going to Okinawa, I decided to only pursue my personal relationship with this woman Takeda Miyuki.

I'd agreed to make a movie about Takeda Miyuki, but I knew deep down that by filming her, I would actually be filming my own circumstances. Logically speaking, that's what it boiled down to. So while my ostensible reason for making the film was to stay in touch with Takeda Miyuki, that wasn't the whole story.

One review of *Goodbye CP* had been more devastating to me than all the others. Saishu Satoru had critiqued us for filming the fight between Yokota Hiroshi and his wife. He said that the way we'd shot that scene and then gone on with the rest of the movie as though nothing had happened was insupportable. That criticism really struck home. It made me think that I needed to re-examine our role in such situations before engaging in any further creative expression. In other words, I'd leapt at the chance of filming the disabled in my first film. I'd filmed the "other." I wanted to return to the question of who or what "I" was when filming the "other."

So after *Extreme Private Eros* was finished, I kept saying that I actually thought of myself as the film's protagonist, even though

---

2 Higashi Yōichi (1934–): Filmmaker. *Those Quiet Japanese*. Ōshima Nagisa (1942–): Filmmaker. *Night and Fog in Japan*, *In The Realm of the Senses*, and others. Nunokawa Tatsurō (1942–): Documentary filmmaker.

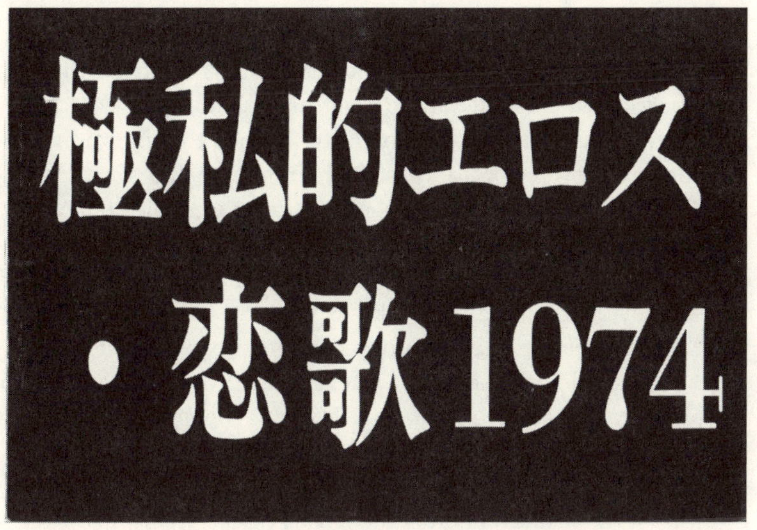

Extreme Private Eros: Love Song 1974's title.
This film begins with a man and a woman in a hostile relationship.

Takeda Miyuki had played the film's heroine; that I'd known, even before making the film—or as soon as I'd decided to make it—that I was about to film myself. Filming oneself doesn't necessarily mean exposing oneself in front of a camera. I thought of it as representing the extent to which I could turn my gaze upon myself in a given situation. I had this extremely strong desire to aim the camera at myself. So I set out to do just that.

THINKING AHEAD WHILE OPERATING THE CAMERA

Going back to what I said earlier about how the camera ignites something, functioning like gunpowder: when I started filming *Extreme Private Eros*, I ended up moving in with Takeda Miyuki and her girlfriend and living with them. As I say in the narration, my moving in with them probably made their relationship worse.

It's not difficult for two people to form a couple, but when another single person enters the relationship, conflict will ensue. In fact, before I arrived in Okinawa, Takeda Miyuki and her friend had already gone through a similar experience. I learned this later, but Takeda Miyuki had been annoyed when Sugako's lover, a black guy, had stayed with them for a while. Then, when I'd shown up, my presence had annoyed Sugako. It's not as though I realized this immediately, but as I rolled camera, the situation became clear to me, bit by bit.

One of the themes of *Extreme Private Eros* is the relationship between a man and a woman. *Goodbye CP* had been structured from the very beginning by the framework of "the healthy vs. the disabled." So I thought that this film called *Extreme Private Eros* would start from the premise that a man and a woman were in a hostile relationship with one another, and that the film would be about how to transcend that hostility. That was what I naively thought as I embarked on the project.

For some reason, I start everything with a hostile relationship.

That's probably because I am obsessively focused on "the individual." For that "individual," everything else becomes the "other." If you're healthy, the "other" becomes those who are disabled; if you're a man, the "other" becomes a woman. There's something in me that's obsessed with "the individual."

I find myself wanting to communicate with others, but somehow not being able to. I'm incredibly warped and twisted. Really. Not just on film sets. One should normally be able to enjoy conversations over drinks, but I get overly self-conscious in such situations, becoming less and less talkative. I become unnatural and awkward. I find myself in such situations on a daily basis. Perhaps I have a habit of thinking too much about what I am—so much so, in fact, that it becomes excessive. I'm too self-conscious. So whenever I make a film, I start off by thinking too much about myself. But the way my mind works, everything I get involved with begins with an antagonistic relationship. The antagonistic relationship comes first. It's a fairly natural routine for me, I think.

In theory, communication is something we *should* do. But perfect communication is impossible. Still, we should at least strive for it. To go further, you could say that I incite action in order to make communication happen.

By creating action, I'm causing all kinds of struggles to take place with the "other." That struggle itself is nothing other than the living, breathing drama of human life. I want to show that drama in my films. In other words, I don't so much want to expose specific issues as I do the drama that comes from engagement—which, to my way of thinking, is what drama in fact is. That's precisely what I'm going after.

I meet someone, I'm fascinated with them, and I want to film them. But before I roll camera, I want to get all the trivial problems out of the way. I don't want to roll camera until I'm at a point where doing so will cause the situation to enter a new phase.

Normally, when making a film, I start filming as soon as I meet an interesting subject. That's how I shot Okuzaki Kenzō and

Inoue Mitsuhara. But with my first and second films, I started rolling camera when my subjects and I were on the verge of entering unknown territory. Past that point, our minds were useless, so I would roll the camera and think about the next steps after that.

"Who cares about what one's personal history might have been before this point, whether it has been introduced wholly or in part? Who cares about that kind of prior knowledge? I'm not going to film that stuff. Throw it all away. What matters is what lies beyond this point." That's how I thought.

It was like that with Takeda Miyuki. She said that she was going to go to Okinawa. When she did, I thought, "OK, everything starts from this point on." All our issues—all the contradictions and conflicts in our relationship as a man and a woman who'd spent three years of our lives together—everything—got thrown into that "from this point on." The camera doesn't describe what's happened in the past. Instead, everything, including everything that's happened in the past, is thrown into the present progressive. I was set on seeing what would come out of everything happening in the present progressive form.

I don't know what will happen when I do this. It's impossible to figure out how to raise the money for production on this kind of a film. Since we have no actual pitch we can use to help us raise funds, Kobayashi, the producer, is always worried. We don't know what's going to happen when; we don't know what the story of the film will be. Still, we have to raise money. So it's always a problem.

DON'T YOU DARE CHANGE YOUR MIND

However, by the time we were trying to raise funds for *Extreme Private Eros*, we'd already made one film, *Goodbye CP*. Because of this, we could make deals with cinema study groups at colleges and with various circles involved in different movements. We borrowed about 30,000 yen from each organization, promising that we would screen the film for them when it was finished. We'd already established our credibility with *Goodbye CP*. The total amount of money loaned to us couldn't have been much, but we still received quite a bit. That's how most documentaries were funded then, I think.

The good thing about documentaries is that they take a long time to make. So you can raise whatever you need for the moment and get started. And you just repeat that process. That's what's good about documentaries: if you continue shooting, you can come up with the money you need to move forward in some way or another.

With *Extreme Private Eros*, Takeda Miyuki specifically promised me that she would go to Okinawa and give birth unassisted, and that she would let me film that scene, which she also wanted to see on-screen. "I'll make the film, but don't you dare change your mind in the middle. Don't quit on me," I said. "I won't," she said. "Promise that you won't, either." I promised. We were both bound by this vow, obliged to see it through. In a way, we'd made and agreed on a contract. So no matter what happened, our promise would persist. In other words, we had set ourselves the goal of doing everything in our power to fulfill our promise.

This meant that even though we had no idea when the film would end, we had a sort of finish line, exemplified by the promise between us: that she would give birth on her own in Okinawa. We said to each other, "Let's do our best, regardless," and got started. We wondered what might happen, or how we ourselves might change along the way. We were going to initiate our own actions towards a common goal, but we had no idea what sort of actions they might be. That's what made it interesting. "So let's get started." That's how we were.

Well, quite a lot did in fact happen.

For example, there's a scene of Takeda Miyuki's face while she's having sex.

The idea was exactly the same as her wanting me to film her giving birth. One day, she said, "I want to see what my face looks like while having sex, so I want you to film me." "Oh, I see. OK," I said, and filmed her. Which shows that she definitely knew the pleasure of being filmed. More than that, though, what was driving her was her extraordinarily intense desire to see what should normally be hidden, what one is supposed to avert one's eyes from. Like someone's face during sex. That desire to see or know what cannot be seen. If someone told you that they wanted to see their own face in the act of having sex, you'd normally be taken aback. People with so-called normal values would say, "What?" But when it came to something like that, Takeda Miyuki's curiosity was extraordinary.

Excuse my vulgarity, but this particular shot required a really unnatural position. If you're holding a camera in one hand, supporting your body with the other, and having sex while rolling camera, you'll almost inevitably throw out your back. I had in fact thrown my back out while I was still working for the Kōmyō School, so I was really afraid that I might do it again. [Laughs.]

You might get the wrong impression because I'm always telling stories about women telling me to film things. That's not good.

IT'S OKAY FOR A MAN TO CRY

Speaking of which, Kobayashi Sachiko also appears in the film. To a certain extent, we found ourselves in a love triangle.

When we first started working on the film, Kobayashi said she was going to try to act only as the producer. When I followed Takeda Miyuki to Okinawa, I didn't stay there the whole time. I would go and come back, go and come back. I'd go there, shoot a scene, and return to Tokyo to raise more money or view the dailies. We were neither fully apart nor fully together.

So—I think it was the second time I went to Okinawa, but when I arrived, Miyuki and a black guy named Paul were living together. I visited their place to film them, then went back the following day, when Paul wasn't there, to interview Takeda Miyuki. I started filming, and I was completely overcome by feelings of jealousy. I couldn't believe it. It was totally unexpected. The day before, when Paul had been right in front of me and the two of them had been talking, I hadn't felt an ounce of jealousy. I hadn't decided to visit Takeda Miyuki the following day out of jealousy: I'd simply wanted to hear more of her story from her perspective. Right about when I asked her why she was with Paul, why she was with this black man, I was suddenly overcome with jealousy. I lost control. I was a little surprised myself.

For my films, it's absolutely necessary that I operate the camera myself. But in *Extreme Private Eros*, I thought that I also had to perform—or rather, that I would also be filmed. This didn't necessarily mean exposing myself in front of the lens; it meant exposing my own situation. In other words, rolling camera was, to my mind, synonymous with revealing myself. This idea came to me because I'm the person operating the camera. As such, I think of the camera, or the screen, or each frame, as my own flesh and blood, my own emotion. I wanted to know how far I could push the idea of the camera itself playing such an active role, of the camera being something identical with me, the cinematographer. So it was a kind of experiment for me as well.

However, I shot that particular scene without looking through the viewfinder. Holding the camera at chest-level, I could more or less tell what was being filmed, because I was using a wide-angle lens. I could tell that by pointing the camera slightly up, Takeda Miyuki would be in the frame. But the camera was loaded with a 100-foot roll of film, so it only lasted about 40 seconds. Also, I was holding the camera by hand, so I had to look at the scale on the barrel of the lens for distance. I had to guess whether the picture would be in focus if I set the distance while also guessing the aperture setting. And I needed to know how many more seconds I could roll camera before it would run out of film. I needed to be absolutely cool and level-headed in order to do all of these calculations. But I was angry and burning with jealousy. I could no longer control my own emotions. That's how that scene came about in which my feelings exploded and I started fighting with Takeda Miyuki. Well, that's what tends to happen when jealousy is involved.

That was the only time during our shoot in Okinawa that a friend happened to be with me. Purely by chance. I remember telling him, “Hey, I’m going to Takeda Miyuki’s place tomorrow to film her. Do you want to come along?” He was also a filmmaker, so the conversation went something like: “Sure, take me with you. I’d like to see it.” “All right then.” His being there was just a fluke. When jealousy had completely overwhelmed me, I entrusted him with the camera and asked him if he would operate it for me. It’s the only time that I’ve appeared in front of the camera as the “object.”

That’s the scene where I cry. Tahara Sōichirō has written that I’m a man who cries a lot. That was the only time I’ve ever handed my camera over to a third party.

Actually, the idea that it was OK for men to cry was gaining currency at the time. A lot of people believed that men had to be strong, but a slogan at the time called for the destruction of such false illusions.

These days, even American superheroes cry profusely on screen with no problem, but back then, in the ’70s, it would have seemed odd for a hero to shed tears. This doesn’t mean that I was crying intentionally in front of the camera. But I’d resolved from the outset not to mind exposing the embarrassing parts of myself. I wanted to be open and honest about such things, and didn’t care too much about how I looked.

It was difficult for me to play the dual role of actor and cameraman. I’d thought that still I’d be able to operate the camera to a certain extent—as long as I wasn’t struck with intense emotion, or I wasn’t in a situation where I was likely to get emotional. But this became much more difficult when the fight taking place on film involved me. My experiment had failed so easily. My next thought was: How the hell am I going to film the next scene?

JEALOUSY BETWEEN A MAN AND A WOMAN

Then it occurred to me: what if the situation were reversed? After all, filmmakers are not always so pure-minded. I hadn't been able to help feeling jealous; what would happen if the roles were reversed?

In addition, I was at a bit of a loss as to how to bring my relationship with Takeda Miyuki to the next level all by myself. Since Kobayashi was pregnant at the time, I asked her to come with me, saying I was at my wit's end on my own. She wouldn't say yes, but I pleaded with her, telling her I was going out of my mind. And so we went to Okinawa together.

Kobayashi had her own ideas about what her relationship with her child would be like. She wanted to explore the issue of community by committing the child to a commune instead of raising it by herself. That was her "theme." So I wondered what would happen if her "theme" collided with Takeda Miyuki's "theme" of going to Okinawa and meeting women there. I was also curious how Takeda Miyuki would react when Kobayashi told her that she was pregnant. She might stay calm, she might not. The key would be when to tell her...

Takeda Miyuki had no idea that Kobayashi was pregnant, so when we arrived, I asked Kobayashi to keep it a secret from her for the time being. Kobayashi said that she wanted to tell Takeda Miyuki about it casually, as if it were no big deal, as soon as she saw her. That way, her relationship with Takeda Miyuki would be less fraught. I told her that I wanted her to wait for the sake of the film. And so she waited.

Soon after we arrived—that very night, in fact—we started fighting with Takeda Miyuki. Nevertheless, I waited until we filmed the scene at the beach—that is, until an appropriate situation arose—to drop the news. That scene happened a few days after our arrival in Okinawa. After a few days, we all ended up going to the beach to talk. I thought we should go to the beach to have a chat, so we did. And so, marvelously, Miyuki fell victim to jealousy of Kobayashi—or perhaps of me.

"Whooa!" I thought.

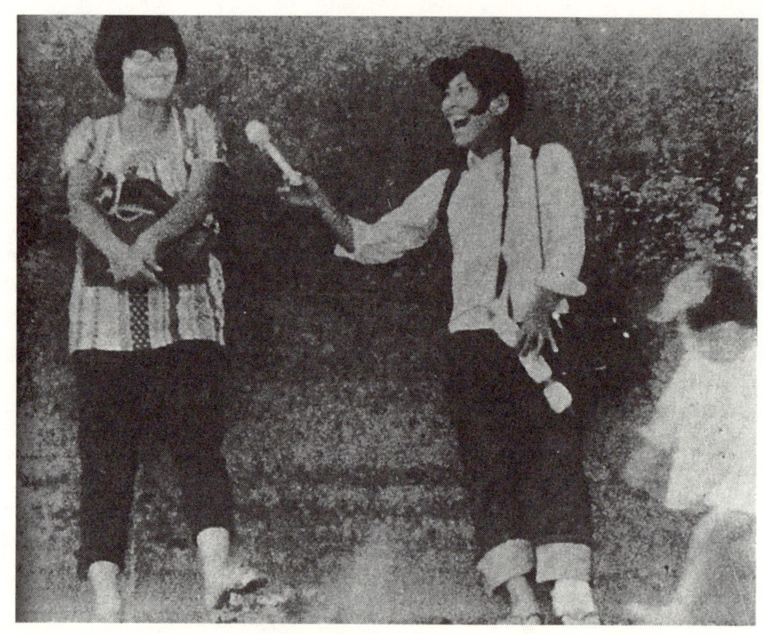

Marvelously, Takeda Miyuki, on the left, became jealous of me—or of Kobayashi Sachiko, on the right.

Again, this is a world you can only glimpse by making a film; and even then, you'd need an especially dramatic situation. That's what I think. Such a moment might have happened even if I hadn't been filming. But there had been a camera. And because there was a camera, each of us had performed our respective "actions" in that scene.

What became visible as a result?

Takeda Miyuki tried to rationalize this and that, but what it ultimately came down to was this emotion called jealousy. When I finished filming, I was surprised by what had happened.

I had wondered how she would react in front of the camera. I was face to face with her, but I was, at the same time, face to face with myself. That's what jealousy means. And that's exactly what happened.

I witnessed this emotion of jealousy surging up in her. I'd been gripped by it myself when that guy Paul had been around. At the time, it made me wonder at how sensitive—and how unfathomable—triangular relationships can be. Takeda Miyuki herself was already clearly pregnant at the time. Still, jealousy towards me had arisen in her. This emotion called jealousy and the way it works in the human heart is quite interesting. Or, to put it another way, it's unfathomable.

I think that Kobayashi had mixed feelings about suddenly being dragged into the film; she was on the production side things, after all. She'd agreed to come because I'd told her that it was for a just cause—"for the sake of the film." Of course, I'm sure she had her own reasons as well.

While I was shooting the scene of the two of them standing against a wall on the beach, deep in conversation, Miyuki turned toward me—toward the camera—and threw a handful of mud at me—that is, at the camera. Then, infuriated, she walked away. Caught between these two women—Takeda Miyuki running away and Kobayashi, puzzled, walking after her—I was at a loss. That moment perfectly reflected our situation at the time. Or rather, the film came together that way. It wasn't as though I deliberately put the scene together like that.

It's really amazing. Takeda Miyuki was walking away from our relationship, and I was wondering what to do. But at the same time, I was worried that Kobayashi Sachiko looked rather downcast. The images I shot clearly reflect the mood of that situation.

Something like this confirms my belief that a person who is making a film is at the same time acting in his own film. Filming while acting is the essence of making a documentary. However, I don't plan ahead, calculating the structure of a film in order to try to capture a scene like the one I just described. I simply try to be true to my feelings in every situation—as a result of which, I'm able to get such images in the can. Once I put these images together, I find that the scene perfectly expresses where I am vis-a-vis the situation I'm trying to capture.

FILMING THE UNASSISTED BIRTH SCENES

The two birth scenes that come up later are, in a sense, the conclusion, or settlement, of the triangular relationship just mentioned.

When I filmed the first of the two—the scene of Takeda Miyuki giving birth—the camera was in a fixed position, and it was basically one extremely long take. I got quite a few shots when I filmed Kobayashi giving birth.

Shooting Takeda Miyuki's unassisted birth was my first time doing something like that, so I was inevitably pretty nervous. We encountered no problems, because the birth itself went well. Yet we were filming an actual birth, and one without a midwife at that. I was naturally worried about what might happen if complications occurred while the child was being born. Of course, we had discussed what to do in case of an emergency. But it was, after all, Takeda Miyuki's decision. She was the one performing the action. Nevertheless, we, the ones shooting the scene, couldn't think that we had no part in it. So of course we thought about what to do in case anything happened while she was giving birth. We even thought about how, if she lost the child, we would, in the natural course of things, be considered accomplices. When discussing the shoot with Takeda Miyuki, we told her that if she were doing everything she could, and there was still a complication with the child, we would have no choice but to call a midwife. Then I said, "The rest is up to chance. Let's try and see what happens." Filled with this resolve to accept the consequences, we moved forward.

We had also basically agreed that we wouldn't help her in any way during labor. She wanted to see how much she could do on her own, so she made me promise that I wouldn't lift a finger.

This was Miyuki's second time giving birth. Also, after moving to Okinawa, she'd worked part-time for a midwife so that she could learn to give birth on her own. She'd observed several deliveries; she'd studied and was properly rehearsed. As for me, it was my first time, so I was nervous, not knowing what was going to happen. Things happened as you see in the film. Seeing the film, you might get the impression that the birthing process took quite a long time, because that's the way I edited it. But the birth itself didn't actually take that long. It only lasted an hour or so from when she started to push to when the baby was born. It was quite easy, since it was, after all, her second time.

The baby came out smoothly and started crying. I was really moved. The only problem was that the picture was out of focus. I've been criticized for that shot being out of focus. One of the people who criticized me for this was Tanaka Mitsu, who wrote that I'd deliberately filmed out of focus because I was scared of how the authorities might view such a scene.

But I'd spent more than a year preparing for the shot. Why would I have thrown the camera out of focus? Not only had I spend a year preparing for the shot, I'd also bought, on a monthly installment plan, a new, more than two-million-yen camera that could hold a 400-foot roll of film.

Honestly, having seen the developed film, we might have said to each other, "Hey, this is a problem. How should we edit it?" That could have happened. But who would throw a picture out of focus while shooting it? Trying to produce such an effect would have been much too unpredictable. I found the criticism outrageous. I was shocked.

Since Takeda Miyuki's delivery was much easier, and had gone much more smoothly than I'd expected, I had the vague notion that the second birth in the film, Kobayashi's, would be the same. You can't help but be influenced by your experiences, so I sort of assumed that it wouldn't be all that difficult. But in reality, Kobayashi went into labor at midnight and gave birth some time in the afternoon of the following day.

The whole process took over twelve hours. Since one of Kobayashi's legs is crippled, her pelvic bone is misshapen. On top of that, it was her first child, so it wasn't an easy birth. In fact, this one was much more dangerous than Takeda Miyuki's had been.

At the same time, since her labor went on forever, I had more leeway in shooting the scene. More time, at least. She wasn't able to deliver the child, so the women who were helping her put their heads together and tried one thing after another. They calmly talked about possible solutions as they sat down and ate, suggesting this and that. I filmed all of this. So when editing, I naturally strung together a sequence of short shots.

Since the action of giving birth was pretty much the same for both Takeda Miyuki and Kobayashi, I knew how to film this second one. I didn't want to film Kobayashi with her legs spread out and all that, since that had been the way I'd filmed Takeda Miyuki. So I decided to string together short takes from different angles, which is why those two scenes were shot differently.

However, one critic said: "What's at work here is the cunning of a man who has no hesitation about showing the private parts of the woman he's no longer with, but who hides the private parts of the woman he's currently with."

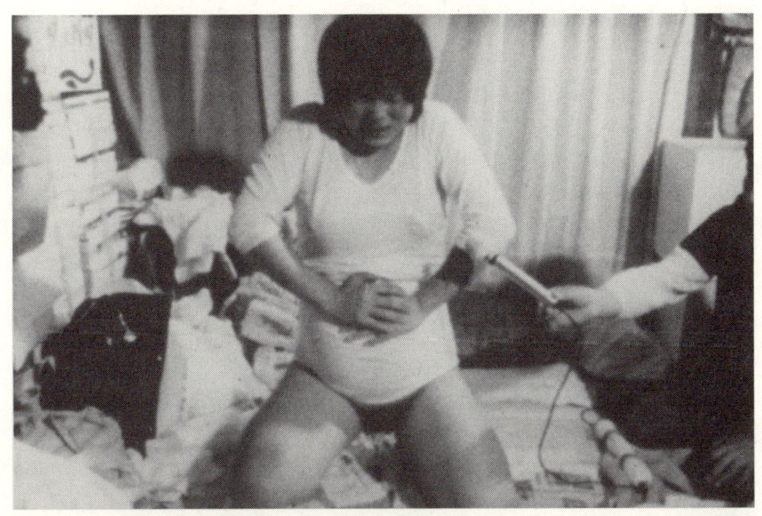

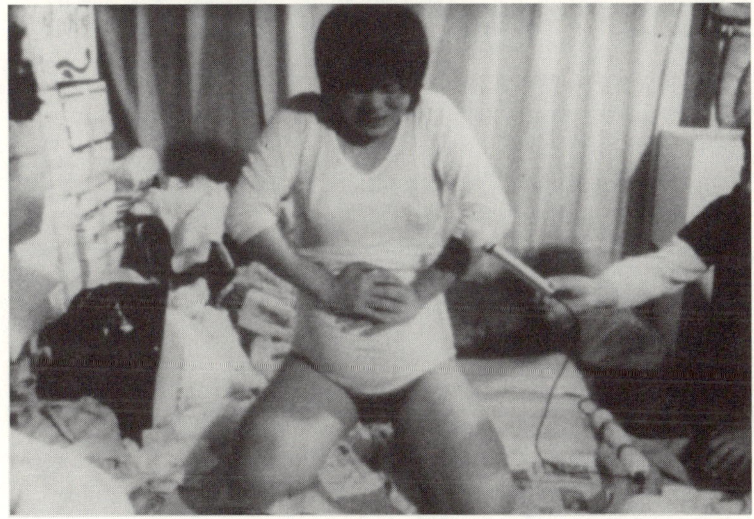

The scene of Takeda Miyuki giving birth unassisted.

It was ridiculous. That hadn't been my intent at all.

I'm amazed at the kinds of things critics come up with. I didn't even think about whether or not to show their private parts. In truth, because Kobayashi's labor lasted for so long, I had time to shoot from various angles. That's all.

Viewers will probably feel more urgency from the first birthing scene with Takeda Miyuki, as though I were filming something unknown. But actually, the second birth, Kobayashi's, was much more dangerous. On screen, it might seem as though everything were peaceful the second time around, but in reality, it wasn't. Looking back on it now, the second time was much more frightening.

THE COLLECTIVE CALLED "THE TOKYO COMMUNE"

The final scene of the film is of the "Tokyo Commune." The "Tokyo Commune" consisted of the child Takeda Miyuki bore on her own, the child she'd had with me and had been raising, and children of mixed blood from Okinawa—children from different backgrounds whom she'd gathered together under her care. The idea was that she would aggressively confront the world by undertaking the care of such children, generating energy for herself and by herself. Other women who shared this way of thinking lived there as well. Actually, some men lived there, too.

She told me to let the commune take care of the child I'd had with Kobayashi as well. Since I was living in Umegaoka at the time, I would carry my daughter on my back, take a train to the commune, and leave her with them a few times a week.

The commune was in Takaido on the Inokashira Line. This was 1974, the mid-'70s, so I think it lasted for two or three more years. But in the meantime, the student movement was fading away. As that era drew to a close, the energy that had sustained that kind of communal living also waned. People's interests were once again brought back down to the level of the individual.

After the commune disbanded, Takeda Miyuki and the women from it began to pursue their own interests. Takeda Miyuki went to Mexico and lived there for a year or two, I think. Just like that, they went back to being individuals again, and the commune inevitably disintegrated.

As for Kobayashi and myself, we felt that we needed to begin a campaign to get the film screened. There were two guys wanted to help us out. We thought a normal campaign wouldn't be much fun, so we decided to do the work required to get the film screened while living a communal life. While Takeda Miyuki's commune had disintegrated, we had ended up moving closer to communal living by renting a house together.

This is because, when discussing what our next film would be, we'd decided to do something about a commune or a community. So we rented a two-story house in Shimotakaido and started a new life: Kobayashi, myself, our newborn daughter, and our soon-to-be-born son. Kobayashi was pregnant again. A room had been assigned to each of the guys who wanted to join our activities, and also to us, and we all started living together. We also started an unauthorized daycare in the big room on the first floor. Many mothers around the same age as us were living in Setagaya Ward like us. The daycare started with mothers chipping in to hire a licensed nurse to watch their children, who would be left at our place during the day.

Our communal life lasted for about six months. I was the first person to get fed up with this arrangement. I felt as though I'd had enough. Living with other people inevitably entailed conflict. I could have predicted this, but the problems that actually arose were about really trivial matters.

I mean, when you start living with other people, you run into issues over meals. Who's going to cook? Who's going to do the dishes after we eat? Who's going to go buy the food? How are we going to pay for it? That's where a communal life really begins. On the one hand, you have your ideals, of course. But while discussing those ideals, you'd end up being swamped with one mundane, bothersome thing after another.

During that time, someone said something jokingly to the nurse, and she took it very personally. She said, "Why do I have to put up with such remarks?" "What? What's the matter?" we all asked, and a discussion ensued.

This kind of thing made me think that communal life wasn't really all that important. Perhaps these seemingly insignificant things are *not* in fact insignificant; perhaps they're the kinds of things we need to distill over a period of one or two years, that we have to overcome through discussions, saying, "Hey, this isn't working. How can we fix it?" But I thought that if I were dealing with such matters, I'd never be able to make another film; that I'd be drained of energy. So I gave up beforehand and left with Kobayashi. We left, rented an apartment, and another child was born, making four of us. We then started our lives together. I spent the next few years of my life living in a space of complete calm. I felt as though I were living in a space of pure, uncontaminated happiness. Even a life such as mine has had a few such years.

In the meantime, screenings were taking place. They began prior to our half a year of communal living, and lasted for about a year or a year and a half after that.

I EXPEND ALL THE ENERGY OF MY TWENTIES

There weren't as many mass-media outlets back then as there are now, but *Extreme Private Eros* was still picked up by a considerable number of venues, and attendance was pretty high. Still, we didn't make much money.

Our first screening was in Tokyo at the Public Hall in Sasazuka. We brought our own projector. The space, which held six to seven hundred people, was overflowing. Our next screening was in a side auditorium at the Nakano Town Hall. This space held about five hundred people. It too was overflowing, which caused a panic. More than a hundred people who hadn't been able to get into the place snuck in during the confusion. After that, we screened the film at the Yotsuya Town Hall. That's how our screening of the film began.

Once the frenzy died down, we screened the film in areas outside the city. Still, everywhere we went, it attracted a record number of people for a self-financed screening. In each region, attendance was slightly higher than anything the local screening facility had ever seen before.

Our budget for this film was six million yen. *Goodbye CP* was about one million. *Extreme Private Eros* cost six million, and it barely did well enough to pay off its debts. It wasn't as if we had money left over to enjoy. In the end, it didn't generate that much income.

But, if we compare ourselves to Ogawa Productions and the like, I think we did super well. [Laughs.] I can't emphasize that enough. We basically paid off our debts. I hear that there was one instance where I couldn't completely satisfy the creditor, but basically, we paid everything back.

In sum, I made my first film in my mid-twenties, and spent the next three years making my second. I had the vague notion that, with the momentum I had then, I should make my third film about a community. But my body wouldn't move. It was as if I'd run out of energy. I felt as though I had nothing left in me.

I truly felt that I had expended all of the energy I'd accumulated during my twenties.

Coincidentally, as I made the film, my feelings toward Takeda Miyuki subsided, or turned into friendship—something other than love. You can tell this if you watch the film.

Even after finishing the film, I would occasionally receive phone calls from her telling me to give her some money because she had none. I'd say, "I see. Let me see what I can do to raise some funds for you." But in the meantime, my love for her had turned into something else. This had already begun to happen during the second half of the filming. My love for her had considerably lessened.

I don't think that that process had any particular significance in and of itself. It was enough that it was something that had developed in the making of the film. However, it's true that I was thinking through a lot of things that were going on inside me, wondering about what had attracted me to Takeda Miyuki, and what Kobayashi Sachiko, my current girlfriend, meant to me—going back and forth between the two women.

I also realized that I'd learned so much from Takeda Miyuki—from being involved with her, from having helped her to sort out her life. While making the film, I couldn't help drawing conclusions from—or, as they say, settling accounts with—all of that. Once, when flying back from Okinawa to Tokyo alone, having left Kobayashi in Tokyo, I remembered the anecdote of Sun Wu Kong doing a cloud-somersault on the palm of the Buddha in *Journey to the West*.[3] I felt as if I were Sun Wu Kong flying back and forth between this woman and that on the Buddha's palm.

Takeda Miyuki now lives in Kunitachi in Tokyo. Also, Yū, the child who was born in *Extreme Private Eros*, was apparently adopted by a family in the United States. Takeda Miyuki raised the child we had together, Rei, and she doesn't seem to be working in the entertainment business anymore, like she was for a time. She's doing... what did she call it? Something about cosmetics, but not exactly sales.

Anyway, she said she was a regional manager, teaching people to sell stuff. What she said they were selling, I can't remember. But she's working in an honest trade.

A MODEST FAMILY LIFE

After finishing the film, we lived together as a family of four in a house. I became a father. I didn't even wonder whether or not this lifestyle would last. I didn't really think about anything for a few years. We had our youngest child. When I held him, he felt

3 *Journey to the West*: Novel about the legendary and beloved Monkey King, Sun Wu Kong. One of the Four Great Classics of Chinese literature.

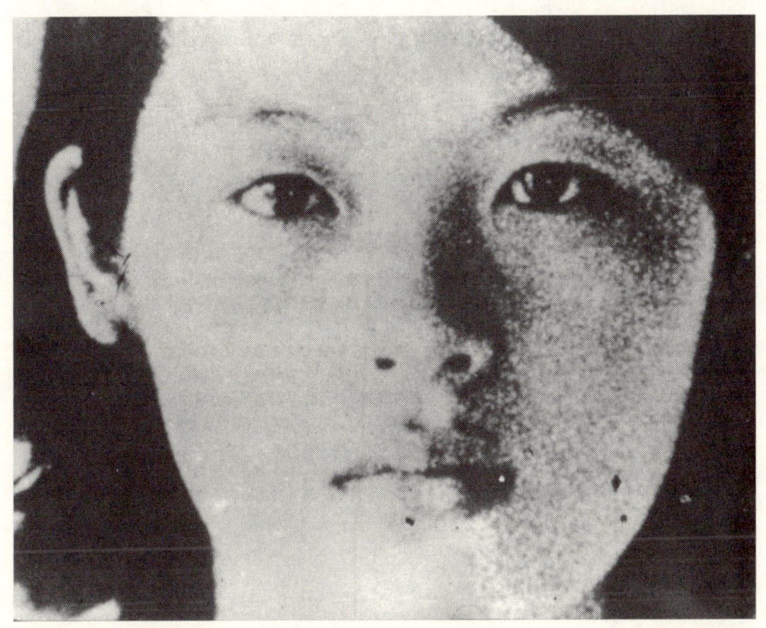

I learned so much from Takeda Miyuki
I settled accounts with her through the making of this film.

incredibly warm. The heat that a body emits is really warm. That warmth gave me comfort. In spring and early summer, I would sit in the sun, holding him, feeling warm. That alone was comforting beyond belief.

I had no desire to work, so I didn't—until we ran out of money. When we did, I went to the pawnshop. I still had my camera, so I pawned it. When that money ran out, I reluctantly went back to work. I would work for two or three days, receive my pay in cash, and not work again until we'd spent all that money. Then we would have to pay rent, so I would go back to work. We did our best not to spend money. The prices in Shimotakaido were cheap, but we would still shop at the least expensive fish shop, buying fish heads and bones or other such cheap stuff and eating quietly at home. We always ate at home, and in our free time, we would go for a stroll in the neighborhood, pushing the stroller. We lived like that for a few years.

Kobayashi basically didn't work either, but since I was so unwilling to do so, she would occasionally take a part-time job.

During that time, we met another filmmaker who was exactly the same age as me. He worked on pink movies, or softcore porn. He would tell me that they were looking for a camera assistant and ask me if I might be interested. I had our living expenses to pay and thought it wouldn't hurt for me to learn some technical stuff, so whenever he asked, I would take the job. That's how I started working in film again.

The four of us formed a tiny but closely knit unit in an apartment right near the Keio Line railroad crossing, halfway between Meidaimae and Shimotakaido. I felt that I had expended all of my energy on making my first two films in my twenties.

I said earlier that I felt at a loss when I became a father. But I only started to feel at a loss after my children formed their own personalities. Until then, I was only perplexed to the extent that anyone is when they become a parent for the first time. When your child is one, two, or three years old, their skin is really comfortable to the touch. It doesn't matter if it's a boy or a girl. Just as a biological fact, I loved holding them.

I grew a bit fat at that time. I grew a belly. My girlfriend was rather skinny, but I was fat. So when I would hold the baby close to me and sit down, we would fit together snugly. I would hold the baby on my lap, and we would just sit there, peacefully cuddling. We did that all the time. I had absolutely no energy to do anything back then. Time passed by peacefully and slowly. Since I didn't work, we didn't have any money. We were poor, but in some strange way, I had a feeling of fulfillment. That lasted for a number of years... into the latter half of the '70s.

MAKING A TELEVISION DOCUMENTARY

When it comes to the question of whether my first two films established me as Hara Kazuo the film director or Hara Kazuo the film auteur—well, it's not so easy to say. Arai Kazuko, who had become a producer at Tokyo Broadcasting System, saw *Extreme Private Eros* and took an interest in it. She asked if I wanted to make a show for television, and let me shoot an episode for a series about the story of Hiratsuka Raichō called *History Begins Here, The Women Are Now...*[4] Kobayashi conducted the interviews.

I thought at that point that I'd finally become big enough to be hired by TV stations; I was hoping that the next offer would just come along. But they never asked me again. "I see. That's how it works," I thought.

That was the first time I had ever worked on a TV show as a director. It was a 30-minute show, so we had only a few days to shoot it. The actual length of the show was twenty-odd minutes. Our style was to spend a lot of time making a film. We would create as dramatic a situation as we could, and the subject would adjust accordingly. Our job at that point would be to condense the footage

4 Hiratsuka Raichō (1886–1971): Writer and political activist. A leader of the women's movement in the early 20th Century.

we'd gotten and create something dramatic out of it. But television shows have to be shot over such a short period that it's impossible to spend a lot of time bringing out that drama. As a result, I felt as though we had to finish the show just as we were beginning the trial-and-error period. Perhaps we needed a different approach. But we weren't about to find it so quickly on our first try. As such, we had to finish while we were still groping our way around. I think the end result was neither good nor bad. I realize that television requires its own method of production, but unfortunately, I didn't have time to figure out what it might be.

The show was part of a series, so we had to satisfy some minimum requirements. Since we had to include historical figures, we had to devote part of the show to explaining who they were. Theoretically, we could do whatever we wanted with the remaining time, as long as it was about women's liberation, which was the theme of the series.

Nevertheless, we didn't want to just give a bloodless depiction of women's liberation through the story of Hiratsuka Raichō. We had just been living in that quasi-communal house in Shimotakaido where people left their children for daycare, so that became the foundation for our show. We visited groups and people involved in various social movements in different regions, interviewing women about their situations. That was what we had in mind for the structure of the show. But, predictably enough, we weren't able to film the kind of action we liked, that we took the most pride in. All we could do was record people talking. The show wasn't that long, so we deftly edited everything together and finished it off. That was all there was to it, I think.

The women's liberation movement was one aspect of *Extreme Private Eros*, and, needless to say, Takeda Miyuki was actively involved in it. But as for us, it was more as if we were running parallel to it; we didn't have any direct contact with the movement itself. While doing the television show, we visited and interviewed three of the several groups engaged in the movement. But this was different from establishing a personal relationship with them, camera in hand. In television, it's impossible to go beyond paying a short visit and doing a bit of an interview.

This wasn't so interesting. Or rather, it couldn't be helped, given that it was a television show. I couldn't transgress the limitations—the physical restrictions—of this thing called television.

If you were to ask me if I liked or disliked television documentaries, I'd have to say that generally, most of them aren't very interesting. But I also think it's meaningless to say that all TV documentaries are boring. The fact of the matter is that in the early days of television, directors worked really hard to produce some stimulating work. But when state power invaded the world of TV production, shows declined in quality and lost their influence. This didn't just happen in television; the same thing happened in the world of film as well.

Given the state that television is in, badmouthing it won't change anything. I feel that television, more so than film, is caught in the snare of state power. I do occasionally find people who are nonetheless trying to find some kind of angle, looking for new, original approaches that would be suitable for television. Some of these new approaches sometimes take me by surprise.

True, the critique that NHK cuts out everything that's inconvenient to them, showing us only what's convenient, is right on target, but I'm afraid it won't get us anywhere.[5] It won't help us change anything.

It's difficult for those of us who are making documentaries in the film world to mingle with those making documentaries for television. We talk to each other sometimes, but we don't quite mesh, or so I feel at least. We do sometimes talk, though. And I do occasionally think that, given the opportunity, it would be better to exchange opinions than not.

5 NHK [*Nippon Hōsō Kyōkai*]: Japanese Broadcasting Corporation. Japan's public broadcasting corporation, similar to PBS.

THE DIFFERENCE BETWEEN TELEVISION AND FILM

A documentary begins from the premise that an existing situation or circumstance must be resisted; it begins from the desire to get free from such circumstances. More so than narrative films, the documentary method requires that you have the resolve to confront such situations directly.

That being the case—and given the fact that state power is a lot more dominant in television than in the films *we* make—I have this idea that our methods, if applied in an appropriate manner to television, might generate more power for non-state actors. Which is why I find it futile to condemn television documentaries indiscriminately.

For example, there was this guy named Tatsumura Jin, who quit NHK.[6] I think he quit because he got himself into a situation where he was going to be fired sooner or later. He made *Carol*, and then he directed an hour-long documentary, the title of which I can't remember. They were *so* interesting. Those were the kinds of programs he would make for NHK. But he quit. Or, to put it another way, he was let go. So one can't deny that television has a hard time accepting talented people like Tatsumura Jin. It's possible to badmouth television documentaries, but all that matters in the end is whether or not doing so re-directs any energy back to us. When you criticize television documentaries, words just go in one ear and out the other. There's no response. I don't find much point in criticism of that sort.

When it comes down to it, it's nearly impossible for film to cross swords with television. Those who make documentaries for television have to start from a discussion about production requirements, or how to get a green light for a proposal. We start from a discussion about having no money. There's not much common ground.

However, when we get together for an hour or two and talk, we

6 Tatsumura Jin (1940–): Filmmaker. *Gaia Symphony*, and others.

inevitably find that we face common challenges. We start examining what television and film documentaries are trying to depict, and when we talk, we find ourselves using the same language.

People working in television say they're interested in people. They want to depict human beings. This means that they're interested in the same things that we are. But the actual works they produce are drastically different from what we produce. So you can't help but wonder where that difference comes from. That's why talking with television people makes me extremely aware of the limitations of exchanging ideas in language.

There's one clear difference between the two: opposition to society, or resistance to power. Or the potency of the venom, so to speak, that expresses any challenge to power. Television cleverly works to control that venom. It exercises so-called "self-restraint."

In film, the more potent the venom, the better the film. Theoretically. But film is not free from "self-restraint," either. As you know, even if a film is laced with venom, you can still screen it, though it's likely to get bashed or criticized or met with some such reaction. It's easier to lace a film with venom. In terms of content, that's the most distinct difference between the two mediums.

For example, documentaries made in countries outside of Japan, such as those made in parts of Asia and Africa, come out of extreme oppression, which means that their enemies can be easily identified. In today's Japan, no such clearly visible enemy exists. Thus, many opt for "self-restraint" in a variety of fields.

If I were working in television, I'd give more concrete thought to how to go about doing what I want in that particular medium. But I'm not. So however much I talk about this, it's like trying to scratch an itchy foot through a shoe. Which is why I probably shouldn't talk about it too much.

When speaking of how much impact a television documentary can have, you've got to consider its various production requirements. The budget gets cut; the content is censored. Most of the time, the final result ends up being spineless, so to speak. Given all that, I don't think a creator who sticks to what they really want to do can get by in television.

In addition, I don't think you can apply the same filmmaking methods to the making of a television documentary. It's already been two years since I made *Yellow Cab* (in 1992), an hour-and-a-half-long program, seventy-odd minutes in total. It aired as part of a variety show called *Friday Star of Television* that was broadcast on the Tokyo Broadcasting System. It was a kind of special, and they told me to make it however I wanted. I had three months to gather material for the program. This amount of time was, I was told, remarkable for television. So I tried to make the most of those three months, spending a good deal of time—though it was only three months—in preparation. However, the subject had already been decided. A certain proposal had been greenlighted, and I'd been hired. So, from the beginning, my mode of selecting my material was itself changed. With film, you tend to pick things that can't be dealt with on television; with television, you're faced with reality first—that is, the approved proposal. That's your starting point.

I say this because my gut tells me that the kind of people television serves up as subjects are only moderately interesting. No offense intended to those who do appear on television, but I bet no one will ever dare to put a superstar like Okuzaki Kenzō on the tube.

When you think about it, people watch television while sitting together around a kotatsu and eating mandarin oranges.[7] So nothing too radical will work. A proposal for a superhero who embodies any kind of radicalism would never be approved. And it's pretty easy to tell what the impact of a product whose theme or hero is only moderately radical will be.

But leaving that aside, I think there *is* a way to make television documentaries interesting—by picking an interesting angle. What, then, is an interesting angle for television? The answer's not to be found in the question of how to make television documentaries, but

7 *kotatsu*: Traditional Japanese-style table, typically outfitted with a small heater, around which families and friends gather.

rather in the question of how to think about television itself. That is, by going back to the questions posed by television's very inception. If we can't examine television from the point of view that it is itself one huge documentary, it may never become interesting. For example, variety shows could be seen as documentaries. The same is true of talk shows, comedy shows, shows featuring impersonations, and so on. I have the feeling that we'll ultimately get to a point where we have to reconsider the documentary elements of all such shows. Thinking about television documentaries only as a genre completely limits your perspective, and forecloses any new horizons for the medium.

Talking about television really isn't that interesting, is it? That's because, in the end, I'm talking about someone else's turf.

WORKING UNDER HIMEDA, KUMAI, AND URAYAMA

After working as an assistant cameraman on pink films, I started getting work, bit by bit, on films shot on location—on the streets, so to speak. The cameraman I was working under was doing niche jobs. I worked on PR films, short films, and video pieces. Initially, television dramas had been shot primarily in studios, but by the time I started doing those kinds of jobs, they were beginning to take small cameras out into the streets and recording onto portable VTRs. So I started to get more and more work as an assistant cameraman on video shoots as well. The number of cameramen I worked under increased from one to two, then from two to three. One of the cameramen I worked under sometimes worked for Imamura Shōhei's production company. He knew Himeda Shinsaku, a cinematographer at Imamura Productions, and introduced me to him.[8]

So I met Mr. Himeda and became his assistant cameraman. I only worked on five films with him. The first was a Kadokawa film,

8 Himeda Shinsaku (1916–1997): Cinematographer.

Proof of the Man. The next was *Never Give Up*. Then I think we did Kumai Kei's *Ocean to Cross*. The last two were Imamura Shōhei's *Vengence Is Mine* and *Why Not?*

Himeda seemed fond of guys like me who had grown up in a somewhat unusual way. His team always had one more person than other teams. There were more people on his team, and you would also be downgraded a notch when you worked with him. [Laughs.] By this I mean that those who were worthy of being cameramen worked as first assistant cameramen, and those worthy of being first assistant cameramen worked as second assistant cameramen. He had incredibly experienced guys working under him.

In that sense, I was just a newbie on Himeda's team, but for some reason, he would trust me with the second unit, saying, "You go shoot it, Hara." Specifically, for example, at the beginning of Kadokawa's *Never Give Up*, Takakura Ken appears on screen flying a hang glider. The main crew filmed the scene with the actor, but the scenes leading up to it, which used people who really could fly hang gliders, were B-roll shots. At the time, my rank on Himeda's team was second or third assistant, but he told me to go shoot all the scenes of non-actors flying hang gliders. I didn't even have an assistant director to work with. So I spent a week on location at Sugadaira, discussing the scene with professional hang-gliders. To make matters worse, I could only film once a day. The hang-gliders would climb to a high place in the morning and fly for me. Then the day would be over. I needed to film them from different angles, so the filming took a number of days. Himeda let me take care of the planning and everything. That's how he let me work.

It was the same with *Oceans to Cross*, too. Normally, the person who was going to be the next cameraman would be the first candidate to operate the B camera. The first assistant cameraman would be the second candidate, the second assistant would be the third candidate, etc. But I participated in *Oceans to Cross* as the B-camera operator. It didn't happen often, but when both cameras were being used simultaneously, Himeda would operate the A camera and I would operate the B camera. That's how we worked.

Around that time, I met Kumai Kei.[9] I also met Imamura Shōhei while working on set with him. But I was in the camera department. You don't get to know the director on set if you're working in a different department. And so that job ended without us ever really getting to know one another.

While working on film sets such as that, the cameraman who had introduced me to Himeda got a job shooting a piece in *A Series Where Japanese Film Directors Compete* for Tokyo Channel 12. The series was to feature directors interviewing people they found interesting. The directors themselves also appeared on screen, and each show in the series was to be thirty minutes long. The cameraman had teamed up with the director Urayama Kiriro, and they hired me as an assistant cameraman. I worked on two shows for Urayama. In one, the person being interviewed was the novelist, singer, and one-time Diet member, Nosaka Akiyuki, and in the other, the actor and singer Kobayashi Akira. While working on these shows, I showed—or rather, humbly presented—*Extreme Private Eros* to Urayama. He liked it, and began talking to me about various things.

Because of that experience, I thought I might like to work as Urayama's assistant director or AD. I'd been working in the camera department, but also wanted to try my hand at being an assistant director. Since Urayama had seen and liked my film, he said he would hire me as an AD. He hired me for *Child of the Sun* as the third AD. But instead of having to be promoted up the chain of command by becoming Urayama's second AD and then his first AD, I was told that I would be his first AD the next time he shot a film. I was told this by Shinjō Taku, who'd been the first AD on *Child of the Sun*, and who would later go on to direct *Okinawa Boys*.[10] Shinjō Taku told me that not many people could work as Urayama's first assistant director. By this he meant that working with Urayama wasn't a matter of skill, but of being able to communicate with him. After all, being first

9 Kumai Kei (1930–2007): Filmmaker. *Apart from Life*, *The Long Darkness*, and others.
10 Shinjō Taku (1944–): Filmmaker. *Okinawa Boys*, and others.

AD is difficult. If you couldn't communicate with the director, you couldn't work in that position.

While we were making *Child of the Sun*, Urayama took something of a liking to me. Before I started working with him, Oguri Kōhei used to work for him pretty often.[11] He was one of Urayama's favorites. And yet I wasn't sure if, after becoming a director, Oguri would like and admire Urayama enough to remain loyal to him. It felt as though Urayama were one of the last giants of filmmaking. But in order to be one of the giants, you have to have people loyal to you who revere you as such. Urayama couldn't be a giant if everyone around him rebelled against him, saying, "How arrogant! Who does he think he is?" And we were already moving into an era when the system that had sustained the giants of filmmaking was no longer viable.

So it was becoming more and more difficult for Urayama to make films. A director's authority requires loyalty, but there were fewer and fewer assistants who could tactfully accept Urayama's authority and team up and work with him. I don't consider directorial authority to be a bad thing. It's probably necessary if you're going to be continuously churning out films. That's what I thought while I stood by and observed both Urayama and Kumai.

So Shinjō Taku told me that I was up—that I would be Urayama's first AD the next time he made a film. But just as I was thinking that I would love to work with Urayama, he passed away. So I wasn't able to establish a close relationship with him in the end. Our relationship ended right before it could even begin.

I'M A BRILLIANT ASSISTANT DIRECTOR

Historically speaking, directing a film has been a job that requires a lot of charisma, similar to being a dictator. You're at the top of a patriarchal hierarchy. At least you have to pretend you are,

11 Oguri Kōhei (1945–): Filmmaker. *Muddy River, The Sting of Death*, and others.

or many things will stop working.

I entered this world, and you might think that I felt repulsed by its patriarchal hierarchy, but I wasn't in the least. [Laughs.] I found it rather interesting, and even found something positive in it. That is to say—and I think this has something to do with the fact that I never really had a father—I have this desire for someone I could call a teacher, someone who could train and discipline me. Despite my desire to meet such a person, I don't think I ever have.

Was Himeda my teacher? Even though I do feel he was a teacher to me, he wasn't the kind of person who would teach with words. Instead, he'd encourage people to steal his techniques while working with him.

I was working in both the camera department and the director's department. I was hoping to meet someone good in the latter department—that is, a director—from whom I could learn about film. But unfortunately, as long as I was working on Himeda's team, which was in the camera department, it was difficult to have a chance to speak to a director. Then I became Urayama's assistant, and I was all set to be his first assistant director, when he died. That's how things went for me.

When good old Urayama was sober, he was like a university professor. He taught me some amazing things using the most precise language. Even now, I remember some of the things he said to me. To call them "gems" wouldn't be an overstatement. But he passed away, so I couldn't fulfill my dream of working with him... That's how I feel. As such, I don't condemn the apprentice-like aspect of the system; as a matter of fact, part of me wholeheartedly longs for it.

However, if I were to ask myself whether or not I could be like Urayama if I were to direct a narrative film, I'd say no. Why? Because, in an apprentice-system-type world, the director has to stand at the very top of the pyramid. In order to stand at the very top, various elements are required—one of which is charisma. Then, perhaps, intelligence, and then... No, there's no "then." I believe that it all comes down to one thing: you either have charisma, or you can't do the job. Because I know I don't, I haven't taken on that role.

Also, a good director has to be a good organizer, or he won't become one of the great masters. I'm not that, either. I'm not an organizer. I think Ogawa was. So the ability to organize people. And the ability to inspire them. And charisma. And, of course, without intelligence and culture, you can't really lead a crew. I have none of these things.

Given that, you might have wondered how I could become a director at all, or what kind of a director I might turn out to be. In fact, I haven't worked on that many films as an assistant director. I started working with Kumai Kei on *The Sea and Poison,* and his latest, *Deep River*, was the fourth film we've worked on together. I was credited as a supporting director, but that's a title Kumai gave me out of kindness. I did the work of a first AD. He let me handle the set to a great degree, which made my job quite easy. So I managed Kumai's shoots pretty much the way I wanted. And this led to good results.

I think I'm a brilliant assistant director. For example, *The Sea and Poison* went extremely well—almost perfectly; right on schedule, down to the last detail, with a surgery scene and other difficult scenes. It's not as though I got my know-how from anyone else. I figured things out on my own: how to set up a scene; how to put together a team of assistant directors; which people to place in which job positions. When assigning jobs, I don't just automatically go down the hierarchy: I ignore the pecking order, assigning this person to wardrobe, that one to props.

Then I coordinate the whole crew. The two engines that run a set are the production department and the director's department. So I put them together as a team. Also, technicians—the cameraman, the gaffer, and the heads of each department—are key to making a successful narrative film. These technicians are skillful but selfish, in the best sense of the word. They're all in their own worlds. Underneath the surface, all kinds of games are going on with them; cold fireworks are always going off. If any of that were to collide with the director, we'd be in deep trouble. It's a given that everyone, including the director, has his or her own egoism. I excel at tactfully drawing out each person's ego, understanding it, and redirecting it towards the energy that's driving the whole. I'm really good at that.

I did my job to perfection on *The Sea and Poison*, so ever since, Kumai has repeatedly said, "I'd like you to do that again," and that's what I've done. I really brag about it. I think I'm close to perfect when it comes to something like that.

What I'm trying to get at is that when I do eventually direct a narrative film, I don't think there would be an assistant director around who could do a better job than what I could do myself. Perhaps other directors feel the same way when it comes to the kinds of things I've talked about. But what will I end up doing when I'm not the assistant director, but rather, the director? What else could I do but manage the shoot using my strengths: that is, as if I were the first AD.

In reality, directing in such a way is nearly impossible. It's extremely difficult, frankly speaking. Then again, is it possible to properly train assistant directors in Japan today? No. Almost everyone goes right into directing.

However, even under the studio system, some people have gone on to make their names as directors after being less than stellar as ADs. An assistant director's talent for managing a shoot is fundamentally different in nature from that of a director. Just because you have phenomenal talent as an assistant director doesn't mean you'll be a good director. But a good director can probably manage a set as well. I think I can say that as a general rule. That's my guess, though perhaps each person is different.

WHAT I LEARNED FROM URAYAMA KIRIRO

I've said that Urayama had seen *Extreme Private Eros*, and that he'd subsequently taught me various things.

I'll tell you just one of the things he taught me. He said, "Hara,

Extreme Private Eros is a good film. I like it. The female protagonist, Takeda Miyuki, is a good character." He went on to say that you'd have to invent or create that kind of appealing heroine in a narrative film. In a documentary, the premise of the film is to shoot someone who already exists. In a narrative film, that person has to be created. "Therefore, making a narrative film is a masculine job," he said. Then he said, "Hara, be sure make a narrative film one day. A narrative film is fascinating, I tell you." According to him, documentaries were feminine by comparison. For some reason, that's the way Urayama thought of them.

Then he taught me something else that I'm not sure if you'll be able to understand. We'd gone to shoot on location on Hateruma, the southernmost tip of Japan—that is, the southernmost island of Okinawa. By that time, our funds were running low, and there were only two assistant directors left: myself and Shinjō. For about a week, we ran around on that tiny island preparing everything for the shoot. Just the two of us, running all over the place.

There was absolutely no entertainment, nothing to do on that island, so we thought we should bring a film to screen or something. So Urayama brought a 16-mm print of a television documentary he'd shot on Borneo or some place. We were going to show it to the people on the island at some sort of town hall, and he put me in charge. But even though I'd been put in charge of the screening, I still had to go from one place to another on the island to rent costumes and do other jobs in preparation for the shoot. At the time, there was a guy in the lighting department named Yasukōchi, who's now working as a gaffer. He teamed up with Kimura Daisaku for a while as a director of photography.[12] I wonder what's the latest film he's worked on. He's become a gaffer now. At the time, he was still a best boy. I got along with him somehow. He said, "Don't worry. I'll take care of the screening." So I said, "Thanks," and left it to him.

I was running all over the island preparing for the shoot, but I was worried about the screening, so I went to the hall and was

12 Kimura Daisaku (1939–): Cinematographer. *Nippon Chimbotsu, The Rage of Love,* and others.

relieved to find that it was going on as planned. A fair number of people were watching the film, so I went back to my preparations. But something did in fact go wrong. That night, I went to the inn where Urayama and others were staying. He was drinking, and everyone who was a member of the main crew was there, even the actress Ōzora Mayumi.[13] The moment I walked into the room and Urayama saw my face, he blew up.

"You! What the hell were you thinking?! You fucking idiot!" He threw a can of fish, mackerel or something, at me, I didn't know why he was so upset, but he was infuriated. Apparently, in the middle of the screening, the projector had crashed to the floor. It had fallen because when Yasukōchi from the lighting department had set it up, he'd put it on one of those poorly made backwoods tables, and the legs had been weak. So it had fallen to the floor, and the sound drum had apparently been bent out of shape, making a fuzzy noise whenever someone on screen would speak.

I had no idea that this had happened. Urayama barked at me, "I felt completely humiliated. I left you in charge of this. Why the hell didn't you do what I'd asked?"

While he was yelling at me, I began to understand why he was so angry. But you couldn't defend yourself at a time like that. However, as he was yelling at me, I was somehow moved. Tears welled up. I realized *how* important showing the villagers his film had been to him.

Now his yelling took on a different meaning: "Why can't you understand how I feel?" or "You don't get it, do you!" As he was dressing me down, I understood. Objectively speaking, I could have said that it had been impossible for me to take care of the film screening because I'd been running around preparing for the shoot. But I didn't. The profundity of his attachment to films moved me. "I'm sorry," I apologized.

Ōzora Mayumi did her best to intervene, saying, "Now, now. Let it go, Mr. Ura." Then another amusing incident took place. After

13 Ōzora Mayumi (1940–): Actress. Most active from the late 1950s to the mid 1970s.

Urayama finished yelling at me, he said, "Well, I guess it's OK. I understand what happened. Come here, drink with me." Everyone in the main crew was there, and in a friendly manner, they all said, "Have a drink!" I said, "OK," and had a few drinks. Then Urayama got wasted. And he fell asleep with his head in my lap. Using my lap as a pillow was Urayama's—how should I put it—his way of letting his anger with me run its course. I'd been chastized by him, but the way his emotions worked... I'll never be able to forget that.

When I told this story to my girlfriend, she laughed and said, "Are you stupid or what? It's called masochism. I'll never forgive Urayama for that kind of tyrannical behavior."

But I can't agree with her. I think my need for a teacher overlaps with my need for a father figure. My desire to meet and have a meaningful relationship with such a person manifests itself not just in my feelings toward Urayama, as I've just explained, but also in my feelings toward others: Imamura, for example, and Okuzaki Kenzō, and also Inoue Mitsuharu.

KUMAI KEI IS LIKE MY BROTHER

But I've never felt that way towards Kumai Kei. Why? It's not as though I don't consider him a teacher. He's just a bit different. He's old enough to be my father, but he feels closer to me on an emotional level. He feels more like an older brother to me.

He's got a bad reputation. It's true: he says so himself. [Laughs.] He always says, "In the film industry, I've got a bad reputation." So I always say, "That's true." He's well aware of why his reputation is bad. Well, it's more like a joke. Nevertheless, there are people in the film industry who love him. Half of them do, that is.

Be that as it may, he feels more like a brother than a teacher for whom one shows loyalty from a distance. So I can joke around with him more. Working with him while joking around is a blast. It's fun.

Kumai knows everything about every film, old and new, Eastern and Western. He'd ask, "What's the first scene of that film? What are the lines in that scene? Do you remember? Do you remember how many shots that scene consisted of?" He remembers. His memory leaves me speechless. My memory isn't that good, so every time I hear him talk about a movie, it stuns me. But more than that, on a personal level, he has a sort of approachability. So whenever we've gone on a shoot, it's been entertaining, a lot of fun. People in the film world might say they can't believe it, but it's true.

Viewed from outside, you might find it difficult to associate Hara Kazuo, the documentary film director, with the guy who manages film sets while mixing with these patriarchal and brotherly figures.

To add to that, I've been thinking that for my next film, I'll finally make a narrative feature. When I'm reading a script to work on someone else's set, I can read it without objections. The lines of dialogue are written down, of course. I simply take them for granted, thinking, "Oh, these are the lines the actors are going to speak." But if I have to think up a line for myself and feed it to an actor, I get very hesitant, wondering if anyone would actually say something like that. That's why I haven't been able to make a narrative film until now.

So you could say that when I'm on set, I'm working under the notion that I'm there to make a living. In other words, I must draw some kind of a line between the work I do for myself and the work I do for others. The sets are not *mine*, after all. In a sense, my skills have been hired. Skills are the only things that matter in that world, so it's a place where my skills are put to work.

It may be true that I maintain a kind of professional detachment when working on other people's films, yet I don't necessarily approve of everything that happens on their sets.

I've always wondered how I would tell the actors to say their lines if I were directing. But I don't butt in and tell each director what I think: I just keep it to myself and think about how I myself would do it. Now that I've done *A Dedicated Life*, I finallly feel ready to try it out on my next film.

I WANT TO LEAVE A FILM FROM MY THIRTIES

So I had a period of peace. Then I started to get more and more work, and I found myself in my late thirties. It wasn't as if I made a conscious effort to force myself into doing something. Nor did I feel pressed for time. But I had the vague realization that my thirties were coming to an end. Anyway, I'd made two films in my twenties. So the thought that I wanted to make at least one film in my thirties occurred quite naturally to me. I was thinking this when I visited Imamura Shōhei one day. While we were talking, I told him that I wanted to make a documentary. I wasn't desperate or anything, or thinking that I had to do this or that.

I just went to see him one day. So I think by the time I saw him, my desire to somehow make at least one film in my thirties had naturally grown much more intense. I had a few ideas... I think this was about two years before I started the film on Okuzaki.

Then, Kaneko Shōji saw *Extreme Private Eros* and liked it.[14] He contacted me and said, "Hara, let's make a film together." "Okay, yeah, yeah, let's do it," I replied. I think what he really wanted to do was to make a narrative film. But he told me that he didn't care what kind of a film it would be, or whether he would be in it or not. At the time, I kept wanting to make a film about a crime for some reason.

There had been an incident at Salesio High School: a student there had decapitated one of his classmates. I had been researching the incident, so I invited Kaneko to make a film about it with me. We investigated the crime and did some preparatory work. But we eventually abandoned the project.

Why did we abandon it? Because we'd tracked down the actual person who'd cut off his classmate's head. It turned out that he had changed everything, even his family registry. Making the film would have re-opened the past and... after all he'd done, I didn't want to ruin his efforts. On the other hand, I had no interest in making a

14 Kaneko Shōji (1949–1983): Screenwriter and actor. Wrote and starred in Tōru Kawashima's 1983 film, *Ryuuji*.

completely fictional film out of this story. I thought that if he didn't mind talking with us, I'd still try to make the film. But that didn't work out either.

I had another aborted idea for a film as well—in fact, quite a few of my ideas were aborted.

There was an incident of arson at the Fuji Evening High School. A homosexual guy had been suspected, but it turned out that he'd been falsely accused. I thought the homosexual aspect of it might be interesting, so I met the person, and even filmed him a bit.

He was obsessed with uniforms. It was a kind of fetishism.

I spoke with him about this and that and started to film, but filming someone's fetishism was even beyond what I would eventually have to go through with Okuzaki...

The guy loved police uniforms, so he would put one on, and have his boyfriend wear one as well; he said hugging his boyfriend like that was the ultimate pleasure for him. So I rented a kind of studio, had them put on the uniforms, and filmed them. They acted as though it were all extremely pleasurable. Watching them, I felt like a complete fool. It was great that they were having so much fun, but if that were all there was to it, I didn't find it interesting at all. I said, "Have fun, the two of you," and lost interest in them. So I abandoned that film, too. I had absolutely no interest in filming them any more. This was before gay culture became as interesting as it is now.

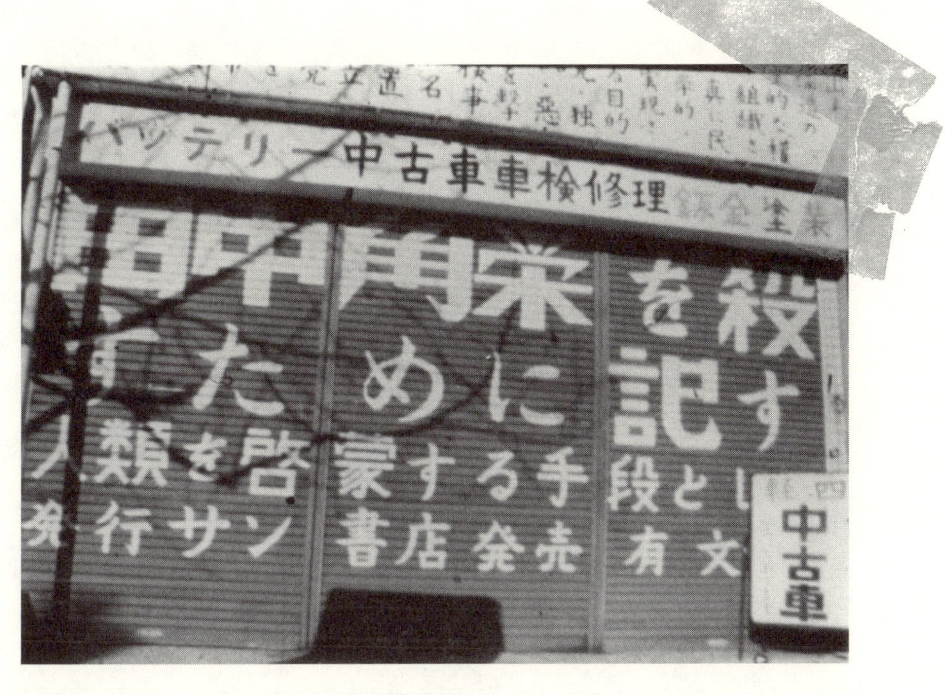

05 The Film that Summons God

The Emperor's Naked Army Marches On[1]

1 The English-language title of this film is a remarkably imaginative take on the original Japanese, or "Yukiyukite, Shingun," which could be more literally translated as "God's Army Goes Marching." Here, "god" refers both to the "kami" or Japanese protective deities, and the Japanese emperor, who was supposed to be descended from the gods, and who was the figurehead of Japanese propaganda efforts during WWII.

According to Kobayashi Sachiko, the film's working title was something like "The Last Will and Testament of Okuzaki Kenzō, Equal Soldier in God's Army," and was derived from Okuzaki's characterization of himself as such. When the time came to decide on the official title for the film, they felt that the working title was a bit too coarse. They wanted to keep "God's Army," but they wanted to make it softer.

Incidentally, the name of their production company, "Shissō," was taken from a poem that Kobayashi-san liked; this time, too, they wanted to use soft, poetic language reminiscent of the writings of Orikuchi Shinobu, who advocated for the use of indigenous Japanese language as opposed to words imported from China. So the choice of the word "Yukiyukite" is a bit unusual. It basically means "go" but has a softer, slightly antiquated ring to it.

Typically, the local distributor comes up with the English title for a foreign film, but in this case, a famous and authoritative Japanese person picked it. As such, they felt they couldn't disagree. Still, they felt from the very beginning that the English title misrepresented the film (after all, Okuzaki belonged to God's army as an equal soldier, fighting against the emperor).

THE MAN NAMED OKUZAKI KENZŌ

I'd been trying to make films on a variety of topics when I met Imamura Shōhei and told him that I wanted to make a film while I was still in my thirties.[1] Imamura said, "Oh. OK, that's great. Then there's someone I would like you to meet." That's how I met Okuzaki Kenzō. It was really nothing more than a chance encounter.

Okuzaki had initially been imprisoned for a crime he'd committed on a very personal level. But while in solitary confinement, he'd experienced what might be called a human revolution. After this transformation, he realized that his actual target should be the emperor of Japan, so after being released from prison, he went and shot pachinko balls at the emperor using a homemade slingshot. [2]Afterwards, he printed and distributed flyers with obscene images of the emperor on them. He subsequently went on doing this and that, or at least trying to. But with each attempt, his targets gradually declined in significance. He was aware of this, too. Why was this? Because he was growing old. Also, his neighborhood police were vigilantly monitoring him, so even if he thought about attacking prominent figures, he couldn't just do as he pleased. Still, if Okuzaki had been able to think something up, he would have been able to carry it out easily enough. But he wasn't quite able to come up with a suitable target. He was the kind of person who couldn't act without just cause. So the basic scenario we had in mind when we met Okuzaki was to do a portrait of the postwar life of this man who had become physically worn out by the passage of time.

This is how we met: Okuzaki had already self-published his *Proclamation to Kill Prime Minister Tanaka Kakuei*.[3] That's the way he works: first and foremost, he makes clear what his target is and declares

---

1 Imamura Shōhei (1926–2006): Filmmaker. *A Man Vanishes*, *Black Rain*, *The Eel*, and others.

2 *pachinko*: Small metal balls that are used for gambling in the Japanese equivalent of slot machines. It's other definition, "slingshot," was, ironically, the device used by Okuzaki to launch the pachinko balls at the emperor in his infamous attack.

3 Tanaka Kakuei (1918-1993): Japanese politician and two-time Prime Minister from the ruling Liberal Democratic Party. Known as the "Shadow Shogun."

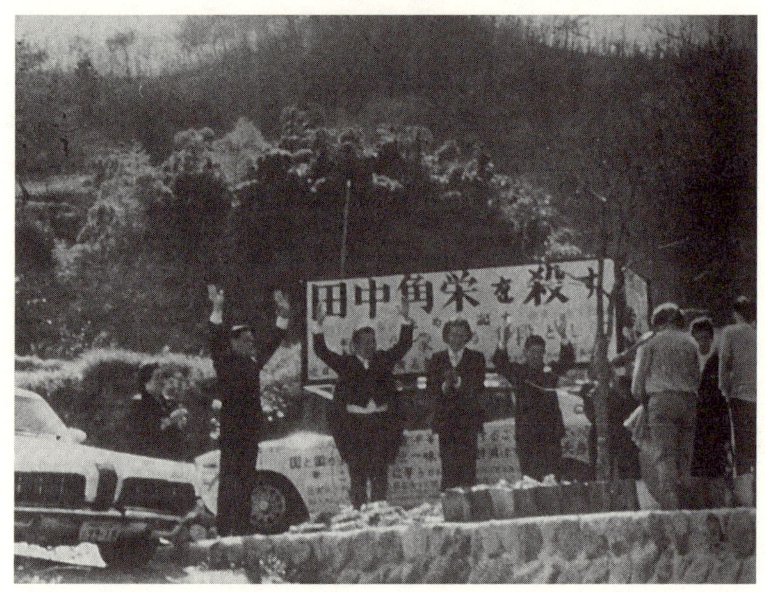

Okuzaki plastered the phrase "Proclamation to Kill Prime Minister Tanaka Kakuei" all over his car.

his resolve. But he's not just announcing this to others; it's also for himself. That's why he'd published the book using his own funds.

The contents of this thick book announced Okuzaki's determination to "kill Tanaka Kakuei" and explained his reasons for wanting to commit the crime. And he sent copies to everyone he knew, including Imamura Shōhei. After sending out the books, he went to Tokyo. He even plastered the phrase "Proclamation to Kill Prime Minister Tanaka Kakuei" all over his car as a kind of commercial for the book. You see it in the film. That's why the name of the book's publishing company, "San-shoten," is also displayed on the car.

When he got to Tokyo, he actually went to Tanaka Kakuei's estate with his wife. When they arrived, they weren't quite sure if they were in the right place. But, having traveled all that way, they figured there was no reason not to take a commemorative photograph in front of it. They needed someone to take the picture for them, so they asked the security guard or some such police person who was there. This photograph was subsequently considered an act of "reconnaissance." Okuzaki had, after all, published a book entitled *Proclamation to Kill Tanaka Kakuei*, and then he'd actually gone to Tanaka Kakuei's mansion and had had his photograph taken in front of it. It was decided that he'd gone to scout out the place, so he was arrested for intent to kill. But he obviously couldn't be convicted on that charge alone, so he was never prosecuted.

Okuzaki was a man who had no regard for consequences. According to Okuzaki, consequences were the will of God. The most important thing for him was to make a decision and see it through.

So that's where Okuzaki was coming from. When I told Imamura Shohei that I wanted to make a documentary, he handed me Okuzaki's *Proclamation to Kill* and told me to read it. So I did. But I could barely understand the book. I had absolutely no idea what Okuzaki was trying to say. So I said to Imamura, "OK then, I'll just go and meet him." That's how we came to meet Okuzaki.

Okuzaki has published several books, by the way. One of his other books is called *The Philosophy of "God's Army."* They're all hard to understand, but I think *Proclamation to Kill Tanaka Kakuei* is the most difficult of all.

When Okuzaki shot pachinko balls at the emperor, a journalist at a weekly magazine wrote an article about the incident. That was Okuzaki's first appearance in the media. The journalist, a leftist, introduced Okuzaki to Imamura. After meeting Okuzaki, Imamura tried to make a film about him. But he wasn't able to.

I heard that Imamura and his crew had brought a camera into the courtroom to record Okuzaki's hearing. The cameraman had apparently disassembled his Filmo, hidden it in his coat, and snuck it into the courthouse. He then went to the restroom, put it back together, and brought it into the courtroom to record the proceedings.

But cheap cameras like that usually make a buzzing noise, so he was immediately discovered and thrown out of the courtroom. Depending on who you ask, some people say he actually managed to record something, others say he didn't, but no one actually knows. Anyway, even though the cameraman tried to film Okuzaki, he wasn't able to in the end. Making any kind of a movie with a protagonist like Okuzaki, a man who shot pachinko balls at the emperor, would be, from a financial standpoint alone, almost impossible.

So, in the end, Imamura wasn't able to make a film about Okuzaki. Instead, he made the film *The History of Postwar Japan as Told by a Bar Hostess* (1970). His premise for the film—which I didn't hear about from Imamura himself, but rather from his crew—was apparently to "interrogate the emperor system and the entire history of postwar Japan."

The heroine of the film is a woman who's supposedly from the outcast slums of the buraku. Imamura had planned to examine postwar Japanese history and the emperor system through a film about both this woman and Okuzaki. When he realized he wouldn't be able to film Okuzaki, his only recourse had been to make a film solely about the woman from the buraku, which is what he did.

Throughout the decade following the making of that film, Okuzaki continued to pester Imamura about making a film about him, and Imamura considered various possibilities. He apparently submitted a proposal to do a piece about Okuzaki as part of his famous *In Search of Unreturned Soldiers* series for Tokyo Channel 12. But getting a proposal about Okuzaki accepted for television was even more impossible, so he never ended up making anything about Okuzaki. He was very sorry about this, and even paid Okuzaki a visit to apologize. They'd kept in touch ever since. Enter me, who casually visited Imamura and told him that I wanted to make a documentary. He said he would introduce me to Okuzaki. That's how we met.

BECAUSE WE'RE "IDIOTS"

I'm now going to tell the end of the story first: after finishing *The Emperor's Naked Army*, a number of directors came up to us and said that they'd been fascinated by Okuzaki and had wanted to shoot a film about him. Some of them said that Imamura had actually approached them to make the film. But they had all declined. Really.

I could only think to myself, "Why tell me this after the film's been finished?" Since Imamura had tried and failed so many times to follow through on his own plans to make a film about Okuzaki, he'd asked others if they might be interested in taking on the project. I had no idea that Imamura had asked anyone else; that story only came out after I had made the film.

Nobody would do it. Why not?

Because they were scared. I was scared, too. But we did it anyways. I can't help but wonder what separated us from them.

The answer is that we're idiots.

Really. I'm not saying this as a joke. The people whom Imamura asked were all smart, so they were able to understand the situation. What would happen if they made such a film? The very act of making it would be dangerous. To begin with, the proposal would never be accepted. Everyone else could naturally foresee all these things. Because they were smart, they could objectively analyze the situation, and they'd come to the conclusion that the film would be trouble. So they decided not to do it.

Why did we do the film? Because we were idiots. Because we never considered the objective circumstances. How do I put this? And I'm not joking when I say this, I'm telling you honestly: We make films because we're idiots. We're driven by this idea of making the kind of films only idiots could make.

Well, leaving this "story of idiocy" aside [laughs], we went ahead and met Okuzaki. The moment we met him, we thought, "This is going to be a fascinating film. Let's do it." We were already talking about doing the film on the bullet train home.

By the way, since Imamura had introduced us to Okuzaki, I'd presumptuously assumed that if we decided to do the film, Imamura would finance us. Someone who asks a director to make a film normally pays for it. So on the train home, our conversation turned to how much Imamura Productions might give. "Imamura Productions is poor, so maybe about ten million yen?" "We might be able to finish the film in a year or two. Still, ten million yen won't be enough, so we'll probably have to raise half a million or so ourselves." Talking about such things, we made our way home.

On the following day, I went to Imamura Productions and talked with Imamura, telling him I'd met Okuzaki the day before.

"Oh. You did? How was it?" he asked.

"Good. WE'LL... WE WANT TO UH... WE'LL UH... DO IT. We... we're going to give it a try." I told him.

"Oh. OK. What are you going to do about money?"

I should have said right there and then, "What? What? What do you mean by that?" But as soon as I thought, "What does he mean by that?" I spat out, "We'll come up with something." I couldn't help it. You know what I mean, how responses sometimes just blurt out of you.

So Imamura, without hesitation, said, "Oh. OK. Sounds good. Good luck!"

"Oh no!" I thought. Totally depressed, I went home. When I

told Kobayashi that things had turned out differently than we'd expected, she replied, "You're a real fool, aren't you?" But she's big-hearted with things like that, so she continued, "Well, it's OK. We can't turn back now, so let's just do it." And that's how we started on our path to making the film.

Now this might sound like a joke, but if we had known from the beginning that it was going to be a self-financed production, I'm not sure we would have gone through with it. We had a serious misunderstanding with Imamura. It's like a joke now, though, so we can just laugh it off.

I subsequently went to meet Imamura again for a second time to discuss the finances for the film, and to get advice on various things.

I also needed to discuss the content of the film, so I went to meet Okuzaki again. We discussed a number of issues. His biggest concern was, of course, the money. He said that he'd be delighted if we were to make the film, but that he would decline the offer if we were counting on his financial support. My heart skipped a beat. We'd actually been expecting some level of financial commitment from him. But, putting on airs yet again, I replied,

"No, no. Don't be ridiculous. We don't have the slightest intention to worry you about the money for the film." Then Okuzaki responded, "Is that so? If that's the case, then I'll cover my own expenses for the film. I'd feel guilty if you were paying for everything." It was decided that Okuzaki would come up with the money he needed for his portion of the expenses, and that we would come up with the money needed for the production of the film.

I WANT TO FILM THE PAST IN REAL TIME

At the time, Okuzaki candidly told me something to the effect that although he'd been thinking about who and what to attack next after shooting pachinko balls at the emperor—and although he'd continued to act out his defiance throughout the entire postwar period—he had, in all honesty, begun to grow weak. He said that if we were going to make a film about him, he would devote every ounce of energy he had to it. In fact, he said that making the film would give him strength and motivation again. We went back and forth about this, with him saying, "So I'll do everything I can; let's do this," and me saying, "Thank you."

But little did he suspect at the time that he would end up going after his company commander. He just meant to do his best. He said, "The character for the word 'monument' consists of the radical for 'stone' and one for 'despicable,' and the film you're going to shoot is going to be a monument to me." So that's where that famous line of Okuzaki's came from: "As my monument, this film will be far from despicable; rather, it'll be a testament to my rectitude." He would go whole hog like this whenever he was given half a chance, saying things like the fact that a film was being made about him was his reward from God.

Okuzaki had a slew of famous lines: for example, everywhere we went, he would say, "My film is being made thanks to the famous director Imamura Shōhei, who introduced me to director Hara Kazuo of Shissō Productions." He would never fail to follow this up with: "This film is going to be a monument to me, so I'm going to try even harder." In short, this film was necessary to Okuzaki as a way of reviving his determination, of refreshing himself.

When we started the film, he had one specific aim: to go back to New Guinea again. He wanted to go back to the place where he had been captured as a prisoner of war in 1944. From 1944 until the end of the war, Okuzaki's fellow soldiers had found themselves in the tragic situation of having to eat human flesh. Okuzaki had been captured by local villagers just before they reached that point, so he hadn't actually seen his fellow soldiers cannibalizing each other. Being captured had been tantamount to being saved.

After Okuzaki mentioned that he wanted to go back to New Guinea, I did some research on the situation there. The People's Liberation Front was waging a guerilla war in the area where he wanted to go. Access was prohibited, so Okuzaki knew as well as I did that getting permission to enter the region wouldn't be easy. This only strengthened his resolve—he wanted to get there no matter what. In short, going there became the specific goal of the film we were making together. This was essentially the same as the promise Takeda Miyuki and I had made to each other about doing everything we could to film her giving birth unassisted. So I specifically promised Okuzaki that we would go to New Guinea.

Discussions about how to get to that point involved Okuzaki coming up with Okuzaki-like plans: for example, pleading with Yamada Kichitarō to get involved. At the same time, he himself wasn't eager to confront the war again after so many years. In fact, he was saying at that point that he wanted to engage in something like missionary work. He had a number of ideas about propagating and actualizing his beliefs. More specifically, incidents would occur that had nothing to do with the war—for example, a parent would kill his or her child, or a child would kill his or her parent—and he would want to go to the homes of those who were actively anti-death penalty or lobbying for reduced sentences in such cases. He wanted me to film him telling these people to stop doing what they were doing. In short, he was interested in contemporary events.

In other words, Okuzaki believed that great evils such as wars existed because the world was messed up. So he wanted to rectify the world. It was as simple as that. He wanted to act in a way that fulfilled that simple principle. Thirty years had passed since the end of the war, and after all that time, Okuzaki seemed to think that the war wasn't worth making a film about.

But this was the man who'd shot pachinko balls at the emperor. Where did the core energy that had provoked such an act come from? That's why I, for one, could not disregard the war. I wondered how best to depict it. I didn't want to show events from the past in the form of simple interviews; I was trying to find a way to show the past from the perspective of the present. I couldn't let go of the war.

WE'RE WORKING WITH A CONVICTED CRIMINAL!

I'd heard the name Yamada Kichitarō quite soon after meeting Okuzaki. Yamada was someone Okuzaki often visited, so I decided to visit him myself. Yamada showed me a roster of ex-soldiers, so I looked up their addresses, located their homes, and paid each of them a visit. During these visits, I learned about the cannibalism and the execution. I then went to Okuzaki and told him that I wanted him to visit his fellow former soldiers. All I said was, "Something definitely took place in New Guinea, but I'm sorry, I'm not going to tell you what it was. It's very important for the documentary that we capture your reaction when you learn what happened for the first time. So I can't tell you what took place. Please forgive me. But something undoubtedly did take place. Let's just go and see, OK?

Apart from the company commander and the first guy Okuzaki meets, the one who's incredibly humble, I'd met with all of them. The content of the story that you see in the film is nearly the same as what I'd heard. Okuzaki wasn't able to get anything more out of his old comrades than I'd been able to. It basically unfolded just as I myself had heard it.

In other words, *I* was the one who told Okuzaki that something had happened during the war, even though, in the film, it appears as though Okuzaki decided to investigate the events by himself.

It was almost as if I already had the basic outline for a screenplay. I expected the film to depict the process of Okuzaki investigating the execution, and then I wanted to end up in New Guinea.

At first, Okuzaki wasn't interested in the idea I'd proposed. "Well, if you insist, I guess I'll do it," he said. That was the extent of his interest at first.

So he started visiting the former soldiers. They were hiding something from him, which is why his second visit turned out the way that it did. He was incredibly perceptive and sensed that something was going on. But he never asked me about it. He never uttered the words, "What's going on, Hara?" After the second visit,

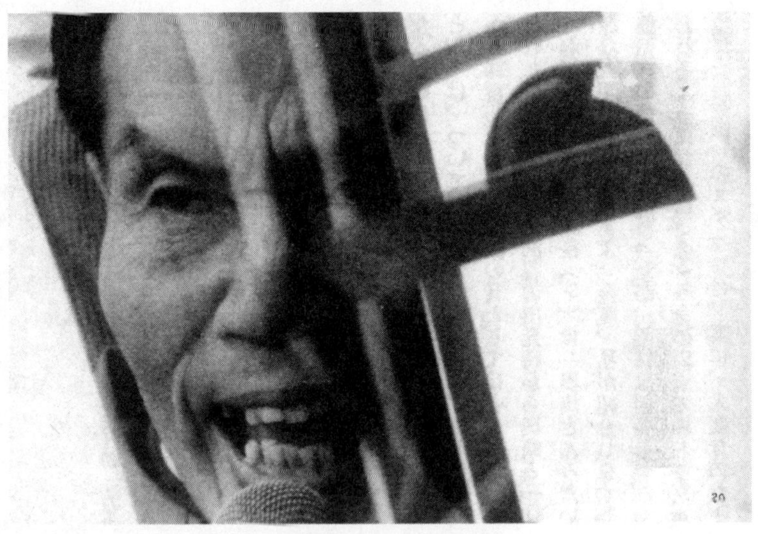

It struck me suddenly that we were dealing with a convicted criminal.

he stopped visiting the ex-soldiers and called the rest of them on the phone by himself.

Okuzaki called everyone I had already visited and questioned in person, so he got to hear over the phone most of the information I had become privy to. His phone bill for that month was more than three hundred thousand yen. It was quite something.

Most significantly, Okuzaki clearly grasped the importance of the execution incident. When he discovered that his platoon had executed two of their own soldiers twenty-three days after hostilities had ended, it was as if he'd been given a green light. At that moment, he was determined to create a scandal—or rather, he'd found his target. In other words, he'd said when we began making the film that he would do his best; now he'd specifically discovered what doing his best would be for.

That's when he asked us if we would film him committing murder. (I've written about this in the *Production Notes* to the film.)[4] Before approaching me about this, he'd actually already talked to the two relatives of the soldiers who'd been executed. I had no idea that he'd already spoken to them; I only learned about this after the fact. Once Okuzaki decides on a target, he makes his decisions very quickly.

It was so dumb of us: after Okuzaki asked me to film him committing murder, Kobayashi and I discussed our options from all possible angles. However, the fact that Okuzaki was planning to commit a crime—that he was a convicted criminal—escaped us for a long time. It escaped me at least. This might seem odd, but it really was the case.

Then it suddenly struck me: we were dealing with a criminal—a convicted criminal. We were preparing to witness, or to go along with, the process of someone making up his mind to commit a crime. This didn't occur to me until after I'd been asked to film the murder. The fact that we hadn't thought of this before shows how dumb we were. We didn't realize that we weren't working with your everyday Joe until

4 A full translation of the *Production Notes* appears in the second half of this book.

late, right in the middle of the production. [Laughs.] That's how dumb we were, frankly speaking. Well, it's precisely because we were so dumb that we were willing to make a film with someone like Okuzaki.

This has no particular significance, but because we were so big-hearted—or so dumb—we didn't realize how dangerous making a film with Okuzaki would be. We just jumped right in. So I don't think that that's necessarily a bad thing.

PEOPLE ARE ALWAYS ACTING

When you start making a documentary film, you generally have in mind some vague notion of what the last scene will be, whether things in fact end up that way or not. You wonder what that final scene might be like, and you work towards it. Of course, if things change, they change.

When we began filming, Okuzaki said he wanted to participate in some kind of missionary activity. A note from that period that I looked at recently clearly states the name of the religion that Okuzaki was thinking of propagating: "The World-Reforming Teaching." Since Okuzaki had said he'd been thinking about undertaking some sort of religious activity, he was completely against taking the film in a darker direction. He wanted it to end with a bright image, with a sense of having come through something. I thought that if he wanted to act out something religious, well, that was fine by me.

The image of Okuzaki as a god or a guru, doing heaven knows what... Okuzaki with a halo. [Laughs.] He's part of the masses—at least he's definitely not an intellectual—so I thought that the image of him with a halo, as incoherent as it might seem, might have some merit.

So we never conceived of Okuzaki going in some kind of a darker direction. But when Okuzaki discovered his target...

I think you'll see it if you watch the film a second time: the expression on Okuzaki's face grows increasingly grim. It takes on a tinge of madness.

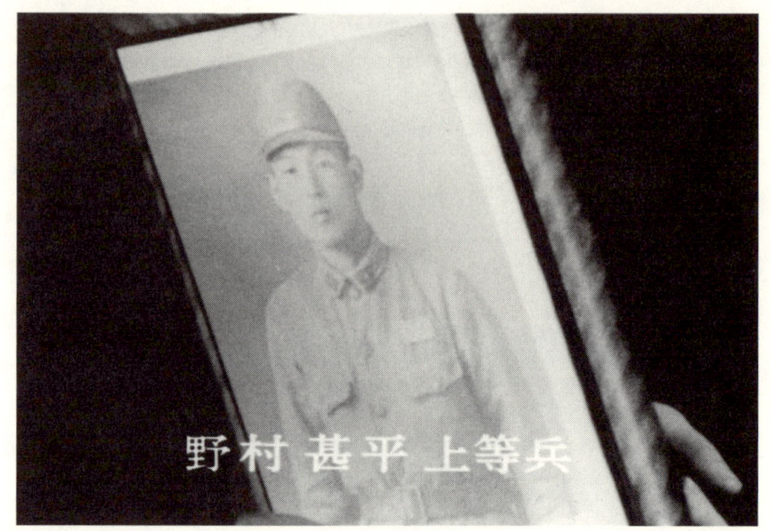

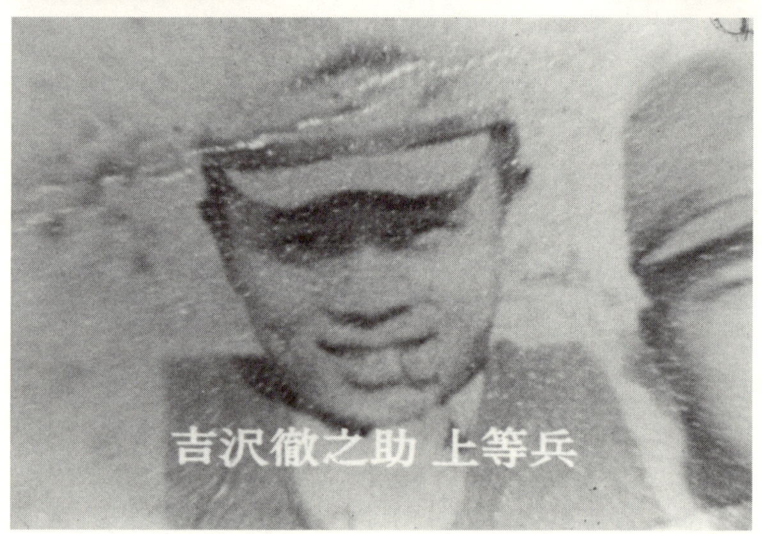

The two soldiers who were executed.

I wrote about this in the *Production Notes*, but after we finished filming in front of the Kobe Detention Center, I interviewed Okuzaki, who asked: "How was my acting?" I was stunned.

Then, in the scene where he visits the second of his fellow ex-soldiers, Okuzaki gets pinned to the floor. I explain the whole story in the *Production Notes*, but in brief, he accusingly asked me, "Hara, do you plan on using the scenes where I'm being defeated?" What he meant was that the film was supposed to be about the "cool" things he did. He told me he wouldn't be able to trust my judgment if I was going to use images of him being defeated. That's when we understood what Okuzaki had in mind in terms of "acting" for the film.

On top of that, Okuzaki hassled us throughout the entire production, insisting that we film every act he wanted to perform. It eventually got to the point where Okuzaki said, "Hara, it's ten years too soon for you to decide what to shoot and what not to shoot."[5] He got really emotional. He said that since this film was, in any case, a record of his actions, he wanted me to get footage of everything he did. Things went on like that for the entire shoot.

This goes to show that, for Okuzaki, the film was a form of PR; it was his own propaganda. And deep down, I can't deny that the film might in fact be just that. Whether it's a documentary or not, you make a film about someone because you're fascinated by them. There's no reason why you should depict that person negatively, since making a film about someone means that you're somehow affirming them; you're raising money for the project and spending a lot of time with them. A film can't be made with negative energy.

But I think that a true PR film is one that stirs up powerful emotional reactions in its viewers. A truly powerful PR film would be one in which I succeeded in depicting an individual as a whole, including his or her negative elements. That's my take on PR films. However, Okuzaki didn't want me to film his weaknesses and

5 "ten years too soon": Okuzaki means that Hara is not yet old enough to be telling him what to do.

shortcomings, or him getting beaten up—anything that he thought might present him in a negative light. He only wanted me to film the parts of him that were "cool." That was a fundamental difference between us.

At first, Okuzaki wasn't all that conscious of my camera work. But it's not that difficult for the person in front of the camera to grasp how or from what angle he is being filmed. He can see where the camera is, what the camera is aimed at when it's facing him, how he should act. He'll think, "Oh, the director wants to shoot the scene like this." The more time he spends in front of the camera, the more he'll understand what sort of action causes the camera to roll. That's how it works. It's not that hard: it's not like I'm filming with a hidden camera. The person being filmed can learn to calculate all of this.

Which means that it's not as though I'm making judgment calls as to whether or not something is good or bad. Whoever's in front of the camera will just pick up on this. And when he does, what will he do? If he knows all this and still has to continue some action, he'll inevitably start performing. It's only logical.

But Okuzaki's not the only one who wants to look cool while being filmed. People argue tooth and nail at the top of their lungs when it comes to Okuzaki's acting in *The Emperor's Naked Army Marches On*. Most of the time, someone being filmed—no, make that *anyone* being filmed—is *always* acting, so this wasn't an issue specific to Okuzaki. But I think the reason why people argue over Okuzaki's acting in particular is because there's more to it in his case. It repulses some people; others find it interesting.

Throughout the film, Okuzaki always says that justice is on his side. Also, there's the way he reasons in order to justify violence. These two arguments prick the audience like thorns, and when combined with the issue of Okuzaki's acting, they excite certain kinds of responses. In truth, I don't think the audience actually reacts to the fact that Okuzaki is acting; instead, they're disturbed by his self-righteousness and his theory of violence.

ENTERING INTO COLLUSION

Take the example the famous work of Hani Susumu, who once put his camera in a box and placed it in a classroom.[6] Once children stopped reacting to the camera, he started filming them. In other words, the camera became more and more invisible, and the children began acting as though the camera weren't even there. My ideas about filmmaking are perhaps the polar opposite of Hani's.

A single theory of documentary filmmaking techniques can't be universally applied to all films. In Hani's case, I think the camera was able to become invisible in a classroom full of children because they *were* children. As Hani said, children are sure to become engrossed in something if it's stimulating enough. I have absolutely no intention of discrediting Hani's techniques—how could I? But with adults, those techniques won't work. The difference is subtle. For instance, even Ogawa Productions didn't wait for their subjects to stop being aware of the camera before filming them. Their subjects are always conscious of the camera.

In that sense, Ogawa Productions' approach to their subjects is no different from ours. The difference is that having made his subjects conscious of the camera, Ogawa brings out something different from the people he films. We make our subjects conscious of the camera, then try to capture "unintended consequences." If I could describe things like this well, I'd be a film theorist, but I can't quite find the right words. Should I say "unintended consequences"? Or "dissonance"? In Ogawa's films, I don't think it's either, actually. The word "collusion" comes to mind, but in his case, I think it's more of a friendly, peaceful collusion.

In my case, I'd say it's a negative form of collusion. Once our subjects become aware of the fact that they're being filmed, I try to see the "unintended consequences" of this. So what's different about our approaches?

6 Hani Susumu (1928–): Director. Part of the so-called Japanese New Wave. Directed *Nanami: The Inferno of First Love*.

Perhaps it's a difference in how we feel vis-à-vis the world. In Ogawa's films, the filmmaker and the people he films try to create some kind of a myth together. It's an incredibly positive perspective. He turns his camera on the beauty of humanity—and I'm not being trite when I use the term "beauty." Together with his subjects, Ogawa creates a rich, dense, communal space in order to get at what is beautiful—what is trustworthy—in humanity. And he records this with his camera. That's his method; that's the direction he wants to go in. I'm not sure if I can bring up "the view that humans are inherently good" here, but that's what he seems to be aiming for. To be honest, I'm attracted to that kind of filmmaking. Someday I'd like to give it a try. Someday.

Ogawa doesn't simply make positive, heart-warming films; they also have history, folklore, ties to the land, and ties of blood. And his space keeps expanding. All of this can be seen in Ogawa's camerawork, or the way he establishes relationships with his subjects. There's something convincing about that way of working; I have a high opinion of it.

But what I'm interested in right now is the gigantic reality of the day-to-day. Without facing this, we can't live: we can't breathe. And I truly believe that we almost suffocate under such oppression. The impulse to tear that oppression up is what drives me.

Which is why I bring my camera to that battle. In a sense, my camera becomes a weapon. I use it to tear apart that oppression. When I say "day-to-day reality," I'm talking about human relationships, not the objects around us. So I bring my camera into living, flesh-and-blood relationships. With all my physical strength, I rip open whatever it is that is masking things that are "unintentional." I want to see what it is that people are hiding—what novelist Inoue Mitsuharu was referring to when he said, "People have many things that they're embarrassed about, that they can't talk about." I can't help it.

In theory at least, when people strive to liberate themselves, they inevitably, in one way or another, bring the things that they want to hide, that they feel embarrassed about, into the open; they inevitably want to talk about such things. One can hardly do that by oneself, so we try to pry open that part of ourselves through our relationships with others. That kind of thing requires force; it's hard to do alone. As such, I think the power of others is indispensable.

Still, I'm keenly aware of the fact that when I pry open a relationship, I'm not doing so for the sake of the other person. But I forcibly involve that other person anyway. Ultimately, I go so far as to believe that having a relationship with someone means getting that person into trouble.

"Once you've set your mind on something, you should bet your life on it," is something people often say. I say, "You, on whom I've set my mind, forgive me for having done so." That's how it feels. "I'm truly sorry. But I can't help liking you. I like you, so please allow me to pry you open." I guess that's what it all boils down to.

WHEN DOCUMENTARY REACHES A BOILING POINT

When taking on a subject like Okuzaki, you have to wonder what he might be embarrassed about. The thing is, Okuzaki isn't embarrassed about anything. [Laughs.]

The problem we encountered with Okuzaki—not on a social level, but strictly vis-à-vis ourselves—arose when he visited the ex-soldiers' homes and pried open their private lives. If we had been the ones to do this, we would have been directly responsible. But because Okuzaki was the one doing the prying, we were one step removed from total responsibility. That was frustrating. We couldn't logically justify our position.

We—Okuzaki and ourselves—were headed more or less in the same direction, and we went to the soldiers' homes together, but he was the one who got to do the prying.

A film has a general framework, and as long as the protagonist acts within that framework, the director doesn't necessarily have

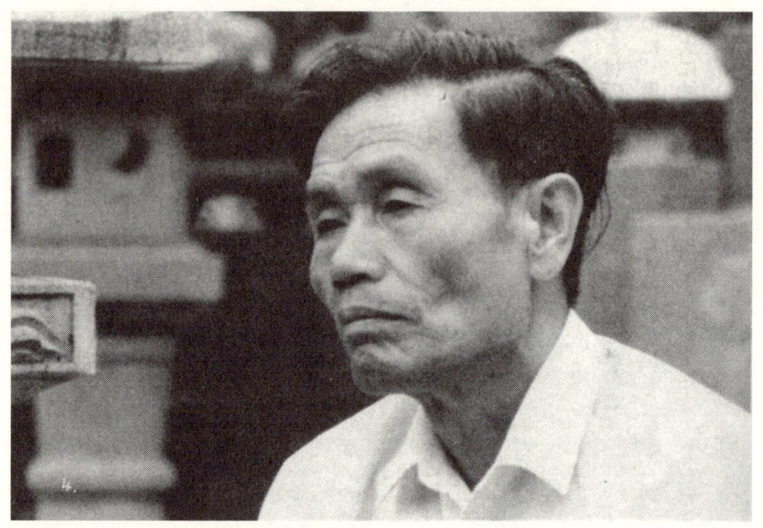

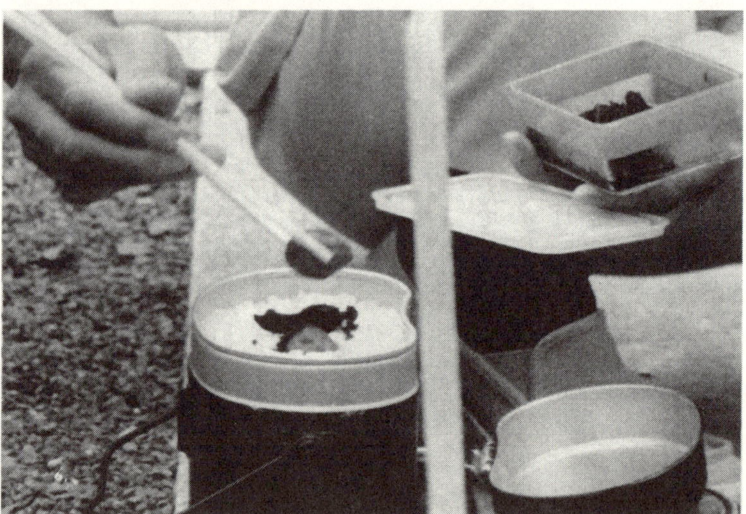

"I want to die after a meal that fills my stomach.": Offering rice to the dead soldiers.

to direct him. The director has to go on the offensive only when the protagonist doesn't take any action. Thankfully, Okuzaki kept taking action, and thus stayed within the framework of the film. To be more precise, the camera of a documentary film will, by its very nature, incite whoever's being filmed to act independently. And it necessarily accelerates action; it necessarily brings action to a boiling point.

Okuzaki was quite aware of the camera's effect. I wouldn't say he was aware of it from the start, but he's a perceptive person, so I think he soon realized how a film works and quickly grasped the nature of the medium. Absorbing this, he used it to his own advantage. As a result, I didn't have to tell him how to act; he acted within the framework of the film.

Or rather, as people have pointed out, he acted more swiftly than we did. When people say that we couldn't keep up with Okuzaki, I have to agree. Yet because he was acting within the overall framework of the film, it was all right for him to be acting that way.

I've digressed a bit. I think the only thing Okuzaki might feel embarrassed about is the scene where he's pinned down. Other than that, I think there's absolutely nothing he should be embarrassed about. Okuzaki understood his role according to each situation, and he played it.

For example, he went to the grave of one of his fellow soldiers and cooked rice in a military camping pot in order to present it as a kind of offering. In that scene, he says, "I don't have to say anything here, do I?" He perfectly understood his role, its purpose, and how to play it.

So he placed the pot in front of the grave. He precisely calculated the meaning this act would have for those who saw it, right down to the impression that viewers of the film would take away from the scene. It was fine for him to calculate all that.

We weren't critical of what Okuzaki did. We thought his acting was so-so, not too bad. It would have been okay if he had cooked rice each time he made an offering, but he didn't the second or third time around. We had no money back then, so we would cook rice for our meals with an electric rice cooker and carry it around with us. He'd come to us and say, "Hara, can I borrow some of your rice?" [Laughs.] And he'd put our rice in the camping pot. Then he'd offer it at the grave. When we finished shooting, he'd say, "Now that we're done filming, I'll give you your rice back." [Laughs.] That gives you some idea of what one might call Okuzaki's mercantile sense, his materialistic way of thinking.

Well, I probably should have filmed those scenes, but you don't think about rolling camera at such times. That's why I wrote the *Production Notes*.

However, if you overlook these things, you won't see the essence of Okuzaki.

To talk about my camera work first: when we began visiting the homes of the former soldiers, I would begin rolling camera as soon as we arrived. And I was going to film each and every visit in the same way. Okuzaki would wait for us as we all prepared our equipment, and I'd ask, "Is everyone ready?" I'd be holding my camera, and there would also be a sound mixer and an assistant cameraman, and when everyone was ready, I'd say, "All right, Okuzaki, let's go." And he'd respond, "Yeah. Oh. OK. Let's go." He was usually quite calm.

Then he'd say, "Hello?" and announce himself. I'd be filming him the entire time. The ex-soldiers would be astounded: the looks on their faces would say, "What the hell is going on?" Then Okuzaki would say he had some questions he wanted to ask. "By all means," the soldiers would say. They'd agree to answer his questions. Almost all of them invited him in, but they would ask me to turn off the camera. And I'd film the entire exchange.

Therefore, as soon as the soldiers would say, "By all means," Okuzaki would jump in and say, "Wait, these people are kindly filming my movie. I know very well that it's impolite of me to just show up with them. Let me fully apologize for this later. For now, though, I'd appreciate it if you'd allow them to film us." He'd then tell them that the film was about him pursuing the truth about an execution that occurred twenty-three days after the end of the war.

He'd say, "As far as you or I are concerned, there can be nothing problematic about such a film." Then Okuzaki would reveal his philosophy in full. Even if the logic of his philosophy didn't entirely convince the ex-soldiers, they knew that Okuzaki Kenzō was someone who had shot pachinko balls at the emperor, so they couldn't resist for long. Frankly speaking, who could? I'd film the entire situation. They'd say, "Well, you're already here. Come on in." Then we'd enter their houses and film everything.

As you see in the film, when we shot the scene with Hamaguchi, the owner of the eel restaurant, we took him out to another restaurant, where the scene unfolded.[7] Then we finished filming. I've already written about the events that ensued in the film's *Production Notes*, but after we finished shooting that scene, Okuzaki told everyone, "Well done. I've ordered some food, so let's all take a break and have a bite to eat." There was a shift in the atmosphere; Okuzaki was now in charge. Hamaguchi said, "Oh, is that right? The filming is over? Then, everyone, let's have a toast." Okuzaki was there, along with Hamaguchi, whom Okuzaki had tracked down and interrogated, the siblings of the executed soldiers, who'd also interrogated Hamaguchi, my crew, and myself. Okuzaki then said, "OK. All together. Cheers!" [Laughs.] There was something strange about that situation... Some scenes you can film, others you can't, honestly speaking.

---

7 Hamaguchi Masaichi: Former medic who, in the film, eventually confesses that soldiers resorted to eating human flesh during the war.

THE LOGIC OF PRYING OPEN RELATIONSHIPS

I've talked before about prying open relationships. The strangeness of *The Emperor's Naked Army Marches On* doesn't have to do with Okuzaki Kenzō per se; rather, it can be described as an instance of the dissonance that we, together with Okuzaki, managed to pry out of the various situations we were in. I basically believe that as much as possible of whatever we're able to pry out should be included in a film. This applies to the scene that I've just described as well. At first, the congratulatory toast was indeed included in the film. We cut it out only because I got into a disagreement with the editor, who insisted that the film be shorter in length.

I've said that we force open areas in people during filming: that we pry them open and film as much of the resultant action as we can, presenting as much of this as possible in the form of a film. In principle, we believe that we should show action as it occurs, which is why we do our best not to organize it according to our own standards. We also don't dismiss criticism about the ethics of we do.

In other words, I don't do what I do believing that it's justified or justifiable. In fact, I know that this method of filmmaking is bound to be criticized, that criticism is unavoidable. And I know that people might wonder why, knowing that I'll be criticized, knowing that it's not the right thing to do, I still do what I do. If someone were to ask me, "Isn't that the kind of logic that terrorists use?" I would have to admit that it might be. But having admitted it, I would still stick to my method of "trying to go for the chestnut in a fire that might explode at any minute." This is something I haven't been able to sort out for myself. I really wish someone else would sort it out for me.

But I also can't help but wonder what other methods might be out there. It's not as though I completely disregard all other possibilities. When thinking about this, I recall what Okuzaki said after that long, long fight with Yamada Kichitarō. He said that he would continue using violence in the service of what he believed to be the right thing. I had to cut that scene short in the film, but Okuzaki said that

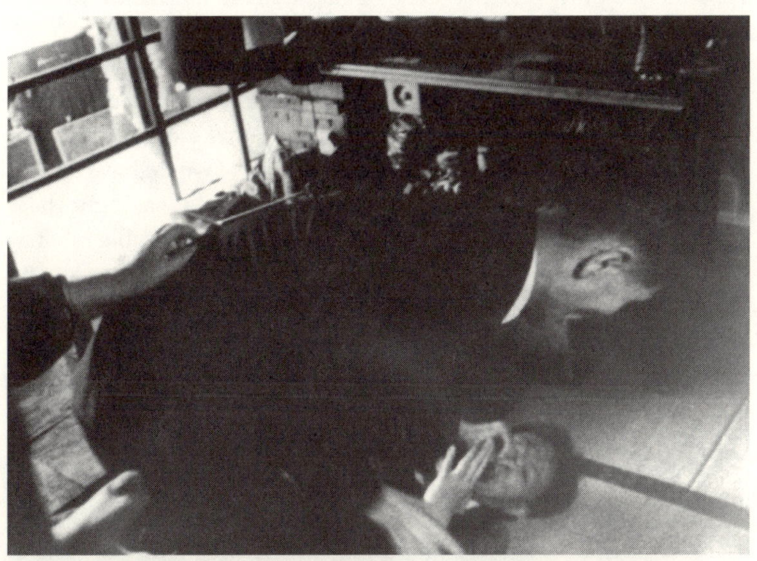

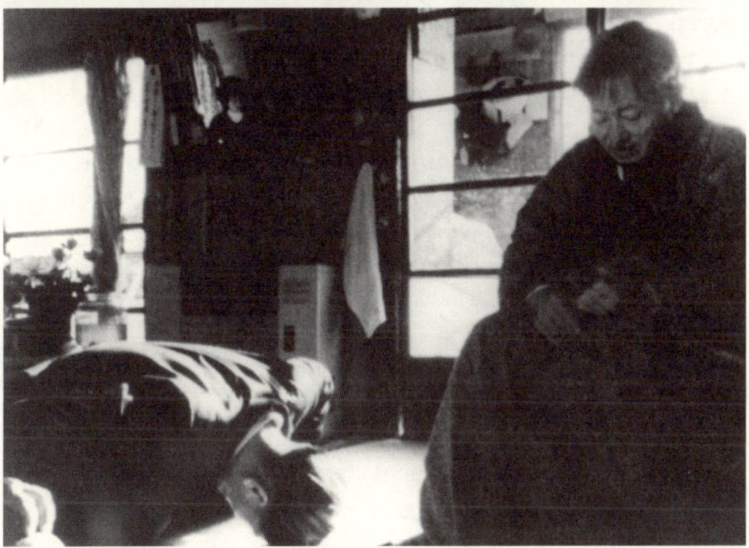

Okuzaki says he will continue using violence for what he believes is the right thing.

Yamada had only talked because he had used violence on him, and that he would continue to use that kind of violence.

I think Okuzaki is right in a way. In other words, it's sometimes necessary to use shock treatment on people. If the scene where Okuzaki was kicking Yamada had escalated to the point where someone's life had been threatened with a knife or something, I would have known about it, even though I was operating the camera. I was right there at the time, but I didn't find anything exceedingly horrible in what was happening in front of me.

Moreover—and I might upset people by saying this—I basically believe that when communication becomes deep enough, it can, under certain circumstances, take the form of violence. That is, in essence, what I believe. So I don't think that you can categorically object to violence. When Okuzaki said that Yamada had only talked because Okuzaki had violently assaulted him, I think he was right. In that situation, absolutely.

That's the principle of prying someone open. In that sense, Okuzaki's method of creating action, his mode of acting, actually resembles our style of shooting a film. No, it doesn't *resemble* it; the two are exactly the same. I'll admit it.

Here we encounter the issue of "the sanctified realm of the director." Pretty early on in the process, Okuzaki understood—I should say, completely understood—how I was moving the camera, what kind of situation I was waiting for. So he would tell me all the various ideas he'd thought up for the film.

Ultimately, however, I was the one who decided whether or not to shoot something; I could accept or reject his ideas. And Okuzaki couldn't stand that. When he realized that we wouldn't just do whatever he told us to, he gradually began to distrust us. Still, when it became clear to him what his next target would be, his desire to go as far as he could after that target became quite intense. So even though he thought of us as bastards and said this and that, he still wanted us to film him. That was the bottom line. And so our discord intensified.

The desire to control every aspect of the film grew within him.

He even went so far as to say that he would edit his own version of the film. That's when our struggle over the authority of the director began.

I thought that in order for people to truly understand who Okuzaki Kenzō the man really was, it would be necessary to film both his pleasant and his repellant sides. Good, bad, positive, negative—people encompass a number of qualities. They have parts that are extraordinarily sacred and parts that are vulgar; parts that are rational and parts that are unbelievably obscene and chaotic. A single individual is defined by multiple opposing poles. I believe this down to my very core. So I naturally wanted to see both sides of Okuzaki.

Which is why we wanted to film the entirety of the space made dissonant by Okuzaki's actions. We wanted to make films in a way that left things open to the audience's interpretation. That's why we were making the film. On our part, we naturally felt that the film was *our* film. Okuzaki thought that it was *his* film, which was fine. However, because we were the ones *making* the film, we couldn't just hand over directorial or editorial "authority" to Okuzaki. That was our last fortress. Thus, much of what I write about in the *Production Notes* recounts how I resisted Okuzaki's incessant attempts to infiltrate my territory as director. I think I can say that.

In my opinion, if Okuzaki had edited the film, it would never have been what it is now. That's for sure. I'd like to add that such a film wouldn't have had as much appeal, either. I'll admit that Okuzaki has a fair understanding of how to make a film, but as a creator, I'd also like to let him know that there are certain aspects he still doesn't understand.

Anyway, Okuzaki told us that he wanted to make *The Emperor's Naked Army Marches On, Part 2*. As soon as we finished the film, he said he wanted to make the sequel. And he wanted us to film it. So we are debating with ourselves right now about whether or not to do it. If we did, Okuzaki would probably try to take complete control. That's what he'd want to do, at least.

If that were the case, I think it would probably be better for him to direct the film himself and to put together a crew that would do whatever he wanted. On the other hand, I know that a film made in such a way wouldn't be able to match the quality of a film directed by an outside party, whether it was myself or someone else. I still waver on this point. I can't say which would be better.

If Okuzaki were to make a film the way he wanted to, it would inevitably become a kind of propaganda piece. The audience would probably see it that way as well. But it's all right for a film like that to exist. It's perfectly fine. And I don't think I can say that a film like that would necessarily be inferior. So long as Okuzaki were to let his his interests lead him... Because the most important thing for him would be to find something that interested him. The audience should just view such a film as presenting another aspect of filmmaking and film viewing.

THE EDITOR VS. THE DIRECTOR

We hired an editor, Nabeshima Jun, for *The Emperor's Naked Army Marches On*. Nabeshima Jun is the same editor that the director Yamamoto Satsuo relied upon for his later, big-budget films.[8] Yamamoto Satsuo was an entertainment-oriented filmmaker who made dynamic, more or less commercial films, and Nabeshima provided him with technical support. I consider Nabeshima to be one of the most skillful editors out there, so I asked him to edit our film. While he was working for us, we had a number of disagreements and subsequent fights. Because Nabeshima belongs to an older generation, he had a distinctly different take on the war.

Specifically, the issue we fought over most was whether or not to include the scene in which Okuzaki explains his theory of violence. Nabeshima said it would be better not to include it in the film. *Better* not to, he said. He reasoned that including Okuzaki's

8 Yamamoto Satsuo (1910–1983): Filmmaker. A leftist who made socially conscious and anti-war films.

theory of violence would serve to undermine Okuzaki's pursuit of the injustices of the war. That was the kind of reasoning he used.

This was definitely an example of his generation's perspective on war. But for us, there was no way we could drop that scene. We believed that the film shouldn't be constrained within the framework of "war is bad." That was not what the film was about.

In short, as the film unfolded and Okuzaki began pursuing the war in the present progressive form, I realized that what I really wanted to see were the ripples of disturbance he caused everywhere he went. I wanted issues such as postwar Japan and our identity as Japanese to emerge from those ripples. That's what I wanted to show more than anything else.

Therefore, I really didn't want to cut the scene of Okuzaki explaining his theory of violence, or the scene of everyone toasting after we shot Okuzaki interrogating Hamaguchi. Really, thinking about it now, I wish I hadn't cut those scenes. At the time, I clashed with the editor about this. He insisted that those two scenes would muddy the point of the film. As a result, the film finally settled on the form it has now.

Which way would have been better? That is, if the two choices were placed side by side? But such a choice is impossible. Well, that's not strictly true. Okuyama Kazuyoshi did something along those lines with *RAMPO*.[9] If such a thing had been possible, it might have been interesting to release both Nabeshima's version and the one we wanted.

Another scene we wish we had edited differently is the one in which Okuzaki and the people he'd been questioning line up tangerines on a table. There'd actually been quite an argument at the entrance of the house when we filmed this scene. Seeing my camera, the people being questioned had said, "All of you out! Only Okuzaki can stay..." Okuzaki had retorted, "Why? Please let them come in, too." And of course, I'd filmed the entire exchange. I would

---

9 Okuyama Kazuyoshi (1953–): Producer/Filmmaker. The producer of *RAMPO*. Unhappy with what the director had done with the film, he released both the director's version and a version in which he credited himself as the director.

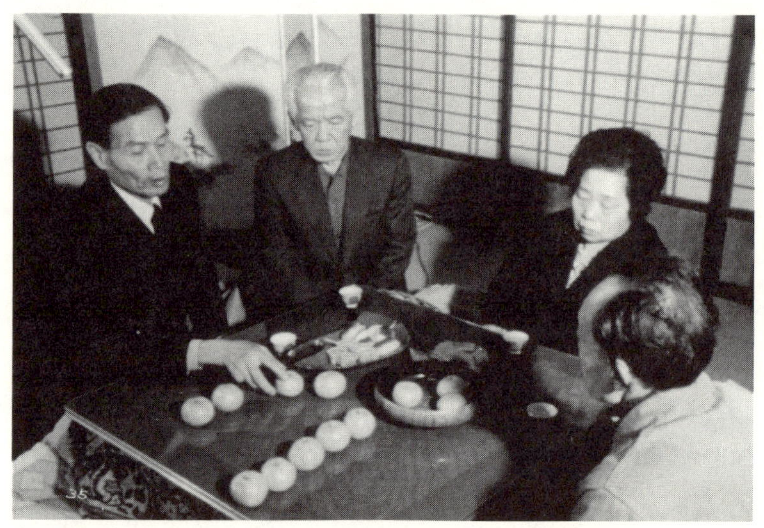

Okuzaki Kenzō recreating the execution incident, using tangerines as soldiers.

definitely have liked to keep that bit in; it would have changed the whole tone of the film.

I've said that we actually had no justification for entering the soldiers' homes as we did, that we hadn't established a just cause; basically, we just wanted to show as much as possible of the situations we'd created. The actions we take when making a film are multi-faceted, and many things should become visible as a result; simply saying that "war is bad" cannot possibly encompass all of them. Human egoism is one such thing; also the the fact that we're the ones creating the situations we film. And the character of each of our individual subjects would also be revealed, along with the relationships they combine to form. We would see different personal qualities. I think the real pleasure of making a documentary lies in revealing such qualities in a person.

But the work of an editor is to shave off these elements. Of course, including all of the different elements we were able to gather on location would be impossible, so it's necessary to organize them to a certain degree. But while organizing these elements, we try to retain as many of them that defy organization as possible. Those elements that resist organization are, to my mind, more interesting. To use a term I invoked earlier, I think such elements are linked with "madness," a state in which many layers of things happen simultaneously and develop together.

So what it ultimately all boils down to is the difference between the responsibilities of the editor and those of the director. Added to all this is the personal taste or the personality of the editor. What I mean is that because Nabeshima's background is in narrative filmmaking, his professional instinct is to make a solid story out of the footage we've shot. That's what I realized as I watched him. On the other hand, we believe that a documentary is about integrating as many as possible of the elements that have fallen out of a story back into it. Or even about seeing how many such non-fitting elements can be drawn out from our subjects. In a sense, the more difficult it is to integrate certain elements into a story, the more valuable they are. It may be that we think this way because we're documentary filmmakers, and that Nabeshima doesn't think this way because he comes from a narrative film background.

HOW TO INVOKE MADNESS

We were with Okuzaki for a long time... and he's... what do you call it? The "stress-prone type" perhaps? I mean, people naturally feel stress when they find themselves in dicey situations. At such moments, they start to tremble. One might call this "a warrior's tremor," or a tremor of excitement, but it might simply be "fear" that makes one's body shake at such moments. It's a well-known phenomenon.

I often found Okuzaki trembling. When I saw this, I thought that perhaps Okuzaki was in fact a timid person. He was aware of his own timidity, but, on the other hand, when confronted with something unreasonable, he stood his ground and faced it. He felt he had to.

In his book, *Yamazaki, Shoot the Emperor!*, Okuzaki recounts being sent to New Guinea crammed in a boat with fellow soldiers. Night fell, and everyone crowded together and went to sleep. An officer who was going to the bathroom strode over Okuzaki as he slept. Okuzaki woke up and thought, "That jerk's pretty rude." Of course, he couldn't forgive him. But he put up with it. And he thought to himself, "I can handle this three times. If it happens more than that, I'm going to rip into that guy." In other words, he set a limit for his self-restraint. But the officer went to the bathroom a fourth time, striding right over Okuzaki. Infuriated, Okuzaki got up and punched him.

But he wasn't accused of insubordination. Typically, when a low-ranking soldier attacks an officer, he's court-martialed. But this didn't happen to Okuzaki. Similar encounters happened several times on the battlefield. Consequently, Okuzaki came to believe that the "laws of humanity" superceded those of the military.

Okuzaki's style is to determine his adversary and to direct his emotions toward that adversary in a controlled manner. When his opponent crosses the line, he has to attack. When the moment comes, his energy, which has been building up inside him, is locked and loaded.

On another occasion, Okuzaki was driving around town when a van of right-wingers pulled up alongside him. They stopped his car and approached him. At that moment, Okuzaki thought to himself, "If these right-wingers look like they might try to harm me, I'll be ready for them." He had a screwdriver hidden in his pocket. But they didn't try anything harmful, so he never tried to stab them. In other words, he's prepared to attack when threatened.

As these examples show, Okuzaki has something like an instinct for protecting himself when fighting alone without any backup, or when he finds himself in sketchy situations. He reads each situation and, determined never to lose, he takes the necessary steps to emerge victorious... This doesn't involve finding a more powerful weapon, however; it involves controlling his nerves. He's well aware of his own cowardice. He controls it, uses it to his advantage, and transforms it into a form of power.

I think that that's the most important lesson I learned from working with Okuzaki. Just like Okuzaki, I'm a coward. I really am spineless. I'm the kind of person who starts to shake as soon as I think something dangerous is about to happen. I'm not at all the type to waltz into a situation without any concern for my own safety. Instead, I feel as though I'm on the verge of a panic attack; I'm terrified. And in the various situations I experienced with Okuzaki, I saw how he turned those emotions into a strength.

To put it in a much broader context, Okuzaki's targets were always big: the emperor system, the state, then society, then evil. Whenever he fought against such adversaries, he did so alone, as an individual, so he was powerless. In order for powerless Okuzaki to be able to pick a fight with an intimidating power, it was absolutely necessary for him to have his own "logic."

For Okuzaki, this logic, which derived from God, was superior to that of the emperor. He assumed the role of an "equal soldier in God's army" and went to fight. His logic enabled him to fight.

I think he used his own madness in order to muster up enough power to compete with his adversaries in the fights he picked, filling himself with that kind of energy. He did this quite deliberately.

When it comes to Okuzaki invoking madness within himself, I think it's something he's done in a variety of ways on various occasions. For example, the incident with the right-wingers and the screwdriver, or his experiences on the battlefield, or when he shot pachinko balls at the emperor. If he hadn't invoked his own madness, he wouldn't have had enough power to challenge his formidable opponents. Through his experiences with all of that hell, he probably acquired something like his own methodology.

Okuzaki's real strength lies in the fact that the madness he invokes is something that he consciously manufactures. It's not real madness; it's on this side of that line.

Some people may leap into the realm of madness without any conscious effort, but what amazes me about Okuzaki is that he commits himself to the madness that he invokes in himself. And then the moment comes when he goes truly insane. He invokes madness knowing in advance that he'll go truly insane. He knows what's going to happen. That seems to be his pattern whenever he causes a scene. In sum, you have to invoke madness in order for it to have the potential to become real; otherwise, no madness arises.

It's hard to make a general statement about this since situations vary, but specifically, while making this film, Okuzaki asked me to film him murdering someone. And I declined because I was scared, as I've written before. He never mentioned this request again. But the expression on Okuzaki's face grew increasingly dour after that. That expression was nothing less than him getting closer and closer to true madness. Okuzaki had said he would do his best for the film. That commitment specifically culminated in him asking me to film a murder scene. When he made this request, his eyes truly glittered; and it was without doubt an expression of real madness.

At that point, the murder was already a done deal in his mind. Therefore, in hindsight, the fact that he had said he would do his best pointed to the same pattern responsible for all of his scenes until then. He didn't explicitly say so, but he'd followed his own pattern all along.

THE DIRECTOR OF THIS FILM IS GOD

While observing Okuzaki's progression in this way, I contemplated what it meant to make films. When I understood that I was no match for Okuzaki, I realized that, like Okuzaki, we too needed to invoke madness. Nowadays, I feel that if we don't try to invoke madness, we'll lack the power to go on the offensive. I truly do. Okuzaki, who'd been growing old, needed our film for much the same reason. Frankly speaking, *Goodbye CP* and *Extreme Private Eros* are rather unrefined cinematically, but in terms of the power they contain, I'm pretty sure that these first two films are more powerful than *The Emperor's Naked Army Marches On* and *A Dedicated Life*. It's true that the latter two are technically more sophisticated; sadly, you can't help getting more skillful. But on the sole point of power or intensity, I've come to think that, unfortunately, the latter films manifest a kind of decline. And I can't think about that without thinking of Okuzaki. Really.

Therefore, watching it from up close, Okuzaki's way of picking a fight really made sense to me: it became clear to me that he was a coward at heart. He might say, "That's ridiculous. You don't understand me at all," but to me, it was obvious. I'm not saying that it's right or wrong to be a coward; I'm just saying that I observed up close how Okuzaki transformed his internal energy into outward energy, and that this taught me something. Which is reason enough for me to humbly call him my "sensei" or "teacher"; I can say that

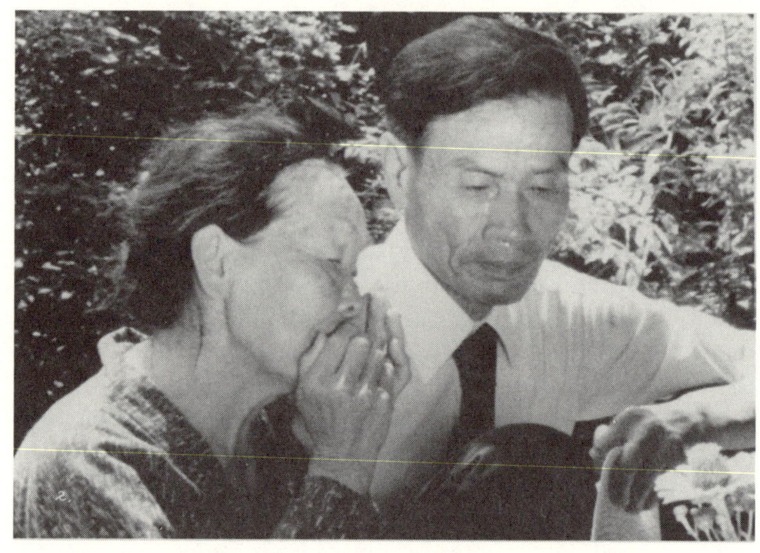

“The director of this film is God,” says Okuzaki. Some inexplicable power affected the film.

now without any hesitation.[10] He really is.

So when shooting my films, my targets—those with whom I try to create dissonance—tend not to be small in scale. Facing them, I flinch. But you can't make a film if you recoil from your subjects, so I try not to. I find myself wanting to call out, as if in a cheap movie, "God! Give me strength!" But whenever I get that desire, I remember Okuzaki. His madness, of course. Whenever I ask myself how I could possibly muster such strength within myself, I remember the way Okuzaki would pick fights with others.

God, according to Okuzaki… This would probably be easier to understand if I started by explaining the context in which he used the word "God."

When the film was completed, Okuzaki said to me, "You're not the director of this film." To be honest, he probably wanted to say that *he* was the director. But leaving that aside, he would tell me that "the director of this film is God." I think he half believed this, too. And I don't think I can deny its truth.

For one thing, encountering Okuzaki, that meeting, owed so much to chance. But for some reason, by the time we finished the film, that encounter had become a necessary occurrence. If you asked Okuzaki, he'd say that God had made our meeting necessary. I wouldn't say it was God, however. I'd say that it was the era that brought us together. After all, Imamura Shōhei had introduced Okuzaki to a number of other directors, and they had all declined to make a film about him. Years later, we met Okuzaki and made the film. Then, not long after we finished it, the Shōwa Emperor passed away.[11] Okuzaki said, in reference to these things, "This is all because God is here, and he's controlling us." That's how Okuzaki interpreted things. But there are moments when I believe that the era, not God, is what's controlling us. That's the sense in which I've

10 *sensei*: "Teacher" in Japanese. Honorific used for one's teacher or superior, or to anyone for whom you want to show respect. Indicates a higher degree of respect than the more common "Mr." or "Ms."

11 Shōwa Emperor: Emperor Hirohito, in whose name the Japanese soldiers fought during WWII.

used the term "God's doing" to describe this inexplicable power that moves us. That's what it feels like.

Now, to give you another, smaller-scale example, here's something that Urayama Kiriro once told me: You're shooting a narrative film on location, rolling camera, and a bird happens by. That is, you capture something very interesting by chance. Whether you're blessed with good weather or hit by a storm is also all up chance. Or so it seems. But transforming chance into necessity is what narrative filmmaking is about. That's what Urayama said. Narrative filmmaking is the transformation of chance into necessity.

What I'm trying to say is that I want to invoke some incomprehensible power within me by believing that an encounter, which can only have occurred by chance, occurred in fact out of necessity. I don't mean this rhetorically; I can even use the word "God" here like Okuzaki did. I want to see God's power at work, I want God to move what only God can move. Now I'm beginning to sound religious. But that's how I truly feel. Or rather, given that it's become so difficult to see the enemy, I'm anxious not to lose. I'm getting impatient because I'm scared that I'll have to be incredibly powerful if I don't want to lose the battle. I feel that whatever it is that keeps me from being absolutely free is growing bigger and bigger by the minute. Feeling this, I can't help but want some enormous power that will enable me to surpass it.

It may be that, in general terms, something that could be called power is invisibly growing larger and larger, but ultimately, what's at issue is my thematic stance. I started out by taking on a very easy-to-understand theme: the healthy vs. the disabled. Many phenomena fall out of such a framework, of course, and you could say that I've been slowly sliding sideways towards such things. Or that my search has been shifting towards the less simple, the less clear-cut. As human existence continues, various fundamental contradictions that are inherent to humanity arise. A human being contains many contradictory elements: joy and sadness, for example. An infinite number of such contradictions exist, and an incredible amount of power is required when preparing to dive into this vortex. So I can't help but wonder with a sigh at how enormous an undertaking making a film is.

Or it might simply be that my body has sadly aged of late. It might very well be that, frankly speaking. [Laughs.]

YOU CAN'T SCREEN THE FILM HERE

As soon as the film was finished, it was invited to the Berlin International Film Festival. Horikoshi Kenzō of the Tokyo arthouse Eurospace saw the film in Berlin, and said he'd screen it at his theater.[12] But he kindly went on to say that if we found a better offer somewhere else, we should by all means screen it there. At that time, documentary films like ours were seldom if ever screened in actual movie theaters. We finished the film and began previewing it anyway. And it seemed as though news of the film started to spread like wildfire from the get-go.

At the same time, we didn't think anyone would actually screen it. Everyone was too scared. Word had spread that if anyone tried to show our film, the right-wingers would make a fuss and cause lots of trouble. But as I said, Horikoshi Kenzō told us early on that he'd screen the film at Eurospace. So, taking up his kind offer, we thought we might as well shop around a bit anyway.

In that sense, it might have seemed as if we couldn't find a distributor for a while. To be honest, Eurospace's offer gave us a sense of security, and since the film was creating a buzz, we thought that we might as well enjoy it a little. Also, given the opportunity, we thought it wouldn't hurt to check out the state of film distribution. It's impossible to learn about such things in the abstract, so we thought we'd see if anyone would in fact distribute our film. As

12 Eurospace is one of the oldest arthouse cinemas in Tokyo. Established in the early 1980s, it screens films through its own distribution system. It has produced films in Japan and co-produced abroad since the 1990s. Horikoshi Kenzō is still the president.

such, we shopped it around to different places.

Actually, quite a few distribution companies came to us. They'd call us and say, "We'd like to distribute your film." "By all means," we'd reply. Take Shochiku, for example. They told us they wanted to distribute the film, and asked to see it. So Kobayashi took it over and screened it in their projection room, waiting there until the screening was over. But what Shochiku ended up saying at the time was, in short, that right-wingers might very well cause problems for them if they distributed our film through their theaters. They said that the right-wingers would probably attack Shochiku first, not us. So they declined to pick it up.

Up next was Cine Saison, which said that their president would like to meet us. But he couldn't actually make the final decision; he had to consult with someone higher up. I don't know if he ever actually did so or not, but he also said, "We can't screen it."

Then someone suggested we try Tokyu, so we took it to them, too. We screened it at Cinema Square Tokyu, and they said, "As a film, it's very interesting. But we can't show it."

Then we of course brought it to Iwanami. They didn't reject it outright, but they said their schedule was completely full, or something to that effect. In other words, they couldn't show it immediately. Which we could only interpret to mean that they wouldn't be able to show it at all.

Oh, by the way—the first place we took the film to was the Art Theater Guild. The people at ATG said, "To tell you the truth, we really want to distribute it to our theaters. But, as you know, Tōhō is our parent company. Your film wouldn't really fit the Tōhō brand. We want to do it, but... you know..." That's how we made our rounds.

The fact of the matter is that the right-wingers hadn't reacted to the film at all. We'd made the rounds of all the distributors, and they'd all rejected it. So it landed where it was supposed to, at Eurospace. Horikoshi had devised countermeasures for the right-wingers in case they did come. He'd thought of everything. Based on previous experiences, he said that the right-wingers would try to make the screen unusable by throwing things at it. Eggs had been thrown at his screen before. Raw eggs. He said he would have a spare screen standing by, in case this happened. And he went ahead and did just that.

The most serious problem was that the theater was in a business district. Right-wingers making noise in the street outside of the theater would have caused the most trouble. And there was no way to prevent this. Horikoshi said that if that happened, he'd be in hot water, with no recourse.

Well, opening day arrived. We had asked almost everyone we knew to come and support the film, telling them to wear sneakers so that they could move easily in case something happened. But nothing happened. Absolutely nothing.

However, there's an interesting story about this that really took me by surprise. Some time after finishing *The Emperor's Naked Army Marches On*, I was commissioned to film a group of rightists for a television project that was eventually aborted. I was following around this group of right-wingers, and I got to know one of their top officials, who probably didn't know that I was the director of the film. During one of our conversations, he told me that his chairman loved movies, and that it was his job to select three videos at a time for his chairman to watch. Then he said, "Yesterday, I chose three videos to give to the chairman, and told him they were fascinating. One of them was *The Emperor's Naked Army Marches On*." This guy, a top-ranking right-winger, said our film was fascinating.

There was also another case. A screening of the film was being prepared in Shimane Prefecture, but the prefectural government—the bureaucrats—called it off after having second thoughts.

Then there was this story. I think this happened in Kurume. A group of citizens wanted to screen our film as part of a kind of festival that the local government funded. But a right-winger complained that using public finds to screen a movie like ours was not right. He was apparently infuriated, but the local group stood up to him and screened the film anyway. I heard that the right-winger took a front-row seat at the screening and expressed his outrage. That was about it.

In other words, the only ones suppressing the film were distributors and the prefectural governments. And there was one more group: the Marunouchi Police Department. Around the time the emperor died, Namikiza in Ginza screened the film. We received a phone call from Namikiza saying that they had received a call from the Marunouchi Police. The cops had said that they thought something might happen if the screening took place, and that they, the cops, wouldn't take any responsibility for it if it did.

Now, you may ask, why wasn't the film attacked by the right-wingers? I think it was perhaps because, when they saw the film, they sympathized with Okuzaki's actions and ideas, or even with Okuzaki himself.

To give you an actual example of this: when the film was screened in Kyoto, a right-winger came to see it. The group that was showing the film was nervous that something might happen. But the film ended, and the right-winger came out. He then bought three copies of Okuzaki's book, which were on sale, and left the theater saying, "I understand exactly how Okuzaki feels."

Perhaps when reasonable people watch the film, they somehow grasp Okuzaki's reasoning. [Laughs.]

However, I have another interesting story. I was filming the right-wing politician Akao Bin, who I think didn't know at the time that I was the director of *The Emperor's Naked Army Marches On*.[13] A foreign station had asked me to do something interesting that would be descriptive of Japan for a television series, so I'd said that I would do something about the right-wingers, since quite a fuss about them had been made regarding my film. Akao Bin seemed to like me, and was really nice to me while I was filming him. But the project eventually fell through.

I learned later that Akao Bin gave a stump speech at Sukiyabashi in which he said something to the effect that an appalling film like

13 Akao Bin (1899–1990): Extreme right-wing politician. The first president of the Greater Japan Nationalist Party.

The Emperor's Naked Army Marches On was being screened, etc., even though he had probably never seen it. But that was about as far as it got. No actual harm at all.

The Emperor's Naked Army Marches On went on to win a number of awards. At the awards ceremonies, I said that I wanted to make a narrative film. Everywhere I went, I asked for a job, half-jokingly. I thought at least one job might come along. Apparently, a producer for some small production company said, "If Hara wants to make a narrative film, why don't we let him?" and took the idea to Shochiku. But it didn't happen. They declined, saying, "We have no idea what kind of film he'd do." I heard about this after the fact. Another producer also tried to help arrange things so that I could make a narrative film, but I heard that that also fell through.

Even then, I had this desire to make a narrative film. Only I didn't know at the time what it would be about. I just had a vague desire to make one. I now have material I want to deal with, and a much more specific plan.

What I'm trying to say is that in the West, once you make a documentary that's critically acclaimed or does so-so box-office-wise, you won't have such a hard time getting your next job. Even if it's a narrative film that you want to do next, quite a few opportunities will come knocking on your door. I know this because I've been to the US, and I heard that that's how people get their breaks. I'd made *The Emperor's Naked Army Marches On*, but in Japan, narrative films and documentary films are two separate worlds. No matter how much praise your documentary gets, no one will think of letting you shoot a narrative film.

GOING TO NEW YORK

We completed and released *The Emperor's Naked Army Marches On* in 1987, and not too long after that, I got to go the United States.

The film critic Yomota Inuhiko had received a fellowship from the Asian Cultural Council and had been to New York for a year. He said that if I had any interest in applying for the fellowship, he'd introduce me to the people there. I accepted his offer, filled out the application, and sent it in. Yomota had received a fellowship for a year, but for some reason, I was only awarded a fellowship for three months. Such results are influenced by a variety of factors, such as what topic the applicant wants to research. Still, it meant that I would be going to New York for the first time.

Around that time, I found out that I'd be eligible for a similar fellowship from the Agency for Cultural Affairs. I'd actually heard about their program earlier. After finishing *The Emperor's Naked Army Marches On*, someone at the Directors Guild of Japan had said, "Now that you've won the New Directors Award, you'll have to join us," and had talked me into signing up. Then someone from there had told me about the Agency for Cultural Affairs' program to send new talent abroad. There was an age limit, and I was almost at the cut off point, so I told them I wanted to go. But that year, they sent Yokoyama Hiroto instead.[14]

I said I'd try the following year, but I got pretty busy, and then I heard that Suzuki Junichi had already applied for the program, so I was told that perhaps I could be next after him.[15] Rumor somehow spread that there was a general consensus that I was next line. So I said to myself, "Wait a minute, I'm going to New York for three months on the Asian Cultural Council fellowship, but that will probably be too short. This would be a good time to apply for the Agency for Cultural Affairs." I took the necessary steps, and I got that fellowship as well. So I went for three months and then a year. I received two fellowships. I don't think many people have done that.

It all worked out perfectly.

I went to New York on both fellowships, living in apartments in different neighborhoods each time, downtown and uptown. But I

---

14 Yokoyama Hiroto (1948–): Filmmaker. *Jun*, *Manji*, and others.

15 Suzuki Junichi: (1952–). Filmmaker. *Lonely Affair of the Heart*, and others. Runs a production company, New Island Cinema, in Los Angeles.

basically stayed in New York the entire time.

Pretty much all I did there was watch movies. The Museum of Modern Art has a collection of about eight thousand films, including early films such as Edison's inventions, Méliès, and the Lumière brothers. I started with the silent films, and got as far as I could, watching everything chronologically. I went once or twice a week.

They have a tiny room with a 16-mm projector sitting in the middle of it. I basically watched all the films alone, projecting them myself.

Not everyone is allowed to do what I did; it's decided based on your personal connections. Someone introduced me to the people there, and since MOMA had screened *The Emperor's Naked Army Marches On* in their "New Directors/New Films" series, my work was recognized, and I was allowed to watch all the films in their collection. Normally, this would have cost something, but I didn't have to pay a cent. So I watched a ton of early films.

I had never studied cinema like that; I didn't even have a habit of watching such films in cinématheques. It was the first time I had watched those kinds of films in such quantities. It was fascinating.

Also, as a documentarian, I wanted to get involved with various communities in the city, but I didn't speak a word of the language, so it wasn't easy. I met a number of filmmakers and artists. But unfortunately, without being able to speak the language…

I went to quite a number of screenings of *The Emperor's Naked Army Marches On* accompanied by Q&A sessions. The most interesting event was at the University of Iowa, which, I was told, has an amazing film department.

They invited me over and screened *The Emperor's Naked Army Marches On* and *Extreme Private Eros*. I can't tell you for sure what the whole thing was about, but Karatani Kōjin had also been invited, and I think I met the film scholar Iwamoto Kenji there too.[16]

I was delighted that Karatani Kōjin spent about an hour of the hour and a half he'd been allotted talking about my two films.

16 Karatani Kōjin (1941–): Philosopher and literary critic.

I think his lecture was about the development of the "I-novel" in Japanese literature.[17] He discussed a number of actual I-novels by different writers, then discussed my work in the context of "I-films." It was great that he talked about my films, but in the United States, there's no distinction between sadism and masochism. The two are combined. For some reason, Karatani discussed my films in the context of sado-masochism, so after the films were screened, everyone teased me, which I didn't appreciate. I'm grateful that he talked about my films, but...

The people in the audience weren't Japanese, they were all American, so Karatani gave his presentation in English. So I don't actually know what he said.

Karatani had been interested in *The Emperor's Naked Army Marches On* before that as well. He and I, along with Itō Seikō and another person whose name was something like Nakamori Akio, had talked together about Okuzaki for a magazine. Karatani later told me that he'd received a letter from Okuzaki as a result of that conversation. "I didn't know what to do with it. It was *intense*."

I WANT TO MAKE FILMS USING A NEW METHOD

While filming Inoue Mitsuharu for my fourth documentary, *A Dedicated Life*, I traveled between New York and Tokyo, which was against the fellowship rules for the Agency of Cultural Affairs.[18] If you go abroad for a year, you can't return until that year is over. You have to stay there the entire time. But I received detailed reports of Inoue's condition, and came home often. It won't be good for that information to get out, but... [Laughs.] I guess I'll never apply for the fellowship again, so who cares? [Laughs.] I guess it's all right.

---

17 "I-novel": A novel characterized by a self-revealing narration in which the author, or a character whose life resembles the author, is the central figure. The earliest Japanese "I-novels" date from the middle of the first decade of the 20th century.
18 Inoue was dying of cancer at the time.

Right after we finished the film, when the answer print was struck, I asked Kumai Kei and Inoue Mitsuharu to come to Nikkatsu Studios to watch a preview. I was certain that Inoue would have a high opinion of Okuzaki, that he would speak positively of him. But he was completely disparaging.

He admitted that the film was good, and praised our work. saying that he had a high opinion of it. But he said he couldn't condone Okuzaki's methods. He sounded as though he felt that Okuzaki was a rival. But perhaps it's inappropriate to say that. However, Inoue's blunt criticism of Okuzaki left a lasting impression on me. At the time, I was amazed that someone who people thought of as a left-wing writer should speak so negatively of Okuzaki. Inoue was of the opinion that I should have gone further in depicting the soldiers whom Okuzaki had tracked down, *their* psychologies, *their* situations.

Before shooting for the film began, I thought that I was finally going to be able to shoot a film the way I would a narrative feature. What do I mean by this? Since I was going to be operating the camera as well as directing, I thought I'd film Okuzaki's movements using a tripod. However, it wasn't as though I had a strict definition of what it meant to shoot "like a narrative film." I thought it would be simple enough.

In short, I think creators in general tend to want to use different methods for different projects. Every time they embark on a new project, they think, "Hey, let's try something new." And I think I was feeling this same desire when I started making *The Emperor's Naked Army Marches On*.

Then why didn't I shoot the film differently?

I had in fact planned on using a tripod for the scene of Okuzaki going to the Kobe Detention Center. I wanted to get a precise shot of Okuzaki's car approaching, and then Okuzaki getting out of his car and walking. I told my young crew, "OK. The first shot. From the top of the hill. Place the camera on a tripod, and we'll shoot Okuzaki's car arriving. OK?"

As soon as I said this, my crew began to scoff. "Hara, you must be joking. It's not going to work; something unexpected is going to happen..." I replied, "It doesn't matter. That's how I'm going to shoot it, no matter what." I had my way despite the crew's objections. We arrived at the location, and I said to Okuzaki, "OK. Okuzaki, please wait a second, I'm going to go on ahead." I jumped in my car, flew to the top of the hill, and stopped. But just as I was getting the tripod out, guards came running out of the building saying, "What are you all doing?" So I didn't have enough time to set the tripod up. My crew made me feel like an idiot, saying, "We told you so, Hara."

Things turned out exactly as they had predicted. In other words, from that point on, we never had time to film Okuzaki with a tripod, because we never knew what would happen next. I realized that I couldn't keep up with the action unless I reverted to a style I was familiar with, so I had to use the handheld camera after all.

As you can see from this anecdote, I always want to use new methods on new films. At the same time, the methods I've used up until now are deeply ingrained in me.

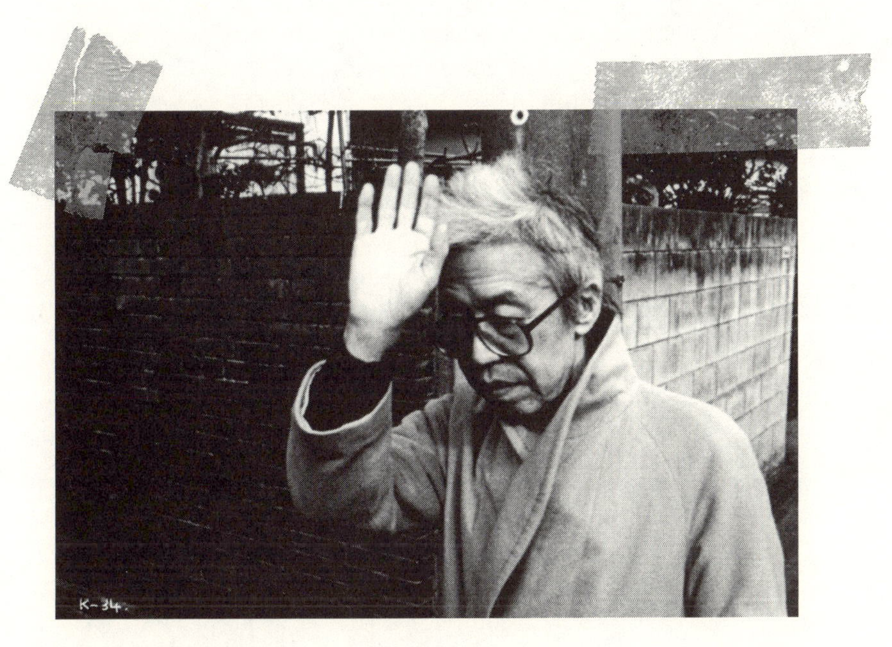

06 A Fictional Person, A Fictional Era

A Dedicated Life

INOUE MITSUHARU, A FICTIONAL PERSON

When I made the decision to do a film about Inoue Mitsuharu, I once again had the vague inclination to shoot it like a narrative film.[1] However, when it came to the question of what method to use, I was counting on Inoue to take action as Okuzaki had done. So I was probably still using *The Emperor's Naked Army Marches On* as a reference point. At the same time, I also wanted to change my style.

The approach I had in mind for the film was to have Inoue Mitsuharu play the part of Inoue Mitsuharu. He would write a script for the film using himself as source material, and we would then follow him around with our camera. But we wouldn't strictly adhere to the script he'd written. Since the script would tell us in advance what each scene was going to be about, I had a vague notion that I should wait until the script was finished before deciding on what kind of gimmicks to use in the film—for example, throwing a real person into one of the episodes. My initial, rough idea for the film was to find something cinematically interesting in Inoue Mitsuharu playing Inoue Mitsuharu.

So I told Inoue my idea, asking, "You'll write the script, won't you?" "Yes, I will. I'll write whatever you want. Just let me know," he said. So I trusted that he would. When I asked what he might write about, he said, "Let's see. I like stories between men and women—so if possible, I'd like to write a story about sex." And so we discussed this rather abstract idea of writing a story about sex.

We were throwing around terms such as "Inoue playing Inoue" and "a story about sex," but by that point, I think Inoue understood what they implied: that if he were to depict his actual circumstances, his true self would probably be revealed. It seems to me that he was wary of this.

---

1 Inoue Mitsuharu (1926-1992): One of the prominent figures in postwar Japanese literature. After WWII, he joined the Japanese Communist Party, but was later expelled for criticizing it. Two of his novels, *Chi no Mure [Apart from Life]* and *Asu [Tomorrow]*, were made into films directed by Kumai Kei and Kuroki Kazuo respectively. Hara was in fact introduced to Inoue by his mentor, Kumai.

In Okuzaki's case, it didn't matter how much of his true self was revealed. However, Inoue was a writer. I only realized this later, but because he was a man of fiction, he was the kind of person who couldn't present his true self without first putting it through the filter of fiction. He was an author, after all.

So he clearly announced to me: "I'm not Okuzaki Kenzō." Those were the exact words he used. I think what he meant by this was what I was just talking about. "If you're thinking about making this movie the way you made *The Emperor's Naked Army Marches On*, then I won't do it." I have to admit that, in the back of my mind, I did expect Inoue to act like Okuzaki somehow. I think Inoue saw right through me.

Not wanting to be like Okuzaki Kenzō meant, I think, that Inoue didn't want our camera to capture his raw emotions the way it had captured Okuzaki's. So when, a little way into the production process, he told me that he wasn't Okuzaki, he also told me to write the script myself.

This was a problem. My approach had been rejected. How was I supposed to move forward? What other angle could I use for the film? I racked my brain, but was unable to find an easy solution.

Inoue had told me to write the script myself, so I had no other choice but to do so. I tried, but I had no concrete material with which to work. By concrete material, I mean that I wanted to make a trip to his hometown and look into anecdotes from Inoue's past, from his childhood or adolescence. But I wasn't able to.

It had became more and more clear to me that if I went to Sarayama, a town famous for Imari porcelain and the locale of many of Inoue's novels, I'd be able to discover something about Inoue himself. So I told him that I wanted to go, and that I was in fact planning to go. He replied, "By all means, by all means. It's a nice place. But I would advise against mentioning my name there." If I couldn't mention his name, though, I wouldn't be able to ask any questions about him. I wouldn't be able to research his past.

I fretted for quite a long time over this impasse. It was an

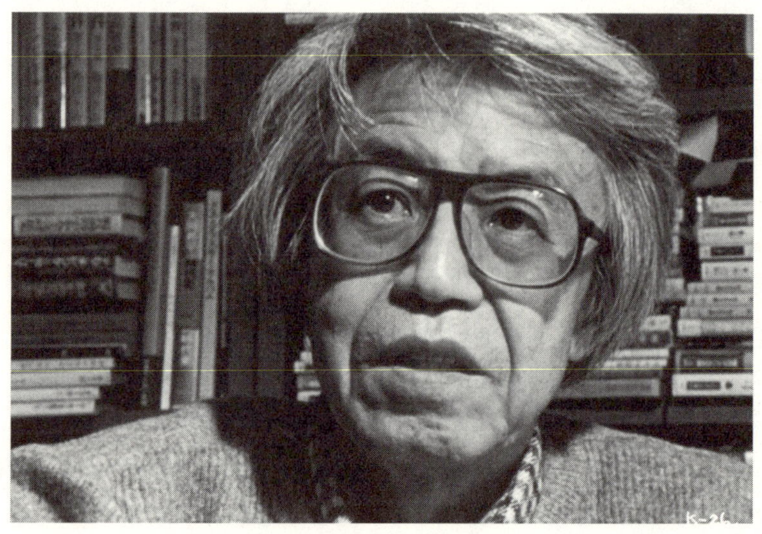

"I am not Okuzaki Kenzō." Inoue Mitsuharu rejected our approach.

impossible situation. But Inoue insisted that I should be able to write *something*. So we started arguing a bit. He said that it was only natural that we follow some kind of a script even though we were making a documentary, that there was no reason for there *not* to be a script. He said he didn't know what kind of film I wanted to make, so he wanted me to show him the structure of the film by writing the script and giving it to him. I responded by saying that the only way this could be a documentary was if I had no idea how he was going to act. We could find no meeting ground; we completely disagreed with one another.

And we dragged this disagreement into the film. Since he was sick, all I could do at the time was film the progression of his illness. He also allowed me to film him when he went to his workshops. So I could film him speaking at his workshops and lectures, and the progression of his illness. That was all.

When I met Inoue for the first time, I had wanted to film him because I saw the other subjects I'd filmed up until that point reflected in him. I never thought of him as a leader of workshops. However, after shooting actually began, I realized that I couldn't depict him without filming those workshops. So I thought about how to deal with them, what angle on them to take. But this only happened after I started making the film.

In the end, though, I didn't go in that direction. You get a tiny glimpse of what might have been in the form of interviews with the women and the men from his class. We did in fact at one point think about focusing on the significance of the workshops as collectives, as examples of group dynamics. But we were ultimately more interested in examining this individual named Inoue. At least in our minds, that's where we wanted to go.

However, when Inoue told me he was not Okuzaki Kenzō, I felt that a door had been shut in my face. I was really in a bind. And while in that bind, unable to find an alternate way of approaching the film, Inoue's illness progressed. Still, we didn't just fold our arms and do nothing. Inoue kept saying that once he recovered his health, he'd do what he'd set out to do. So we kept waiting for the right opportunity, thinking all the while of how to get Inoue to play himself.

And the time came when, after camping together for a week in Sakito, he said, "I'll do anything, whatever you tell me." So I thought that I could at last go on the offensive. Then it was revealed that his cancer had spread to his lungs. So that idea fell through. Every potential opportunity fell through, and, in the end, I couldn't achieve what I wanted.

Therefore, I was at a loss from the moment Inoue said he wasn't Okuzaki Kenzō until he was on his deathbed. When it became clear that he was about to die, the question of what would happen to the film took on even more urgency.

In the end, I'd misunderstood Inoue; or rather, I'd imposed my own ideas upon him from the very first time we'd met. I'd expected him to be a continuation of the heroes and heroines we had filmed up until then. That was why I'd been drawn to him, why I thought I could make a film with someone like him. But I was wrong. He had two sides: one that had something in common with our previous heroes and heroines, and another that didn't.

I didn't know what to do with the side of him that didn't...

So I have a sense of regret to this day when I think of how, if Inoue had not taken ill, if he had been healthy, I could have stepped further into him with the camera, as I'd done with Okuzaki. No one knows what might have resulted; you can only know the outcome of something when you actually do it. But, had he lived, I have a feeling that I would have used that method of stepping right in...

I made my first two films during the 1970s. It wasn't until *The Emperor's Naked Army Marches On* and later that I started saying that the films we made were practically narrative films, even though they fell into the category of documentaries. I never used to say that in the '70s.

Nowadays, I positively assert that our films are fiction, and have no qualms about saying this from the get-go. It wouldn't mean much if I were to say that "some people say this, and I don't object."

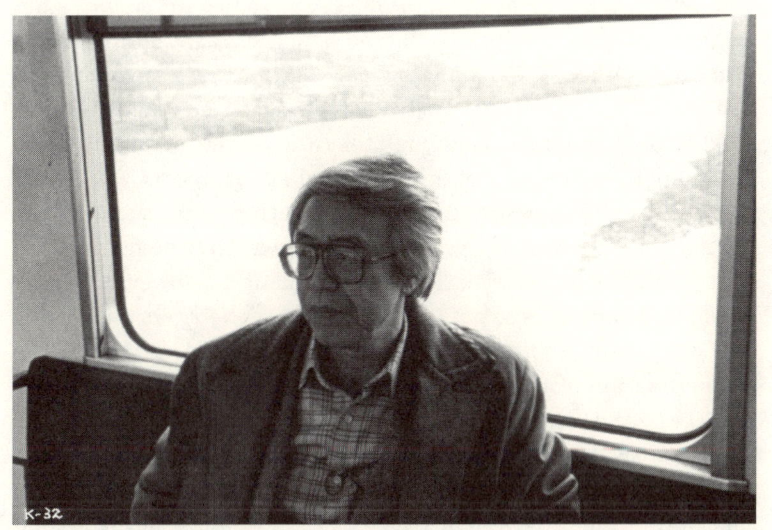

If Inoue had been healthy, I would have stepped further into him with my camera.

But from *The Emperor's Naked Army Marches On* onwards, I started taking a kind of so-what attitude, saying, "We just made a fiction film." Now I've changed so much as to say, from the very start, without hesitation, "In fact, the four films we've made are all practically fiction." My feelings towards my films have changed.

Still, my first two films and my second two could be said to be slightly different. I've said that the relationship between the filmmaker and the subject—for example, between the healthy and the disabled in *Goodbye CP*—is an antagonistic one. In *Extreme Private Eros: Love Song 1974*, the antagonistic relationship is between a man and a woman. In other words, the questions I posed in *Goodbye CP* and *Extreme Private Eros* were practically the same. At least in principle. In terms of chronology, too: only about a year—no, just a few months—had passed after finishing *Goodbye CP* before I started making *Extreme Private Eros*. Therefore, even though they are two separate films, I feel as though they were part of the same production process.

I'm sure I was obsessed at the time with phrases such as "the relationship between the person being filmed and the person who films" and "the transformation of relationships." However, when I would try to apply these phrases to *The Emperor's Naked Army*, I realized that they didn't quite make sense. People would ask how "the transformation of relationships" applied to *The Emperor's Naked Army* and *A Dedicated Life*, and I would try to answer them. I knew that I could give an answer if I tried hard enough, but I couldn't help thinking that, frankly speaking, I myself would be left unconvinced. When considering the difference between first two films and the second two, I've come to the conclusion that I'm the one who's changed, however subtly.

EXPOSING ONESELF

I am, according to my own observations, a painfully self-conscious person. Not only that, but I can't help thinking that I'm incredibly warped. Even when I'm walking down the street: of course, no one is looking at me, yet I'm conscious of being looked at. This consciousness of being looked at is oppressive; it deprives me of freedom, it makes feel awkward. Even when I'm alone.

For example, I'll brood over something I said or did. And I do this quite frequently. Without fail, this process is accompanied by feelings of embarrassment, as if my face were on fire. I'll say something and then brood over and regret it. I do this all the time. That's what I mean when I say I'm painfully self-conscious.

My desire to free myself from that self-consciousness is pretty strong. The more I think about freeing myself from self-consciousness, the more I find myself wondering what I should do next. Since I always feel as though my face were on fire, I try to act in a deliberate, conscientious fashion. I practice how I'm going to act in my next encounter, and so on. I think that's why I feel like I'm always acting. I *am* acting to a large extent.

In my daily encounters, that self-consciousness makes me extremely awkward. It exhausts me to the point where it adversely affects my relationships with others. I once opened up to a friend of mine about this. When drinking alcohol, people are generally able to talk openly about things that are on their minds. But when I spoke like this without being drunk, my friend said: "Hara, you're abnormal."

I don't think I'm abnormal,though. Nor do I think that this kind of self-consciousness is particular to me alone. Still, as an individual, I guess I'm on the more self-conscious side of the spectrum. Therefore, whatever I do, I'm incessantly conscious of the fact that I'm acting. That's the kind personality I have.

For me, making a film means emphasizing that "performative" aspect even more. Therefore, not only does making a film involve dealing with the person in front of the camera, the very act of filming is itself part of the performance. So in a sense, my camerawork is also a kind of performance.

Even when you're filming someone else, you are, so to speak, exposing your entire personal history. In that sense, though I'm aware that I'm going be exposed, I think quite a bit about how to work around this in order to really make an impact with my next film.

I make a film knowing full well that people will see through me regardless of what I do. But at the same time, if I don't act in a way that overwhelms my opponent, my opponent will get the better of me. So I'm always constantly thinking about how to perform in such a way that my opponent will be overwhelmed.

I also know that when I pair up with an intense opponent, our synergy multiplies exponentially. That synergy won't take place if I pair up with someone who's weak, so I have to pair up with someone strong. When I do, there's no doubt that I'm stimulated to try even harder to hold my own. That's when I start thinking about how to conspire with my opponent so as to put on a performance that will overwhelm the viewers of my next film. Where does this sensibility of mine come from? I don't know how to explain it.

SUPERIMPOSING MYSELF ON THE PROTAGONIST

When I was a kid, I suffered from what is commonly called anthrophobia, or fear of people. I was poor at communicating and socializing with others, so I was a pretty morose kid. Even today, I consider myself to be fundamentally gloomy. Back then, there was this book that I was engrossed by and would read repeatedly. It was Dale Carnegie's *How to Win Friends and Influence People.*[2]

It's one of those how-to books on forming human relationships. In addition to *How to Win Friends and Influence People,* there was another book by Carnegie that I think was called *How to Stop Worrying and Start Living*. Anyway, it was a diptych, and I read both books zealously in order to learn how to change myself—my morose self, that *me* who was shy and afraid of strangers—so that I could relate to people better.

2 Dale Carnegie (1888–1955): American writer and lecturer who developed courses and methods for self-improvement, public speaking, and salesmanship.

"Influencing people" means guiding your communications with others in a positive way. It doesn't at all suggest using people the way a manager would. It means communicating in a way that's good, bright, constructive, and optimistic. Since it's a how-to book, it has specific advice on how to influence people by praising others, acting cheerfully, etc. I forget the details, but I read that book as though my life depended on it. And, looking back, I've conscientiously followed the advice it gave throughout my 20s, 30s, and 40s. I'm sure I'm still following it today.

So when I go out to meet someone, I tell myself, "I'm going out now to meet someone. So I'm going to do my best and act as cheerfully as I can." [Laughs.] To tell you the truth, before going out, I make an admirable effort to prepare myself. But when I find myself alone again, I get overwhelmingly depressed. The more cheerful I act, the more depressed I get when I'm alone. And this range of fluctuation has grown wider over time. To be honest, there's that side of me, too.

Making a film thus forces that aspect of myself that acts cheerfully, that puts on a performance, into an inescapable corner. The first two films I made in the '70s represent the process of me desperately trying to alter myself through relationships with others. Such films were possible because I was able to conceive of themes that were at once social and topical, such as "the healthy vs. the disabled" and "man vs. woman." But I made *The Emperor's Naked Army Marches On* in the '80s. So rather than examining my relationship with Okuzaki in the context of "transformation," I, as the film's creator, felt that I was superimposing myself onto Okuzaki. Of course, it's possible to look at the film in the context of the relationship between Okuzaki, who continues fighting, and the former soldiers, who have quit fighting. Still...

With *A Dedicated Life*, I once again wanted to examine my own male sexuality, this time through Inoue. At the same time, because trying to see masculinity is practically the same trying to see femininity, I wanted to see the femininity in him as well. So that tendency of mine to superimpose myself onto others, to see deeper and deeper into myself through another person, has begun to predominate.

People have pointed out that Okuzaki and I resemble each other. Having spent so much time with him, I actually do feel that resemblance. His cowardice, his transformation of that cowardice into power, coincides with the methodology I've devised over time for myself. Only he's much more powerful than I am.

The same goes for Inoue. What makes him care so much for others... I mean, we differ in many ways, but the fact that we both grew up in a mining town, and the way we treat women... I can't of course flatter women to death the way he could: I'm more like his opposite in that respect. But the way he controls his mind, or the way his mind would find its way through things, is more or less identical to the way I search for myself.

I think those are the differences between my first two films and my second two. Of course, certain similarities run through all of them.

In the context of what I've just been saying, the "fiction" part of the "fiction and reality" dichotomy applies to how you relate to or communicate with people—then goes even further, until it applies to your whole way of being. What I mean is, when you wake up in the morning knowing that you have to meet someone that day, you think about how you're going to conduct yourself, how to direct the conversation this way or that.

At night, I get into bed and turn the lights off. What I think about then is a lot of "what-ifs": what if I had said this instead of that in that situation on that day? I actually find myself doing this quite often. So while making *A Dedicated Life*, I would sometimes say, "How shall I play *my* part next time?" That's how I really felt.

So while filmmaking is about how those who are being filmed play their parts, I ask myself how *I'm* going to play my part in my next film. I find myself studying for the part I'm going to play for the unknown people out there who will be my audience.

In short, there's a sense in which my raison d'être is sure to be simultaneously affirmed and negated by others; and I search for

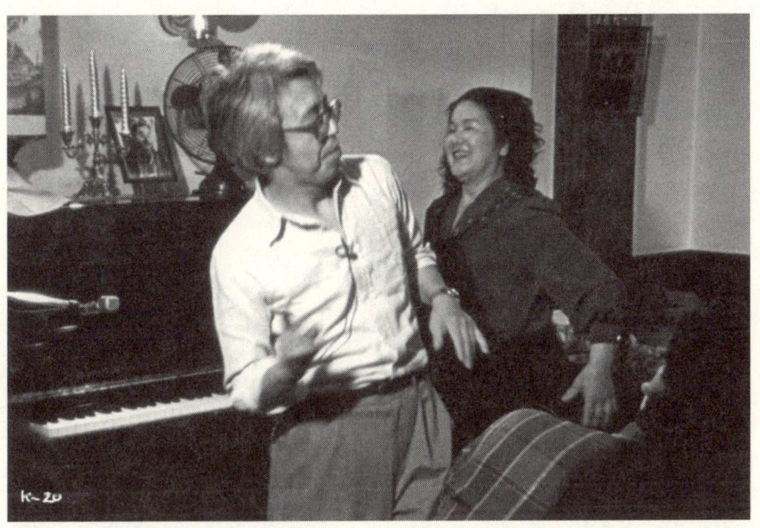

"Fiction and reality": Perhaps human relationships,or human existence itself, is "fiction."

myself in this certainty.

Everyone wants to search for themselves, but if you enclose yourself within the frame of yourself, it's impossible to do so. I believe that the only way you can find yourself is in relation to others.

For example, I'm a man, so I have relationships with women. I can't help but be the center of any relationship I might have, so I can only begin to see myself by relating to others. By relationships, I don't just mean chatting with someone else, of course. Also, I believe that relationships are, in and of themselves, always essentially in motion. And I make a point of consciously setting them in motion. Or, to be more precise, I force myself to do so. Otherwise, I would never discover myself. Therefore, since I believe that I can only see myself in relation to others—and furthermore, only when those relationships are in motion—the best way to achieve what I want is to make films. I feel very strongly about this.

FEAR OF SOCIETY

I began by discussing my self-consciousness, but perhaps it's just that I'm afraid of society or the world.

For example, suppose I got into a fight with someone whom I thought I could physically overpower, someone younger than myself, for example, or a woman, since women are physically weaker than men. And suppose that person grew angry. Even if that person were much weaker than I am, I'd be really frightened if they became angry and directed that energy at me. I'd be seized with fear. Or... but now I'm getting into something I'd rather not talk about...

We had a son. I use the past tense because he committed suicide when he was thirteen.

I guess I have to talk about him.

Previously, I said that it felt really good when my child was born. He was a good kid. He continued to be a good kid for some time, but he enrolled in elementary school and moved into the higher grades, gradually developing his own sense of self. As he moved into junior high, that sense of self became more clearly defined at an accelerated rate.

Then—and I rarely talk about this, but—I gradually began to feel that I was... how should I put it? I was afraid of my son. He was still in the higher grades of elementary school, or barely in junior high. I started to imagine that he would be able to physically overpower me when he reached high school or was old enough to go to college, though I don't know if he would have gone to college or not. So even when he was only in fifth or sixth grade, I began to wonder how long it would be before I would no longer be able to discipline him as I had until then.

I wasn't just afraid of his physical strength. Physical issues aside, what I was really afraid of was what would happen when he entered the inevitable period of rebellion: that he would quite simply step right into me or see right through me and know that I had absolutely no confidence in how I should treat him as a son. I'm not exaggerating this at all. I felt this more and more frequently as he grew older.

And, like I said before, I didn't have a father. So I didn't know what principles I should use when facing him. I didn't know how to relate to my own child. If I'd had a father as a model, I could have tried to be better than him, or I might have approved of him as he was—I wouldn't have had to simply imitate him. But if I'd had a model, I could have incorporated it into myself, into my own way of doing things, and then I would have known how to deal with my son. But I didn't have a father as a model.

So what happened? Ultimately, the values imparted by the 1970s were our point of reference, and I treated my son accordingly.

Friends from my generation who lived around us at the time also got into similar situations once they had children. The more I listened to their stories, the more I realized how similar our situations were. So it wouldn't be wrong to call this a generational issue.

That is, we would express all of our emotions to our children, letting them know everything we were feeling at a given moment. That's what the values of the '70s were like. We thought that giving vent to our emotions—so that they couldn't possibly be misunderstood—was a way of communicating sincerely with others. Even with children. We would direct our energy towards others with as much force as possible. People do think this way, you know.

It would be wrong for me to say that children aren't strong enough to endure this. I wouldn't say that our way of thinking was wrong, but unfortunately, children can't handle this kind of excess as well as we might expect them to. It's an unfortunate fact.

Children try, within their own limits and as best they can, to cope with the energy of their parents. I'm sure a lot of kids deal with it well. Each case is undoubtedly different, but many children must be able to cope with such things as they grow older. However, there are also a number of cases where the children don't handle it well. Our family was one of them. Asking around, I hear that my friends have also had children who've become delinquent and so on. The kids just couldn't handle all the energy that spilled over onto them from their parents. At such times, many children don't know what to do.

Children have various other relationships besides the one they have with their parents; their relationship to school, for example. So they don't always know how to digest their parents' energy and transform it into their own. When our generation became parents, we steadily and excessively vented our energy onto our children, exceeding their capacities. It seems to me that some kids became delinquents as a result, while others, like my son, just up and killed themselves. So I've failed in that regard as well.

In short, we didn't see our children as children, distinct from us adults. According to the values of the '70s, we couldn't. Our generation believed in the golden rule of putting everything we had into everything we did.

But I think our children couldn't bear such overwhelming expectations and desires. Not all of them at any rate. In my case, I didn't know how to be a father, and when my son grew older, I also didn't know how to respond to his "strength." My lack of preparation and my incredible weaknesses, mixed with the ideas instilled in me by the 1970s, led me to turn on my child in the worst way. This is not something I can just look past.

It's not as if my failure was the inevitable result of all that; it's not that simple. But I can't help but think that I failed spectacularly, and that as far as my son's suicide is concerned, I was deservedly punished.

RECORDING THE MURDEROUS "KI"

The values of the 1970s also extended into the community called "the home." In my case... it's broken, as you might expect. In reality, my girlfriend and I registered our marriage, so we're legally married. And it's not as though we're in the middle of an all-out emotional crisis. But even though we're a family in form, the illusion, or rather the "illusory community" that underpins that idea of home, is, in my case, very weak.

Or rather, that's precisely what I'm constantly taking aim at. I'm always grappling with it, this thing that resides within me. I'm "anti-illusion." I deconstruct the unstable conventions of the gender system, the parent-child relationship, the relationship between man and woman, husband and wife... precisely those things that constitute the core of human relationships. I thrust myself again and again and again into the question of those relationships and gaze at it. I never take my eyes off of it.

To gaze at something is to drive it further and further towards its complete deconstruction. The subtle difference between my first two films and the second two is that the first two focused on "relationships." They focused on how the energy I directed at my subjects ended up being turned back onto me.

But when it came to people like Okuzaki and Inoue, it was a whole different story. True, a kind of power struggle may have taken place between Okuzaki and myself over the "authority" of the director. I've also talked about the conflict that emerges between two things that are alike. But Okuzaki had his own world. It's not as though his world completely clashed with mine.

In my first two films, my subjects and I confronted one another to the fullest extent possible, social positions and all. For example, in *Goodbye CP*, my subjects were disabled and I was healthy. Again, in *Extreme Private Eros*, I, a man, and the subject, a woman, were able to completely confront one another. This wasn't the case, however, with *The Emperor's Naked Army*; and it was even less so with *A Dedicated Life*, where the methodology we had used until then was unequivocally rejected by Inoue. He clearly stated, "I am not Okuzaki Kenzō. I can't stand that mode of filmmaking." So relying on our previous methods of making documentaries became impossible.

That's another way you could say that the orientation of the first two films differed from that of the second two: to the extent that the latter two films did *not* attempt to confront their subjects, they went in another direction instead—that of contemplating the multiple layers of their subjects' ways of being. In other words, I didn't want to deconstruct the subjects of my second two films; I wanted to contemplate them.

At the same time, I'm aware of the dualism that allows me to discover myself by examining someone else's energy, though not necessarily in a violent way.

Perhaps a film, or the medium of film itself, especially a documentary film, could be said to record "ki" or "energy flow"—that is, the "ki" of both the subject and the creator.[3] Film is basically a recording. So the kind of "ki" you see in *The Emperor's Naked Army Marches On* and *A Dedicated Life* is not the kind to be found between two warriors facing off against one another, alert and focused, swords in hand, the air between them charged to the point of generating sparks. It's true that Okuzaki and I had our disagreements, as I wrote

3 *ki*: A word with multiple, somewhat ambiguous meanings. Coming from the Chinese concept of "qi," it often refers to a type of energy force or life flow that permeates all things.

in the *Production Notes* to the film. But what was recorded on film was not the "ki" of confrontation; it was Okuzaki's murderous "ki."

Triggered by that murderous "ki," I think I directed the same energy inward, towards myself. Moreover, Okuzaki and I resemble one another. So I'm convinced that I was looking at Okuzaki as though he were a mirror I could peer into in order to analyze myself.

In the end, when trying to deconstruct something, you can't help but go inward, towards yourself. I think it's just a natural thing to do. To an audience, this might not be evident, though. They're probably too enthralled by the intensity of the film's protagonist.

SHOOT YOURSELF!

When I say that a documentary records "ki," I also mean that it records the "atmosphere of a place." The atmosphere of a place is the specific "ki" of each setting, each situation; at the same time, if you connect those single moments of "ki," you begin to see a certain kind of flow. Over the span of several years, the "ki" of an era becomes visible. Consequently, I think that my films have done their share of work in capturing something like the "atmosphere of an era." I think the atmosphere of the '80s runs through *The Emperor's Naked Army*, and *A Dedicated Life* probably has something very '90s about it. Perhaps the change from one subject to the next, from Okuzaki, who embodied a kind of vitality, to Inoue, who was a fictional being, also reflected the times. Looking back on it, that's what I think.

When I push my thinking a little further, I realize that we've entered an era that's incredibly difficult to film. In a word, the readily understandable nature of shooting pachinko balls at the emperor, as embodied in the phrase "Yamazaki, Shoot the Emperor!" no longer exists. That is, we can no longer simply say that the emperor or anything else is the enemy. If you push this logic to its conclusion, you inevitably end up screaming, "Shoot yourself!" You do—at least for a time. It's true.

What I mean by this, of course, is that you thus examine yourself. But you need someone else in order to be able to do this. The only way you can see yourself is in relationship with another being. Precisely *because* you want to see yourself, you need someone else. Communication is based on this principle.

In that sense, our camera inevitably goes after others. But there are a number of occasions when the people we are filming don't want to be filmed. In situations like that, our camera has no choice but to become violent, so to speak. It's only logical.

As such, when making this kind of film, it doesn't mean much to simply say, without context, that "violence is bad." Using a word like "love" makes me feel bashful, but communication is the act of pursuing "love," which necessarily includes an aspect of violence. That's what a relationship boils down to.

Even back in the '70s, I more or less understood that much. I did, but... I also knew that society would be critical of that kind of viewpoint...

That's why, when faced with exactly this dilemma, I gather my strength and make a stand, telling everyone, "OK. Let's go." We tell one another "Let's do this" knowing full well that we're about to engage in work that exists in a gray zone. Which means that we'll have to work really hard. That's what it means.

I've said earlier that I don't in any way want to justify my actions or my reasoning—that I wouldn't be able to if I tried. I really think it's better that I not do so. Therefore, I'm "defenseless." I don't care if people laugh at this or question why I prefer not to defend myself. But for that very reason—*because* I'm defenseless—the things I'm able to see when I lunge forward with my camera become all the more precious, all the more dear to me.

I experience the same day-to-day problems as anyone else; that's a given. In other words, before I start making a film, I experience the personal, internal agony and conflict that accompanies my existence. I take all of this in, concentrating it into energy to use for the action of filming with my camera. And then I go in one step further, condensing our "ki"/"intention" in order to film a moment, in order to step right in and capture something on film. For us, the act of making a film, of rolling camera, is the same as Okuzaki hiding a screwdriver in his pocket.

The "ki" we bring to a scene forcibly opens up the gap that exists between reality and our protagonists' points of view. Needless to say, this causes them to react. And it's impossible to see this highly complex, multi-layered gap between reality and delusion without examining yourself.

That's what a documentary is about; or rather that's the role our camera plays in our methodology. A camera accurately captures the "atmosphere" of wherever we're filming. So if the "ki" of that place is weak, the images we capture will naturally be powerless. That's why we make a stand, holding our ground as if our lives depended upon it.

HOW TO FILM A NOVELIST

A Dedicated Life takes up the literary world or literature. But in spite of that, it doesn't make any reference to Inoue's own writings.

There have been reviews or critiques of the film to the effect that, despite its title [literally, *Every Bit A Novelist*], it doesn't mention any of Inoue Mitsuharu's literary output. These reviews often question the validity of a film about an author that doesn't deal at all with his writings. This criticism isn't necessarily a comment on the quality of the film, but it's something that people who react negatively to it tend to bring up. They say that the film doesn't depict the novelist at all; that the Japanese title, *Every Bit A Novelist*, is misleading, or rather, too exaggerated—a misnomer. Negative reactions to the film usually stem from this particular point.

It's not as if we were determined from the outset to not take up Inoue's literature. I considered more than once how best to integrate Inoue's works into the film. Indeed, all of his novels contain vivid imagery: for example, a chicken coop set on fire, every chicken inside burnt to death; or a worker at a public health center who's standing motionless, wire in hand, in preparation for a stray dog hunt.

I considered quoting some of these images from his novels for the film, but I came to feel that this would be little more than a literal translation of words into images, so I abandoned the idea. What, then, could we do? Should we visually recreate an entire scene from one of his novels? That didn't seem interesting to us, either. We even considered adapting an entire novel, but that would have been no different from making a film based on a novel.

Then we came up with the idea of doing something in real time. We discovered that Inoue was just about to start writing a piece entitled *A Record of Young Michio Kamisaki*. So we decided to ask Inoue for updates about the novel as it progressed, interviewing him a few times on that topic. I considered filming fictional pieces based on each of these updates, but this still felt like little more than a translation of written passages into images, and we concluded that it wouldn't be very interesting.

We also tried another strategy. For example, one of the novels Inoue wrote when he was young is set in Sarayama, a town famous for Imari porcelain. It was, as a novel, really interesting. So we went to Sarayama and started talking to the people there. Through that process, it became apparent that the chronology of Inoue's life that would often be published in the back of his books was basically a lie.

Once we had done some more research on this novel, which we had picked as a way of showing the relationship between the author and his work, we were able to figure out to a certain extent who the models had been for some of the characters in the novel. One of the characters resembled Inoue's grandfather; another resembled his father; yet another resembled the woman with whom his father had had a relationship, and so on. But these characters only "resembled" the real people; they didn't represent facts.

Moreover, integrating one of Inoue's novels into the film would have required explaining the relationships between the characters.

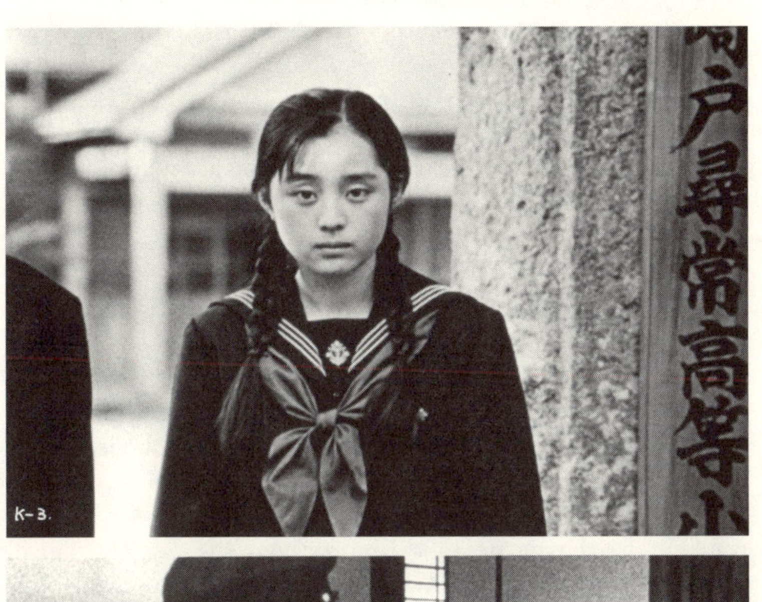

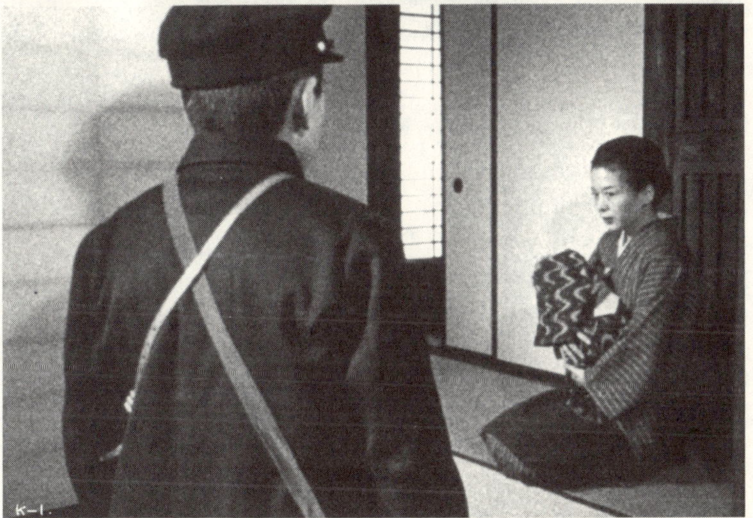

Characters from Inoue's novels were reminiscent of people from his past.

We would also have had to present the actual facts they were based on, and to illuminate the connections between reality and the work. Then we would have had to go so far as to analyze the mechanism by which that reality had been fictionalized.

We thought that, for the time being at least, we might as well put aside Inoue's work in order to investigate his actual relationships with people. As much as possible, we decided to pursue facts rather than fiction.

And we learned that he'd definitely used some real people as models for his characters; that certain human relations had provided the background for some of his stories. People who had been only peripherally involved in these anecdotes were pretty cooperative, agreeing to be interviewed, but some of the people who had played more central roles declined to be interviewed on the grounds that the past was the past.

Such anecdotes are possible to write about in novels, but they wouldn't be convincing in a film without the participation of those more central players. Inoue uses rumors, investigations, and legends to narrate the stories in his novels, so we thought there was no reason why we shouldn't use similar techniques in the film. So we filmed interviews with the people around Inoue, even though all they could talk about were rumors they had heard. But I eventually had to abandon these interviews; without the participation of the people central to the events being described, they wouldn't have been convincing on film.

At the same time, this meant that there was no way we could touch upon those writings by Inoue that were based upon those facts. This was unfortunate, because he had some interesting works, and the reality that served as a model for them was rife with astoundingly fascinating events.

The only part of this effort that remains in the film is that anecdote about Inoue's first love, the pretty girl.

As a result of the process I've just talked about, we concluded that if we could present a piece of Inoue's universe, a piece of his world, we could say that we had incorporated his literature into the film, even if we didn't specifically reference any of his novels.

We also thought we could counter the criticism that we weren't depicting his literature by invoking characters from his novels, quite a few of whom were reminiscent of Inoue in his youth. We figured that, once people saw the film, those familiar with Inoue's writings would more or less catch on. However, critics have an image of Inoue as a leftist. What they didn't understand, quite predictably, is that this image of Inoue as a leftist is another one of his fabrications, and is in fact deliberately refuted in the film. So to those who criticize us for not depicting Inoue's fiction, I say that you are completely mistaken.

INOUE MITSUHARU WAS NOT A NOVELIST?

We first began preparations for the film thinking that since Inoue was "a man of letters," we couldn't tell his story without referencing his "literary works." But, as I just explained, that mode of thinking didn't quite work out. Inoue himself would repeatedly say in his workshops that literature or "a literary style" was nothing less than a way of life.

When I heard him say this—that "literary style" was not a matter of literary technique, but rather of how one lived one's life as a whole—I realized that the film's vision could come from the idea of depicting Inoue Mitsuharu's very way of being.

For better or for worse, I don't think of myself as a bookish person. Precisely for that reason—that is, *because* I'm not a lover of literature—I was able to disregard that side of Inoue, to put it tentatively aside and decide that depicting a human being would be enough. Because of this, we never thought of the film as dealing with or not dealing with the place occupied by literature in Inoue's life.

Of course, we don't think our film is perfect. Moreover, we didn't set out to present a "thesis" on Inoue Mitsuharu. We had no intention of discussing his literature in a way that would clarify the significance of a certain expression in a certain work of his. I think our film is nothing beyond the story of a man who happened to make his living writing literature.

I think the film will have served its purpose if it can convey what it meant for Inoue to express himself through literature, or rather, what it meant for him to have chosen literature as the means for accomplishing his ends.

In an interview I did with Tanigawa Gan, he made a very significant point.[4] It's extremely interesting. It's more than that—it's astonishing.

What follows is Tanigawa's remark:

> ...I think that Inoue Mitsuharu could have been something other than a novelist; that *that* possibility was in fact greater than him becoming a novelist. Or rather, I wish he had *not* become a novelist. Let me explain.
>
> It goes back to the problem of choices that came up earlier. In sum: Imagine Disney World. Inoue could have created something like a Disney World, and it's fun to imagine what Inoue's version of Disney World would have been like. But no one really dares to do so...
>
> If you ask me, the vastness of Inoue's actual, full-of-lies spirit is slightly under-represented by Inoue Mitsuharu the author... And in that sense, I think he failed in his life—or rather, he's an example of that kind of failure.
>
> —(A Dedicated Life *Production Notes/Transcribed Script: Another Version of Inoue Mitsuharu*. Kinema-Junpo-sha: 1994)

This was the most interesting interview of all the ones we shot because it has the potential to overturn everything we think about

4 Tanigawa Gan (1923–1995): A leftist poet and social critic who joined the Communist Party in the late 1940s and became involved in party activities with Inoue Mitsuharu.

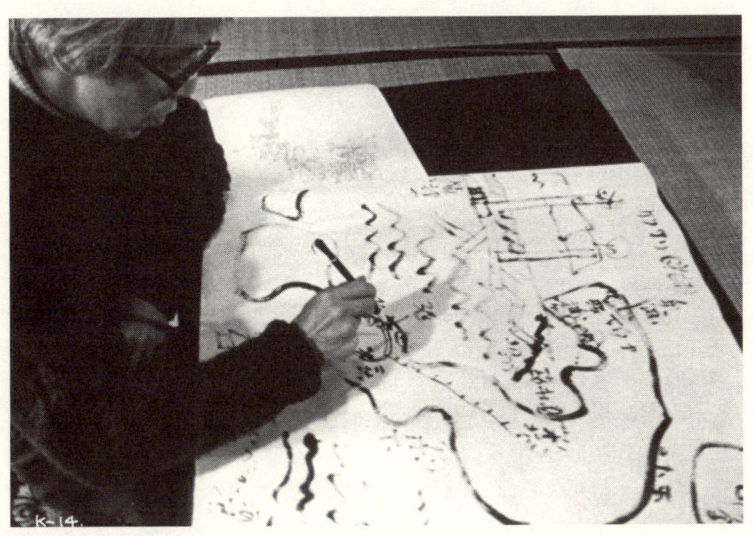

Did becoming a writer under-represent Inoue's vastness of spirit?

Inoue's persona. However, we couldn't include it in the film for one simple reason: we couldn't roll camera. Tanigawa allowed us to record sound, but he refused to be filmed.

His reason was that because his health was not so good, he couldn't bear to sit under the lights in front of the camera for prolonged periods of time. Actually, prior to our interview, he'd been interviewed by NHK and had spoken at length, but NHK had ended up using very little of the footage they'd shot. Well, we would have used very little ourselves, had we been allowed to film him…

When Tanigawa said he would only allow us to record his voice, there wasn't much else we could do. We'd agreed to his conditions because we thought we'd be able to run the sound over still photographs of him. But we subsequently realized that the section with Tanigawa would take on special significance if we were to do that, since we were using footage with synchronized sound for everyone else.

So there was a practical reason why we couldn't use Tanigawa's interview. Beyond that, we felt that we couldn't establish the specific context needed to make the most of his lines. We had a limited amount of time, of course, and using Tanigawa's lines to their fullest potential would have required gathering more material. But if we had included Tanigawa's interview, the film might have deconstructed Inoue Mitsuharu's very identity as a novelist. If we'd begun the film with that approach in mind, it probably wouldn't be what it is now.

I kept saying that I didn't want the film to be one of those cancer patient documentaries, but, fortunately or unfortunately, we began filming Inoue after he'd had been diagnosed with colon cancer. So I ended up filming the progression of his cancer. That alone took up quite a bit of the film.

We also had footage of the process by which we came to see his fictional persona, so we used that as well. Ultimately, we could only use what footage we'd been able to shoot; we had to live with what we had, interviews included. Consequently, this film had to be… well, something like "An Introduction to Inoue Mitsuharu." To be honest, given the circumstances, I thought that something like that would have to suffice.

The main reason I felt like publishing the *Production Notes* for this film was that I wanted to make use of our interview with Tanigawa. On top of that, each and every time Inoue said something, some part of what he said would be quite impressive. The things he said were undoubtedly the words of an author. Those were the two main reasons why I put together that book.

THE SPIRIT THAT SURPASSES REASON

However, there's an unwritten rule that you can only make a film with the footage you've been able to shoot.

Nabeshima Jun, the same editor who'd worked on *The Emperor's Naked Army Marches On*, edited this film as well. Now, it's an editor's job, or rather his instinct, to try to put things together into a coherent whole. He's expected to put together a story, so that's what he tries to do. On the other hand, we'd been at every single scene we'd filmed, so we placed a great deal of significance on things that defied organization. Also, we're the kind of people who go in for whatever strikes us as interesting. So we fought constantly. The truth of the matter is that each scene in the film was ultimately decided on through a kind of tug-of-war, not according to who had the better logic. Decisions were based on people's attachment to a given scene, on whoever's spirit prevailed.

For example, there are scenes that, invoking my authority as the director, I insisted upon including. But it's not as though I did that from the beginning to the end of the film. When you team up with someone, that person's views and sensibilities will inevitably also be projected onto the film. I'm not saying that this is a bad thing; "teaming up" means working with someone whose personality you respect so much that you *want* his or her views or sensibilities to be projected onto the film. So sometimes you end up going along with your editor's ideas. It's not as if I would just compromise, though; we argued pretty fiercely. If we weren't arguing, we would be silently hating one another... Oh, it wasn't hate, we just thought that the other person was completely clueless. [Laughs.] It was really intense.

We edited our first two films by ourselves. For some reason, we didn't think of hiring an editor. We thought we could just splice the shots together in the order we shot them, and that's basically what we did. We didn't think that any refined editing technique would be necessary.

Nevertheless, an editor has his or her own sensibility. And Nabeshima isn't the most articulate person I know. I'd tell him what I wanted, and he'd just respond, "Hmm, hmm, hmm," as though he were listening. But in fact he wasn't.

Nabeshima only edits the way he wants to. This would at times make me furious. At other times, the way he would edit our footage would be surprising and eye-opening. It's fifty-fifty. Actually, he sometimes "rediscovers" material that I myself have shot but have since forgotten. A few times per film, he'll discover an unexpected way of using such shots, and it's like, "Wow, are you going to use that here? Like that?"

Therefore, while a film is a director's work, it's also at the same time the work of each person involved in production. And any great director, in order to shine as a great director, must in fact incorporate other people's ideas into their films. I'm not saying I'm a great director; it's just that I truly believe that that's the way you enrich the worlds that are portrayed in film. No ordinary editor could have edited *A Dedicated Life*—and the same could be said of *The Emperor's Naked Army Marches On*. It was very difficult.

Towards the end of the film, right before Inoue dies, there's a scene of him getting a massage from some women. At the end of the sequence, you get a glimpse of his wife working, shot from behind. At that moment, I wasn't operating the camera. The cameraman was someone else, this guy named Mizuno. You get a slew of images at the shooting stage, you know.

That image of Inoue's wife takes on a lot of meaning when used in that context. Editors can more or less foresee such things. It comes from their experience, their instincts.

There's a similar instance in *The Emperor's Naked Army* when Okuzaki and Yamada Kichitarō are fighting with each other, and Okuzaki's wife all of a sudden shows her leg, which had been kicked. I was operating the camera at the time, so I could only see what was going on in front of the camera, but the two wives were showing their injuries to one another behind the camera.

Earlier, I'd made a point of telling the assistant director to inform me if anything ever happened behind the camera, where I'd be unable to see it. This was because of a previous incident, a scene I ended up not using, where we shot Okuzaki going to apologize to one of the ex-soldiers from his company. I'd been operating the camera, and after we finished shooting, the assistant director told me that the soldier's wife had been crying behind me. I yelled at him, saying, "I'm both the director and the cameraman. The director should be paying attention to what's happening behind the camera, but unfortunately, as the cameraman, I can only see what's going on in front of me. Why the hell didn't you tell me what was going on?!" Ever since then, I would tell my crew to inform me if anything was happening behind me. So when Okuzaki's wife got kicked, I heard the AD whisper to me, "Hara, behind you, his wife..." and I spun the camera around and got a shot of her. That's how I captured that image.

Of course, in the editing session, I wanted to use that shot. But a picture has its own rhythm. So figuring out how to fit a shot smoothly into the flow of things—finding the exact spot where it won't disrupt the rhythm—is ultimately up to the editor's intuition and innate sense of things. It's like that saying: "If you want bread, go to the bakery." The director can tell the editor where he wants a certain shot to go, but in the end, it's not his specialty; editing is, in principle, Nabeshima's territory. As far as possible—that is, insofar as I *could*—I had to let Nabeshima have his way, to respect his opinions. After all, I was the one who'd hired him. That was the basis of our relationship.

When Nabeshima edited the film about Okuzaki, he seemed to be able to relate to it on a personal level, since it dealt with the war, and he himself was nearly of Okuzaki's generation. With *A Dedicated Life*, however, he said he could barely understand the parts of the film that dealt with Inoue's fictionality. So he said that if I came up with a concrete plan for how to edit those parts, he would follow it.

For that reason, this film was incredibly difficult to put together. Without disrupting the film's overall rhythm, we had to dramatize Inoue's fictional aspect as part of the film's structure, transposing his fictionality into that of the film. This was extremely hard to do. So I must say that once the overall direction of a film has been decided upon, Nabeshima is quite an editor when it comes to using a splicer to execute that vision. I'm not exaggerating when I say that he's one of the best.

THE EXISTENCE OF IKUKO, MRS. INOUE

We always decide on the titles for our films after they've been completed. Once most of the editing is finished, we come to the stage where we need to place an order for the title. That's when we begin to discuss what to call it. For this film, we had a number of ideas.

"The Mitsuharu I Loved" was one candidate. Another was "Inoue Mitsuharu, Every Bit a Novelist." Kobayashi Akira, who had been both assistant cameraman and assistant director for the film, mentioned that Haniya Yutaka had used the phrase, "Inoue Mitsuharu, Every Bit a Novelist" in his eulogy for a newspaper.[5] Then he suddenly said, "Why don't we call the film *Inoue Mitsuharu, Every Bit a Novelist*?" "That's a good idea, too," we replied. So, for a while, we

---

5 Haniya Yutaka (1909–1997): A leftist author and social critic who, in 1946, founded the journal *Modern Literature*, which became one of the most influential literary journals of the postwar period. Most famous for his nine-volume novel, *Spirits of the Dead*.

used that as the film's working title.

When it came time to finalize the title, we narrowed it down to those two. We heatedly debated which one was better and, in the end, decided to drop the "Inoue Mitsuharu" and simply title the film, *Every Bit a Novelist*. *Inoue Mitsuharu, Every Bit a Novelist* would have been good in its own way, though. We could also have used *The Mitsuharu I Loved* as the main title, giving it a secondary title along the lines of *Every Bit a Novelist, Such and Such*. Various combinations would have been possible, but we decided that it would be better to keep things simple. So it was decided.

The Mitsuharu I Loved may have added a different nuance to the film. A slight one. We felt that that title better matched what had been going through our minds while we were filming Inoue. It better represented him as he was to those who got involved with him—including us, the makers of the film, of course.

Speaking of *The Mitsuharu I Loved*, various women from Inoue's workshops appear in the film. Then there's his wife, a charming and quite mysterious woman who's definitely one up on them. I'm sure lots of people would be curious to know what was going on in her mind regarding her relationship with Inoue.

Naturally, we hoped to be able to interview her sometime, but she's... how should I put it? She's not the type of person who's eager to go in front of a camera. She kept saying, "If possible, I'd prefer not to be filmed." Inoue would then tell her, "Come on, it's all right." So she'd reluctantly agree to be filmed.

After Inoue passed away, we decided to look into some events from his boyhood, and wanted his wife to go with us. We visited her once and politely asked her if she'd come, but she said she didn't want to. After that, we persisted in asking her several times to tell us some of her own stories about Inoue. But she told us that if she did, what she had to say would be considered the final word on him, since she was his wife.

She said that the film as it progressed carried with it many questions pregnant with multiple possible answers, and that

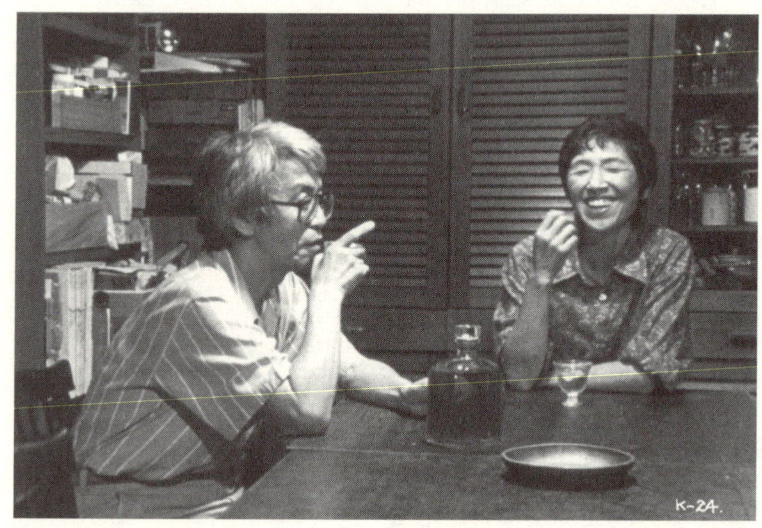

Ikiko, on the right, didn't want to have the final word on Inoue; she said it was our film.

anything she might say would be regarded as conclusive. She also said that just because she was Inoue's wife didn't mean that she necessarily knew everything about him. And, indeed, she was right. Furthermore, Inoue's boyhood and youth preceded her meeting him, and Ikuko wasn't the type of person to pry into Inoue's past. In that sense, she was—how should I put it—pretty modern.

On a daily level, too, she didn't seem to have insisted on knowing what lay behind Inoue's fictionalized persona. She even believed that he had been born in Manchuria. The truth about that came to light almost by accident, just before Inoue passed away, surprising everyone.

The "accident" happened like this: when Inoue was in hospital, his younger sister, Tazuko, came to visit him. While they were chatting, stories about their past came up, and she said, "In fact, my brother wasn't actually born in Manchuria." The family was shocked. "What? Is that true?" they asked. Areno, Inoue's daughter, has written in one of her books that her father had lied even to his own family. So Inoue's wife didn't learn of this until just before he passed away.

In short, Ikuko didn't know that much about what had actually happened in Inoue's life—which was another reason why she thought the viewers of the film would be better able to freely imagine things if she didn't say anything. And, to be honest with you, she was right on the money about this. In hindsight, she was spot on.

She also said, "No matter how you depict him, it's your film." I think she's the kind of person who can perceive a situation objectively. I don't mean that she's a "cold person," nor that she's overly intellectual. I think the term "objective" describes her best.

In other words, she understood the limits of making a creative piece about someone, of telling someone else's story. I think she knew that the image a person might have of Inoue from his work would necessarily differ from, or couldn't *possibly* be the same as, the image she had of him. Good or bad, she knew that that was the nature of artistic expression. After all, she had spent all those years with Inoue; she probably knew those kinds of things inside and out.

Also, when Inoue went out in public and lectured to his workshops, he was quite a fire-brand, full of enthusiasm. But one could easily imagine that when at home, he would show a different side of himself. Though he was apparently like that even at home. So... it must have been quite difficult for his family to live with him.

NEXT, I WANT TO FILM WOMEN

My relationship with my mother hasn't changed much.

The Emperor's Naked Army Marches On was screened where she lives, so she came to see the film. We rented a public hall or something, and she came to see it. But she didn't say much about it. I didn't really ask her what she thought, either.

I've constantly... pitied my mother. She's been with the guy she's with now for almost thirty years. He's more than a dozen years younger than she is, so he probably wanted to have a child with her, but because of her age, he couldn't. She married him after we, her children, were already adults, so we found it difficult to call him "Dad." He does sometimes act like a father, but we all know that he's not. Then I left for Tokyo, and my younger sister married into another family and had a child—so, for all intents and purposes, they weren't our family any more.

Then, as the two of them grew old by themselves, he took a mistress. My mother suffered tremendously from this. While she was suffering, I would occasionally call her, and I could tell that she was sad, even over the phone. Seeing her in that state, I, as her son, should probably have blamed that man for doing such a terrible thing to her. But I could also understand the desires he had as a man, so I couldn't reproach him. I could only pity her. I mean, she's not in good health: she's pretty fat, on the verge of becoming diabetic, and she has heart problems.

She puts it bluntly: "Suffering has been a part of my life for as long as I've been alive." She's pretty straightforward about such things. So every time I call her, I'm filled with pity; I feel really sorry for her. Realistically speaking, though, despite what I feel, there's nothing I can do for her. So I feel apologetic. Then again, could I move back to where she lives, stay with her, find a job, and live there taking care of her? No. All I can do is tell her "I'm sorry."

However, there's one thing I feel that I absolutely must do regarding my mother. That is, I have this urge to ask her at least once about her personal history: to hear her tell, in her own words, her story from her girlhood to the time she became an adult at about the age of 20. This would not be unlike what I did with Inoue. But I haven't been able to do so yet. For one thing, she doesn't really want to talk about it; apparently, she has some really difficult memories from that period.

I've heard some fragments of something painful that happened to her—painful not in financial terms, but in terms of human relations. I recall hearing about one incident that was pretty shocking. I feel hesitant to ask her about this, so I haven't, but sometimes I'm struck with the realization that she might pass away before I can get around to it.

When thinking of my mother, the woman who's been closest to me in my life, I can't separate her out from her constant financial difficulties. It seems as though she'll live that way for the rest of her life. She often says about herself that she has no luck with men. Since she's never been all that blessed with financial fortune, either, I would have to say that she's had a pretty miserable life. It's true enough that, going from man to man as she did, she's had precious few peaceful periods in her life. Each man came with his own baggage. Despite that, I think she's lived with each new man as honestly as she possibly could, though I'm not sure how conscious she is of this.

So the image I have of my mother is that of a woman who, while complaining of her own bad luck with men, has lived as sincerely as she could, given her abilities.

In addition to my mother, the woman to whom I most owe my view of women, from the bottom up, is Takeda Miyuki. There's no denying that. She's the kind of person who relies on nothing but her own ego, who lives in order to bring her ego into full bloom. She's always wanted to live a more intense life, to go forward forever in that way. And she would heedlessly and relentlessly throw her body into everything that she did, seizing on whatever it was that she had put her mind to. For that reason, she became very sensitive to the institution of monogamy, which is why she deliberately did things to defy that convention when she was with me. Being with the kind of woman who would go through that much trouble in her quest for independence was something that I, for my part, couldn't help but accept. Or rather, I was challenged to find out how much of her I could accept...

The moment I accepted Takeda Miyuki, I would be challenged. During our time together, she taught me that in order to challenge myself, I had to keep accepting what she did, no matter how many times this was required. Of course, I must have taught her something as well.

But that's what she taught me. Then again, this very personal encounter of mine with Takeda Miyuki took place in that period from the late '60s to the early '70s. So there were two different elements at work. The fact that my own personal relationships meshed together perfectly with the era ended up forming the basis for the films I would make in the coming years. In other words, that's how my view of women took shape.

If I'm going to make a narrative film next, I want to re-examine my view of women through it. In fact, I want the film to take on the issue of "women." In both *The Emperor's Naked Army Marches On* and *A Dedicated Life*, women appear as wives. Various women from Inoue's workshops also appear. Men were the protagonists of those two films, but women do feature in them in that way... In other words, even when we make films about men, we still keep an eye on women.

So, in my next film, I want to further question the things I've said and thought about women in order to think about them on a deeper level one more time. Schematically speaking, examining women is equivalent to examining my own sex as a man. I also intend to fully express the image I have of my mother in this next narrative film.

I'm not sure what kind of narrative film it's going to be, which is only to be expected. However, as far as form is concerned, I want it to be a narrative film.

And I want to depict women. You might ask why I want to make a narrative film. In the documentaries that I've done so far, the reality that was the premise for each film was guaranteed from the beginning—all I had to was forcibly grab it. But in a narrative film, we would have to create every situation from scratch. On our own. And I want to give that a try.

I'M NOT A POLITICAL PERSON

I don't feel much enmity toward women, but there's one thing I haven't mentioned yet about Takeda Miyuki. When we rented a house together in Yamato City, there was this guy she used to date in high school, a former classmate of hers that was still a good friend. Apparently, she still liked him a lot. When we started living together in Yamato, we'd established a complete home, a home in compliance with monogamy. The era being such as it was, she was naturally sensitive to that kind of closed space containing just the two of us—or rather, the idea of home as an institution. So she felt like destroying it.

One day she announced: "There's a man I used to go out with in high school. And I'm in love with him. So I'm going to sleep with him tonight." Then she went out. She had a tendency to make declarations and take action against institutional things like that.

How was I supposed to react? Yeah, I understood her reasoning. Rationally speaking, it made a lot of sense. But having agreed that it made a lot of sense, what would I do? All I could do was shut up. Since that was all I could do at the time, I gave her my consent in the form of silence.

And, well—she went out. I probably should have put up a fight right then, but I found it utterly impossible to do so. So I passed that night suffering, unable to sleep.

It really tore me up inside. And as I was being torn up, I tried really hard to think. That's basically my method for getting through tough times. [Laughs.]

I really tossed and turned, suffering. I mean, there was this part of me that understood her philosophically and intellectually—and another part of me that, quite realistically, felt otherwise.

However, I didn't think I was being "hurt." How can I describe it... At that time, we shared the same awareness about various problems. So basically, on a intellectual level at least, I was of the opinion that it didn't matter if either of us got ahead of the other. Except that she was always the one getting a step ahead of me. Truth be told, women always get a step ahead of men in such matters. Men are more conservative. Or rather, women are more radical; they can make leaps using nothing but their own bodies.

When she said what she did, she was saying it to me, but in fact, she was directing her words at social institutions. That was the kind of era it was. So, intellectually, I thought I had to agree with her. That's what I thought, but in reality, it was difficult to accept. So I ended up just thinking. I thought because there was nothing else I could do.

This isn't simply a random anecdote from my life; it became one of my methods for coping with difficult situations. This relates to what I said earlier about influencing people. It's possible, to a certain extent, to see the institutional elements inside you that need to be destroyed. You might be able to see what your problems are, and you might even know that you have to do something about them. However, it's not easy to destroy your own weaknesses. Because of this, when you're challenged in a relationship with someone else, all you can do is tell yourself that now's the time for you to hold your ground. Or rather, you seek relationships in search of such challenges. I could even go so far as to say that I make films to seek out such challenges. No matter how eagerly you want to change yourself, it's not easy to do so; you need the devastating counterpunch of another person.

In other words, only when you subject yourself to some kind of attack—only when you see yourself in someone else, or when you yourself are being torn up from the inside—can you see who you really are. The question then becomes how much strength you can manage to muster in such situations. What's revealed at that point is what you're truly after. Because, in theory, I understand that much—because I believe that I have to subject myself to whatever is taking place at the time—I swallow the pain and subject myself to that challenge. But it is painful.

Things like that happened several times with Takeda Miyuki, culminating in *Extreme Private Eros*. In fact, there's that one scene in the film where I'm overwhelmed with jealousy.

When you decide to deconstruct institutions and relationships, you end up experiencing a great deal of suffering. This suffering is human.

I am by no means a political person. In my youth, however, as far as *Goodbye CP* and *Extreme Private Eros* were concerned, I wasn't completely indifferent to political themes; I won't deny that. Still, even then, politics were secondary, so to speak. Human dramas were what I was really interested in showing.

So to me, that's what politics means. I'm only political in the sense that "embarrassment" and "institutionalized emotions" are political. I have a feeling that the reason why I've been making films is in order to figure out the way such things work. To a large extent, I believe I was able to capture that on film in *Extreme Private Eros*.

Therefore, the issue at the very end of *Extreme Private Eros* was not whether or not the childbirth should have been filmed or anything like that. Given the triangular relationship involving Takeda Miyuki, Kobayashi, and myself, I'm not even sure that I celebrated the birth of the child. So when we finished shooting the film—when we made it that far—I didn't feel some kind of gratification or sense of accomplishment.

If anything, the sensation I felt was that of something leaving my body—of being deflated, so to speak. That's what it felt like more than anything else.

This isn't to say that it's a feeling of calm, however. When we struggle to make a film, we project energy at one another until we're on the verge of exploding. So it's really exhausting. But if you continue to do that for a while, you hit a sort of a peak where a dramatic confrontation takes place; then you feel as though you've gotten over it. That's the point when you feel that you've done enough, and the shoot comes to an end. After a while, you edit the film, and it takes on its final form. After that, you feel as though you were melting down—as though the air's been let out of you, so to speak.

I'm not sure if I can say that I experience some kind of transformation. That's essentially a question of how you define "liberation" or "freedom." But regardless, it's not as if once you've transcended something, you're then "free" for the rest of your life. Whenever I go through something very dramatic, there's a certain sensation I feel immediately afterwards; a moment comes when I suddenly find myself liberated from both time and space.

I think this sensation is freedom itself. Instead of being measurable in reference to the axis of time—because you can't measure freedom that way—it's the moment when you experience the sensation of air being let out of you.

From the point of view of regular people, it may seem as though something were just a triangular love relationship; or that they're bearing witness to a clash between Okuzaki and Yamada. Things may seem immoral or totally outrageous. But when I've lived through such experiences, such scenes, I have in fact gone through some *process*, and I get this sense that something I've been stuck with is melting down within me. It's an ephemeral sensation, but it's very real. In fact, it's a very nice sensation. Without a doubt.

WHAT IS ACTION DOCUMENTARY?

I wish life were filled with such moments, but it's not; they never occur under normal circumstances. That's why we decide to make yet another film, to search for something more dramatic. These moments can't possibly occur in your everyday life. There's no way.

Tsuchimoto Norikai once said that the act of making a film is like going into labor. The crew debates, gets drunk, pulls sleepless nights, and argues tooth and nail for the entire nine months; then, in an instant, you go through labor and give birth to the film. The work of making a documentary film is a kind of living creature.

I like action films, so I often use the phrase "action documentary." What I mean is this: Let's say I begin by initiating things, as I did in the early stages of my relationships with Takeda Miyuki and the people with disabilities. Those who are provoked take in my words and filter them through their bodies, then take action. I believe that to take action with your body means to see things that you would otherwise not be able to see—and to see things is better than not to see things.

The flip side of this is that I also want to be provoked. All the time. I want to keep my body in action and thoroughly examine what becomes visible as a result. I want to see a lot of things, but for that to happen, I need to be stirred up. I need to have stimulation injected into my body. I want to take action with my body, because a body that takes action is a wonderful thing. There's a whole world out there that can only be seen through action, and I want to see that world.

Therefore, our films are not action movies: they are action itself. We want to see what will unfold when the camera takes action, when bodies take action. Our films don't just depict actions; our act of making films is nothing less than action itself. That's the ideal that I always have in mind.

Ultimately, since we're Japanese, we spend Japanese money and make films in Japan. So people classify our films as Japanese films. But we got started in a place outside of the "film industry," so all we have to rely on is ourselves. It's true that we've been influenced by Ogawa's films, Ogawa Productions' films, Tsuchimoto's *Minamata* series, and television documentaries from that period. Such works have influenced us quite a bit. But our decision to actually start making films was merely an extension of what we'd already been doing—that is, searching for ourselves in the era. I mean, we had no teachers; nor did we become filmmakers in order to overcome something we'd been taught. For us, filmmaking has been, more than anything else, a kind of self-pursuit. I think that best describes how we feel about it.

So while there are moments when we wonder about what roles we have played or will play—or what place our films might occupy—in the history of cinema, thinking about such things is rather futile. Also, I feel that most film critics regard our films as oddities. That's fine by me, and it's certainly true that we are rather "odd" in the world of cinema, that we're never orthodox. We know the place we've been assigned to—that of being on the margins, of brewing up "unusual" things. Nothing more is expected of us. So of course we have a sort of so-what attitude towards all that.

For example, the director Shindō Kaneto has said that making a film while being intensely conscious of a certain filmmaker is to kill that filmmaker.[6] The filmmaker to be killed in his case was undoubtedly Mizoguchi Kenji, but I've never felt that I had to do anything like that.[7] On the other hand, I'm not so cool as to say, "I go my own way."

Also, the kinds of films I like watching are different from those I make. I love to watch action films, films for pure entertainment, so I watch those kinds of films all the time. However, would I want to develop my filmmaking technique in order to make such films? Well, that's a whole different story.

Which means, I guess, that I shouldn't be talking about these kinds of things. I bet someone someday will talk about how this means this and that means that.

6 Shindō Kaneto (1912–): Filmmaker. *Children of Hiroshima* and others.

7 Mizoguchi Kenji (1898–1956): Filmmaker. *The Life of Oharu*, *Ugetsu*, and others.

Still, I can't help feeling that people look at me as if I were some kind of a freak.

MASCULINITY AND FEMININITY

Kobayashi Sachiko tells me that I'm not masculine. She really does; she says that I'm not at all manly. So the male principle, or the patriarchal principle, is probably completely missing in me. She, on the other hand, is rather manly. So together we become neutral; we even each other out...

As for Takeda Miyuki, she was definitely more masculine than I was. That's true. I hear that Inoue had his masculine side and his feminine side, but I think I saw more of his feminine side.

And Okuzaki is feminine. In his gestures, for example. Also in the way his emotions would shift.

However, even though he had his feminine side, Okuzaki had a very patriarchal side to him as well. That's what my battle against him consisted of; that's why I couldn't call him "sensei." If I did, I'd have lost. But he tried his utmost to make me do so. And this battle developed into a struggle over who had power over the film. It was, fundamentally, a battle over who was going to succumb to who's authority—namely, whether Okuzaki could subjugate us, the filmmakers, to his will, to his own emperor system.

On a conscious level, Okuzaki hinted at the fact that he would reject anything that seemed like "male-chauvinism." This was because he had hung out with members of the All-Campus Joint Struggle Committee. They had approached him in the context of the struggle against the emperor system, and while hanging around with them, Okuzaki had picked up their jargon. So, for example, he would call his own wife "kimi" for ideological reasons.[8]

8 *kimi*: A form of "you" that, when used towards one's wife or someone close, implies the equality of the speaker and the person being addressed. Traditionally, Japanese men would call their wives "*omae*," implying the superiority of the speaker.

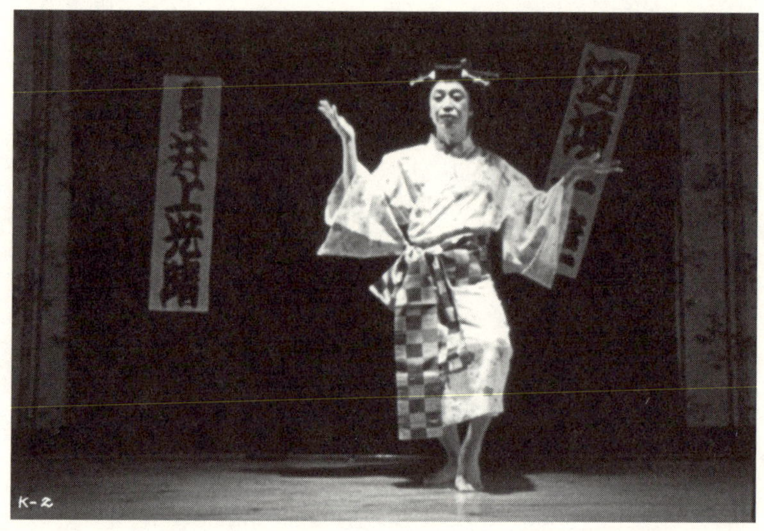

I think Inoue showed more of his "feminine side" to me.
Inoue Mitsuharu dancing, dressed as a woman.

Along these lines, whenever I would call my assistants simply by their family names, Okuzaki would protest, saying, "Mr. Hara, why do you call them without saying 'Mr.' or 'Ms.'? Shouldn't you be a little more polite to them?" That was the kind of "sensibility" he'd acquired by hanging out with student activists. But the true Okuzaki definitely had a streak of "male-chauvinism," which would suddenly manifest itself when, for example, he would demand authoritatively, "Just obey me!" That was another side of him.

To give you another example of Okuzaki's unique way of thinking: in the wedding ceremony scene in *The Emperor's Naked Army Marches On,* Okuzaki didn't want to be the go-between for the ceremony. He agreed to do it on the condition that we be allowed to shoot the ceremony for the film.

Okuzaki, who was about to start work on the film, had probably calculated that a wedding ceremony would be an ideal platform from which to declare his dedication to his cause. And things went exactly as he had planned. His speech was flawless. It seemed as if we had arranged everything just for the film. So Okuzaki's "sense," when it worked out, made for some interesting scenes.

Also, he had no intention of murdering his company commander when we began shooting the film. He discovered his target in the middle of the shoot, then took off after it in a blaze. I think he thought that if he didn't take things to the limit, the film would lack its finishing touch: the black dot in the eye of the dragon.

But strangely enough, part of Okuzaki didn't care if the film didn't have the actual scene of him achieving his goal. It's really strange; in the end, he didn't ask a second time for me to film him committing the murder. However, he knew full well the powerful influence that his committing such an act would have. He figured that, even without the final act, the film would have sufficient cinematic value as long as it contained the process of him preparing to commit murder. It may have been the store-owner in him that made such calculations. His shop may have been a small one, but he'd been running it for quite a while. His reckonings about such materialistic matters were quite accurate. He had a very good sense of balance.

That's why he could keep the shop afloat. Also, he lived very modestly, because there were only two of them, him and his wife.

He said that his sales had increased because he had shot pachinko balls at the emperor. And this was apparently true. Some people hung out with him just because they found him entertaining. Ordinarily, he would never do anything radical to upset such people; in fact, he was very polite.

I'LL TAKE AN INDIVIDUAL OVER A COMMUNITY

In terms of subject matter, I tend to direct my camera at individuals who are sticking it out by themselves, not at gatherings or groups of people. I never intended this, but, in retrospect, that's definitely the pattern.

I feel that no group can escape the dynamics inherent to all groups. Speaking of groups, I'd always wanted to film a commune, so I tried to approach the workshops we shot for *A Dedicated Life* as if they were a kind of commune. But unfortunately, the workshop members weren't the kind of people who could cross swords with my camera as equals. I realized this as I was filming, so I abandoned the idea. Consequently, if you were to tell me that I deal with groups in *A Dedicated Life*, I'd say that though they do appear in the film, I didn't go far enough in examining their inherent logic.

That's because I realized that it would be impossible to really delve into the communal aspect of the workshop community with my camera. So I stopped. Instead, I pursued the "individual," which is what I've always done. The people from Inoue's workshop who did appear did so as "individuals." Naturally, a bit of the group dynamics seeped through, but our emphasis was on "individuals."

I want to try making a film about a group, but filming it would be meaningless if I weren't able to aim my camera at its dynamics. The choice of which group to film would also be absolutely critical. If

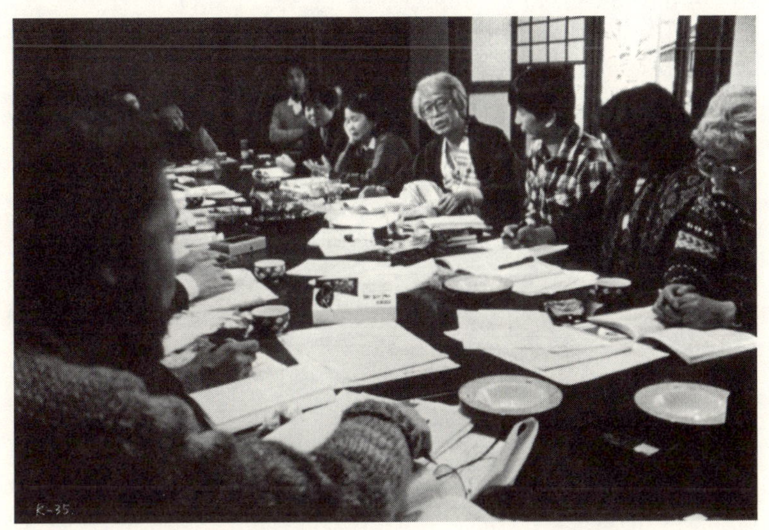

I realized I couldn't depict Inoue without filming his workshops.

I were to depict a collective, an organization, or a group involved in a social movement, then I'd also be dealing with the ideology of that movement. And let me tell you: I've actually been involved in such things a little bit myself, so I already know that I'd be exhausted even before I got around to making the film. My energy would be wasted. As such, I'm not... I'm not that interested.

To put it bluntly, it would be boring. I want to make films because I have my own romanticism about filmmaking, which I can share with the protagonists of my films. I'm sure a social movement has its own romanticism as well, but when you deal with a group that is too movement-oriented, you get worn out in too many ways. I can't find the energy to do that, so I'm not inspired to try.

Instead of a movement, I'd like to try filming an organization. Among the subjects that I would like to tackle one day are, for example, a religious organization and an organized crime group. While depicting the "individuals" within such organizations, I'd like to deal with their internal workings, their group dynamics. However, I've never yet encountered a group I've wanted to film, so I haven't yet made a film about a group, though I'd like to someday.

Ogawa went to Sanrizuka, then to a village in Yamagata. And I think I share something of the sensibility that drove him to make films about regional communities or groups.

The young guys at Ogawa Productions shot *Dokkoi! A Song of the Bottom* in Yokohama's Kotobuki-chō.[9] Nomoto Sankichi, the author on whose non-fiction book the film was based, actually asked me to join them. I even met Nomoto and talked with him for a bit in 1975 or thereabouts. I thought it was interesting. I think this was after I'd finished *Extreme Private Eros*.

This means that I was actually somewhat interested in making a film about a community at the time. Why didn't I do it? Because my energy had been utterly depleted.

But I do think that a time will come when I'll have to do an

9 Kotobuki-chō: a town in Yokohama with numerous cheap rooming houses, known for its large population of day laborers.

about-face and direct all my energy at communities. And even though I've primarily filmed individuals, in doing so, I've also paid attention to a variety of communities. In *Extreme Private Eros*, you see the Tokyo Commune. Through the lives of the former soldiers in *The Emperor's Naked Army Marches On*—in the history of post-war Japan, so to speak—you get a glimpse of our community, our nation. That was in the background of what we were consciously dealing with, at least. In the case of Inoue, there were his workshops. So it's not as though communities have been completely absent from our films. But our emphasis has been on the "individual" within those communities. One day, I'd like to shift the emphasis onto the communities themselves. I think that I'll finally face off against one in my next film, or the one after that; I feel that I'll have an opportunity some day to direct more of my energy in that direction.

A JAPAN WITHOUT AN ENEMY

These days, it's become incredibly difficult to see what needs to be attacked. Especially in Japan. This makes it difficult to make films as well.

But that's okay. I have one or two ideas that I want to tackle for the moment, that I think I'll be able to make into films. I have material to work with at least; I'm just racking my brains as to how to handle it.

Another thing is that I can't make up my mind about what kind of subject to shoot if I don't see it for myself. The only way I can know if something is workable or not is by taking a look at it. It's intuitive; I can't quite analyze it in words. So you're wrong if you think we decide on subjects by meeting people, researching their backgrounds, and then determining whether or not we can make a film about them. We're the kind of people who think that we should just start shooting if we find a subject we like. We shoot before we think. Part of me believes that we can't really determine whether or not a certain subject will work for one of our films unless we roll camera.

As far as documentary methodologies go, ours is fairly inefficient. But Tsuchimoto Noriaki has also written somewhere about beginning to shoot subjects that he thought would eventually be made into films, but that ended up grinding to a halt.

So if we're taken with a subject and want to make a film about it, the first thing we do is to start shooting. With film, money starts going out the window as soon as you start rolling camera, so it's not easy. But truth be told, you can't know about something unless you roll camera. There have been times when I've lost interest in something as soon as I started shooting it. When we filmed the gay guy that I mentioned earlier, for instance. I shot him once, and I didn't want to film him anymore. I'd had enough. Such things can happen.

But I think I utilize more footage in proportion to the amount of film we expose than others do. I rarely drop an entire scene. I've been good at not wasting too much.

In *A Dedicated Life*, however, there were a number of people whose interviews I didn't use at all. That was only because they weren't interesting. In general, though, I tend to use a good portion of what I shoot.

I've already talked about the reaction that the right-wingers had to *The Emperor's Naked Army Marches On*, but *A Dedicated Life* received a slew of reactions from people on the left who had their own preconceptions about Inoue as a leftist writer. Then there were those who thought that the Inoue portrayed in the film was quite different from the Inoue they knew. Some found the Inoue who appeared in the film to be quite interesting. Others, especially those who had a high opinion of his early literary writings, were puzzled and made negative comments to the effect that that his literary side had been totally neglected in the film. People were completely divided on this point.

In terms of the general public, the reactions from women have

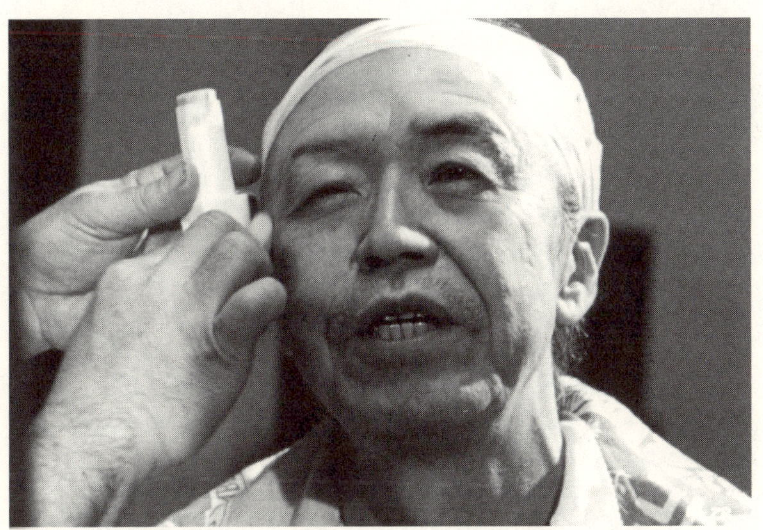

Some people have said that the Inoue they knew was different from the one in our film.

been the most extreme. I've learned that when women see the film, some will find it interesting, and others will loathe it. Some female critics have said in newspapers that they absolutely detested the film,

Quite a few elderly women got really excited when they saw the film. I mean, they were, so to speak, turned on by Inoue... Of course, that kind of thing came up in the film as well.

At the same time, some women were viscerally turned off by it all.

TOWARDS A FILM WITHOUT A SUPERHERO

By the way, I'm turning fifty this year. Fifty years old. I can't believe it myself.

Earlier, I told you about my son. The fact that my son died, that he killed himself, is an incredibly private matter. Therefore, even though this would inevitably mean getting extremely personal again, I think I'll have to think it through via the vehicle of a film.

Until I actually start making it, I won't have any idea how such a film would turn out. And although it's about an extremely personal matter, the protagonist will not be with us. So I won't be able to make the film the same way I've made my series of superhero films.

There's another thing I have to tackle. I touched on this earlier, but the reason why I keep going on and on about the '70s is because I feel that it's time to redefine that era. I believe that redefining the '70s will lead directly to redefining postwar democracy. In a more extreme sense, it will lead to redefining the entire Shōwa era.[10] And my own child's death feels like the most palpable starting point for such a project.

I said earlier that other members of my generation found themselves in the same situation we did vis-à-vis their children. I want to use this fact as a starting point for an examination of the

10 Shōwa era: The period corresponding to the reign of the Shōwa Emperor, Hirohito, from 1926–1989.

meaning of community, or the communality in which individuals live. I feel that this process has yet to begin, that it will only begin for myself if I begin making the film. So I have to search for a new way of making films that will be different from what I've done so far. It's something that I feel obliged to do.

I also want to make a narrative film. We say we like intense stuff, intense people, and intense events. So we're wondering how much intensity we'll be able to generate within the framework of a narrative film, of fiction. This idea relates to the film about women I talked about earlier.

Of course, my interest in action hasn't waned. Even in *A Dedicated Life*, we wanted to get involved with Inoue with that kind of intensity. We wanted to grapple with him, but the opportunity just slipped away from us. We think of our way of making films as a kind of battle. So we wonder: if we were to make a shift to narrative films, how would we fight? We've always given our flesh and blood to making documentaries. Now we'll be in a fictional space from the very beginning. So we wonder what's possible. But it's not as though we can know the answer to this in advance.

Therefore, my reasons for wanting to make a narrative film aren't all that profound. You don't have that much freedom in filmmaking, you know. And you have even less in documentary filmmaking. So I need to give vent to all my frustration, which has accumulated over the years.

Logically speaking, narrative films shouldn't be any freer than documentaries. I know that, but I still feel that you won't know whether or not the grass is greener on the other side of the fence unless you try to cross over. So we're going to try. That's closer to our true motive.

Our experience with making documentaries has shown us that the things you have to go through before you can roll camera, and also after you've gotten the footage... it's important, for sure, but it's also incredibly ridiculous in many ways. Honestly speaking, we would like to make a film for once without worrying about such things.

Furthermore, having made a film about Inoue, I feel that I've come to understand, if only slightly, what fiction is.

To quote Inoue, fiction is a way for you to say who you want to be, it's an expression of your desire for freedom. When he said that, I suddenly felt that I could tell actors how to act in a fictional scene. That's what I mean. An actor says "Good morning" simply because the script tells him or her to. The director has to make the actor say that line. Before, I had no idea what to tell actors—what sorts of facial expressions I should ask for, what sort of tone to tell them to use, that sort of thing. However, now that I've made the film about Inoue, I feel, however modestly, as though I could say to an actor: "Can you move like this next time?" That's why I feel like trying my hand at a narrative film. In order to understand anything beyond that, I'll have to actually do it. That's the only way.

The film that's supposed to begin with my child's story will be a separate film.

So I have two ideas. Two. You never know how these things will end up; production hasn't even begun. But I want to make both these films, no matter what. I don't know which one I'll do first, though. I'll take it easy and... I *can't* take it easy. Actually, I've got to hurry up a bit. I'm going on fifty. [Laughs.] Really.[11]

---

11 After completing *A Dedicated Life*, Hara went on to make the television documentary *My Mishima* (1999, with Cinema Juku), a film about the inhabitants of the island of Mishima, another television documentary about the filmmaker Urayama Kiriro, and his first narrative film, *The Many Faces of Chika* (2004), which follows the protagonist Chika through four different relationships during the political turbulence of the 1970s.

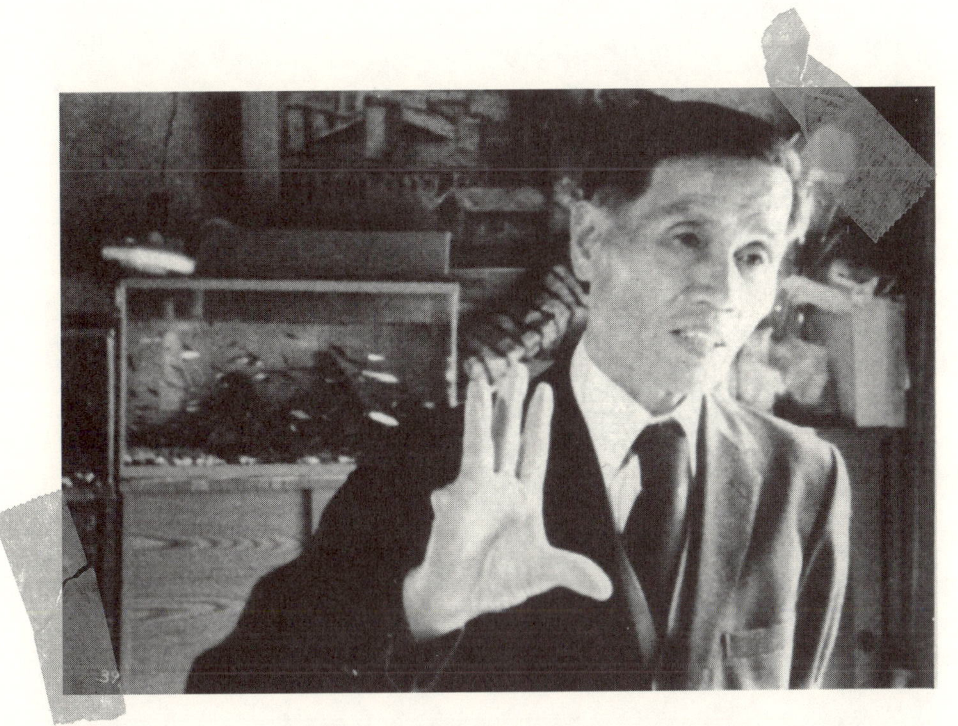

The Emperor's Naked Army Marches On Production Notes

Hara Kazuo

Introduction

When making a documentary, the events you don't capture on film are often more numerous than the ones you do. During the production of *The Emperor's Naked Army Marches On*, the number of scenes I was unable to capture was far greater than in my previous two films. I wanted to record everything, but for various reasons, I wasn't able to. With this film, I keenly realized for the first time that I wanted to speak of these "unrealized scenes."

When Mr. Ikeda, the editor-in-chief of the magazine *Image Forum*, called to ask me if I would write the "Production Notes" to the film, I promptly accepted his timely offer. I began by throwing into note form the anecdotes and events that had left me feeling less-than-satisfied or misled. I filled the pages, struggling to create a "structure" that had a single narrative flow. When I had nearly finished writing the promised 28,000 characters, I felt that there was still more to write. Once the release date for the film had been decided upon, I met with Mr. Yazaki about making these notes into a book that would also include the film's script. I restructured these materials to include the notes originally presented in *Image Forum*, a series of other anecdotes, and a section about our shoot in New Guinea.

Which is how these *Production Notes* came together. Much of what you can see in the film is left out here. I've written as best I could—and with as much honesty as possible—about what was happening *outside the frame*.

I wrote them as a document of us and of our involvement with this fascinating *subject* Okuzaki Kenzō.

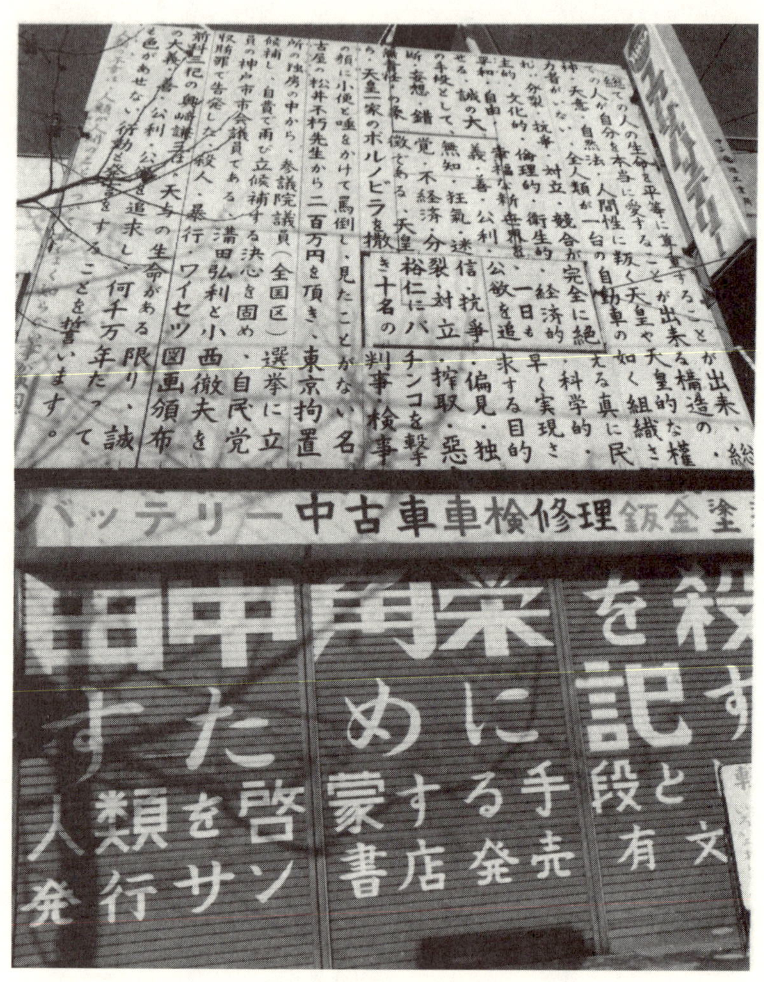

The exterior of Okuzaki's home.

Part 1 – At Home

MEETING OKUZAKI KENZŌ

"I'd like to meet Okuzaki Kenzō face to face."

"You would? Then I'll call and tell him you're coming. Give him this," Imamura Shōhei said. He wrote "Introducing Hara Kazuo" on his name card and gave it to me.

Several days before, Imamura had asked me, "Any interest in this?" and handed me Okuzaki Kenzō's thick, self-published tome luridly titled *Proclamation to Kill Prime Minister Tanaka Kakuei*. I read it and wanted to see what kind of person the author was.

In December of 1981, I went to Kobe with my friend, partner, and longtime producer at Shissō Productions, Kobayashi Sachiko. Okuzaki ran a shop that dealt with small cars and batteries in Kobe.

When I meet someone for the first time, it's normal for my heart to flutter from nerves; this was the man who had shot pachinko balls at the emperor, so I felt my heart screaming in my chest. The taxi we took from the station at Shin-Kobe arrived at our destination. The first thing that caught my eye when I got out of the taxi was a mass of large characters written above the entrance to the store. Within the ordered ambiance of this section of this ordinary city, standing in front of this sign, I felt a strange, vortex-like sensation.

Dropping my eyes from the billboard, I saw in the road in front of the store a man cleaning a rubber car mat with a scrubbing brush as water ran from a hose. He moved his body rhythmically, exuding the energy of a person busily working away. The strangeness of the cluster of written characters and the mundaneness of the man's work created a peculiar contrast. Kobayashi and I called awkwardly to him.

"I'm Okuzaki Kenzō," he said modestly, bowing deeply.

"I'm his wife," said a woman standing next to him. She appeared genuinely delighted by our visit and smiled.

"Please, come in," she said and guided us into the office.

Corrugated cardboard boxes and for-sale car batteries were piled everywhere. There was a single steel desk. It was a simple room, perhaps no larger than 150 square feet. It made me feel the vitality of the business itself. Okuzaki put away his work and began speaking to Kobayashi and me as we sat on round stools…

About five and a half years have passed since that first meeting. It's now July 1987, and I can't remember what Okuzaki said to us that day. But I do clearly remember that he started talking in the office, then said, "We're getting hungry, aren't we? Let's go get something to eat," and that we got into a car with a huge sign affixed to it that read, in enormous characters, "Yamazaki, Shoot the Emperor!" Also that Okuzaki continued to talk fervently as he was driving—and that even when the shrimp tempura over rice we had ordered arrived, he continued talking, as if he didn't even want to stop to pick up his chopsticks. At first, his tone had been normal, but soon enough, he was yapping away feverishly: the more he talked, the more animated he became. His spit cut through the air with such force that it flew right into our meal on the table.

With his jaw stretched out in an exaggerated manner, and his eyes sunk deeper than those of anyone I had ever seen before, he fixed his eyes on us, his face inches away. He wasn't just running off at the mouth; he spoke with an energy equal to the force of a waterfall. All Kobayashi and I could say was, "Oh. Hmm... Wow." His spirit absorbed the entire room. He wasn't all intensity, though. While talking, he would occasionally flash a strangely charming smile. His countenance, which resembled a "spirit wandering through the jungle," would change, reflecting something strangely friendly, mischievous, kind, and sweet. I thought his smiling face resembled that of the actor Noro Keisuke.[1] Looking back on it now, I think it might have been this smile of Okuzaki's that put me under his spell.

Night fell. He had spoken for about seven hours. He took us to the Shin-Kobe Station. We had finally been liberated from Okuzaki, who had talked up to the moment of our departure. Exhausted, our bodies

1 Noro Keisuke (1937–): Film and television actor.

sank into the seats of the bullet train heading back to Tokyo. But we were in high spirits. It wasn't clear who started talking first, but we found ourselves saying to each other, "Interesting, huh? Should we do this?" That was the start of our movie about Okuzaki Kenzō.

At the beginning of 1982, we visited Kobe a second time. "We'll do the the film," we said, but he still seemed only half convinced.

This had all started because Okuzaki had wanted Imamura Shōhei to make a film about him.

"What films have you made so far?" Okuzaki asked. I explained the overall gist of the two films we had made: *Goodbye* CP and *Extreme Private Eros: Love Song 1974*. I thought it best not to go into the content and themes of these films with him, since he had no reason to know anything about self-financed documentary filmmaking.

"Hmmm…" he replied vaguely. "Do you have any money?"

"No, none at the moment. We're just going to start making the film."

"Hmmm."

I emphasized the part about *going to make money*. "We'll put out a call for investors, 200,000 yen per unit," Kobayashi explained eagerly, giving the details of her plans to raise money.

"I see. I was going to turn down your offer to make a film if you were counting on my money, since I have none," he replied.

I secretly had been hoping that he would put up some funds, so I broke out in a cold sweat. "No, no. Don't be silly. We'll raise all the money for production," I stressed hastily. I realized that he had been wary of our intentions, suspecting that we were after his money.

"If you're making a film about me for my benefit, then I can't count on you for everything. I'll have to chip in something, too," he said with a slightly brighter expression. He told us that he would somehow come up with the money for his own activities.

On another of our many visits to Kobe, I happened to be alone with Okuzaki's wife. I asked her:

"Since when has Mr. Okuzaki been such a lively talker?"

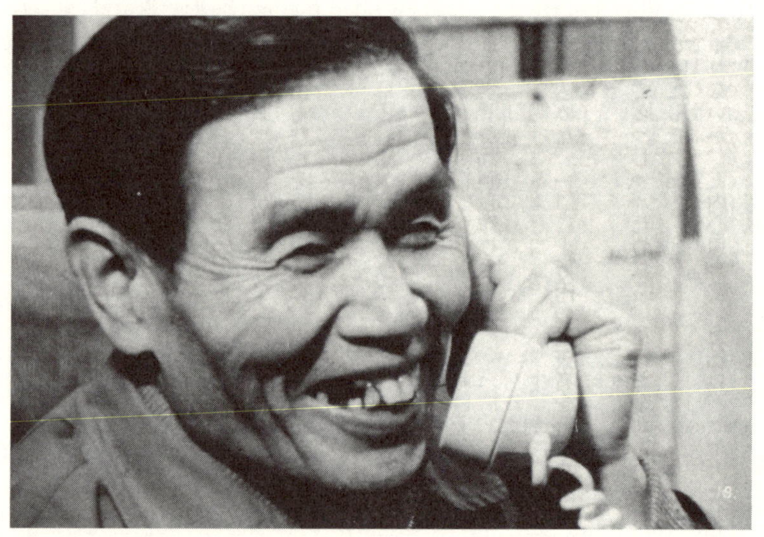

Okuzaki's strangely charming Noro Keisuke smile.

"Well, he killed that real estate agent and was put in solitary confinement for ten years. It was after that. He hardly spoke until then. He was incredibly quiet, didn't say a word. Yeah. Then he started talking, just like that. I was completely shocked."

I, too, was shocked. Had ten years in solitary confinement changed his personality that drastically?

ACTION!

"I want to go to New Guinea."

That was Okuzaki's wish.

We began research immediately. Okuzaki's 36th Special Engineer Corps retreated across the island of New Guinea from east to west. In other words, it crossed the border between what was then known as New Guinea and Irian Jaya. Getting into New Guinea was easy; the problem was getting into Irian Jaya, which is part of Indonesia. A former member of Waseda University's Expedition Club who was familiar with local affairs there told us that a guerilla war being waged by the People's Liberation Front had broken out in the region Okuzaki wanted to visit, so there was no way we could get a permit to enter the area. He said that it would be 200 percent impossible to get permission to bring a 16-mm camera into Irian Jaya to begin with. I was hoping to get footage of a small village in the middle of the Arso jungle where, in 1944, Okuzaki's 36th Special Engineer Corps had collapsed and scattered; I also wanted to shoot the village of Demta, where Okuzaki had been imprisoned. When I showed Okuzaki the reports about the current guerilla war I had collected, he said, with no consideration for my concerns:

"Mr. Hara, I'll cross the border. To me, a border is not worth a fart. I want to interview the guerillas; I'll tell them to stop the war. My philosophy doesn't accept people killing one another. I'll say, 'Off I go!' and go from New Guinea to the edge of the jungle, until I reach those villages. I want you to shoot that scene."

Dumbfounded, I quickly replied, "If you do that, I'm going with you. I can't let you go alone. I'll shoot an interview with the guerillas as well."

Thinking rather irresponsibly about how amazing it would be to shoot a scene of a World War II veteran interviewing guerillas about war, and also feeling that I couldn't turn my back on Okuzaki at such a time, I spoke with bravado. It was as though I'd been sucked in by his beaming, innocent smile. But deep in my heart, I knew that trying to cross the border would be quite risky.

Okuzaki said he would write a letter directly to the president of Indonesia asking for permission to enter Arso and Demta. There was no harm in trying. Shooting on the film began with Okuzaki reading his letter aloud to the camera.

A WEDDING FOR THE "PUBLIC INTEREST"

"Mr. Hara, there's a scene I'd like you to shoot," Okuzaki said hastily over the phone. He said he'd been asked to be the go-between at a wedding, and he wanted me to film the ceremony.[2]

"I already told the couple that if you agreed to shoot it, I'd agree to be their go-between. Day in and day out, I'm always thinking about all humankind. Using the ceremony as an opportunity for me to speak in front of the camera would make this wedding a special one, you know. Weddings are for personal happiness, for self-interest. But I never act out of self-interest; I always act for the 'public interest.' Thus, I'll be speaking for the 'public interest,' and if it's a wedding for the 'public interest,' I'll be the go-between. A wedding ceremony for the 'public interest'—there's never been anything like it before."

He didn't wish for the happiness of the groom or bride; he wanted

---

2 "go-between": In Japanese weddings, the go-between is typically an esteemed older person or couple responsible for arranging the marriage between the bride and groom. The "go-between" may arrange a formal introduction for the prospective bride and groom before their engagement, and during the wedding reception, will often introduce the bride and groom and their family backgrounds to their guests. Similar to a matchmaker.

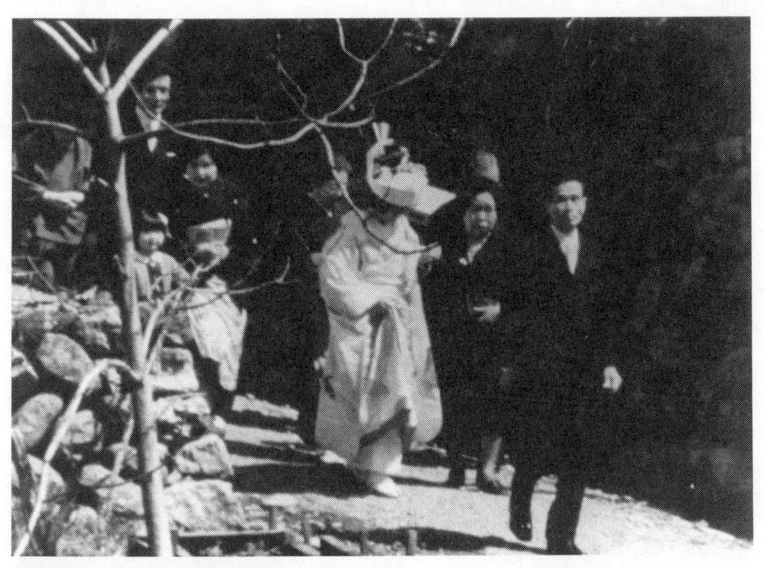

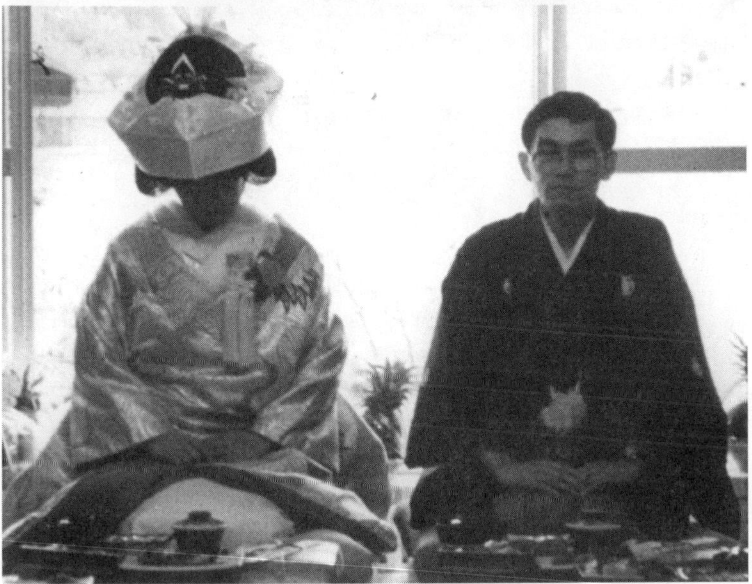

A wedding that could boast Okuzaki Kenzō as a go-between was indeed unique.

to use the wedding as a stage on which he express own thoughts. There definitely could be no other go-between like Okuzaki. At the same time, I was curious to know what kind of people would ask Okuzaki to play this kind of role for them.

Ōtagaki Toshikazu, a former member of Kobe University's faction of the All-Campus Joint Struggle Committee, had been arrested once for throwing a Molotov cocktail in Okinawa. He was now a farmer living deep in the rural mountainous Chūgoku region of Hyogo Prefecture. Though he was going on 40, he was still single. One day, attracted by Okuzaki's sign with its "mass of characters," Ōtagaki went into Okuzaki's store and bought a used car. The two hit it off from the start, and talked through the night. Ōtagaki told Okuzaki that he had no parents, so Okuzaki put up a "wife wanted" sign on the storefront's front shutter. He was sure that no one would ever respond to it, but someone did. She was about the same age as Ōtagaki, and had never been married. A wish fulfilled. The Okuzakis had presided over an arranged meeting for the couple at a city restaurant. And so it had been happily decided upon without a hitch...

I thought it was an interesting encounter. As I listened to Okuzaki talk, I was thinking that I wanted to shoot it as beautifully as I could. I consented to shoot the scene. Okuzaki's voice lit up on the other end of the phone.

As for the part I shot at the wedding and later edited out, it was the footage of Okuzaki saying, "Through the introduction of the famous director Imamura Shōhei of *Vengence is Mine* and *Why Not?*, we have, filming us here today, Hara Kazuo of Shissō Productions..." He kept repeating that phrase "introduced by the famous Imamura Shōhei" during his explanation of his protest on the emperor's birthday, and, later on, in the congratulatory speech of his lawyer, Endō Makoto. Every time he did so, I would be made aware of the fact that he would have preferred that famous Imamura Shōhei to some unknown punk like me. I could brush this off the first time with a wry smile, but after the second or third time, it truly bummed me out.

OKUZAKI'S EXCESSIVE "PERFORMANCE"

After the wedding scene, we shot Okuzaki visiting both his maternal ancestors' graves in the town of Izushi in Hyogo Prefecture, and his paternal ancestors' graves in Miki City, which is also in Hyogo. (We later cut these scenes when editing). We then returned to Kobe.

The following day, we headed to the Kobe Detention Center.

"I think I'm going to build a 'solitary cell' on the roof of my house," Okuzaki said, and I went along with this idea.

Okuzaki had been forced by the authorities to spend ten years in solitary for manslaughter, despite his insistence that he'd done nothing wrong since he'd never intended to kill the real estate agent. This ten-year-long confinement had only led to Okuzaki's realization that his true target was the emperor. After being released from prison, he shot pachinko balls at the emperor and went straight back to solitary confinement. His ponderings grew even deeper as he rested his mind and body. Upon being released for a second time, he was arrested for passing out pornographic handbills of the imperial family, ending up back in prison for a third time. After a brief respite, he was released again. This time, he'd decided to target Prime Minister Tanaka Kakuei. He was subsequently arrested for conspiracy to murder, but was never prosecuted. Then, while considering this and that, and with no distinct idea of what to do next, he met us.

I was still debating with myself about how to present Okuzaki's criminal history, so I thought that this scene of him building a replica of his "solitary confinement" cell might be a good starting point. I could picture Okuzaki thinking in the "solitary cell" he'd built himself. That was a scene right there! Could I get an aerial shot of it? If so, I would also get an aerial shot of Osaka Prison, a real prison built by the state, which I could then use to contrast against Okuzaki's "solitary cell." It might not be half bad!

At around this time, I remember Okuzaki saying sincerely,

but with a bashful smile, "I hate religion, but I'm thinking of establishing a religion that worships the universe, nature, and the gods that I advocate. It could be called 'Okuzaki-ism.'"

A shrine of "Okuzaki-ism?" The altar could read, "Solitary Confinement." It would be great! It had the potential to be a great last scene, I thought, letting my imagination run wild.

We wanted to draw up a blueprint of an actual cell as a reference for the one we would build for the film, so we paid a visit to the Kobe Detention Center. I was, of course, planning to shoot Okuzaki requesting permission to measure the cell; then I would film him making the actual measurements. But a handful of prison guards came rushing out as soon as I tried to set up a tripod in order to get a shot of Okuzaki's car arriving at the Kobe Detention Center. The back and forth between the prison guards, who demanded that we shoot only after getting permission, and Okuzaki, who insisted that we wanted to shoot him *while* he was getting permission, had begun.

After I shot Okuzaki yelling at the prison guards, I interviewed him against a long shot of the prison in the background.

I was stunned by the words that came from his mouth. The first thing he said was, "How was my performance?"

What!? His anger had been a performance!?

Laughing, he'd continued, "Yesterday, I didn't get enough sleep because I had to entertain you and your staff. I've been running around ever since the wedding ceremony, which has only added to my exhaustion. Those prison guards were the perfect target."

Again. What?! The prison guards had been sacrificed to Okuzaki in our place? To save money on lodgings—actually, since we had no money for lodgings—Okuzaki had put us up in his home, and he and his wife had given us the royal treatment. Okuzaki in particular had gone all out. I believed him when he said he was tired because of his relentless hospitality towards us. True, I hated the super-arrogant attitude of the prison guards, but if he had yelled at them on our account, I couldn't help but feel a slight sense of sympathy for them. Still, what could I do?

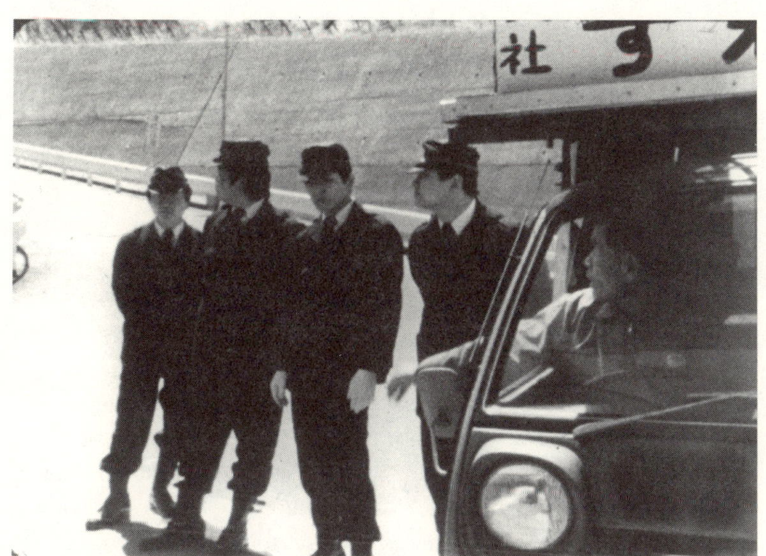

The prison guards at the Kobe Detention Center were unwittingly sacrificed to Okuzaki's irritability and fatigue.

But he had called it "acting." Come to think of it...

Okuzaki, who had gone alone to negotiate with the guards, had driven slowly back over to us. I'd greeted him with the camera rolling.

The buzzing camera seemed to be waiting for something to happen in Okuzaki's eyes. After a brief silence, Okuzaki had started to yell. But there had been something unnatural about this. I remember feeling that the refrain he kept on repeating—"If you're a human being, get angry! Get mad!"—was not particularly well-suited to the situation. Now I see that this *lack of clarity* had perhaps been due to the fact that he had been "performing."

Since then, I've been repeatedly annoyed by Okuzaki's "performances." I was really fed up with the excessive "performance" in everything he did.

THE CAMEO APPEARANCE OF A PATROL CAR

Okuzaki wanted to go to New Guinea with ex-Sergeant Yamada Kichitarō. In order to persuade Yamada, we went to visit him in Fukaya City in Saitama Prefecture.

An unmarked police car began tailing us as soon as we left Kobe. As we drove on the Meishin and Tōmei Highways, every time we entered a new prefecture, from Kobe to Nagoya to Tokyo, a new patrol car would tail us. When we entered the Tokyo city limits, we noticed that we were now being tailed by a Tokyo Metropolitan police car. That evening, we set Okuzaki up at a business hotel in Shinjuku and sent the crew home.

Advice that had been given to me by an older cameraman rang in my ears. He told me that he'd snuck a camera into the courtrom and had secretly filmed Okuzaki during his trial for slinging pachinko balls at the emperor. After that, cops had staked out his house around the clock, following him wherever he went. When he learned that we were going to make a film about Okuzaki, he had warned me to beware of the police. Frankly speaking, I got a little freaked out; it was creepy. After leaving Okuzaki, I went home and timidly peered through my window into the ominous darkness of the night. No one was out there, but I wasn't able to relax.

The following morning, we met up and took off. I immediately noticed the unmarked police car from the day before behind us.

We arrived at the Red Cross Hospital in Fukaya City where ex-Sergeant Yamada Kichitarō had been admitted.

I thought it necessary to get a shot of Okuzaki's car arriving at the hospital. As I was setting up the camera, I was suddenly struck by an idea. I thought there was no way permission would be granted, but what did I have to lose? Maybe my fear, working in reverse, had made me desperate enough to want to provoke the police. I took the idea to Okuzaki.

"I want to shoot a scene of your car arriving at the hospital. And if we're going to do that, we might as well have the patrol car make a special appearance."

Okuzaki nodded and went over to the unmarked police car. I followed a few paces behind him. He said a word or two, in response to which the detectives smiled. What? Okay?! We were somewhat disappointed at how readily they had agreed. Still, my young crew was delighted and amused. We set up the camera so we could get a shot of Okuzaki's car as well as the unmarked police car. I told the assistant director the distance between the two cars and their respective speeds. As I looked through the viewfinder, I made the AD run over to ask if the detectives would mind turning on their patrol lights. "Maybe I got a little carried away," I thought, feeling some regret. But when I saw the AD give me the OK sign and head back, my mood instantly improved with the excitement of shooting an action sequence.

"Okay. Action!"

Okuzaki's car and the unmarked police car started to move past the camera. The first take was good to go!

Immediately after the shoot, we exchanged greetings and

chatted with the detectives. They treated Okuzaki politely and with friendliness. This was probably a technique they used knowing that, given Okuzaki's character, it would make getting information from him easier. I knew that we were being treated in the same manner for the same reasons, but talking with them face-to-face made us feel better than being watched from the shadows on a stakeout.

A VISIT TO EX-SERGEANT YAMADA KICHITARŌ'S SICKBED

I met with Sergeant Yamada Kichitarō a number of times in order to gather information for the movie. He had compiled voluminous records on the 36th Special Engineers Corps. Okuzaki had a fondness for and sense of camaraderie with Yamada that he had for no one else. Because Okuzaki had been captured a year before hostilities were brought to an end, he'd managed to avoid the "hell that was the New Guinea War." But Yamada had wandered around in the thick of it for over a year, just trying to stay alive.

Okuzaki's vitality, as expressed in his book *Yamazaki, Shoot the Emperor!* was phenomenal, but the vitality of someone who'd been able to survive the vortex of that hell, was also something to behold. Yamada and Okuzaki had been dramatically reunited in March 1946 on a repatriation boat from Sydney back to Japan. Yamada was a somewhat diminutive, good-natured man, but as he himself said, he had extraordinary reflexes and instincts. And he'd been able to survive the hell of the battlefield. After the war, he had excelled at catching birds and fish, and had in fact been able to send his children to college using money he'd made with those skills.

I wanted to make a movie that captured the postwar lives of both Yamada and Okuzaki. They stood in complete contrast to one another. One was an "equal soldier in God's army" who was taking on the entire nation all by himself, and the other was an ordinary man who sought peace and worked himself to the bone caring for his family. I wanted to get a shot of Yamada surrounded by his children

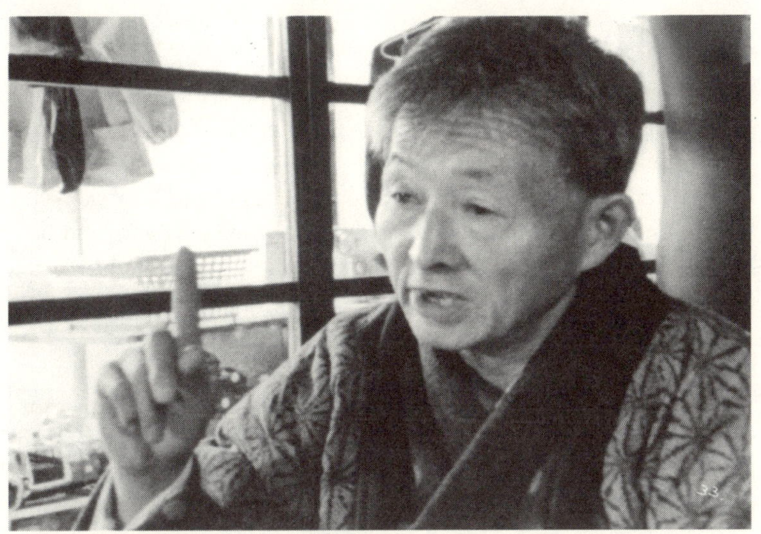

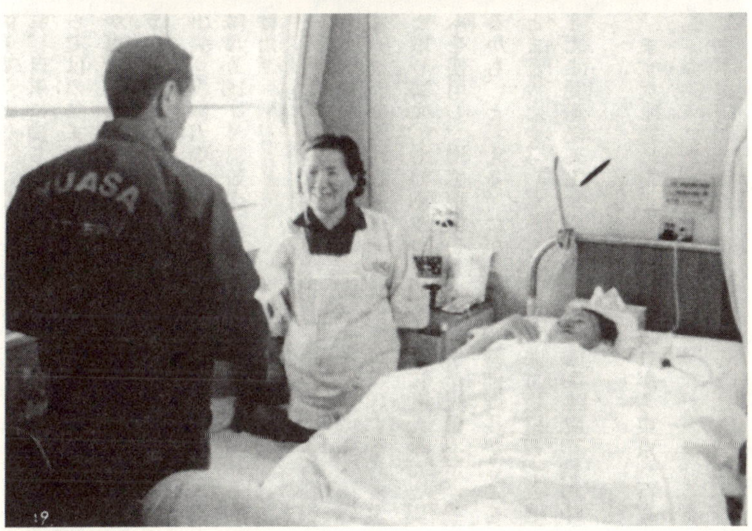

Out of the main force of the 36th regiment,
only Okuzaki and ex-Sergeant Yamada Kichitarō survived

and grandchildren that would, in the structure of the film, function as the polar opposite to images of Okuzaki. I wanted to etch the postwar experiences of all the members of the 36th Special Engineer Corps in the charged field that existed between the lives of these two former soldiers.

The endless work of postwar life must have been impossible for even Yamada Kichitarō to bear. It had weakened his body, and he'd been hospitalized at the Red Cross Hospital in Fukaya City in Saitama Prefecture.

I filmed Okuzaki visiting Yamada to convince him to go to New Guinea with him.

In trying to persuade Yamada, Okuzaki revealed his "theory of heavenly retribution." Okuzaki, who was healthy, told the bed-ridden Yamada Kichitarō, "The reason why you're in this poor physical condition is because of 'heavenly retribution.'" This phrase, "heavenly retribution," shocked the film crew. "He has no consideration for the sick." "He's too insensitive towards those who are less fortunate than him." "What selfish logic." "He's inhuman." General consensus leaned towards hating Okuzaki who, with that one phrase, had upset our morally based solicitude for the sick. Kobayashi Sachiko, the film's producer, disagreed: "We wouldn't normally tell a sick person that their condition was the result of 'heavenly retribution,' but I think that a person who can say such things makes for an interesting human being." She said that Okuzaki was an attractive protagonist for a film *because* of the kind of person he was; he made us think of the many facets there were to humanity. However, the crew's antipathy toward Okuzaki was already fixed.

A SECRET SHOT OF THE HYOGO POLICE DEPARTMENT'S CHIEF OF SURVEILLANCE

"Hara, there's a scene I really want you to film..." Okuzaki broached to me one day.

"I'd like you to shoot a scene of me talking to the person from the Hyogo Police Department who's in charge of me. People who watch the film will understand the kind of person I am if they see such a scene. The police keep an eye on me around the clock. When I go to Tokyo, the Metropolitan Police Department is contacted, and they tail me the whole way in an unmarked police car. The police are always bothering me. This time, I want to beat them at their own game."

"I see. But how would we go about doing this?"

I had absolutely no idea how to shoot such a scene.

"I'm going to install a one-way mirror here, so shoot it from here."

Next to the office in Okuzaki's store was a stairwell that went to the second floor. I went in and noticed that only a thin board divided the stairwell from the office. That's where Okuzaki was going to install a one-way mirror. Okuzaki had already determined what the camera position would be. This wounded my pride, and I was annoyed at his peremptory tone, but I was impressed by his idea. It was the kind of thing that only Okuzaki, who was used to the police, could have cooked up. From the position he'd indicated, I'd be able to capture a face-to-face meeting between Okuzaki and the Chief of Surveillance from the Hyogo Police Department.

"But the one-way mirror absorbs light, so the shot will be too dark. And we can't put up lights..." I protested.

"OK, I'll use brighter fluorescent lights," he replied nonchalantly.

On my next visit to Kobe, Okuzaki brought me into the office as if he'd been waiting impatiently for chance to do so. The one-way mirror had been mounted. As I was looking at it, impressed, he turned on a light switch in the corner of the room. Fluorescent bulbs lit up. It was dazzling, considerably brighter than it had been before. He explained that he'd replaced all of the bulbs with new ones that were double the wattage. I took out my light meter and took a reading. Even if I used high-speed film and pushed the stock, the light level was still inadequate. It was two stops short. On the other hand, I thought, that might lend an air of realism to the scene.

Then I thought: wait a second. This probably won't be the first time the police chief will have come here. Even I had been confused by all this light. In addition, a mirror had suddenly been put up on a wall of planks. He's a pro: he'll have to realize it's a one-way mirror. I felt uneasy. But at that point, I couldn't say that I wasn't going to go through with the scene.

Okuzaki explained how he planned to direct the scene: "I'll call the Hyogo Police Department. When I tell them I'm going to Tokyo, the Chief of Surveillance will come over," he said with the utmost confidence.

Our operation to secretly film the police chief had begun. First, I filmed Okuzaki calling the police department. The first time he did so, the police chief wasn't in. An hour later, he tried again. This time he was there. Just as Okuzaki had anticipated, the Chief of Surveillance said he was coming over. My crew and I waited behind the one-way mirror holding our breath. Our hearts raced. In no time, we heard the chief's footsteps.

We shot twenty-one minutes in a single take with a 400-foot film magazine. Okuzaki was unparalleled against the police chief; I could only take my hat off. In the way he responded to the police chief's questioning, too. He was a fine actor indeed.

PERFORMING A "MEMORIAL SERVICE" IN FRONT OF THE IMPERIAL PALACE

It was decided that we would shoot Okuzaki performing his memorial service on the emperor's birthday in Tokyo. We left Kobe on April 28th, the day before the service, and stayed in a hotel in Shibuya. I have reprinted the journal entry from the 29th. (Assistant Director Yasuoka recorded these notes.)

APRIL 29TH: Cloudy with occasional light showers

09:00 — Shibuya. Crew assembled at Tobu Hotel.

After preparing the camera and equipment, knocked on room 636, Okuzaki's room.

Verified such things as:
- Must take the shortest possible route to the Imperial Palace because the reception of public congratulations for the emperor's birthday ends at 11 am.
- Contact the press. Could only get in touch with Kyodo News. The evening edition has been suspended for the day, so many newspaper correspondents are absent.
- A plain-clothed detective has been genially asking anyone he can get his hands on, including Okuzaki, about our route.

10:05—Left Tobu Hotel. Sound technician Kuribayashi got into Okuzaki's Mark II to set up the public address system. Because of time constraints, he set up the PA while we were on the move. The crew's Cedric was supposed to lead the way until we got to the vicinity of the Imperial Palace. When we turned onto one of the streets Okuzaki was familiar with, his Mark II was supposed to go ahead of us.[3]

Two unmarked police cars followed us.

We took the route from Shibuya to Tameike, then from Tameike to Toranomon. Just in front of Toranomon, Hara stopped the cars to verify the route with Okuzaki. Hara went over to Okuzaki's car. Plain-clothed detectives stood listening near where they were talking. When they heard Hara say the words, "Imperial Palace," their attitudes suddenly changed. They took off in a hurry.

10:30 — Turned left at Toranomon. Upon heading towards Sakuradamon, the Mark II passed the Cedric and took the lead. One of the two unmarked police cars that had been tailing us sped up furiously behind the Mark II, passed it, and pulled it over. Filmed Okuzaki in his car talking to the plain-clothes detectives. He dodged the detectives' questions about where he was going. The Mark II began moving again. Turned right

3 "Mark II" and "Cedric": Car models. The Mark II is a Toyota and the Cedric is a Nissan.

at Sakuradamon and headed toward Shimbashi.

10:40 — As the police car and the Mark II battled for the lead, they turned onto Sotobori-dori in front of the Shimbashi Dai-ichi Hotel. At the Sukiyabashi intersection, the Mark II took the lead. It turned left and headed straight for the Imperial Palace on Harumi-dori.

10:45 — As the Mark II was aiming for Iwaidabashi and Sakuradamon, an unmarked police car overtook it at the Hibya intersection and pulled it over. In a flash, riot police had set up a barricade with their vehicles. Okuzaki was surrounded by police officers in uniform.

Okuzaki began his "Memorial Service." From the speakers atop the Mark II, Chopin's "Funeral March" rang out. Okuzaki's agit-prop had begun. Kuribayashi recorded from within the Mark II.

11:30 — Okuzaki arrested. He seemed to talk on and on. Then, when he got tired of speaking, he got out of the car and went with the police. Hara and Kuribayashi caught up with him and filmed. Yasuoka and Ōmiya were stopped by the police: Ōmiya at the Mark II, Yasuoka at the Cedric. Both were held there. The police asked them for identification. Takamura left the scene to shoot it from a bird's-eye view. After Yasuoka, Ōmiya, and Takamura met up again, they were led to a patrol car and taken to the Marunouchi Police Department.

12:15 — Okuzaki interrogated. Hara and Kuribayashi are also asked to come to the police department for questioning.

Hara's interrogation is nothing more than a "greeting," but they take a statement from Kuribayashi, since he was riding in Okuzaki's Mark II. They try to get Kuribayashi to admit that he was participating in a joint conspiracy with Okuzaki, but he denies it.

> 14:05 — Okuzaki is released.We interview him in front of the Marunouchi Police Station, asking him to comment on his release. He is puffed up with pride. He thanks the crew for the success of today's "Memorial Service."
>
> After Okuzaki, Kuribayashi comes out from his interrogation. Together, we all leave the Marunouchi police department. A single unmarked car follows.
>
> 14:55 — We eat at a Japanese restaurant in Udagawa-cho, Shibuya. Okuzaki congratulates everyone on the success of the "Memorial Service" and treats everyone to lunch.
>
> 16: 05 — We leave Shibuya and see Okuzaki's Mark II off as far as the freeway entrance at Ikejiri. He turns around and says, "Thank you very much," to the unmarked police car. The detective says, "You've had a long day, huh?" and turns back.
>
> 17:05 — Arrive at Shissō Productions.

The fact that Kuribayashi ended up riding in Okuzaki's car happened by chance, but it brought us both "misfortune" and "happiness." When Okuzaki had been stopped at the Hibiya crossing on his way to the Imperial Palace, he had no intention of getting out of his car. He knew that if he stepped out, he would be arrested and taken in. For Okuzaki, his Mark II was his "fortress." Kuribayashi, who looked as though he were trapped there, was lucky; the noise coming from Okuzaki's speaker was so distorted that if he had recorded it from outside the car, it probably wouldn't have been usable in the film. Since he was inside the "fortress," he'd been able to get a good recording. On the other hand, since Kuribayashi had been with Okuzaki ever since we'd left Shibuya, he was suspected of being Okuzaki's "accomplice."

While I was being interrogated, the person questioning me said, half jokingly, "Please don't just film people who resist the system like Mr. Okuzaki. There are a number of good people amongst the police. Next time, I'll introduce you to one of them. Please make a movie about upstanding citizens like us."

Kuribayashi had a hard time clearing himself of suspicion. After this incident, the police would visit his home whenever something happened. Since I'm the one responsible for any trouble that occurs to the crew on set, I apologized to Kuribayashi. Being a crew member on "Okuzaki's film" was not easy!

"MY BROTHER WAS EXECUTED"

While shooting these scenes, we sought out some soldiers' homes and visited their relatives.

In order to find Iseko, the mother of Private Shimamoto Masayuki, Okuzaki's only war buddy, and the soldier whose body Okuzaki had buried in the village of Arso, we relied on a list of names of people from the 36th Special Engineer Corps that we had borrowed from Yamada Kichitarō. Shimamoto's mother had a slight build, but was full of energy; she was a down-to-earth, friendly old lady. She warmly welcomed our sudden visit.

"Yesterday, I had a dream about Masayuki. He must have been telling me of your visit today."

She said it was strange, since she hadn't had a dream about her son for years. She was a kind woman.

Private Yoshizawa Tetsunosuke's younger sister, Sakimoto Rinko, said the same thing when we visited her in Funabashi City in Chiba Prefecture.

"Yesterday, I had a dream of my brother. I haven't had a dream about him in years. He was informing me of your visit."

By the time I visited Sakimoto Rinko, I was more or less aware of the incident in which two soldiers had been shot dead by their company commander. But at that point, research was still in progress, and I had yet to meet with the numerous concerned

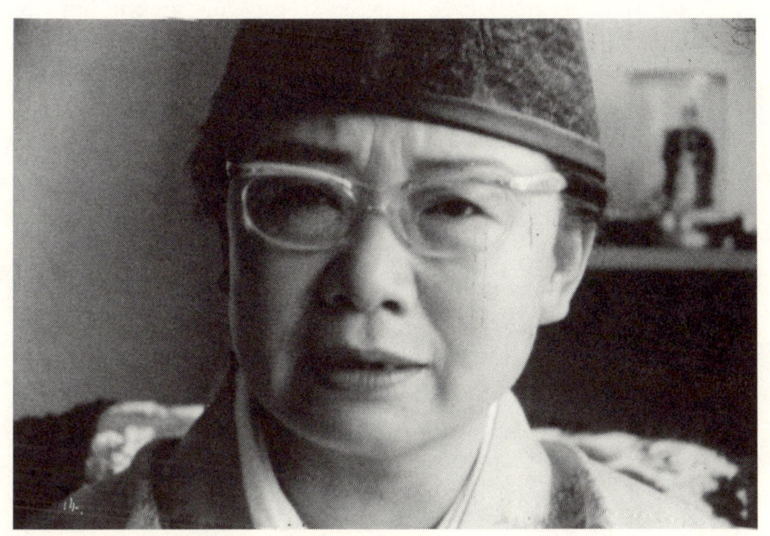

Sakamoto Rinko asked the gods about her brother's death.

parties. Sakimoto Rinko had been told that her brother had died from a "disease contracted at the front"; I had come to inquire about this.

Sakimoto Rinko was a priestess of the Tsuchimikado Shinto sect. As she was answering my questions, she suddenly realized something. "Why do you want to know about my brother's death *now*?" she asked in reply to my questions. Stammering, I told her that Yoshizawa Tetsunosuke's death might not have been from a disease contracted at the front. "If I don't investigate further, I won't be able to say for certain," I answered as best I could. After a brief silence, she said, "I see. I'll ask the gods."

I received permission to film what the gods might have to say. She was going to ask the following day. I quickly set up my equipment. The next day, Sakimoto Rinko wrote her request to the gods on a slip of paper: "I humbly ask you to tell me the cause of death of my brother, Yoshizawa Tetsunosuke, in Eastern New Guinea in September 1945." Then she entered the shrine. I was asked to appeal to the gods with her, so I clapped my hands as she had done, then bowed. I then waited for an hour in the reception room, where I could hear her voice ringing out as she made made further inquiries of her gods. Following her figure with my camera as she came out of the shrine, I waited for the words of the gods to issue forth from her mouth.

"My brother was executed."

A light shudder ran through my body. The gods had clearly pronounced "execution."

"What for?" I asked.

"For food. My brother had become a burden."

As I investigated further, I began to think that the dead wanted to come into "this world." I felt a force urging me on in order that "this world" might take a serious look into the conditions under which the soldiers had died. It was the first time I had ever had such a thought.

A VISIT TO SQUAD COMMANDER TAKAMI MINORU

We had finally come to the shooting of the "execution incident." Immediately after the war, Okuzaki had, coincidentally, run into his former squad commander, Takami Minoru, in a town in Osaka. Separate from my own research, Okuzaki had told me in a casual conversation that his squad commander had shot subordinates to death. After talking it over with Okuzaki, we decided that Takami would be the first person we'd visit with the crew.

"Let's go," I called out to my crew. I concentrated my energy in my lower belly. Let's do this, I thought, mustering up all my internal resources. We didn't contact Takami in advance. We were just going to show up on his doorstep—wielding a camera, no less. From his perspective, there could be nothing more annoying. Okuzaki would probably say that the annoyance suffered by the dead had been much worse. His logic was convincing. It was convincing because it was Okuzaki's. But could I reasonably justify suddenly destroying the *life* of a former soldier, just because he'd been a party to the execution incident? My stomach hurt. No, more accurately, I was afraid. It was the kind of "fear" you feel when you're about to do something terrible.

As we followed Okuzaki from behind, we could hear the rhythmic thuds of his leather shoes moving resolutely forward along the small gravel path to Takami's house. A human figure appeared in the doorframe. Who was it? It seemed to be Takami. "Are you Mr. Takami?" Okuzaki asked. After a pause, an expression of surprise came across Takami Minoru's face.

Takami Minoru had been Okuzaki's squad commander. He didn't act arrogantly toward Okuzaki just because he'd been his superior officer, of course. In fact, he went too far in the opposite direction, brimming with self-depreciation. He even called Okuzaki "sensei" once during their conversation. However, we missed recording that line, which was never to be uttered again.

When shooting with sync sound, it's more important for the

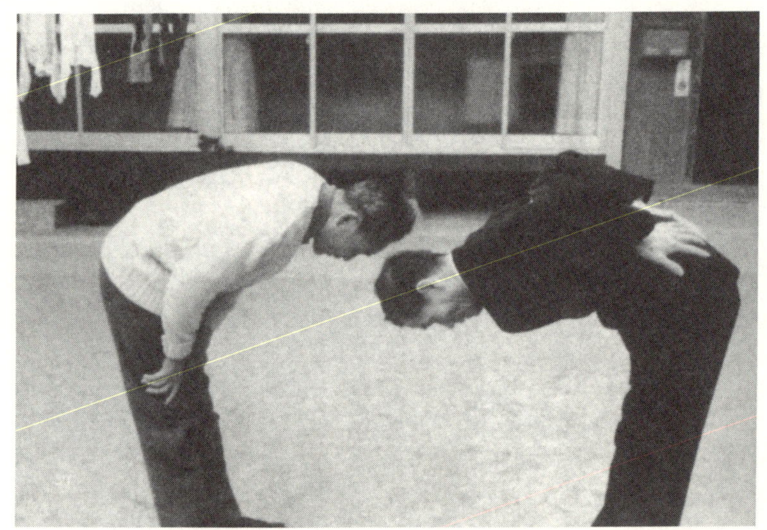

Okuzaki (right) visits his former squad commander.

from yet another blow. Yasuoka, the assistant director, gave me a look, asking me what we should do. Don't move, I replied with my eyes. We just have to keep rolling, I thought. I wondered how things were going to turn out. In the middle of this chaos, time felt endless, though not much actual time may have passed. People from the neighborhood rushed over. Impatient Okuzaki. The tide had turned. At this point, I ran out of film and quickly changed the magazine. I started shooting again. The Seo couple and two neighbors had by now completely pinned Okuzaki down.

"Stop! Can't you see they're defeating me? Stop!!" Okuzaki yelled towards the camera. I wasn't sure if his yell was genuine or not. Okuzaki later told me that they'd been choking him with his necktie. He'd thought he was going to die and had barely been able to slip his finger between the tie and his neck to prevent this. But the room was dark, and, given the limitations of the viewfinder, I couldn't see that his life was in peril. I continued to shoot. Okuzaki yelled for help. I hesitated; should I help or not?

This time, Yasuoka came over and whispered in my year, "What should we do?" "Wait a bit more," I replied. Deep in my heart, I'd decided to continue until Okuzaki asked for help one more time. He gave a heart-wrenching scream. Got it!! That's enough. I told Yasuoka to help Okuzaki. When I saw Yasuoka coming into the frame, I turned off the camera, then turned away from the entrance and went towards the living room. The struggle had ended; Okuzaki sat on the floor.

"Okuzaki, are you okay?" I asked, thinking how stupid that sounded.

He barked at me in an ear-splitting voice, "You idiot!! I almost got killed!!"

I cringed at the power and intensity of his voice. It thoroughly beat me down. The next instant, all the strength in my body withered away. I actually lost my ability to stand and had to sit down helplessly, right where I was. As Okuzaki went after the Seos again, I found myself unable to roll camera. The police will come soon, I thought. I had to shoot, but just holding the camera was difficult. Unseemly though it was, I began pleading with Takamura, the assistant cameraman: "I'm sorry, but the police will arrive soon, so please shoot the scene for me." The next second, a patrol car arrived. The police argued with Okuzaki. The neighbors surrounded them. I just watched in a daze. I managed to regain my strength just as Okuzaki was being interrogated by the detectives in the police car, and began once again to roll camera.

SPILT MILK CAN BE PUT BACK INTO THE BOTTLE

That evening, after we got back to the hotel, Okuzaki called me to his room, "Hara, let's call off this film."

I was shocked.

"I can't work with someone who just indifferently films Seo Yukio beating the crap out of me. My life was in real danger. I survived the war in New Guinea, but I could have died today. I'm impressed with how well you can handle the camera when a person's life is in danger. But though you're a fine cameraman, you're worthless as a human being!!"

As he talked, he gradually became enraged. I became lost in feelings of despair at the thought that the film had come to an end. How would I be able to return the money I'd borrowed? Kobayashi's face appeared before me: "I'm sorry," I thought.

"When I was on top of Seo Yukio, I wanted you to stop us and say, 'Hey, chill out.' First and foremost, I'm the hero of this film. I'm the star. Scenes that show the star being beaten up are embarrassing, and the audience won't like it."

So we were only supposed to shoot scenes that showed him in a positive light? This pissed me off. Who'd be interested in such superficial heroism? Who would want to make such a cheap hero movie? The scene was good *because* you were getting beaten up. Get some perspective. I had a lot to say. But doing so right then would only have added fuel to the fire, so I remained silent. To Okuzaki, it must have seemed a betrayal of his trust. I could only think of how unbearably humiliating it must have been for him to be recorded at his worst. I didn't completely accept Okuzaki's criticisms, but I could only apologize for upsetting him to such an extent. Overwhelmed by humiliation, vexation, and a sense of powerlessness, I felt tears welling up.

I returned to my anxious crew, and informed them of Okuzaki's "decision." I felt sorry for them. Kuribayashi, the sound engineer, suggested we return to Tokyo to think about Okuzaki's decision. I was thankful for his heartfelt words.

The crew went out to eat, and I remained alone in my room. I was exhausted. Okuzaki came to ask if I wanted to eat with him. "Yes," I replied with sincerity, and we went out together.

"You know the saying, 'There's no use crying over spilt milk'? Well, I think spilt milk can be put back into the bottle," he said.

What?!! What was this? I had no idea what he was going to say next.

"You know, when you apologized without reservation earlier, my resentment went away."

A case like this can only be described by the expression, "as if fooled by a fox." He was saying that we should continue making the film. I was dumbfounded. At the same time, I was relieved.

THE UNREALIZED EPISODE OF THE "CASE OF ATTEMPTED MURDER IN SHIMANE"

The Seo Yukio incident didn't end there. It remained a problem even after we'd shot everything we'd scheduled for the day, including Okuzaki visiting the graves of his fellow soldiers, and had once again been tailed as we returned to Tokyo. Several days later, I got a phone call from Kobe.

"I want to charge Seo Yukio with attempted murder, so I need footage of that scene. It's fine if it's a copy, but I want to use it as evidence in a court of law."

I thought that calling the attack attempted murder was a bit outrageous. I understood how humiliated Okuzaki must have felt, but I was amazed at his persistence. However, there was absolutely no way I could agree to present the dailies in court. I promptly refused. Okuzaki grew angry and said, "I'm quitting the film."

Again, several days later, I got a phone call from Kobe.

"Will you edit what we've shot so far? I want to take the film and go to Shimane."

I didn't know what to say. Was he still stuck on "the humiliation of being strangled"? But no matter what he said, editing the footage we had into some half-assed reel would have been unbearable. Again, I had to turn him down.

Several days later, I got another phone call: "If I can't use the film, then we'll act the scene out. I've put a sign up on my car and want to go to Shimane where Seo Yukio lives."

Now he wanted to form a theater troupe? What the hell was this?! What sort of act did he intend to put on?

He continued: "I heard that the emperor is going to visit the Shimane National Athletic Competition. I just want to get near the emperor. But I'm sure I'll be stopped before I'm able to."

I was speechless. Wanting to get close to the emperor was a new request. Even Okuzaki knew he couldn't get near the emperor. What was he trying to accomplish? I thought it was just some flight of fancy. Even so, the force with which Okuzaki continued to insist on going again to Shimane was extraordinary.

However, we had just begun to delve into the "war" that would subsequently structure the film. I didn't want to waste time on anything else.

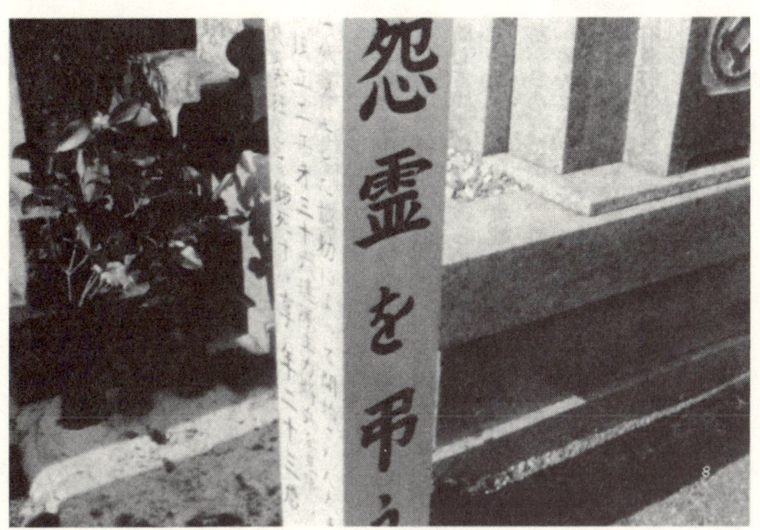

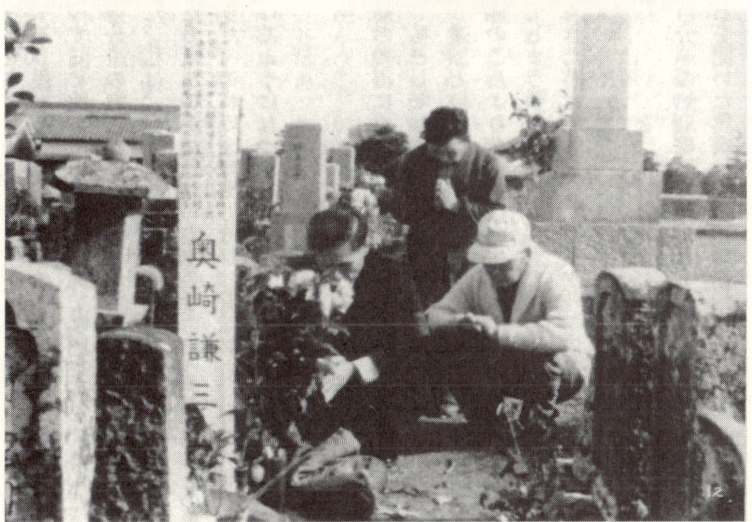

Making a round of visits to console the spirits of fallen comrades.

WHIMSICAL WAKE-UP CALLS

Going backwards in time a bit, I want to talk about Okuzaki's phone calls. As soon as we'd decided to make the film, he began bombarding us with phone calls. He would call early in the morning at about 6 am. He would wake up with these idea and call us right away. Since these "whimsical wake-up calls" were a manifestation of Okuzaki's desire to make the film, I thought we should welcome them. But the frequency of the calls was abnormal. And each call was long, taking at least an hour. He'd say whatever had popped into his mind, and in order to show how important it was, he'd fully expand upon its meaning. I would hold the receiver to my ear and just put up with it. All that mattered to Okuzaki was whatever he happened to be thinking or feeling at the moment. He wanted to speak, so he spoke, whether in person or over the phone. I'm only human, so I would get sleepy at times and start to respond absent-mindedly. He would immediately ask if I were tired, then blame my sleepiness on not paying enough attention to him. As a result, I couldn't let myself relax. When I would finally put the receiver back, my ear would often be numb, paralyzed with the pain of having been pressed up against the phone for so long.

The content of these "whimsical wake-up calls" was diverse, and I was often impressed with the fact that he came up with so many ideas. Here are a few of them:

> A while back, Okuzaki had taken a commemorative photo in front of Tanaka Kakuei's house. He had noticed that Tanaka's doorplate was dirty. "I want to clean the dirt off. Will you shoot me doing that?"
>
> — "Someone once told me that my shooting pachinko balls at the emperor was a kind of parody. I want to do it again as an actual parody. I'll set up a life-size picture of the emperor in front of the Imperial Palace, then shoot pachinko balls at it. I'd like you to film me doing this."

— "I want to meet the leaders of the Middle Core and the Revolutionary Marxist Factions of the Japan Revolutionary Communist League. I'd like to interview them. Hara, will you convince them to do an interview with me?"

— "I read in the newspaper that a child has been kidnapped and killed. The mother is calling for the death penalty for his killer. I want to meet her and tell her that I think it's a mistake to ask for the death penalty. I can't accept state violence in the form of the death penalty. I want you to shoot me talking to the mother."

- (Around the time when Minister of Education Sakata Michita was in the headlines regarding "textbook issues").[5] "I want to crash my car into the Minister of Education's car. Hara, will you find out where and when the Minister drives his car, then shoot a scene in which I crash my car into his?"

— "The annual memorial service at Yasukuni Shrine is approaching.[6] I want to disrupt the ceremony. Since I myself won't be able to get near the shrine with a weapon, I'll have my wife carry a bouquet with a knife hidden in it. Once we're close, I'll take the knife from my wife and attack. Will you shoot that?"

Everything Okuzaki said surprised us. Some ideas sounded like jokes, but there were others that seemed worth doing despite the risk. We would call an emergency meeting of the crew, have a heated discussion, organize our ideas, and prepare for the next phone call, during which we would give him our answer. But by then he'd be babbling on enthusiastically about his *next* idea, as if he'd forgotten

---

5 "textbook issues": There's been an on-going debate in Japan about how Japan's responsibility for World War II should be portrayed in school textbooks. Sakata was one of the people advocating less transparency about Japan's aggression during WWII in textbooks.
6 Yasukuni Shrine: Another contentious issue in Japanese politics. The Yasukuni Shrine is dedicated to Japan's war dead, but since these "eternal spirits" of the war include WWII class-A war criminals, it has been criticized both domestically and abroad as an affront to victims of the war.

the one he'd brought up previously.

Initially, when I would ask for some time to think about his proposals, he wouldn't say anything about it. But gradually, he began to show his impatience. "What do you mean you need to think about it?" he would demand as if appalled. Then he would say: "I want to know what *you* feel about this." He would try to put me on the spot by saying that it didn't matter whether or not I would actually shoot whatever he'd suggested. However, this was just a trap. If I said, "That's a good idea," he would immediately say, "Then let's shoot it." If I responded negatively, he would accuse me of not understanding him at all. But we didn't have the time or money to shoot random scenes. I wanted to stick to the "war"; I didn't want to dally. Okuzaki felt differently. He just wanted to create a scandal. The gap between the two of us was growing larger.

"My actions and judgments are correct. Because of this, I was able to come back from New Guinea alive. I make the decisions; you follow them. I'm a man of action; you're a storyteller. It would be best for the storyteller to shut up and film the man of action." Now that we were in the middle of the film, Okuzaki had begun ordering me around with increasing frequency. My frustration with his tone grew.

"A PRISONER OF THE EMPEROR'S ARMY": HAMAGUCHI MASAICHI

When shooting the scene with Hamaguchi Masaichi, there was a line I regretted not getting on film, though I knew that doing so would have been close to impossible physically.

Okuzaki had provoked Hamaguchi, and had managed to successfully bring him outside. It was then decided that we would move him to a different location by taxi. Hamaguchi Masaichi, Sakimoto Rinko, and Nomura Toshiya went as one group; I rode in the taxi with Okuzaki and our sound engineer, Kuribayashi.[7] We drove through the evening streets and headed towards an inn Okuzaki had in mind. The taxi carrying Hamaguchi and the others drove directly ahead of us. Okuzaki, looking straight ahead, said jubilantly, "Hamaguchi is a prisoner of God's army."

I wanted that line. But even though the sound engineer, the cameraman, and I, the director, were riding together, we couldn't get it; it was just one of those things that suddenly pops out. What was I to do? I could ask him to repeat the line, but I didn't want to do that, because Okuzaki was sure to overact the second time around. I could only wait for another chance. But in the end, he never said it again.

After we had finished shooting the scene with Hamaguchi, Okuzaki treated us to dinner. Our meal was brought to us in a separate room on trays that were loaded with dishes that seemed quite lavish.

It was bizarre beyond description. Hamaguchi, who had just talked nonchalantly about having eaten human flesh; Sakimoto and Nomura, the executed soldiers' family members who'd just been doggedly interrogating Hamaguchi; the Okuzakis; and Nakagawa and Ōtagaki, supporters of Okuzaki who were visiting the shoot—were all raising their glasses and smiling at Okuzaki's toast of "Thank you all for your hard work today." It was exactly the kind of atmosphere you might get when proposing a toast to the actors and crew of a feature film after shooting on location. I shot this uninspiring scene. (It was later edited out.) Okuzaki poured Hamaguchi some beer as Hamaguchi looked bashfully towards the camera. What had that excited scene just before been about? Was it just that *the actors had put on a heartfelt performance*?!

Actually, that was in a sense exactly what had happened. Before we'd shot the scene with Hamaguchi, Okuzaki had rehearsed it with him.

---

7 Sakimoto Rinko and Nomura Toshiya: Sister of Yoshizawa Tetsunosuke and brother of Nomura Jinpei, the two soldiers whose execution Okuzaki investigates during the film.

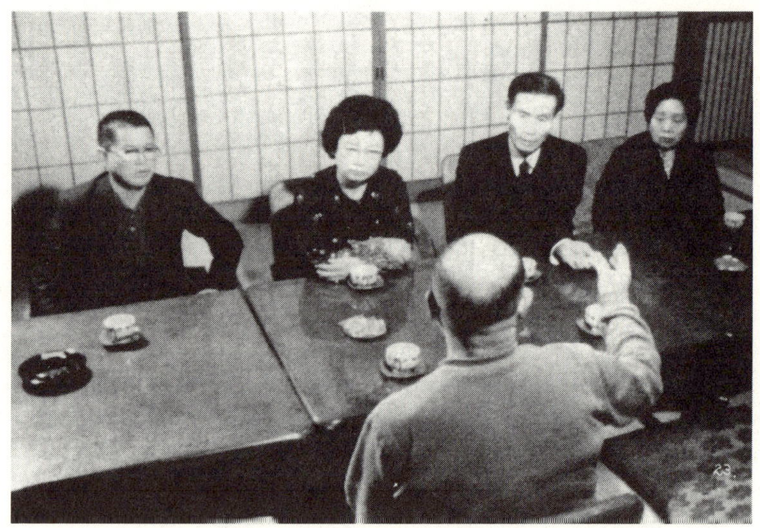

The Okuzakis (right) and the two relatives of the deceased soldiers searching for the truth about the execution incident.

Okuzaki, his wife, and his supporter, Nakagawa, had gone together to visit Hamaguchi's restaurant before the film shoot, and had talked with him about various things. Had Okuzaki gone there because, having dealt with Hara Toshio's evasions, he'd learned his lesson?[8] Was he hoping to put in some legwork so that Hamaguchi wouldn't try to talk his way out in front of the camera? At the shoot, Hamaguchi had ended up saying nearly the same thing he'd said at this preliminary meeting. Okuzaki had come to the shoot having already found out what there was to know.

Later, when I found out about this, I understood what had happened. During the shoot, Okuzaki had lost energy, becoming silent as the two relatives had relentlessly accused Hamaguchi. Okuzaki had been extremely enthusiastic about taking Hamaguchi as "a prisoner of God's army," but even he couldn't keep his interest up when pursuing something he already knew. Around this time, Okuzaki began to resist being directed by me.

"Mr. Hara, it's ten years too soon for you to direct me," he'd say to me over and over. He probably thought that since I already had some prior knowledge of what was going on, he would also do some preliminary research before showing up at the shoot. That wasn't necessarily a bad idea, I thought, but look at what it had all come to. I'd wanted him to shine when he accused Hamaguchi, but it had all backfired.

"I THINK I'M GOING TO KILL KOSHIMIZU"

Okuzaki asked to see the dailies. I didn't want to show them to him. If I did, I felt he would say something ridiculous. I was also afraid that this might further increase his tendency to over-act. But in the end, I couldn't refuse.

I borrowed the office of his lawyer, Endō Makoto, and showed

8 Hara Toshio: Former soldier interviewed by Okuzaki in the film.

him the footage of Aikawa Riichi, Hara Toshio, and Seo Yukio.

He said he wanted to see more. The next night, I borrowed the house of one of Okuzaki's supporters. I brought in a projector and showed him footage of him visiting his ancestors' graves and of the wedding.

The sound of the turning projector wheels filled the room. Images played on the improvised screen of white paper that had been posted on the wall of the Japanese-style room. Okuzaki watched the screen, utterly engrossed. The roughly one-hour preview ended.

"Wow!! It's amazing!! I'm thoroughly impressed."

He seemed to especially like the wedding scene. His expression changed entirely, and his Noro Keisuke smile filled his entire face.

"I've yelled at you a number of times; I'd like you to forgive me," he said, bowing deeply. I didn't think anything I'd just screened was particularly good, so when it made Okuzaki this happy, I actually felt embarrassed.

"I'll never say I'm quitting again," he continued.

There was no way I was ever going to believe that, so I said, "No, no. If I ever displease you, please just tell me that you want to stop."

I made my remark as sarcastically as I could, but he was too delighted to notice. He went to call his wife in Kobe and tell her how amazing he thought the film was. When I had put away the projector and was getting ready to leave, Okuzaki came back into the room and said, "Hara, there's something I need to tell you." He led me to another room, and we sat face to face, a kotatsu between us.

Okuzaki stared at me as though he were going to shoot me in the eyes. His eyes shone. Full of a sternness uncommon for him, he pressed his lips tightly together and assumed an attacking position. Science fiction films often have these scenes of demons or monsters who shoot bluish-white rays of light from their eyes and threaten, attack, and destroy their opponents—facing Okuzaki, that's exactly the kind of situation in which I found myself. He leaned forward until the distance between our faces was a mere 50 centimeters. The glint in his recessed eyes grew sharper.

"I think I'm going to kill Koshimizu."[9] He said this much and fell silent. He was waiting for a reply. I remained speechless; there was no way I could say anything. He continued,

"I want you to shoot the scene when I kill Koshimizu."

I cringed, desperately enduring his gaze. My mind went blank. I didn't know what was what.

"No film has ever had a scene like this. I think the greatest present I can give you is to have you film me killing Koshimizu."

I desperately wanted my camera at that moment. I'd thought I would just be showing him the dailies, so I hadn't brought it. A feeling of regret coursed through me. I wanted to shoot him talking, his face. I *must* shoot this, I thought. I itched to, but there was nothing I could do.

Various thoughts rushed through my mind about whether it was right for Okuzaki to kill Koshimizu, and whether it would be right to film it. Would he attack with a pistol in one hand? The figure of Koshimizu would appear and, in the next instant, tragedy would strike. Would I be able to roll camera? Image aside, what about sound? Would my crew come? No, I couldn't involve them. The police would come immediately. They'd probably confiscate the film as evidence, and I might also be arrested as an accomplice. It would be fine for me to be arrested, but would I be able to protect the film? Possible scenarios kept flitting in and out of my mind.

"I'm not going to say a word of what I've just told you to anyone else. So pretend you never heard anything, Mr. Hara. How about it? Will you shoot the scene?"

He told me to pretend I hadn't heard anything, to just shoot the scene as if it had all happened by chance. But I had no confidence in my ability deny absolutely, in all the places I might be asked, that I'd been completely in the dark.

How could I get through this situation? With my mind in complete turmoil, I strained just to think. Would I somehow be

9 Koshimizu Masao: Former captain of the 36th Special Engineer Corps. Koshimizu gave the orders that led to the execution of the two soldiers that Okuzaki was investigating.

able to shoot Okuzaki asking me to film the murder? Would I have another chance? Okuzaki had said, "I want you to shoot a murder." Given Okuzaki's persistent character, he'd probably ask me one more time. Then I'd have another chance. Since I wanted that chance, it would be better to refuse him this time. OK, I'll say no. I'll wait for my next chance. In the meantime, I'll think hard about whether or not to agree to shoot the murder... After finally coming up with this plan, I replied nervously,

"Okuzaki, I'm afraid. I don't have the confidence I'd need to shoot the scene."

My body was quivering. I tried to stop myself from shaking, but couldn't.

He listened to my reply. "Ahhh," he groaned, giving free reign to his disappointment and putting his head in his hands.
"Hara, you really are worthless!!"

I just remained silent.

"There are a million other cameramen with your skills. It's not as though your technique is anything to boast of." He said this just to provoke me into shooting the scene. He acted as though he'd be doing me a big favor by letting me film him. I knew the shortcomings of my camera technique, but I didn't think technique was what made a film good. I wanted to ask him if anyone with exceptional technique had ever tried to make a film about him.

"I said I wouldn't quit the film again, but I'm taking that back. Let's pretend as if the film never existed. That's it; it's over. Please, burn all the film you've shot."

He spat.

I wanted to get the hell out of there. As I was hastily preparing to leave, Okuzaki, who had returned to himself, said, "Hara, how about staying here with me tonight? I promise I won't ask you to shoot the scene of me killing Koshimizu again." Okuzaki had already arranged to stay at the hotel for the night. No kidding. With our futons lying side by side, he was sure to beg me, this time with humility; just the thought of him relentlessly grilling me was unbearable. I adamantly insisted on going home. He still wouldn't give up, and tried to detain me. I finally shook him off forcibly and went out. It was past 3 am.

Omiya, the assistant director, was kindly waiting awake for me. I was parched. "Let's grab a beer," I said, and we went out to an all-night Chinese restaurant. I recounted the story. Omiya must have been shocked, but he remained silent, listening to me talk.

"Okuzaki is an idiot! If he wanted me to shoot that scene, he shouldn't have bothered telling me about it; he should have just gone to the spot and done it out of the blue. Then I would have been engrossed in shooting it, I think," I muttered. After saying this, I was shocked by what I'd said. Did I actually want to shoot the murder?

I left Omiya and went out into the street as dawn broke, the night turning white. I jumped into a taxi and headed home. As I watched the scenery flow past the window, I fell deep into thought.

I had told Okuzaki that I was scared, that I wasn't certain I could shoot such a scene. Those were my true feelings; I was definitely afraid. Who wouldn't be? Every time we went into the homes of the former soldiers, I tasted fear, so how could I remain calm heading into a murder scene, the height of chaos?!!

Did I become stronger, did my nerves become tougher, the more chaos I experienced?? No. I grew increasingly cowardly. *No one gets used to chaos.* At least that's how I felt. But if that chaos were, dare I say, necessary—if it were somehow satisfying—I would have to come to terms with it, despite being afraid. I'd told Okuzaki I was scared that I wouldn't be able to shoot the scene, but I also thought that I would have to shoot it precisely *because* I was afraid. My cowardice made me try even harder. On the other hand, there were times when I couldn't shoot things even though I knew I should. This act of examining oneself is, I think, what documentary filmmaking is all about. The question was, would I be satisfied? Hearing me say that I was scared, Okuzaki had decided I was worthless—a coward. But I'd only really given him half an answer.

When I returned home, I told Kobayashi what had happened in detail.

"It makes me feel ill. I don't want to shoot a murder. It's horrifying to just think about it. Okuzaki is sick. He must be possessed. I can't believe you're wondering whether or not to shoot this. If you shoot this murder scene, I'll quit."

Kobayashi had clearly stated her position on the matter. But I couldn't completely deny that I might still shoot the scene. "Why do you have to do something like that? Is it even essential to the film?" Kobayashi asked. I couldn't reply.

"Let's at least look into what would actually happen if I did shoot it," I argued forcefully. She nodded reluctantly.

I consulted with a lawyer first. What would happen to the film? Would it be confiscated as evidence? Would I be arrested as an accomplice? Would I be able to screen the film? "Hmmm," the lawyer said in response to my rapid-fire questions. "Since there's never been a case like this before, I can't anticipate what the actual judgment might be," he replied. It was understandable that he couldn't say in a 30-minute consultation what I might be charged with, or that I didn't have anything to worry about. But this left me feeling frustrated.

I consulted Imamura Shōhei as well.

"I think that filming Okuzaki holding a blood-soaked knife and killing a man would be pointless," he said.

I met with other friends and elders in whom I confided, but I only ended up strengthening my conviction that I had to find the answer myself.

A few days later, Kobayashi said to me, "I want to meet with Okuzaki. I'm going to tell him that I don't want him to kill anyone."

We headed to Kobe. We worried a great deal over whether or not to bring the camera. I wanted to film Okuzaki asking me to film the murder, but I felt that even if I brought my camera this time, I would only end up with something rather distorted. In the end, we didn't bring the camera. We arrived in Kobe in the afternoon, but weren't able to meet with Okuzaki until after 7 pm, after he finished work.

"I don't want to kill Koshimizu out of hate, but out of principle. My act will be completely justified. Letting you shoot this murder scene is an expression of my appreciation for everything you two have done for me." He calmly went on like this for four, five, six hours without tiring.

Kobayashi, who always plays the role of a quiet listener, objected. "Until now, I've liked everything you've done and thought; you've had ideas that most people could never dream up. And they were all tinged with humor!! A scene of you killing Koshimizu would just be gruesome. I don't want you to kill anyone!!"

Her voice trembled as she began to cry. She turned to Okuzaki's wife, who'd been watching from the sidelines.

"Why don't you stop him from saying he's going to kill Koshimizu? Are you okay with this?" Kobayashi asked, almost shrieking. Tears streamed down her face. Okuzaki probably wasn't good at handling crying women; he appeared troubled and fed up.

Even though it was 3 am, I said to Kobayashi, "Let's go." Okuzaki entreated us to stay, telling us that the bullet train had stopped running, but we said we'd fill the time somehow. He didn't insist. As we staggered around the empty nocturnal Kobe streets, Kobayashi remained silent. She had held to her opinion, but I had only watched silently. I kept thinking that it was my turn to come to a decision.

I was discussing Okuzaki with Kobayashi when it suddenly occurred to me: The man we'd been shooting this entire time was a criminal! And a moral one at that! Someone who was fully aware of what he was doing! Stupidly, I'd never before been conscious of the fact that Okuzaki Kenzō was a criminal, despite having filmed him uttering the refrain: "Okuzaki Kenzō with three prior convictions: murder, assault, and distributing obscene images." I was shocked at my realization. What an idiot I'd been. I'd been so soft. Not that the way I dealt with him was going to immediately change as a result. Still, I had to prepare myself. We had quite a difficult character to reckon with—ourselves!

BURN ALL THE FILM YOU'VE SHOT!

Toward the end of '82, we visited Hamaguchi Masaichi and Maruyama Tarō about the execution case.[10] Sakimoto Rinko, Nomura Toshiya, my crew, and I were all staying at a hotel in Kobe. Okuzaki had returned home. We were going to leave Kobe early the next morning to visit the grave of Sergeant Hashimoto in Nagoya, then pay a visit to Kojima Shichirō in Kakegawa City in Shizuoka Prefecture. The entire story of the execution was gradually coming to light. It felt as though we were about to fulfill our objective: to visit all of the related parties in order to get their stories, and, after gathering enough definitive evidence against the company commander, to confront him with his responsibility for the execution of the two soldiers.

"I don't want to go to Hashimoto's grave. I'd rather visit Kojima Shichirō first," Sakimoto Rinko said to me. "I've talked this over with Mr. Nomura, and we both feel this way."

Nomura Toshiya managed a small factory. It was a tiny business. The year was coming to a close, and he was running around trying to get loans to help with a cash-flow problem he was having. Despite all that, he had come on this trip to pursue the truth about the execution of his brother. Sergeant Hashimoto, who had been a friend of Okuzaki's, had nothing to do with that case, so I understood the desire to visit Kojima's house first. However, for Okuzaki, pursuing the execution and visiting the graves of his war buddies were equally important. Both the scenes related to the execution case and Okuzaki's visits to his war-buddies' graves had to be efficiently integrated into a single schedule. And in fact, we had already made visits to the graves of several soldiers who had nothing to do with the execution case. But for the blood-relatives of those who had been executed, such visits seemed irrelevant.

I saw Sakimoto Rinko's point, and told her that I would discuss

10 Maruyama Tarō: Former soldier interviewed by Okuzaki.

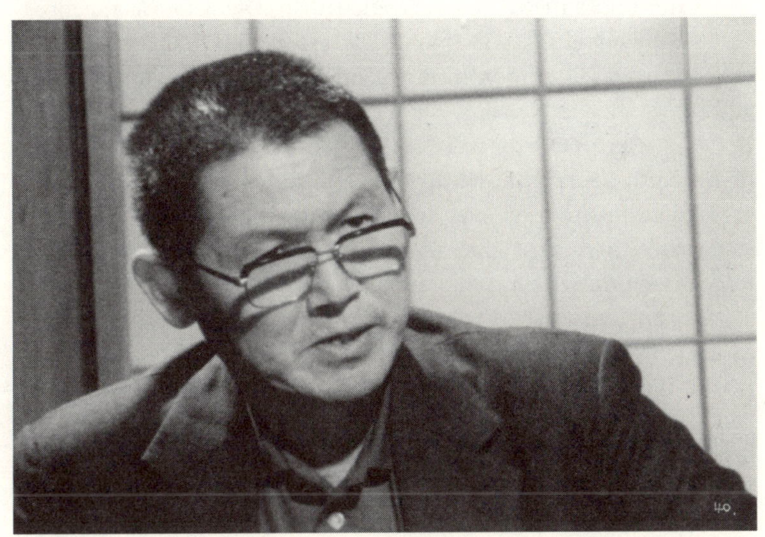

Nomura Toshiya, brother of Nomura Jinpei, one of the executed soldiers.

the matter with Okuzaki that morning. By that point, the discord between Okuzaki and myself had gotten worse; the repulsion for him that I'd been repressing had grown. So when Okuzaki's interests stood in opposition to those of the two relatives, I was on their side. This is something I can see now.

The next morning, I stepped out into the dark Kobe streets and headed to Okuzaki's store. When I arrived, he was loading a wooden monument he intended to place in front of Hashimoto's grave into his car. He had been up all night making it. I went over to Okuzaki.

"Ms. Sakimoto and Mr. Nomura say they want to go to Kojima Shichirō's house first." Before I could finish, Okuzaki was incensed.

"Suit yourself!!"

There was no approaching him on the subject. He started his car and left.

This was an unexpected development. What was I to do? I went to a nearby restaurant with Omiya, the assistant director, and discussed the situation over breakfast. "Let's go after him," Omiya suggested. Later on, I came to realize that Okuzaki had wanted me to go after him with Sakimoto and Nomura, but by that point, my distaste for Okuzaki had grown out of control. Okuzaki was speaking to me only in commands, and would repeatedly threaten to quit the film if I made the slightest objection. He'd chastize me, saying, "You're worthless." I would silently battle against him, saying to myself, "Don't think I'm at your beck and call!!"

I went to tell my crew of the most recent development.

"Let's leave Okuzaki alone. It's fine. We'll go to Mie and shoot Nomura Jinpei's gravesite."

My crew listened with worried expressions.

Once I was in the car on the way to Nantō Town in Mie Prefecture, I began to worry about what Okuzaki was doing. Had he gone to Sergeant Hashimoto's grave in Nagoya and then on to Kojima Shichirō's house in Shizuoka as planned? Or had he turned back and gone home? I forced down my feelings. I shot footage of Sakimoto Rinko and Nomura Toshiya in front of Nomura Jinpei's grave, conjecturing about what might have triggered the execution. That night, we stayed at Nomura Toshiya's house and returned to Tokyo the following day.

I received a phone call the next day from Okuzaki. He was enraged.

"You idiot!! You went with the relatives. I was waiting for you at the interchange in Ōtsu. Don't think I can't do this stuff on my own!! When I was putting up Hashimoto's grave post, the police who were tailing me came to help me set it up!! They dug a hole for me. The cops are a hell of a lot more useful than you. I even met Kojima Shichirō!"

He ranted on and on in his Kobe dialect. The blood rushed to my head. Was I going to concede to him? The lump that I'd been suppressing for nearly half a year suddenly exploded, let loose by his outburst.

"What the hell are you talking about?!"

I have no recollection whatsoever of what else I said at the time; I just yelled back at him at the top of my lungs. It was the first time I'd fought back against Okuzaki with such raw emotion. But lo and behold: my response simply added fuel to the fire of Okuzaki's rage. He now came at me with magnified energy.

"Burn all the film that you've shot thus far! I'm going to come to Tokyo and light it all on fire!!"

I'd been defeated. His power had completely overwhelmed me. As he yelled at me, outraged, I realized that Okuzaki's power could not be matched; I had to admit defeat. Realizing this, I suddenly felt relieved. I fell silent, waiting for Okuzaki's anger to pass. Sergeant Hashimoto had been a soldier in the same 36th Special Engineer Corps as Nomura, and had died on the same battlefield. Wouldn't it have been appropriate for the two family members to pay their respects to him alongside Okuzaki? I was angry; they had only thought of their own families. Okuzaki was right, I thought. I apologized to him.

This incident definitely changed how I behaved toward Okuzaki. I realized how foolish it was to resist him with power. He seemed fed up with me as well. For the rest of the film, we would meet and part on location; Okuzaki avoided being with us outside of the shoot as much as possible.

THE GREAT DEBATE: A "SUBSTITUTE" RELATIVE

We had at last arrived at the stage when we were to visit the company commander's home. Despite Okuzaki's repeated insistence, the two relatives of the executed soldiers refused to accompany him. In response, Okuzaki severed all ties with them. I had decided that they were to play a large role in the film, so their exit was painful. Okuzaki must have understood well enough the pressure that their presence would have placed on the perpetrators of the incident. But when left to his own devices, Okuzaki tended to favor questions of general postwar morality over the specific truth behind the execution incident. As such, I thought it would be unfortunate if we ended up having to abort our investigations into the execution.

Okuzaki suggested over the phone that we find "substitute" relatives. A great debate erupted within the crew over this proposal. Let me talk a bit about the "substitutes."

The first "substitute" suggested was Yuuki Shoji.[11]

Why Yuuki Shoji? To sum up: when Nomura had been around, he'd said that he'd seen a television show dramatizing a story that recounted a similar execution. The author of the original story was Yuuki Shoji. Upon hearing this, Okuzaki had immediately called Yuuki to ask if he would make a "special appearance" at the scene at the ex-commander's house. Yuuki seemed interested, and had agreed. However, now that the executed soldiers' relatives were decisively out of the film, Okuzaki had promoted Yuuki Shoji from a mere "special appearance" to being a possible "substitute."

I was the person who most objected to the idea of "substitutes."

11 Yuuki Shoji (1927–1996): Crime fiction author.

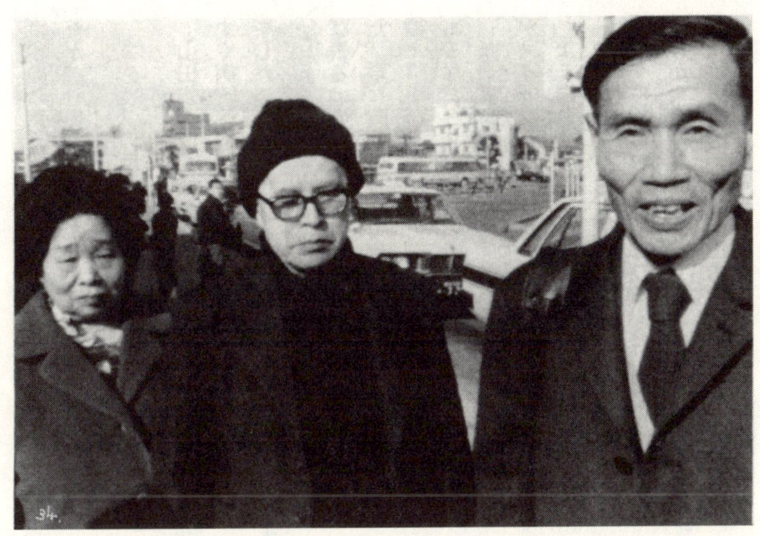

Okuzaki's "substitutes" for the relatives of the executed soldiers included his own wife (far left).

According to my sense of ethics, using "substitutes" was beyond the pale; it meant lying to our opponents. I was adamantly against this idea. Why even have substitutes? And why Yuuki Shoji? Wouldn't this mess up everything we'd done in the film so far? I was yelling. But my partner, Kobayashi, objected. "Don't you think Okuzaki's proposal to use a 'substitute'—something none of us could even close to dreaming up—is what makes Okuzaki interesting?" Hmm?!! I choked. During the shoot, Okuzaki and I were never on the same wavelength, and kept running into trouble with one another. But Kobayashi was different. She always emphasized the fact that each of Okuzaki's ideas and performances were so Okuzaki-esque, making him a wonderful subject.

Her words hit a nerve. Maybe she was right. We didn't want this film to end up simply being a commentary on war. More than anything, we recognized that investigating Okuzaki the human being was a subject unto itself. Because Okuzaki's ideas and actions challenged my moral principles more often than not, I would get emotional about them. But I was convinced by Kobayashi's point. Since using this "substitute" in the film was an action that Okuzaki had decided to take, I had no choice but to shoot it, despite my hesitations.

Several days later, Okuzaki called to inform me that Yuuki Shoji had declined to play the "substitute" because he had fallen ill.

Okuzaki's next phone call a few days later literally stupefied me.

"Please ask your mother to play the 'substitute.' Your mother lives in Yamaguchi Prefecture, right? Yamaguchi is near Hiroshima. It wouldn't be that much trouble..."

Was this supposed to be another of his super-utilitarian ideas? I wanted him to put himself in my shoes. I'm not the kind of person who will just use his own mother as a "substitute" and roll camera!! Stupid!! I absolutely refused to go along with Okuzaki's brilliant idea.

FOR MOVIES OR FOR PEOPLE?

Our crew consisted of: myself as director and cameraman; Kuribayashi, the sound technician; assistant director Omiya, who did the lighting; assistant director Yasuoka, who carried other necessary machines and bags; Takamura, the camera assistant for the first half of the film; and Hirasawa, who helped us as camera assistant for the second half.

When shooting, we would begin to roll camera and record sound before we entered a location. We would then follow Okuzaki as he went to visit someone's home. When that person appeared, we would try to capture their reaction, then shoot Okuzaki's response, and then really just capture everything about the scene that we could. That was our style. Lighting was the problem. We had no way to light the entrance to a house other than with a handheld battery light. And the battery didn't last long at all. It would go out after about ten minutes. When we entered the house, we had to plug an "eye lamp" into an outlet as quickly as possible and light the scene with that.

On this visit, we entered the house as expected and began shooting.

Koshimizu's living room was dark. The situation was moving along, so we couldn't wait for the lights to be turned on. As I rolled camera, I silently screamed, "Omiya, hurry up and get the lights turned on!!" A moment later, the room was illuminated. OK, they were on. But a moment after that, the lights went out again. What happened?!! "Omiya!!" I roared to myself. Turn the lights on!! I was growing frustrated. A moment later, they went on again. Okay! All right! But then they went out again. At that moment, out of the corner of my eye, I caught a glimpse of Koshimizu's wife pulling the cord to our light out of the outlet. I noticed Omiya standing a few feet away looking perplexed. Whenever Omiya would turn the lights on, Koshimizu's wife would unplug the cord. A heated battle was being waged over the outlet.

We were all aware that we were intruders; we knew we weren't going to be welcomed and ushered in. The only way for us to use the outlet was to take it by force and get consent after the fact. So in moments like this, when we met resistance and refusal, we were helpless. Omiya must have been feeling the pressure, since he knew that the longer he waited, the more underexposed footage we would end up with. But, faced with the wife's resistance, he was powerless.

I prayed that Omiya would be able to do something. But, on the other hand, I was also rooting for Koshimizu's wife. Strangely enough, her resistance pleased and amused me.

This tough-willed woman remained cool and calm throughout the filming. Near the end of the shoot, she didn't hesitate to appear right in front of my camera with a Polaroid in hand. In order to capture evidence of our outrageous trespass, she prepared the flash on her camera and took a shot. Seeing her in the middle of the frame, I respected her boldness and guts.

Here's another of her "heroic" episodes. Sitting next to her husband, she stoically watched as he and Okuzaki argued fiercely. Okuzaki asked Koshimizu's wife: "The police called me 'sensei' even though I've only graduated from elementary school. Why do you think they do this? Do you know why?" Okuzaki kept emphasizing this "why." He'd already decided on the answer he wanted to hear. But contrary to his expectations, she retorted, "Why don't you research this properly?"

Okuzaki, taken by surprise, didn't know what to say for a moment. A second later, he responded ferociously, "It's because I've lived a life worthy of being called 'sensei.'"

This phrase "the police call me 'sensei'" was a typical refrain for him. He would repeat it almost everywhere he went, but the only person who'd thrown it right back at him, unflinchingly, was Koshimizu's wife. As I rolled camera, filming this exchange, I thought it would probably make for some of the film's best humor.

Let's think about this phrase, "the police call me 'sensei.'"

Okuzaki would often precede this statement with: "It's probably just flattery, but..." Even Okuzaki knew that it was something the police did to flatter him. Still, he seemed to believe that being called "sensei" by them made him worthy of such a title—that they called him "sensei" because they valued or felt a sense of reverence for what he had done.

I don't actually think that the police called him "sensei" simply as a professional tactic. There were, of course, those who did refer to him in that way in order to please him; I met one policeman who admitted to as much during the shoot. But the Hyogo police were different. Whenever they responded to Okuzaki, they were polite. After all, they went to his house on a regular basis. They knew him as the Okuzaki who didn't drink or smoke, who had no hobbies, worked with devotion, and was humble. Okuzaki Shimizu, Okuzaki's wife, told me that whenever they had a problem at home, the Hyogo police would come straight over and help them out. I wouldn't have been surprised to find out that some of them had what Okuzaki would call "respect" for him.

For Okuzaki, being called "sensei" was, more than anything else, a kind of invisible decoration. For him, it signified an appraisal of his life accomplishments. Nothing pleased him more; as a result, he took action in order to live a life worthy of always being called "sensei."

I had a hunch that his "desire to be called 'sensei'" would one day be directed at me. Although he never actually said as much to me, I could sense it. But I made a point of not calling him "sensei." Why? Because I was making a movie. If a filmmaker enters into a relationship in which he refers to his subject as "sensei," he'll lose all artistic freedom. Okuzaki would criticize me, over and over again: "Hara, you probably think we're equals, but it's ten years too soon for you to think that!" In terms of the amount of energy each of us had, I think I fully acknowledged his incomparable superiority, but in terms of our relationship, we *had* to be equals, no matter how much Okuzaki might reproach me for this. From Okuzaki's point of view, this was yet another thing about me that irritated him.

Let me add in passing that I would resist him at every opportunity by saying, "For the sake of the film..." or "When it comes to filmmaking..." This would infuriate him.

"Hara, though the film may be your goal, for me, it's only a means to 'the greater end of making humankind truly happy.' You always refer to yourself as someone who's 'crazy about films.' Me, I'm a battery salesman. But every time I take action, I drop the title of 'battery salesman.' If I just thought I was a battery salesman, I'd never be able to do anything to achieve my final goal. I would even go so far as to say that I work as someone who's 'crazy about people.' So, Hara, I want you to drop the title of 'movie fanatic' and start acting like a 'people fanatic.'"

"PLAN TO KIDNAP" SHIMAMOTO ISEKO

As we were shooting the scenes about the execution incident, we were simultaneously making preparations to go to New Guinea. While meeting with Okuzaki about this, he said, "I want to take Shimamoto Iseko to New Guinea. She said she wanted to go, but her daughter objected because she was worried about her mother's health."

Shimamoto Iseko, the mother of the friend whom Okuzaki had buried during WWII, was 77 years old. I'd heard that New Guinea was incredibly hot and humid, so I was also worried about whether or not her body would be able to withstand the climate. I understood her desire to go to New Guinea, and Okuzaki's desire to bring her along, but her daughter's concern was reasonable. I listened to Okuzaki, thinking that it would probably be impossible to bring Shimamoto Iseko on our trip. He went on, as if he saw right through my misgivings.

"We'll take her to New Guinea. Perhaps she'll die there. But even if she does, I think she'll be satisfied with such a death. So I think we should take her."

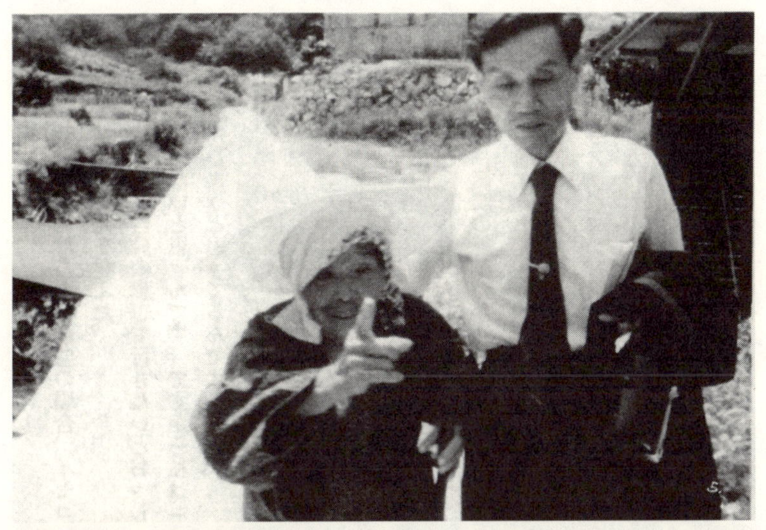

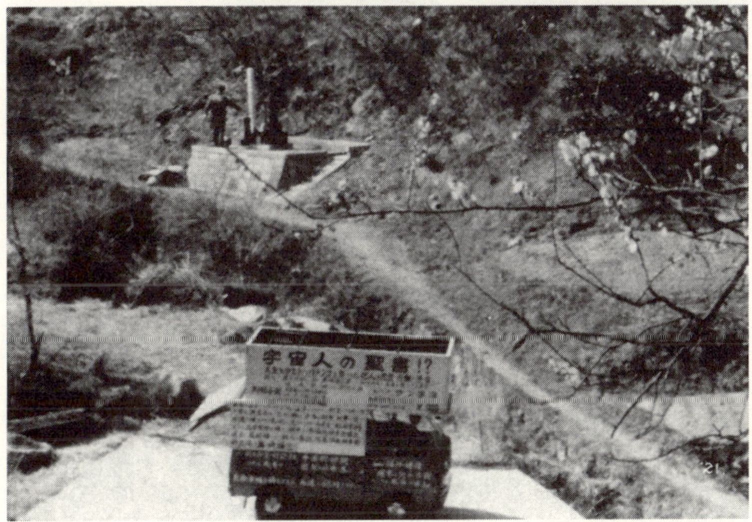

Shimamoto Iseko saying she loves *enka*, popular Japanese ballads.
Okuzaki visiting the grave of the late Shimamoto Iseko (bottom).

Even if Okuzaki wanted to take her to New Gunea, this would be impossible without her daughter's consent. When he said he knew full well that, in the worst-case scenario, Shimamoto Iseko might die there, I felt slightly repulsed.

"Her daughter refuses to let her go, but she's not a child. Shimamoto Iseko said of her own free will that she wanted to go, so I don't think her daughter has the power to prevent her, even if she is her daughter. So I'm going to prepare everything for our trip, and on the eve of our departure, I'm going to kidnap Mrs. Shimamoto."

I was dumbfounded. "Kidnap" her? Weren't the police still following us? This was bad. Was he that determined to take her to New Guinea? As thoughts about whether or not a kidnapping scene would be relevant to the film swirled around in my confused mind, I grew tense. Basically, I thought we should film it. But the next words to come out of Okuzaki's mouth totally threw me off.

"Well, I won't be able to kidnap her on my own. Please, Hara, I'd like you to help me."

I was utterly disappointed. Me, help you?! Who would shoot the scene then?!

I thought I should shoot the "kidnapping" as an example of the profundity of Okuzaki's obsession, but this would only make sense if Okuzaki were the one carrying it out. Since I would be shooting him performing the kidnapping, I, too, would be participating in it in a sense. Thinking about myself as part of an abduction gave me chills. He'd once said, both praising himself and belittling me, "I'm a man of action. You're a storyteller, Mr. Hara. The storyteller should just shut up and film the man of action." But how did he think I could function as a storyteller if I were helping him out?! Sometimes, Okuzaki would politely ask my crew or me to help him. He wanted us to act like his assistants. This pissed me off. To "kidnap" Shimamoto Iseko and take her to New Guinea, though she might die there... What would happen if she did die? Okuzaki's "ethics and logic" aside, I had to think about my own "ethics and logic." Moreover, our relationship was growing increasingly awkward. It was depressing.

But I never uttered a word that might have revealed any of this inner conflict. I simply repeated vague responses.

In the end, the "kidnapping" never took place. Just before our departure, Shimamoto Iseko passed away.

THE CREW HAS SALT THROWN AT THEM

On our second visit to the house of Okuzaki's old squad commander, Takami, we barged in on him with no prior notice, rolling camera in our usual style, and found him with a visitor. He was in the middle of meeting the go-between for his son's wedding.

Just as I began filming, a woman's voice rang out behind me, hysterical. I sensed that the assistant director, Omiya, was dealing with whomever it was. For a moment, I wondered what was going on, but most of my energy was focused on the viewfinder. A moment later, Yasuoka whispered in my ear, explaining that Takami's wife was behind me. I turned slightly in the direction of the "voice." "I see, it's his wife," I thought. She sounded as if she were crying. I understood the situation immediately. She was outraged, furious at our irreverence. She was reproaching us and pleading that we stop filming. I wondered if I should turn the camera, which was focused on Okuzaki and Takami, onto the voice behind me. Technically, this would have been easy. I could have gotten a shot of Takami's wife by just turning my body around. But I hesitated. Her trembling voice grew louder.

A situation like this is really tough. Her entire body was saying that it refused to be filmed. If I ever became more accustomed to chaos, would I one day be able to shoot in a situation like this?

In the end, I couldn't make myself pan to Takami's wife.

The shoot ended. We said our goodbyes and left the house with Okuzaki in the lead. I brought up the rear. After a few steps, on a whim, I turned around. Takami's wife was standing in the doorway. With a big sweep of her arm, she threw salt onto the ground as if to hit us with it!![12] I was shocked. I saw that Takami had noticed, and, turning back towards his wife, hastily ran over to her, pushed her back inside the house, and shut the door, bowing his head. Had Okuzaki noticed? It seemed as though he hadn't. Thank goodness.

Hirasawa, the camera assistant, had also noticed what had happened. "I've worked on a number of films before this one, but this is the first time I've ever had an interviewee throw salt at me," he said, crestfallen; apparently, it had been quite a shock for him. "I don't want to work on this film anymore," he continued. Since we would have been in a real bind without him, I tried to console him and stop him from leaving. I explained to him the importance of the film, but I myself knew how empty my words sounded. I felt exactly as he did.

THE CREW REBELS

After shooting the scene where a wailing ambulance carries Yamada Kichitarō away, I thought it would be obvious that we would also be heading for the hospital as well. I called to my crew: "Let's follow the ambulance!" But my crew's reaction seemed to say, "Are we still shooting?"

About six hours had passed since we'd arrived at Yamada's. From the very beginning, Okuzaki and Yamada had butted heads. Okuzaki had resorted to violence, then made a lengthy speech trying to persuade Yamada to talk. The police had appeared. The crew had been subjected to constant tension the whole time. The problem wasn't simply the length of time; Okuzaki's use of violence on Yamada, who was still convalescing, had been unbearable to them. I could see from the expressions on their faces that, while repulsed by Okuzaki, they'd been equally repulsed by the fact that I'd continued to film the scene. But I vigorously urged them on to the hospital.

12 In Japan, salt is commonly thought of as a "purifier." It is placed in front of one's house after a wake or a funeral to cleanse out bad luck and to ward off evil spirits.

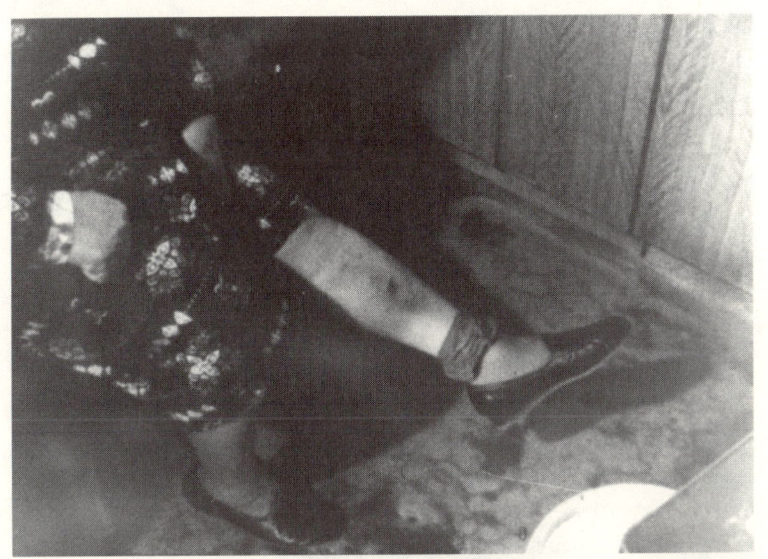

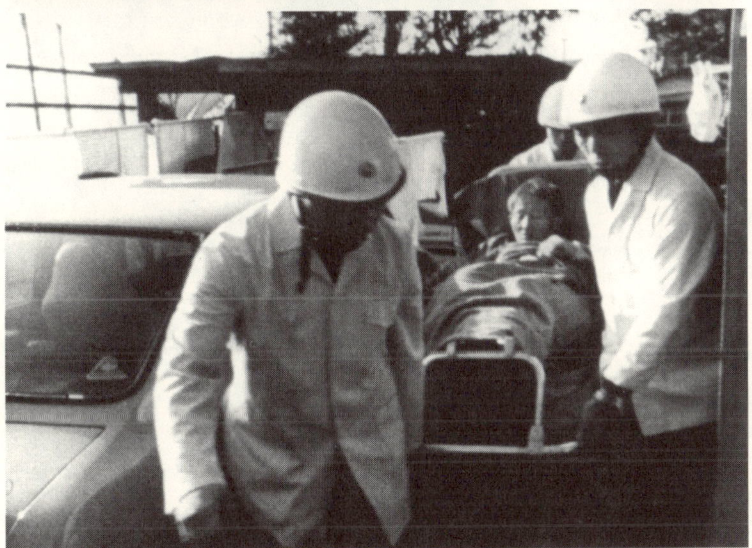

Okuzaki's wife showing where she'd been kicked (top).
My crew didn't want me to shoot Yamada in the hospital (bottom).

When we arrived at the Red Cross Hospital, I jumped out of the car, camera in hand, and readied myself to head in. But my crew wouldn't budge.

"Let's go shoot this."

"Let's not, Hara," they replied. I shrank back.

"OK. Then I'll leave the camera here and go see how he's doing."

I ran into the hospital and found Yamada right away, his wife standing next to his bed. "How are you?" I asked.

"I won't know until they take an x-ray, but I think I'm okay," Yamada replied feebly, though in a livelier tone than I'd expected. His response seemed to indicate that he felt better than I would have thought. I took a look at the room. Nurses moved about, as though they were preparing to take an x-ray. I would probably be able to shoot that if I wanted, I thought. I left the room and returned to where my crew was waiting. Their faces, which showed that they knew what I was going to say before I even opened my mouth, expressed refusal, silently telling me, "Go shoot all by yourself if you want to."

My spirits sank. I felt that there was nothing I could do but give up.

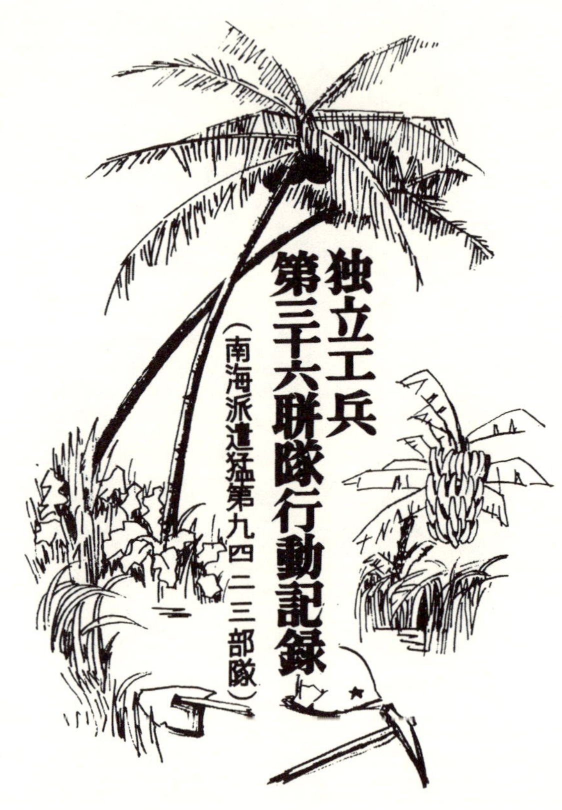

The Battlefield Movements of the 36th Special Engineer Corps

At last—or should I say, at long last—we ended up making our trip to New Guinea. By this point, about a year had passed since we'd started filming. Okuzaki had shouted several times that he was quitting the film, and I'd thought in return that it was all so stupid that I was going to beg him to quit. Nevertheless, *the film was still on*. It was impressive that we'd managed to get to that point.

Okuzaki had a proposal regarding our trip to New Guinea. Since we had to cut our budget to a minimum, only Yasuoka, the assistant director, and I could go. Okuzaki suggested that we play Shimamoto Iseko's grandchildren.

"I'm not *asking* you to do this. Just do as I say," he said.

He sounded as though there were no room for discussion, as though his decision were final. Okuzaki told me to copy and enlarge Shimamoto Iseko's passport photograph. The day before we left, Okuzaki arrived from Kobe at our hotel in Tokyo and ordered Yasuoka to buy a picture frame. The next morning, Okuzaki appeared before us with the framed photo of Shimamoto Iseko tied tightly to his chest with string.

Okuzaki kept this frame tied to his body throughout our journey to New Guinea until we returned home.

Seeing him with this picture of Shimamoto Iseko tied to his chest, and remembering his insistence that Yasuoka and I play the roles of Shimamoto Iseko's grandchildren, I finally understood what Okuzaki had in mind. But I had absolutely no idea if it would actually work. In the past, Okuzaki had strongly declared that human emotions could be understood despite national or ethnic differences. I suppressed the unpleasant realization that finally even I had been made to play a substitute.

Kobayashi sent us off with the words "Do a good job," and we were on our way to New Guinea.

On March 16th, we flew from Narita to Jakarta. We stayed there for a day, and flew from Jakarta to our destination, Jayapura's Sentani

Airport in the province of Irian Jaya.[1]

I considered how to best capture Okuzaki taking his first steps into Western New Guinea. I figured that after landing, I would probably be able to film him stepping down the plane's stairs only if I followed him out from behind. I consulted with Yasuoka. He was dead-set against this. He said that since we didn't have a permit to shoot at the airport, doing so might cause trouble; we'd be arrested immediately. His fears and concerns made sense. We'd brought our 16-millimeter camera into the country without asking for permission.

Mr. O, who was well-informed in matters pertaining to New Guinea, had told us that when creating a travelogue or TV exploration program with villagers living in the interior of New Guinea, he'd had to apply in Indonesia for a license, pay an exorbitant amount of money, and wait for over two years before they finally gave him the OK. We didn't have that kind of time or money. The day before, I'd been nervous while going through customs in Jakarta with the camera and film stuffed into the bottom of my bag; when they let me through without thoroughly checking my stuff, I'd been very relieved.

Maybe we should forget about shooting at the airport. I still hadn't been able to make up my mind by the time the plane touched down at Sentani Airport. We landed, and I noticed that the passengers had started to de board. "I'm going to roll camera," I said to Yasuoka. He looked shocked and furious. I ignored him.

I brought Okuzaki's figure into the viewfinder as he headed down the aisle and turned the camera on.

He walked out of the airplane. The light was dazzling. A panorama of the entire airport, a modest building, filled the viewfinder. He stepped down the stairs. Rolling camera, I followed

1 At the time this book was originally published in Japanese, the current province of West Papua in Western New Guinea was known as the province of Irian Jaya.

the line of passengers. I wanted to catch a bit more of the airport terminal in the shot. "Just a bit more," I thought when suddenly someone tapped my shoulder. My heart stopped. The gig was up. "Yasuoka, I'm sorry, I should have stopped," I repented. I turned off the camera and hesitantly turned around. A man in an army uniform was pointing. "Over there," he gestured. I had strayed a little off the course to the terminal. I took a deep breath. "Okay," I said, nodding. I hadn't been busted for filming. Still, it made my blood run cold. With that, I took my first step into Western New Guinea.

As expected, it was truly hot. The thick heat engulfed my entire body. Wiping off my sweat was useless; I'd just sweat some more. Having briefly greeted Iskandar, our local interpreter who'd come to the airport to meet us, Okuzaki asked him to take us to a lumber dealer. I got a number of shots of Okuzaki looking for the proper wood with which to build a memorial to the spirits of the dead. We then headed to our hotel in the city center. Upon arriving, Okuzaki called us together for a meeting.

He demanded with a stern expression that we go to the village of Arso.[2] We'd been guaranteed that it would be 200 percent impossible for us to enter the region, but perhaps the picture of Shimamoto Iseko tied to Okuzaki's chest—an unquestionable indication of his determination—had had an effect. Iskandar responded to this impossible demand by suggesting that we go to the police department the next day and ask them if we could enter Arso.

(The only time I kept a journal of the film was during our shoot in New Guinea. What follows is a reproduction of that journal, along with supplementary notes and commentary on Okuzaki's exploits in New Guinea.)

---

2 Arso: The name of the village where Okuzaki and the 36th Special Engineer Corps disbanded after retreating from the US advance into New Guinea during World War II. Also where Okuzaki buried his friend Shimamoto Masayuki. Refers also to the district south of Jayapura municipality, east of the Papua New Guinea border. During the 1980s, when Okuzaki and Hara visited the area, the Indonesian government was beginning to transform Arso into an palm oil plantation.

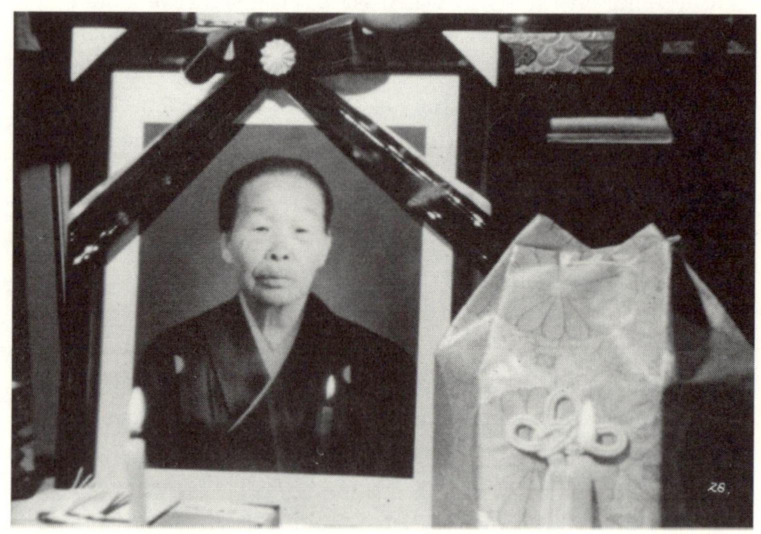

Iseko's photograph, which Okuzaki tied to him during the whole trip to New Guinea.

MARCH 18TH (FRIDAY)

7:20: Breakfast. 8:00: We go first to the police department with Iskandar. We talk with a man who seems like the chief. He makes a series of phone calls for us.

We then go to what seems to be Irian Jaya's military police headquarters. The first in command is not around, so the second in command attends to our request. But we get nowhere. We decide to go back another time.

I walk around with the camera wrapped in a garment bag, but find no opportunity to shoot anything. I wonder how to capture this situation—that is, Okuzaki wanting to get to Arso.

Afternoon, we wait. We nap and lie around idly.

At Okuzaki's request, we cook rice using a military camping pot.

After dinner, I search the city for a light so we can shoot a scene of Okuzaki making an international phone call.

When I arrive back at the hotel, the first commander, whom we weren't able to meet, is engaged in a conversation with the brother and sister from Japan who are also staying at our hotel. The sister, when she sees me, flashes a promising smile.

Iskandar sits down with them and goes to work. Getting a glimpse of them from time to time, we hold our breath in anticipation and wait.

But no new developments.

Okuzaki had begun his activities by trying to get a permit to enter Arso. I didn't think we'd be granted permission, so I thought I had to film Okuzaki trying to obtain the permit. As such, I was holding the camera the whole time, wrapped in black cloth. I wanted to be able to shoot him immediately if an opportune moment presented itself. However, I couldn't help but think that taking out the camera in the middle of the police department would invite trouble. When we got to the headquarters of the army, the most powerful institution in the state of Irian Jaya, I became incredibly nervous—much more so than when we'd been at the police department. I was worried that they might find the camera wrapped in the black cloth, making it impossible for me to shoot anything that day.

As for the scene of "Okuzaki making an international phone call," I'd always planned to somehow capture the relationship between Okuzaki and Shizumi, his wife. Okuzaki was continually calling Shizumi at home. I'd seen this when on location in Japan, and I'd come up with the idea of using two camera crews to shoot a phone conversation between New Guinea and Kobe, like a live broadcast from two different locations, and editing the footage together. A new camera crew had been formed on the Kobe end, with Kobayashi at the helm, and they were standing by, ready to go at any time, as soon as I gave the word.

In documentaries, people don't usually shoot both sides of a telephone conversation because it looks contrived and false. In narrative films, however, it's a very common technique. I deliberately wanted to use this common narrative film technique. Would it look artificial? I thought that when it came to this film—in which Okuzaki had used substitutes as many as three times, and in which he himself had been so excessive as to have seemed to have been "acting"—too much artificiality wouldn't be a problem. Or rather, that that artificiality, combined with Okuzaki's excessive "acting," might end up making things seem more real.

As for the "brother and sister," we'd met them at Biak Airport on the way from Jakarta to Sentani Airport. The girl, in her mid-twenties, desperately wanted to visit the uncharted wilderness smack in the middle of Western New Guinea. Since it was unsafe for a woman to travel there alone, her brother had come with her. Like Okuzaki, she also hadn't gotten permission to enter the region. She was thinking about just going there directly and seeing what would happen. No Japanese person had ever been there, which was the very reason why she wanted to be the first to visit the area. Okuzaki appeared to be quite pleased with the girl's spirit. She and her brother were staying in our hotel. It seemed that the person responsible for granting the brother and sister permission to enter the heart of the New Guinea jungle was the same person who'd be granting us permission to go to Arso. I figured that the reason why the sister and brother had been given the opportunity to negotiate—over dinner, no less—was because the sister was quite attractive.

MARCH 19TH (SATURDAY)

Woke up at 6:30 am. Shot a scene of us meeting with Iskandar. He leaves to negotiate with the police by himself. We just wait. About three hours pass. Some time after two in the afternoon, he returns, and I shoot his report. Okuzaki's way of asking questions of Iskandar is great. But no good. We didn't get the sound. Yasuoka has been functioning as both interpreter and sound technician; he was trying the best he could to interpret, a task unfamiliar to him, and he failed to record Iskandar's report.

Obtaining permission to go to Arso is proving difficult. Iskandar informs us that the case has been sent up the chain of command to the big boss in Jayapura, but that today is Saturday, and nothing can be done until Monday. All we can do is wait.

At night, I go into the city to buy the light needed in order to shoot the "international phone call" scene. I look all over the place, finding only a red, uneven light. It's an awful lamp. But I have to make do with what's available.

Yasuoka looks rather exhausted, mentally fatigued from interpreting. Iskandar is also wiped out.

When I've returned from shopping, I shoot Okuzaki cooking his rice in his room using military camping utensils and eating it.

MARCH 20TH (SUNDAY)

Mid-morning, Okuzaki builds his memorial to the dead. I shoot him carefully applying paint to the wooden post he bought immediately after our arrival here.

A nap.

Negotiating to shoot Okuzaki's "international phone call" in the evening does not go well.

Later in the evening, I summon Iskandar, who's on holiday. He negotiates with the hotel manager, but is told no. I want to shoot in the hotel lobby. I can shoot in the lobby, but I can't dismantle the phone to install a device to record Okuzaki's conversation. Our only hope it seems is to shoot Okuzaki asking to make the phone call at the front desk, and then, without permission, installing the device in Okuzaki's room, in order to record his conversation with his wife in Kobe.

Just as I'm about to consult with Okuzaki about this, he beats me to it. He says he wants to do the phone call at the front desk no matter what. He goes on to say that even if we have to sacrifice the sound (i.e. his wife's voice on the phone in Kobe), the image of him is important. I get upset and wonder why he won't listen to what I have to say, to my plan. But since I'd instructed Kobayashi to make sure she'd record his voice over the phone on her end, I calm myself down and agree to his plan. I shoot him asking for permission to use the phone at the front desk anyway. Iskandar is kind enough to hold the light for us. When I'm in my room, changing rolls of film, Okuzaki shows up and asks if we should shoot the rest of the scene in his room.

This pisses me off. Why does he say that now? He didn't even listen to me. He should have done as I'd said from the beginning. I talk back to him. Then he gets enraged, saying, "This just occurred to me now. If you'd thought of it earlier, why didn't you tell me sooner?" Because you wouldn't listen. At any rate, we decide to shoot the scene in Okuzaki's room. We inform the manager of our decision, but he's distrustful of us dismantling the receiver and wants Iskandar to attend the shoot. "Dismantling" means taking some screws off and installing a simple device. But the manager is afraid we might break the phone. Iskandar and the manager are close friends, so he's not on our side right now, he's a watchdog looking out for the hotel's interests. I'm not pleased with this, and neither is Okuzaki.

Because we have no other choice, we stand by in Okuzaki's room. We give up on the idea of installing a device in the phone. We shoot the "international call" to Kobe anyway. Despite all the trouble, the shoot is more or less successful, so Okuzaki is in a better mood, his bad temper soothed.

I wonder if they got the scene in Kobe? Kobayashi Sachiko, I'm counting on you.

MARCH 21ST (MONDAY)

Okuzaki's morning whims have become a problem again. He thinks the Indonesian government has been disrespectful for making none other than Okuzaki Kenzō wait as long as three days. "We've left everything up to Iskandar, and that makes me feel like I'm not trying as hard as I can. For me, the result isn't what's important, it's the satisfaction of knowing that I've done my best. I'm going to negotiate with the Indonesians myself." Iskandar is puzzled by Okuzaki's outrage, but decides to arrange for him to speak directly to the people in the government.

However, Okuzaki's shorts are a problem. He's been wearing shorts in the hotel because of the heat. When Iskander asks him to change, he starts putting on long pants. But a moment later, as if having second thoughts, he asks angrily,

"Why are shorts disrespectful? What's disrespectful is making me wait for three days. I'll respond to their disrespect with disrespect of my own." Hearing Okuzaki screaming, the hotel manager comes over to discuss something with Iskandar. Yasuoka, who's been interpreting, looks annoyed with Okuzaki. He feels that "When in Rome, do as the Romans do."

The situation is turning into a personal struggle between Okuzaki and Yasuoka. This, too, is a part of Okuzaki's character; I shoot with a rather heavy heart. Poor Yasuoka. But since he's the one bearing the brunt of Okuzaki's fury, it should be possible for me to film. However, Yasuoka's temper flares up in return. As expected, so does Okuzaki's. This is bad. Sure enough, Okuzaki tells Yasuoka that he is no longer needed as an interpreter, that they will part ways here, and that he should go home. Once again, Okuzaki threatens to abandon the film. He storms down to the lobby.

When I go to check on him, a policeman is in the lobby. It appears that as a result of their previous discussion, the manager and Iskandar have reported Okuzaki to the police. Iskandar is begging Okuzaki to change his shorts. "No, I won't!!" says Okuzaki. The people in the lobby are alarmed, wondering what's going on. Okuzaki paces around the tiny lobby, shouting. Once he gets like this, there's no way to stop him. Iskandar is talking feverishly to the policeman. Okuzaki calls Kobe and tells me to take the receiver. Kobayashi, on the other end of the phone, asks me what they should do. I tell her that they can go back to Tokyo, and that I'll call her back in the evening.

Upon replacing the receiver, Okuzaki yells at me "All of you can go back to Japan tomorrow!!" The policeman steps forward. He tells Okuzaki, "I've just informed the proper authorities of your request. The decision will be made this afternoon, so please wait."

At 3 in the afternoon, the same policeman returns. He tells us that we can only enter Abepandai. Iskandar, knowing that Okuzaki won't be satisfied as long as his request to go to Arso is denied, pleads with the policeman again. After listening to his explanation, the policeman says he'll look into it further and leaves. Iskandar follows him out.

Iskandar returns after 7. He says that to go to Arso, we have to get a permit from two police departments, and that we've gotten one from the local police here. He's going now to the big boss's house to get the permit from the military police.

8:30 pm. Okuzaki has started to say that he's going to go to Port

Moresby.[3] If he can't enter from Western New Guinea, he'll enter from Eastern New Guinea. He says he wants to cross the border and enter Arso unrestricted. He tells me to come with him to Port Moresby if I want to—but only me. He tells Yasuoka to go home.

I know he doesn't actually want Yasuoka to go home. And I don't think we'll get permission from the military police. Still, I tell him that I'll grant his wish and go. Right then, Iskandar returns. When he finds us, he gives us the OK sign. "What!!" I couldn't believe it for a moment. Well done, Iskandar!! You could see his delight in the smile that filled his face. But then there's Okuzaki's response. He frowns and says, "Good. Thank you." Shouldn't he at least express some gratitude for all the trouble Iskandar has had to go through? "I was sure we'd be able to go to Arso." What a lie. Hadn't he been talking about going to Port Moresby just seconds earlier? He actually thought we wouldn't be granted permission. "We got permission to go to Arso because I got angry today. You have to get angry sometimes. That's my way of doing things."

I couldn't help but think that Okuzaki actually had a point. Because he'd been shocked by Okuzaki's outrage, Iskandar had fought tooth and nail for permission. Even the policeman, when he knew how strongly Okuzaki felt, had gone and told his superiors. But that doesn't mean that our problems have come to an end. Our visas are going to expire tomorrow at midnight. We've already received permission to visit Arso and Abepandai, but Okuzaki couldn't care less about our visas. He's going to Arso tomorrow, come what may. The day after tomorrow, and the day after that, he wants to go to Abepandai. On top of that, he's demanding that we go by canoe. He continues to address poor perplexed Iskandar, telling him to call the Japanese embassy for visas so we can go to Port Moresby.

Watching this exchange, I figure it would be a good time to restore the relationship between Okuzaki and Yasuoka. So I call Yasuoka down from his room. But it's a mistake. Yasuoka's appearance revives Okuzaki's anger. Signaling with

3 Port Moresby: The capitol of what is now known as Papua New Guinea.

my eyes, I let Yasuoka know that there's nothing we can do about it, so he should stay away from Okuzaki a while longer.

Even after Iskandar, now further burdened, leaves, Okuzaki's excitement persists. But he gradually calms down and begins to show a smile. He says he's going to call his wife to tell her the news about being able to go to Arso. I tell him I'm going to shoot the phone call. He replies with a nod. "I'm going to have Yasuoka help, OK?" I tell Okuzaki. He grimaces but consents, saying that it made him sick but couldn't be helped. Because Okuzaki had rebuffed him earlier, it's Yasuoka's turn to sulk. I manage to persuade him to rejoin the shoot. The younger employees on the hotel staff hold lights for us and help us with the shot.

Today has been truly a long day!!

I'm glad we're clear to go to Arso!!

MARCH 22 (TUESDAY)

I'm not able to sleep very well. I'm worried sick. When I wake up again for the umpteenth time, I hear the sound of rain. I get out of bed at 6 am. The rain continues to fall. I become concerned that the rain might prevent us from going to Arso as planned. Then Okuzaki comes into our room. "It's been called off for today." I wonder who could have told him that so early in the morning. But he returns to his own room, so I couldn't find out.

Just after 8 am, Iskandar comes to our room. It's become customary for us to console one another about the difficulty of dealing with Okuzaki at the beginning of each day. As I was informing Iskandar about the cancellation of our trip to Arso, his face suddenly went pale, and he headed straight for Okuzaki's room next door.

I'm not sure what happened between the two of them, but it was decided that we are going to Arso as planned.

We leave the hotel, buy an artificial flower, and head for Arso at 10 o'clock. Two local police officers escort us. We head straight for Arso. It's stopped raining. The white road that pierces the forest looks wide enough to accommodate two lanes. It's not badly paved. Okuzaki, recalling when he'd been there during the war, says that it wasn't the path he'd taken back then; Iskandar says that it's the only way out there. We come across a river along the way.

"In 1944 I swam across a river, but was it this one? No, it wasn't. That one was much bigger. It definitely had a U-shaped curve in it," Okuzaki says, repeatedly shaking his head at the gap between his memory and what lay in front of him. Several minutes after passing the river, we arrive at our destination: Arso. It's at the end of the white road. "Here we are," we're informed. "What!? Here!?" I yell without thinking. A bulldozer moves across the landscape. It has the feel of a land about to be deforested for cultivation. Okuzaki also has to make sure. "Is this it?" Of course, I had no reason to know what the place would look like, but I had at least expected to find a fragment of the horror, something reminiscent of the fact that, during the war, the 36th Special Engineer Corps had begun its march into the hell of starvation here. But the place utterly defies that image. There are a number of soldiers in military uniforms. A crowd of barefooted men who look like natives surround us, staring from a distance.

Since we'd arrived in Arso, I thought I might as well get at least one shot of it, so I shoot Okuzaki reeling in the threads of his memory. One of the soldiers levels his gun right as I start shooting. Quickly pushing my camera down, Iskandar informs me that filming there is prohibited. "That won't do for me," I retort. The soldier hadn't actually aimed his gun at me, but still, it wasn't a good feeling. Eventually, they agree to let me film Okuzaki performing the ceremony he had gone there to do. What a relief.

Because of the rain that had been pelting the ground since the previous night, we struggle through the thick mud to get to the soldiers' office. I grow frustrated at not being able to film the Arso landscape. I think, the moment that soldier with the gun takes his eyes off me, I'm going to roll the camera without looking through the viewfinder. But I never get a chance.

Their office is more like a slightly upgraded shack on a construction site: it's like a barracks. They lead us into the office for introductions; inside is a small platoon of soldiers, about 20 to 30 of them. An arrogant, chubby soldier with a Che Guevera-like beard receives us. The information I'd been given about a guerilla war being waged by the National Liberation Front is in fact true; the reality of this strikes home.

The young soldiers chats away while kindly guiding us through the forest. Okuzaki appears to be desperately searching for the path he himself had taken when he'd been there as a captured soldier. He repeatedly mumbles to himself, "This is completely different." Before long, he gives up, and, after getting permission, sets up a wooden memorial marker in a corner of the garden in front of the office. I film Okuzaki from many angles as he digs into the earth with a shovel. He plants the memorial marker and gathers some wild flowers as offerings, working quietly all the while. The soldiers watch us. As I move around, I casually try to get an angle showing Okuzaki with the soldiers in the background.

Okuzaki says he wants to give the village chief money as an expression of his appreciation for caring for him 39 years before. The soldiers then lead us to the chief's residence. Okuzaki politely hands the chief a shockingly thick 10 cm roll of rupiah bills (when I ask him later how much he had given, he says it was about 200,000 yen). The chief is speechless with surprise at Okuzaki's unexpected offer. Of course, I shoot this. Profound interest is visible on each of the surrounding soldiers' faces.

Lunch. Okuzaki eats the rice cooked in the military camping pot with delight.

I want to capture the current atmosphere of Arso. I wonder what might be the best way to accomplish that. I proposed taking a commemorative picture of the soldiers. They show interest. I take still shots and moving ones. Naturally, the latter ones are what I really want. I want to film anything I can.

Okuzaki then says he wants to give the soldiers some money. He distributes money to each of the soldiers, who look dumbfounded. I feeling uncomfortable, wondering if we weren't being rude.

At night, while we're eating dinner, Okuzaki says, "I feel like I've banished a demon." He's in a really good humor.

MARCH 23RD (WEDNESDAY)

Today, we decided to call off the trip to Abepandai. Okuzaki hadn't completed his inscription on the memorial he was to erect. At breakfast, Okuzaki said he was going to Vanimo via Port Moresby to charter a Cessna or a helicopter so he could look from the sky for the road he had walked from Vanimo to Arso 39 years before.[4] I'm shocked. He's still stuck on the fact that while heading to Arso the day before, he couldn't find the actual path he had taken back then, even though he did get to Arso. I'm becoming anxious again. To go from Vanimo to Arso we would have to cross the border between New Guinea and Indonesia...

Mid-morning, we prepare for our trip to Port Moresby.

Evening. Okuzaki makes an international call to Shizumi, his wife in Kobe, and informs her of his successful journey to Arso.

MARCH 24TH (THURSDAY)

Off to Abepandai, a small village on the coast. It's one of the destinations for our trip, along with Arso and Demta. There's a memorial to the Japanese soldiers there. That's where Okuzaki erects the wooden memorial he made. The people of the village crowd around him. "Cut down this banana tree for me, so the fallen soldiers can see the ocean," he says. The massive leaves of the banana tree,

---

4 Vanimo: Village in northeastern Papua New Guinea near the border of West Papua, where Japanese troups retreated after the American attack on Wewak, the site of the largest Japanese airbase on the island of New Guinea during World War II.

about four to five meters from the ground, covers the area, casting a dark shadow so you can only get a glimpse of the ocean just a few meters away. The banana tree is the village's staple crop; it's their staff of life. I think this is selfish of Okuzaki, even if it is to give the soldiers a better view of the sea. He tells the villagers he'll pay them the worth of the tree if they cut it down. A number of villagers then go to work. With one or two swings of the machete, they easily fell the tree.

As I film, I'm overcome with an awful sensation. A drunken man is screaming: "JAPAN!!" He's protesting the cutting down of the tree. I feel a growing sense of melancholy. I gesture to the officer who had escorted us to show how horrible I think all of this is. He nods. In an instant, the horizon opens up; a view of the sea spreads out before our eyes. I stop filming. The drunken man, still yelling, has come closer to me. He's young. We stare at each other, eye to eye.

I say to him in English, "You're right. I'm sorry." Perhaps he understands. He asks to shake my hand.

The work has finished. Okuzaki hands over the money. I feel disgusted. Money again. After debating with myself about whether or not to film this part of the scene, I eventually decide not to. Or rather, I can't bring myself to do so.

MARCH 25TH (FRIDAY)

Today was one of Okuzaki's worst. He was angry all day long.

First. It all began after our morning greetings, when Okuzaki asked me if I had noticed and filmed one of the old men from the village in Abepandai cementing a chip that had fallen off the stone monument back into place. I said I hadn't noticed it. This was the beginning of his tirade.

Hara, you should have been focusing on the area inside the fence around the memorial," he said. This had apparently taken place when I had left the others to get some scenery shots of the village.

"The old man was doing this without being asked. That's what's most important to me. Hara, you didn't even notice such an important scene. You really are good for nothing." As I listened to Okuzaki saying this, it wasn't as if I thought the old man's actions were without value. Still, it wasn't a necessary scene for the film.

Second. "Hara, did you or did you not shoot me giving money to the police officer and then him distributing it to the villagers?" I certainly hadn't; I couldn't possibly have brought myself to film that scene. As soon as I said, "No," Okuzaki, looking furious, screaming, "Do you think my money is that dirty?!! My wife and I scrimped and saved in order to raise that money. Why the hell didn't you shoot that scene?!!" As he was yelling this, I realized that for Okuzaki, that money was like a religious offering. Because I'd been so repulsed at what I'd thought was a reenactment of the bad habit that Japanese people have of getting what they want through money, I hadn't shot the scene. Clearly, I had misunderstood Okuzaki's true intent. The amount of money he paid out of his own pockets to console the spirits of his fallen comrades was, for Okuzaki, a concrete measure of value. Our feelings about money were completely different.

I openly admitted my mistake. I should have rolled camera at the time, despite my repulsion. That was the least a documentarian should do in order to qualify as such. Okuzaki was furious with me, and I had no grounds on which to defend myself. When he said he wanted to end the film project and asked us to return to Japan, I simply listened. Okuzaki's anger had started at 6:30 in the morning, and, since it seemed to have ended here, we went and ate lunch together at the hotel restaurant while continuing our conversation. A little after noon, it eventually came to an end. Yasuoka and I kept apologizing. Somehow Okuzaki managed to calm himself down.

But that was just the first stage of his fury. He started saying that he wanted to take the Japanese siblings to Eastern New Guinea with him. Okuzaki emphasized that the sister's determination to be the first Japanese to set foot there had something in common with his own determination to push for something that only he could achieve. No matter how he rationalized it, I didn't think this girl had any relevance to the film. But since we'd been dealing with his temper up until that very moment, arguing with him was bound to just re-ignite his anger, so I simply nodded.

The siblings were supposed to have attained their goal of going to the unexplored New Guinea highlands, and were returning to Jayapura today. Okuzaki went to the airport to meet them. I just had to film him. I knew that they would be surprised to see us suddenly start filming, but there was nothing I could do. I started shooting.

Okuzaki's face, expectant. The sister and brother, surprised. Okuzaki approaches them with a welcoming smile on his face. The sister seems surprised but touched by the fact that Okuzaki has come to meet them. Then she starts crying. She puts her hands together to Okuzaki and prays. It probably wasn't a prayer, but rather her imitation of the local manner of greeting people. But it would look like a prayer to someone who's Japanese. Maybe Okuzaki saw it as I did. That she hadn't simply shed tears, but had put her hands together to greet him.

In the car from the airport to the hotel, Okuzaki began telling the girl in a single burst about everything that had happened. Maybe because her tears had moved him so, Okuzaki also began to cry, gradually raising his voice as though he were possessed. He told her about having been convicted three times, about having been to Arso, about his plan to kill the company commander, and his conviction that such violence was justified, about his experiences during the war, etc. He properly identified us, Yasuoka and myself, not as the grandsons of Shimamoto Iseko, but as the assistant director and director who had come to New Guinea to shoot his movie.

I was a little embarrassed, so I stopped the camera and greeted her, saying, "Nice to meet you." I think she had believed that Okuzaki was going to explain that he, an old man with a picture of Shimamoto Iseko strapped to his chest, and we, Shimamoto Iseko's grandchildren, had simply come here to memorialize the dead, so she must have been flabbergasted at his introduction of himself, without any preamble, as a man who had shot pachinko balls at the emperor. I sympathized with her. But I was astonished myself by what Okuzaki said next.

"I confess I've had sex twice since I got here," he said. Come to think of it, two or three days earlier, Okuzaki, who was feeling exhausted and whose joints were stiff, had called a masseuse to his room. I remember thinking that filming him getting a massage would be a nice souvenir shot of him on location in New Guinea. Was that the woman?! "I wasn't going to tell you two about it, but since I do believe that it's more respectful as a human being to admit a mistake rather than to hide it, I'm telling you now."

As soon as we arrived at the hotel, Okuzaki said to the siblings, "Please call your family in Japan and let them know. I'll pay for the call." The sister hesitated, but eventually she asked for the phone. Okuzaki went on, "In exchange for paying for the call, I would like you to let us film me talking to your parents." The sister started saying, "I was bitten by mosquitoes out in the jungle. It really itches, and I want to go to the hospital." The brother said they'd have to go to the hospital before making the phone call. Okuzaki didn't like this one bit, but we called off the phone call.

Moments later, the brother came into our room. Since we had wanted to discuss the situation with him also, this was a good opportunity. We began by describing Okuzaki from our perspective. He said that although he had been surprised by the welcome at the airport, he had also been quite glad. But he couldn't understand what Okuzaki had said in the car. He wondered if Okuzaki was insane. Just as he was saying that he didn't want us to use the footage of them, Okuzaki burst into the room. Seeing the brother there, he inquired into his sister's condition. "How's your sister?" he asked. Okuzaki said he wanted to talk to her, but the boy, doing the best he could to protect his sister, said that when you're sick, you don't want to see anyone. His face clearly displayed the antipathy he felt for Okuzaki. This response irritated Okuzaki. He screamed, "Tell your sister I wish to speak to her!" The brother, at a loss for words, stood up abruptly and left the room, violently slamming the door behind him.

This reaction added further fuel to Okuzaki's anger. Filled with rage, he screamed, "Wait! You bastard!" and flew out of the room in pursuit. The boy fled downstairs. Okuzaki trailed after. Yasuoka and I looked at each other. Damn, we had to stop him. We stood up. Since I was wearing sandals at the time, I quickly changed into my shoes, and so was a step behind Yasuoka, who had already rushed out of the room. When I went around the stairs leading to the lobby, I caught a glimpse of the brother heading from the front desk to the manager's office. With both arms thrust forward, Yasuoka was pushing back at Okuzaki, who was trying to catch the boy.

"You still haven't learned, have you? Are you going to tell me what to do? Get out of the way!" Okuzaki yelled, beside himself. "Where'd he go?!" The hotel manager and Iskandar rushed over. "It doesn't have to be long! Just let me talk to your sister!" Okuzaki continued screaming.

I thought that in this state, Okuzaki would never relent, so I called the sister and said I would like for her to briefly meet with Okuzaki. She was not pleased, but understood the situation. She came down to the lobby. Although he softened his voice once he saw her, Okuzaki nevertheless expressed his dissatisfaction. He told her that since she was sick, she didn't have to come downstairs. Chatting at her bedside would have been fine. She'd probably figured out that letting him go to her room would have been worse.

She stepped closer to him and bowed silently. Then she turned her back on him and started sprinting up the stairs leading to the second floor. Okuzaki showered her with abuse, yelling, "You're a spoiled brat!!" The sister stopped dead in her tracks in the middle of the stairs and turned towards Okuzaki. Her body trembled. After a moment of silence, determined not to yield to Okuzaki's harassment, she erupted in a torrent of words. She was speaking in English.

Okuzaki's rage continued. "You're Japanese. Speak Japanese!" But she continued to spit English at him. Then Okuzaki himself retorted, "Sick! Sit down!" I was quite impressed by Okuzaki's attempt to quarrel in English, but as I watched him fighting with someone who was, after all, a mere girl, his spit flying all over the place, furious, I couldn't help but feel a sense of sadness.

Okuzaki had invited the police officer who had accompanied us to Arso and Abepandai to dinner that evening as a way of showing thanks for his having taken care of us. The police officer watched the argument between Okuzaki and the girl, looking perplexed. I apologized to him. In any case, I had to bring the situation under control. I asked the hotel manager to take the girl back to her room.

Then the officer and his wife, Iskandar with his wife and kids, the hotel manager, Yasuoka, and I all began our dinner hosted by Okuzaki. Everyone looked unnatural, and awkwardness prevailed at the table. Okuzaki had yet to calm down. From time to times, he would raise his voice at Yasuoka and me. Everyone in the hotel glared at our table. There was no way the food could taste good.

That night, Okuzaki asked the hotel manager to deliver a message to the siblings saying that if they changed their minds and wanted to go to Eastern New Guinea, he would pay for the trip. The manager agreed, but said that it would be better for Okuzaki to write them a letter than to have him explain the situation. "I'll write it tonight," Okuzaki said and returned to his room.

Today has been yet another unbearably long day. When I lay down in bed, I thought about Okuzaki. The more Okuzaki cared for someone, the more profound that person's rejection of him became. It was natural that the siblings should reject him. I've gotten to a point where I think I finally understand how Okuzaki feels. But I also think that no one would probably accept Okuzaki's feelings. I haven't been able to shake off the sense that this man Okuzaki will repeatedly try to care for someone but will end up being rejected for the rest of his life. Nowadays, the more Okuzaki screams, the more my heart aches with sadness. How am I supposed to relate to him?

MARCH 26TH (SATURDAY)

I woke up to Okuzaki's knock on the door. I looked at the clock. 5:15 am. He said he didn't want to yell in the room, so we should go out. I sighed in my mind and obeyed. Outside, it was still dark. We went over to a nearby lot. "I'm still angry," he began. "I'm not trying to manipulate you to my advantage. And this is not a threat. If you don't agree to my terms, let's call the film off," he continued in a subdued voice.

He had two requests. The first: he wanted me to give the siblings his three books and a three-page letter he had written the night before, and to talk them into going to Eastern New Guinea with him on his dime. The second: he wanted me to tell the army commander that he wanted to meet him.

If he was that fixated on the girl, I thought I'd see what I could do, but I wasn't exactly sure what to do about the army commander. The sun was beginning to rise. I returned to our room and called the siblings anyway. I asked the sister if she would briefly meet with him. The sister obstinately refused, saying she didn't want to have anything to do with him anymore. The brother repeated his request for us not to use the footage of them. Click. She hung up the phone. I hadn't thought there was any chance that they would accompany Okuzaki, but I'd been hoping that they might have a peaceful talk with him in order to assuage his anger.

As I gave him the news, I wondered if Okuzaki would lose it again. "If that's how it's going to be then that's how it's going to be. As long as we do everything we possibly can, the outcome makes no difference," he accepted. The siblings were to return home that afternoon. Since Yasuoka and I weren't sure what else Okuzaki might try to do before they left, we passed time until their departure by drinking coffee in the hotel restaurant and nodding at everything he said. When, before noon, the hotel manager gave us the sign that they had left, Yasuoka and I exchanged glances and exhaled.

In that fleeting moment of relief, Okuzaki broke in.

"At any rate, let's part ways here. I'm going alone from here on. Please go back to Tokyo. I'll film the rest of my trip with my 8-mm camera."

He had brought an 8-mm camera with him. His voice was calm and composed. This was different from his usual tone. He was typically angry when he'd tell us he wanted to stop the film or that he wanted us to go home. I sensed he was determined to cause some serious trouble here. I wondered what to do, but there was nothing I *could* do. There was no knowing what might happen next, so I decided to wait and see.

Without saying where he was going, Okuzaki stood up and left. As I watched him leave, I worried that he might barge in on someone, but all I could do was wait. A while later, he returned. He said he had been about to go to the bookstore, but had turned back. He asked if we would give him our English- and Indonesian-language books, now that we no longer needed them.

He decided to compile a "conversation book," and chatted up a group of kids in the lobby. He had become the center of attention at the hotel. He was a hit. He asked for the phone. He wanted to call the Japanese Consulate in Ujunpandai. Whoa. I ran back to my room, grabbed my camera, and went back to the front desk. Okuzaki was holding the receiver and spouting obscenities. I got the camera rolling as quickly as I could. Everyone was watching him, wondering what was going on.

"I'm the man who shot pachinko balls at the emperor!" He played his best card. "You need to put on the pressure so I can go where I want to!" he yelled at the top of his lungs. But there was a degree of composure in his voice. He was well aware of the stares from the people surrounding him in the hotel. "Putting on quite a show," I thought. "Keep it up!" I cheered him on silently as I rolled camera. When he finished his phone call, he paced back and forth in the lobby and, gesturing wildly, kept screaming into the camera. "You get it?! Here's Okuzaki's real value!"

But just as I was thinking that I'd definitely gotten the shot of

Okuzaki screaming at the camera, I heard the tone indicating that the film had run out. I called to him, "Okuzaki, the film is out so I'm going to change rolls." "Okay. Got it. Thank you very much," he replied. He even bowed to me. I was elated. We were in perfect harmony. This was what is called being "in perfect sync." The person being filmed and the person filming were now accomplices.

I changed the film and went back. Okuzaki now took out his passport and raised it high in the air. Then he threw it to the floor. He picked it up, spat on it and began destroying it. The hotel guests and employees who were his "audience" gasped. Even they must have thought that destroying a passport was too much. Yasuoka flew at Okuzaki, tearing the passport from his hands. Okuzaki screamed, "You still don't get it!" I wanted to tell Yasuoka to let Okuzaki do what he wanted, but I didn't have the chance.

Yasuoka had made all of our arrangements for our trip to New Guinea. He must have been seriously worried that Okuzaki might be deported if he destroyed his passport. I understood his sentiment, but I didn't think that Okuzaki's destroying his passport was that big a deal. I wanted to tell Yasuoka, "Okuzaki is in the zone, he's giving a grand performance and you're in the way!" but he was already holding the passport tightly to his chest. Okuzaki, with the look of a Yaksha, leapt at Yasuoka.[5] Chaos broke out. The hotel employees did their best to restrain Okuzaki. The manager called the police. At this point, my film ran out again.

When I went back to the room to change rolls, Okuzaki followed. "Don't you want to film the Demta village chief?" he asked. "The village chief? Who's he talking about," I wondered. But I responded, "OK," and we went back to the lobby together. A well-built young black man was standing there. Just to make sure, I asked him if it was okay for us to film him. According to Okuzaki, he was the "captain" of Demta. I had no idea what "captain" meant, and, given Okuzaki's interpretation abilities, it was no use trying to enquire further. We

5 Yaksha: Protectors of Buddhist teachings and guardian spirits of nature that can be both benign and demonic. Yaksha statues are known for their ferocious expressions.

only had to shoot. We then went to the restaurant.

Okuzaki ordered one dish after another, pouring beer for the "captain" of Demta village. In a magnificent feat of drinking, the man managed to leave a row of over a dozen empty bottles on the table. He had apparently witnessed Okuzaki's earlier performance, and when he'd learned that Okuzaki wanted to go to Demta, he'd gone over to talk to him. Okuzaki entertained him as extravagantly as possible, thinking that this might open the doors to Demta. He told the man that he had a present for him. He handed him a work uniform with "Yuasa Batteries" embroidered on it and a camera. But, as if that weren't enough, he looked at Yasuoka and me and asked, "Why don't you give him your watches?" Yasuoka looked at me and shook his head. What could I do? I took my watch off my wrist.

Naturally, the man was delighted. Perhaps because of the effectiveness of this present, the "captain" of Demta said he himself would take us there. "What? Really!" I thought. Things seemed to be looking up. Okuzaki shook the man's hand vigorously. Looking back on this later, I could see that this wasn't something the man could decide upon by himself, but at the time, I felt as though I'd run into the Buddha while in Hell... Okuzaki implored the man to drink more and offered more beer. By the end, over two-dozen empty bottles filled the table.

The manager came to tell us that the police had arrived. When we went back to the lobby, the officer who had allowed us to go to Arso was standing there. He was in fact a soldier, not a policeman—a lieutenant. He was a young man who appeared to be just out of school, an elite candidate with a promising future. Nevertheless, his attitude toward Okuzaki was one of respect. I wanted to film the exchange between Okuzaki and the lieutenant, but I had to be careful about bringing out a camera in front of him, so I kept it hidden. Let's wait and see, I thought.

The lieutenant wanted an explanation, so Okuzaki began talking, repeating all the good old refrains we'd heard so many times before. As Okuzaki spoke, he grew feverish. In a moment, tears mingled with his passionate defense. I have to shoot this, I decided. If the lieutenant were to say anything to me about filming, I'd deal with it then. Frankly speaking, I was a bit scared, but I exchanged a look with Yasuoka. We went and grabbed the camera and tape recorder we had left in our room and started shooting.

Okuzaki had taken his rhetoric to another level. The lieutenant simply remained silent, listening. He didn't stop us from filming. When Okuzaki finished his hour-long monologue, the lieutenant said, "I understand exactly how you feel. I'll see what I can do for you one more time." The lieutenant told us to wait until Monday for the "decision." As I watched him leave, it was as if I'd caught a glimpse of sunlight.

While we were talking with the lieutenant, it was revealed that the "captain" of Demta we'd just met was in fact no such thing; he was just some boy from the village. After the lieutenant left, Okuzaki yelled at Iskandar and the hotel employees for not telling him this, but I kept thinking that he was barking up the wrong tree; his hasty judgment was to blame. I could only smile bitterly, thinking that such a blunder was just like something Okuzaki would do. He was still harping on this, but eventually his tone shifted, and he started saying, "But I still believe him." Perhaps because the lieutenant had provided him with ray of hope and, with it, some peace of mind.

Anyway, I think Okuzaki did admirably well today. I want to tell him, "Good job." I mean it. That's how I'm feeling today. On one level, he'd put on a big performance against a clerk at the Japanese Consulate and a young lieutenant, but in fact they had been directed at the nation-states of Japan and Indonesia.

I strongly feel that I want Okuzaki Kenzō to start a fight against opponents as large as nations.

MARCH 27TH (SUNDAY)

8 am. We've been granted permission to go to Abepandai because

the lieutenant from yesterday was senior enough to be able to grant permission for this area. Much obliged. As for the boat, we were able to charter a canoe with an engine, as Okuzaki had wished. Churning up waves, we sped across the bay. Okuzaki had his eyes cocked above the bow, trying to find the road he had taken to Abepandai during the war. It was a pleasant jaunt across the bay beneath the southerly sun, the soft wind blowing on our faces. I couldn't tell this to Okuzaki, but I felt refreshed for the first time in a long time. He couldn't find a definitive trace of what had happened 40 years ago, but he seemed satisfied that at least he'd searched all day. Today, remarkably, we had no troubles.

MARCH 28TH (MONDAY)

This morning, at 7 am, Okuzaki's knock woke me up. He began by saying, "We can skip breakfast this morning. Let's go straight to the police headquarters and wait for the lieutenant. Once permission is denied, I'll lose my chance to charter a Cessna and fly over the route I walked during the war. If you don't want to come with me, that's fine. I can go alone. The two of you can go back to Tokyo whenever you want."

He kept talking on like that for an hour at the door to our room. I offered him a seat, but he stood the entire time. He heard both of us consent to his wishes, then left, then immediately came back. "I just realized this, so I'm going to tell you now. While I was standing here, the two of you were sitting on your beds the entire time. That's a sign of your disrespect for me. If I were you, I would have stood until you sat down." He went on for another hour. I wanted to say, "Didn't I offer you a seat?" but since any response would just prolong his speech, I remained quiet and simply listened. Being with Okuzaki is really exhausting.

As Okuzaki was writing his request in the restaurant, Iskandar and the lieutenant arrived. Okuzaki said that we didn't have to bother going to them, since they'd come to us. Smiling, he said, "I'm going to make them wait on purpose." He finished his breakfast leisurely and, about thirty minutes later, the meeting began. Okuzaki made Yasuoka translate what he had written. He wanted to charter a Cessna and search from the sky for his route from Arso—through Hollekang, Abepandai, and Genjem—to Demta. The lieutenant told him he could go to Demta the following day. I listened nearby, hoping Okuzaki would thank the lieutenant for granting him permission to enter Demta, which he'd been longing to go to. But he expressed no such gratitude. He persisted with the matter of chartering a Cessna. The lieutenant told Okuzaki that granting him permission to charter an airplane was beyond his authority, and that he would have to take him to headquarters to speak with his superior officer.

This was our second visit to the headquarters in Irian Jaya. The second officer in command, with whom we were already acquainted, attended to us. Again, I decided that it was still a good idea to refrain from filming inside the office. Okuzaki started in on his stories with the second officer, just like he'd done with the lieutenant. At first, shedding tears, he said, "In 1945, with nothing to eat, we began our wretched retreat from one village to the next, one soldier after another dying of starvation." The second officer listened kindly, responding, "I see. I see." But when he brought his "sob stories" to the next level, telling the officer that he had shot pachinko balls at the emperor and that, without fearing punishment, he'd continued his campaign to memorialize the dead in his own way—and especially when he told the officer that, considering who he, Okuzaki Kenzō was, it was disrespectful for Indonesia to not grant his wish to go where he wanted—the officer's face gradually hardened.

"This is Indonesia. Here you follow Indonesian law," the officer said in a hostile tone. "Chartering a Cessna can only be dealt with in Jakarta. If you insist on chartering one, go to Jakarta and see the Minister of Defense!" Okuzaki, refusing to budge, responded, "I don't have the money or the time to go to Jakarta, so I'm going to call the Japanese Consulate and make them pressure you into allowing me to charter a plane." In response to Okuzaki's persistence, the officer said, "Tomorrow, I will let you go to Demta. The day after, you have to leave this country. Your visa has already expired. That's an order! I don't want to have to deport you, but you'd better follow my orders!!" Okuzaki went as far as to say, "If you won't heed my demands, I'm going to commit hara-kiri," but it had no effect.[6] The second officer in command said, "That's all I have to say," and left.

We went back to the hotel restaurant. While we were eating lunch, Okuzaki seemed convinced that he wouldn't be able to charter a Cessna. If you do everything in your power, and find out that your goal can't be achieved, it's still a step forward, I think. "You'll regret it if you don't do your best," Okuzaki said with unexpected satisfaction.

At that point, the boy from Demta showed up. "Hey, my friend, Japan, very good," he said cheerily, and took a massive swig of beer. The drink was on Okuzaki. He went along with the boy, with a sort of resignation, saying, "You, with free drinks, number one!" On the boy's wrist was the watch that I had had no choice but to give him as a present the day before. I thought about asking him to give it back to me, but he kept saying "Thank you," so I couldn't broach the subject.

At night, lying in bed, I remembered something Okuzaki had said in the morning: "I'm going to go to Jakarta, stand in front of the Japanese Consulate, piss on my passport, then destroy it." That's something he might actually do. Thinking that there was bound to be more turmoil on the horizon, I dozed off.

MARCH 29TH (TUESDAY)

My body was being shaken. I opened my eyes. When I looked at the clock, it was 11 at night. I went to Okuzaki's room. The young

6 *hara-kiri*: Ritual suicide.

lieutenant was there. "It takes five hours to get to Demta by car. We're leaving at 7 in the morning," he said. I went back to sleep and woke up at 6 am. It was raining. Neither the lieutenant nor Iskandar showed at the appointed 7 am, or even by 8. I was worried. Iskandar was at the headquarters when I called. He told us that the road to Demta quickly turns to mud when it rains, and that he was checking on road conditions. Later, the lieutenant arrived driving a jeep.

"Today, I'll be driving you there," he said. A small gun had been placed underneath a seat in the jeep. We left at at 8:50 am. We sped along, bouncing on the rough road. My ass hurt, but the thought of being able to go to Demta distracted me from the pain. After about an hour of driving, one of the tires blew out. We quickly changed it. The road grew increasingly worse from this point on. Because of the rain, getting stuck was a real possibility, so, at the lieutenant's discretion, we decided to change course and go by sea. We headed for a nearby village on the coast.

The lieutenant made arrangements for us at an office that looked like a police box. Three soldiers holding guns joined us as guards. We climbed into a motorboat and took off. Okuzaki was on cloud nine. "Yesterday's rain and the flat tire have actually brought us good results; this is the best possible route to get there," he said. That's exactly right, I thought. At our backs rose a mountain that, with it's perfectly triangular shape, looked like a mini Mt. Fuji. I got the coolest shot I could of Okuzaki looking ahead with the mountain in the background.

We headed toward the open sea. The waves were rough. Spray flew. My heart skipped a beat at the thought of arriving at our final destination that we'd been told would be 200 percent impossible to get to. We had been on the boat for about two hours. Okuzaki's face showed nervousness. We approached the shoreline. "This is Demta," our guide said. A mountain ran all the way to the shore, leaving a strip of white sand where I could see four or five ramshackle huts. Okuzaki gazed restlessly upon the landscape. Before long, he said as though forcing the words out of his mouth, "There's no mistake.

This is it. This is where I was taken after I was captured. I remember it clearly."

But we didn't disembark there. Demta wasn't the village where he'd been captured: it was the camp where he'd been held as a prisoner. Okuzaki now said that he wanted to go to the village where he'd been *taken* prisoner, a town that should have been right next to Demta. Iskandar looked displeased, his face signaling that he'd only promised to take Okuzaki to Demta. Still, seeing Okuzaki's desperation, he didn't say a word. The boat headed out to sea again. Okuzaki continued to gaze at the coastal landscape as it passed by. Okuzaki asked the man who'd come aboard at Demta,

"Is there a village around here with a road running down the middle of it? On both sides are houses, and there's white sand. I snuck in carrying a green banana."

"There is," the man replied. "That's the village you're heading to now. It's an hour away by boat."

Upon hearing "one hour," Okuzaki cocked his head. He thought it had been the village right next to Demta... When we rounded the cape which jutted out from Demta, we could see houses. There seemed to be a village there.

"It's not that village, is it?" Okuzaki asked the man.

"There's no white sand in that village, that's a reef," he replied.

Okuzaki cocked his head incessantly. Soon thereafter, we arrived at the village the man had mentioned. It was called Tarfia. Since the shallow rocky shoreline would scrape the bottom of the boat, we anchored offshore. From about fifty meters out, soaked in the waves up to our thighs, we waded through the ocean to the shore. The moment he made shore, Okuzaki bolted for the village.

"It definitely has a road. This is it. No question," he said with excitement. As he was about to head into the heart of the village, Iskandar, who arrived just in time, quickly stopped him.

"Wait a second, I want you to greet the chief," he said. He managed to dissuade Okuzaki from proceeding.

Three village elders came toward us. Okuzaki had no sooner

bowed, when he started walking, saying he wanted to go to the edge of the village. Many villagers came out and stared at us with curiosity. With a flurry of gestures Okuzaki desperately asked if a Japanese soldier had been captured there thirty-nine years before. The elders nodded. An old woman stepped forward and said,

"I remember that."

"Ooooh." Okuzaki made an indescribable noise. He fervently grabbed both of the woman's hands and then kissed them.

Okuzaki urged me to go to the beach with him. There he showed me how he'd actually crawled into the village 39 years before. Needless to say, he told me to film him.

"I want to give you money to express my gratitude for taking care of me 39 years ago," Okuzaki said, handing the elders 200,000 yen, this time in 10,000-yen bills.

The time to leave was upon us. Iskandar was worried because the ocean grew dangerous when the sun went down. I wanted to film this Tarfia village. It was much more beautiful than one might expect. It even seemed at first glance like a place that had been deliberately created for tourists. I only got two or three shots. Iskandar rushed me.

We waded through the water again toward the boat. All of the villagers saw us off, waving. I took a long shot of the village as it gradually receded into the distance. The sunset was crimson. It was gorgeous. Showered in the salty air, I thought to myself, "Now we can finally wrap." I was flooded with deep relief. I indulged in a bit of sentimentality, thinking how long it had been, how far we had come.

Wondering what Okuzaki was thinking, I turned around. My heart stopped. He was shaking his head incessantly!! This gave me a terrible sense of foreboding. But I remained silent. The wrong word here could lead to disaster. Okuzaki then looked me in the face.

"I don't think Tarfia village was the one," he muttered.

What?! Are you kidding me?! I screamed inside. Those were the last words I wanted to hear at that point. "It's all over now," I thought to myself. I pretended I hadn't heard him. I said to him forcefully,

"Okuzaki, congratulations. I'm really glad for you."

"Thank you. I owe it all to you and your crew," he said. His words seemed somewhat hollow.

My indulgence in the sunset and the sea breeze had disappeared. What the hell had that outpouring of emotion been that he'd expressed for the old woman earlier, back at the village?

We arrived back at the hotel after 9 pm. Okuzaki invited Iskandar, the young lieutenant, and the police officer who had guarded us for the first half of the trip, to dinner, thanking them for all the trouble they had gone through. He was bowing his head.

The Demta boy showed up. He said he had brought presents for us. He gave us a bamboo spear and a bracelet of woven bamboo used by the locals. "Well, he's got a nice character after all, hasn't he?" I was glad. Okuzaki invited the boy, whose name, he said, was Nixon, to sit on the sofa in the lobby and began showering him with questions.

Was there a road that ran through the village that lay between Demta and Tarfia? Was there a beach? The man who had gotten on the boat at Demta had said there wasn't, but Okuzaki thought that that village had been the one where he'd been captured. He thought it had been closer to Demta, directly at the foot of a mountain. There was no mountain directly behind Tarfia. He went on and on.

I recalled the landscape of Tarfia village. There had definitely been no mountain there. From what I remembered seeing from the boat, there had been a mountain right behind the village between Demta and Tarfia. And alas, Mr. Nixon nodded his head at Okuzaki's description. He told us the name of the place. It was called "Anbora."

Thirty-nine years after the war had ended, Okuzaki had learned the name of the village where he'd been captured.

"No question about it. The village where I was arrested was not Tarfia, where we went today. It was Anbora. Well, that's OK. I'll come back again. Next time, I'll bring my wife. Although I was able to get close, I wasn't able to go to Anbora. I think it's the will of the gods. I'll be able to go to Anbora next time. From now on, the idea of going to Anbora is going to give me the motivation to work hard." Okuzaki was telling himself this, not us. I wanted to film him saying these lines. I started to think that this line, that Tarfia was not where he'd been captured, was so like Okuzaki that it could work as the final line for the film.

I had brought fifty 100-foot rolls of film to New Guinea. At this point, I had used forty-nine of them. Actually, when Okuzaki said he wanted to thank the local police for taking such good care of him, he asked if I would shoot the scene. I willingly consented. Since he'd been working so hard, I happily gave him the OK. I had forgotten that we hadn't gotten permission to bring the camera. Neither the police officer nor the lieutenant had said anything about my filming. I'd even shot footage of them with no problem. It seemed as though I shouldn't have worried about it in the first place. So, without hesitation, I'd agreed to Okuzaki's proposition. I'd kept 100 feet of film just for that scene.

I had a hard time making up my mind about whether or not to save some film in order to shoot the scene of Okuzaki thanking the police. Or should I shoot Okuzaki saying these lines expressing his determination to come back to New Guinea? After much deliberation, I decided to save the film for the following day's shoot. I figured that Okuzaki, content with himself, would be thinking up a heroic act for the glorious stage that was the finale of this New Guinea shoot, and I didn't want to disappoint him.

As I write these lines, knowing full well how useless this kind of thinking is, the phrase "If at that moment..." which I repeated so many times back then, comes back to me along with the *deep regret* that always accompanies it.

"If at that moment," I had used the roll of film that I was saving to shoot Okuzaki's words of determination, perhaps the damned "big trouble" that has been the biggest disaster in my life wouldn't have occurred. However, I'm just an ordinary man, not God, so I couldn't know what the next day would bring. Well, thinking back now, perhaps that "big trouble" was itself "God's way of directing this film..."

MARCH 30TH (WEDNESDAY)

I woke up just after 6 am. Yasuoka was gone. I could hear voices coming from Okuzaki's room next door. Yasuoka returned a short time later. "I'm translating something Okuzaki's written," he said. The note said something to the effect that Okuzaki wished to say some words of thanks at the police station (meaning the general headquarters in Irian Jaya), and to be granted permission to film the scene.

We left the hotel at just past 9 am. After we finished shooting, we were going to go straight to the airport and on to Tokyo, so we had packed our bags. We arrived at the general headquarters. This was our third visit. First, Iskandar and Yasuoka took Okuzaki's letter and went into the office. Yasuoka returned, giving me the OK sign. I prepared the camera.

Okuzaki smiled cheerfully and even said, "Please be on standby. I'm going to come in later."

"Who does he think he is," I thought for a moment. But since it was going to be our last scene, it didn't bother me that much. I took the camera in hand and headed to the office with Yasuoka. The second officer in command, whom we'd come to know so well, greeted us with a smile. His eyes fell on my camera. Suddenly, his expression changed. "Wait here a second," he said, and rushed out of the office, leaving Yasuoka and me behind. Something was about to happen. I was petrified. Our departure time was approaching. How long would he make us wait? The ticking of the clock on the wall was deafening.

Okuzaki arrived. "What's going on? Why does it take you so long to set up?" he said as if to scold us.

"No, actually—" I was telling him what was going on when the officer returned. He was with two other men: an officer from the bureau of information and his assistant. The officer from the bureau of information glared at me and demanded,

"Give me your film."

Oh no! This was the worst thing he could have said. The question of what to do flashed through my mind. But the next moment, Okuzaki screamed,

"What? You want the film? Then take the film!" That was that!! "Go get all of it!! Do what I say!!"

I left the office and went to the parked car. I was desperately trying to figure out what I could do. What should I do?! What should I do?! The 49 rolls of exposed film had been divided in two bundles, wrapped in x-ray-proof leaden material, deep in my bag. As I pulled them out, I said to Yasuoka,

"How about I only give them half?"

Yasuoka decisively shook his head. "It will only make matters worse."

I held the film in both hands and headed back to the office. I felt as though I was about to faint. The sun looked strangely white. Wasn't there anything I could do? If I didn't do anything, everything would be lost!! Maybe I should just deny them outright, tell them I couldn't hand over the film. If I did that, would they throw me in jail? I piled every one of the 49 rolls of film on the reception desk in the office.

Okuzaki climbed on the table and sat cross-legged. "If you bastards think you can take our film, just try!!"

The assistant furiously snapped pictures of Okuzaki and us. He also recorded Okuzaki's voice on tape.

"I'm the man who shot pachinko balls at the emperor!!"

I could tell that Okuzaki was putting on this outrageous act instead of being obedient in order to try and get the situation under *his* control.

The first officer in command arrived. He scowled at Okuzaki. Our 11 o'clock departure time had passed.

"Then I'm in no hurry!!" Okuzaki screamed.

Iskandar, red with anger, said, "The flight's now scheduled to leave at 2 o'clock. Please, get out of here."

"What! The powers that be are so desperate to get rid of me that they delayed the airplane? Are you trying to make me leave?!" Okuzaki yelled.

I learned this later, but our departing flight had automatically been delayed because the arriving flight had simply been late. With the stack of film between them, Okuzaki, the soldiers of the general headquarters, and the officer from the bureau of information kept the threats flying. I just felt dejected. There was nothing I could do. I prayed that the situation would turn in our favor.

Okuzaki continued with his "reasoning," saying, "This film has nothing in it that could hurt Indonesia. It just shows me memorializing fellow soldiers and giving money, as an expression of my gratitude, to people who took care of me in 1944. Are you trying to take away a film about *me*? You're the ones who are going to disgrace yourselves!" But all this was in Japanese, so there was no way they could understand what he was saying. Finally, the first officer in command said,

"We're confiscating the film. Sign the paper!"

"No way! Never!!" Okuzaki yelled. As if to cut the argument off right there, they gathered up the film and quickly took it away.

(I'm going to summarize my notes—and there are many more of them—from here on out.)

Yasuoka had been called into another room and told me in a whisper that they would probably send the film to Jakarta, so it would be better for us to negotiate through the Japanese Consulate. Okuzaki, who had stormed out of the general headquarters, thought it was better to get a "receipt" for the film, so Iskandar went back to pick it up. When we returned to the hotel, the employees looked astounded. Okuzaki called the Consulate and said in a fury, "You bastards do something about it!" But they seemed to have given up on him. He showed no sign of backing down, saying that he was going to to tear up his passport in front of the Japanese Embassy in Jakarta.

"Please film it. We have to give them *some* trouble, after all." Iskandar, the local interpreter, had devotedly put up with all of Okuzaki's unreasonable demands. After what had happened, he couldn't stand it any longer. He gave back the U.S. dollars that Okuzaki had used to pay him for his services and disappeared, announcing, "I'm through with this."

We flew to Jakarta the following day. We hurried to the Japanese Consulate. Okuzaki, fully ready to fight, was planning to paint the Chinese character for "Small" over the "Big" that appeared on the plaque at the Consulate's entrance. But the Consul General Kakinuma who met us was such a mild-mannered man. He listened calmly to Okuzaki's story for over an hour.

"I understand. I understand the work you've done and how you feel," he said. He would happily do everything he could. But Indonesia was a country where everything took time, so it was best that we go back to Japan and wait. Without destroying his passport or painting over the plaque, Okuzaki left in a good mood.

AFTER OUR RETURN

On the plane back to Narita, while ordering another free whiskey, Okuzaki, face flushed and spirits high, said to me:

"I've never had this kind of drink before. It's delicious." He then asked, "Hara, do you think they'll return the film? I'm sure they will."

"I want them to," I said meekly.

We arrived at Narita airport. We got in line with the other passengers to go through immigration. Before long, it was Okuzaki's turn. When he approached the immigration officer, he thrust his passport in front of the officer and crumpled it up. I was surprised. I tensely waited to see what the officer would do. Was it going to turn

KEPOLISIAN REPUBLIK INDONESIA
KOMANDO DAERAH KEPOLISIAN XVII
I R I A N - J A Y A

T A N D A - T E R I M A

No. Pol. : TT/001/III/1983.

TELAH MENERIMA PENYERAHAN SECARA SUKARELA DARI :

1. N A M A : KENZO OKUSAKI.
2. PEKERJAAN : TOURIS.
3. WARGANEGARA : JEPANG.
4. PASPOR : NO. E 4038928. SKJ MABAK NOPOL: SKJ-1202/II/1983/DIPP TGL. 25/2-1983.

SEBANYAK 52 ROLL FILM 16 MM DAN 5 ROLL SLIDE FILM HASIL PENGAMBILAN DI LOKASI DEMTA DAN ARSO DARI TANGGAL 18 MARET 1983 TANPA IJIN DARI MENTERI PENERANGAN RI.

Jayapura, 30 Maret 1983.

YANG MENYERAHKAN,

KENZO OKUSAKI

YANG MENERIMA,
KEPALA SEKSI INTELPAM DAK XVII / IRJA

S. SAUMAR
MAYOR.POL.NRP.38110013

MENGETAHUI / MENYAKSIKAN,

1. AS. INTELPAM KASDAK XVII/IRJA

KEPOLISIAN R.I.
STAF
KOMANDO DAERAH KEPOLISIAN XVII

. MADONZA
KOL.POL.NRP.31010011

2. A.N. KAKANWIL DEPPEN PROP. IRJA
KABID PERS,

F. MABOSENDIPU
NIP. 050004343.

The receipt for the confiscated film.

into a riot?

The officer just stared at Okuzaki. Okuzaki then spit four, five times into his passport and, with a defiant look, gave it to the officer. What was he going to do? The puzzled-looking officer took the passport, turned through the pages without touching the spit, stamped it, and handed it back.

The sun had already set. I was loading my bags onto the shuttle bus. Okuzaki looked around restlessly. I asked what was wrong.

"Strange," he said. "I thought the police would be here." Hearing this, I looked around, but no cops or cop cars seemed to have turned up.

Somewhat annoyed, and thinking to myself that there was no way the police would be there, I replied, "They didn't know when our flight was going to arrive."

Still, Okuzaki persisted. "No, the Japanese police are brilliant. I'm sure they've been in contact with the airlines the whole time to find out when I was going to return." He continued to stare into the darkness.

I sat next to Okuzaki at the back of the bus. Even after we had left Narita, he continued staring out the back window.

"Hara, I think that's it. The police car."

Wearily, I turned my body around and stared out the window into the night. In the distance, I could see headlights. But there were several cars around, and it was so far off that I had no way of knowing whether it was a police car or not. I thought it was inconceivable that a police car would be tailing us. I was pretty exhausted. My responses to Okuzaki had grown half hearted. I said,

"You really think so?" in a tone that was, inadvertently, openly contemptuous. Okuzaki looked pissed, but he himself wasn't completely sure yet.

"Wait. Nope. No mistake. That's a cop car," he said as he got up on the seat and stared into the darkness, his body pressed up against the window. I had no choice. Keeping my skepticism to myself, I also looked back. Hmmm...

Once you paid attention to it, the car was indeed driving at an unchanging distance from our limousine bus. All the other cars would speed up and pass us. Just one car, just that one car was moving at a steady speed. I still couldn't believe it. Perhaps it was just taking it easy, following the limousine bus at a leisurely pace. Now the gap between the car and the bus was beginning to close. Okuzaki fixed his gaze on it. I, too, gazed at the car. Slowly, it crept up on us. Eventually, it came close enough for me to see its shape. But it showed no sign of passing us. It drove up in the same lane, right behind the bus. The gap between the two closed. Okuzaki was still staring. Drawn by his intensity, I also leaned forward.

It came so close that I could discern the faces of the people inside. At that moment, a man in the passenger's seat turned toward us and gave a short, quick bow of his head.

"Ahhhhhh," I screamed an inarticulate scream in my mind. I thought I'd seen him smile at us. The next moment, the car sped up and, in a flash, passed the bus. The moment it was gone, Okuzaki started screaming at me in a fury:

"Hara, you really are good for nothing!!"

I cowered, but the situation was irreparable. While feeling victorious because his judgment had been proven correct, he was also furious at the contemptuous tone I had taken a while earlier, which had hurt his pride considerably. I didn't even try to defend myself.

"I'm always honing my instincts like this. If I didn't, I wouldn't be able to do my important humanitarian work. You speak to me as though you think we're equals, and your attitude proves it, but if you ask me, it's ten years too soon!"

Okuzaki's face was less that a foot from mine, his recessed eyes glaring at me. I shrank back further and further. The passengers in front of us turned to see what was going on. Embarrassment and the distress caused by my blunder made my blood run backwards. Okuzaki's anger grew.

"Hara. Why, why don't you call me 'sensei'? Hara. No one else has observed my judgment and actions as closely as you. For that reason, I thought you'd be the first to call me 'sensei,' but you've never once done so. Even the detectives called me 'sensei.' Hara, you are less than a cop. If you respect me from the bottom of your heart, you should be able to call me 'sensei.'"

I knew the time would come when he would pressure me into calling him "sensei." "The time's now come," I thought.

I simply muttered meekly to myself, "How can I respect you when call me an 'idiot' and a 'good-for-nothing' with all these people watching?"

The following day, Okuzaki went to the Ministry of Foreign Affairs and the Indonesian Consulate and asked them to make an effort to get the film back. He then returned to Kobe. As I was seeing him off at Tokyo Station, I thought, "I don't want to see him again for a while."

Some time later, I received a phone call from Okuzaki. He said he was going to Eastern New Guinea, which is now Papua New Guinea. Entering Papua New Guinea would be easy. He was planning to enter the country, go near the Western New Guinea border, and charter a helicopter there. He was then going to scatter rice over the jungle from the sky. He said he wanted me to go with him to film the event.

During our earlier trip to New Guinea, he had expressed his desire to scatter rice from the sky to console the spirits of his former comrades who had starved to death. Now he wanted to accomplish what he hadn't been able to before by entering Eastern New Guinea, since Western New Guinea had been no good. I could only feel a renewed sense of awe at his incredible persistence.

I was tempted to shoot the jungle of New Guinea from the sky. I was impressed that Okuzaki knew how cinematic the act of scattering rice from the sky would be. I wanted to go with him. But my memory of the feverish humiliation I had been subjected to on the limousine bus earlier came back to me. The bitterness of that moment made me refuse his proposal. Scattering rice from the sky would surely have made a great shot, but that's all it would be. We had made our trip to Western New Guinea, which had been full of thrills and crises, and which we'd been told would be 200 percent impossible. Safe Eastern New Guinea would be no fun. If we didn't get our film of Western New Guinea back, then this scene would be all the more useless. After thinking it over, I wasn't completely without second thoughts, but I said no.

A while later, I received another phone call from Okuzaki.

"I went to Eastern New Guinea. As planned, I chartered a Cessna near the border and scattered rice over the jungle to console, in my own way, the spirits of the dead soldiers. I do what I have to do, even if you don't film me. I can leave a record of my deeds in writing. So don't underestimate me!!"

He slammed the receiver down.

Kobayashi and I did everything we could to get back the film that had been confiscated in Indonesia.

We insisted that we wouldn't use it for political propaganda, that it was a record of a memorial for those who had died on the New Guinea front. We sought to make connections with politicians who were influential vis-a-vis Indonesia. Whatever our causes may have been, in reality, it was a question of money. We had no idea how much it would cost. At first, we were told that it would cost about half a million yen. Then it went up to a million, then three million, then jumped up to five million. It was a huge sum for us. Kobayashi, the producer, was at her wit's end.

We chose not to tell Okuzaki about what we were doing. We knew Okuzaki was forcefully trying to get the film back by making threatening phone calls and sending threatening letters to the Indonesian Embassy and the Consulate in Kobe.

Half a year had passed since our return from New Guinea.

I happened to be working on a TV job on that fatal day. I was having lunch on location. The voice of the announcer on the TV in the restaurant leapt out at me. "The suspect who shot at the son of the company commander and ran off is Okuzaki Kenzō..."

He did it!! He really did it!! I recalled Okuzaki's face when he had urged me to shoot the scene of him killing Koshimizu. But the announcer had said that the son had been shot. Why not company commander Koshimizu? Why his son?!

The suspect had fled, the announcer went on to say. After committing a crime, Okuzaki had always admitted to it, accepting responsibility and turning himself in, so I wondered why he had fled this time? I ran out to the street and grabbed a pay phone.

"I know, I'm shocked. I received a call from the police department asking if we knew where he was. I told them we didn't. I really don't know, so I told him I didn't." Kobayashi sounded worried.

Okuzaki had set out to shoot Koshimizu. He wasn't home, so Okuzaki had shot Koshimizu's son when the son had answered the door. I was supposed to have been accustomed to Okuzaki's "extraordinary daring," but I was again shocked when I saw the headline that read, "His Son Was Good Enough." But an even bigger shock awaited me.

Two days later, there was news of Okuzaki's arrest. When he revealed the reason for his two-day disappearance, my whole world literally darkened.

Commander Koshimizu hadn't been Okuzaki's only target. Okuzaki had also planned to shoot a certain Diet member of the Tanaka faction of the Liberal Democratic Party who had been a party to the Nanking Massacre and who was living in Shikoku—and, lo and behold, he had also planned to shoot a clerk at the Indonesian Consulate in Kobe! His reason for targeting the consulate was that they wouldn't return the film that had been confiscated in New Guinea!! What did he do?!?

In the end, he didn't harm anyone at the consulate, but now that his "intent to kill" had been reported, there was no way Indonesia would relinquish the film! I felt as though I had been thrown into the depths of despair. Now there was no way the film would come back to me! After we had managed to achieve the goal of "going to New Guinea"! Because I didn't have this crucial final scene, I couldn't finish the film. I'd have to abandon the film! Like a bubble that had burst, everything disappeared!!

After that incident, my heart would race any time I thought of Okuzaki. The first stage of his public trial began at the Hiroshima district court. Kobayashi made the trip down to Hiroshima a number of times. Whenever she went, I'd get curious and ask her how it was going. When I heard her report, my heart would begin to race. I was suffering from "Okuzaki syndrome." Filming had ended. I'd left all of the unexposed film in a corner of my room to collect dust with everything else that was piled there.

About two years passed before I finally felt that I had no choice but to edit the film with the footage I had. My obsession with getting back the reels from Indonesia hadn't cooled with time, but I'd forced myself to get rid of it. Bit by bit, I began to recover from "Okuzaki syndrome."

I asked the editor Nabeshima Jun if he would help me edit the film.

Throughout the editing process, I was constantly debating with myself.

I might have filmed the murder scene. Why didn't I?

I'd answer: because I hated Okuzaki Kenzō.

He had verbally abused me; he had humiliated me. I couldn't possibly bring myself to accompany him on his *greatest scene of pandemonium*.

I continued to ask myself: but what if you had *liked* Okuzaki Kenzō? Would you have filmed him then? I'd answer: If I had liked him? Maybe then I would have filmed the murder...

That part of myself—the part of me that thought I might film a murder—was creepy. It scared me.

At such times, I recalled something Kobayashi had said. She'd mentioned once that Okuzaki was possessed. If Okuzaki Kenzō had been possessed by something and driven to a crime, perhaps I, obsessed as I was with the idea that I could have filmed a "murder scene," was possessed as well? But by what?

By cinema. For cinema... That absolute thing called cinema... Was cinema my god!?

We received a letter from Okuzaki while he was in the Hiroshima Detention Center. "I'm going to wave a hand-held flag from the yard of the prison, and I'd like you to film it from a nearby building," he wrote.

I was at once dumbfounded and impressed. I couldn't help but smile a bitter smile. He went on to say that if I agreed, he would consult with his lawyer so that no one would find out about it... that he would be the only one in the world to send signals by waving a flag from inside a prison.

I think he's absolutely right. In this whole world, Okuzaki Kenzō is the only director who never tires of figuring out how to best present Okuzaki Kenzō.

If I say so, will you say that it's not you who is directing, but God? I couldn't possibly come up with such ideas. I grudgingly surrender to you.

I thought that his proposition would indeed make a great shot. I thought I could use it as the final scene in the film. But I couldn't bring myself to do it. The filming had long since ended.

Okuzaki's wife, Shimizu, who had completely devoted herself to helping us create "Okuzaki's film," passed away just before we finished. She had been eagerly anticipating its completion. By the time we struck the first release print, five years had passed since we'd met Okuzaki.

In February 1987, Kobayashi and I went to the Hiroshima Detention Center. I hadn't seen Okuzaki since New Guinea. About three years had passed. His hair had turned completely white. When

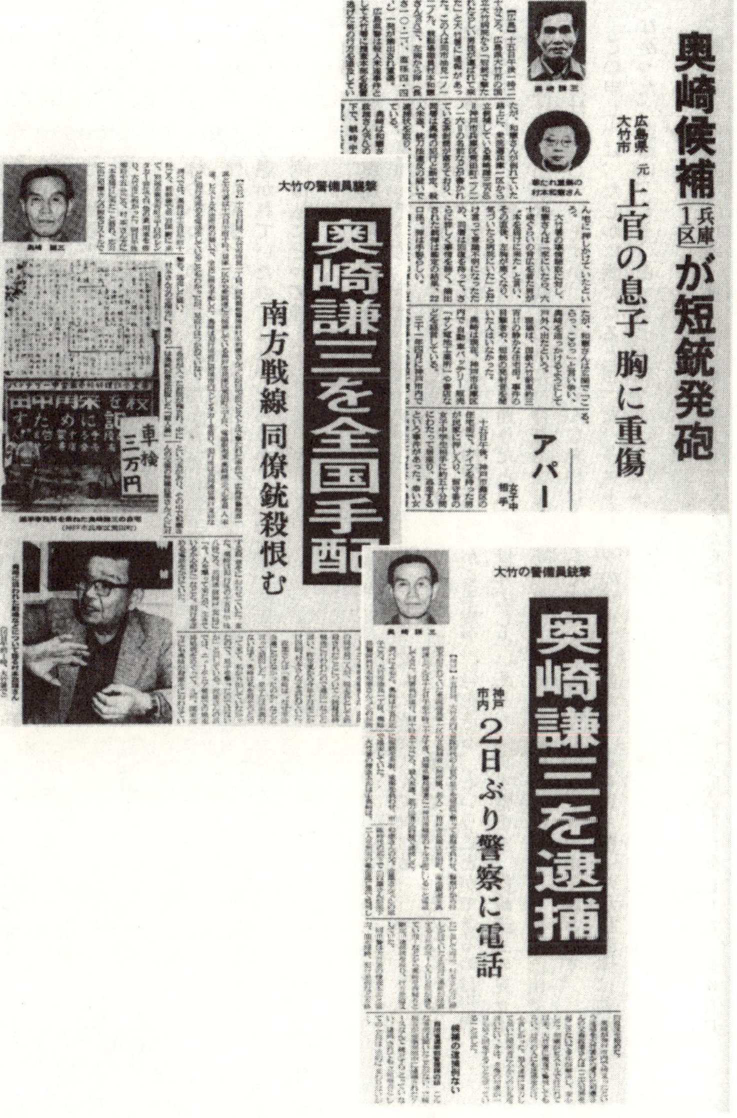

奥崎候補（兵庫1区）が短銃発砲

広島県大竹市 元上官の息子 胸に重傷

大竹の警備員銃撃

奥崎謙三を全国手配

南方戦線 同僚銃殺恨む

大竹の警備員銃撃

奥崎謙三を逮捕

神戸市内 2日ぶり警察に電話

Newspaper accounts of Okuzaki's "greatest scene of pandemonium."

he spoke, his gums bled. He had grown wan, but he spoke, as if in a single breath, throughout our entire 30-minute visit. His energy hadn't diminished. At a pause in his flowing speech, which had poured out of him like a flood, I saw that smile of Okuzaki's, the one that I think resembles Noro Keisuke's. Something welled up in my heart—something overwhelming and nostalgic.

As we were leaving, Okuzaki said to me, "I'm going to get out of here in good health, and I would love it if the two of you filmed the scene of my release."[7]

7 After 12 years in prison, Okuzaki Kenzō was released. He died in 2005.

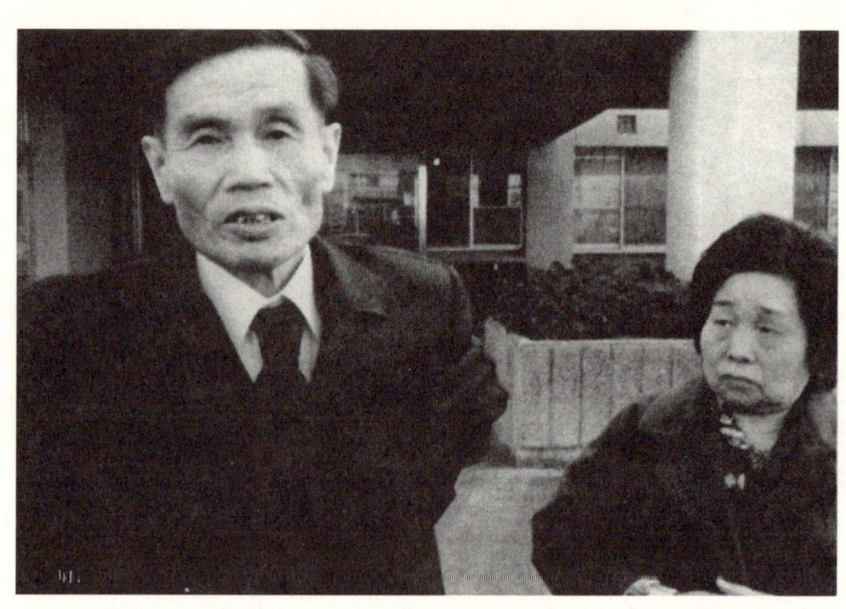

In Place of an Afterword
Kobe's Goddess, Okuzaki Shizumi
By Kobayashi Sachiko

> *Please show the wedding film to my dying wife to make her happy. If possible, please film my wife's pitiful state. Please show the people at the hospital as well. My wife will feel proud and find the courage to fight the disease. Miracles will happen. (Letter from Mr. Okuzaki dated September 11, 1986)*

The film we had begun editing in the summer of 1985 was becoming a four-hour mess of an edit. Every time we received a call from Okuzaki's wife in Kobe, we answered, "We're editing right now. Please wait just a little longer." A year and a half went by like that. The words, "*my dying wife*" jumped out at me with frightening force. I knew that Okuzaki's wife had been receiving treatment for cirrhosis, and that she was awaiting surgery, but I had no idea her ailment was so grave. Forcing myself to act calm, I phoned the hospital. "Please wait a little while longer, ma'am. We really are close this time." I repeated words that were part prayer, part mantra as I listened to the phone ring. The hospital director sounded surprisingly cheery as he explained Mrs. Okuzaki's condition. She had been admitted on September 3rd and had required a blood transfusion for the combination of acute kidney failure and urinary failure, but the surgery on the 8th had gone well. He reported that she should be discharged in a month if things continued the way they were going. I couldn't help but let out a sigh of relief. "Thank goodness!! I'm going to make sure I make some time at the end of the month to go see her." Once I made up my mind, I finally settled down.

"Greetings, I tried to send a telegram but couldn't because I ran out of my cash allowance. I hate to impose, but please expedite its delivery." Mr. Okuzaki was asking acquaintances to lend him money.

"I am almost to the point where I can no longer expedite letters to my wife (because I do not have money or stamps). I would like to expedite delivery of as many letters as I can in order to write her while she is still alive."

Okuzaki knew we were all broke, and he was always very considerate not to bother us with matters involving money. This fact only exaggerated the letter's sense of urgency. Securing money became more of a priority than the film. At that point, I did not have an ounce of doubt with regard to Mrs. Okuzaki's recovery.

However, before I was able to find the means to answer Mr. Okuzaki's plea for help, I received a real telegram six days later.

My wife, Shizumi, has died. I sincerely appreciate all the support you provided while she was alive. – Okuzaki Kenzō

The first time Hara and I visited Mr. Okuzaki's house, Mrs. Okuzaki had waited for us outside. I remember the warmth I felt when I saw her standing there. I believe she was full of natural and unpretentious kindness. After that, we shared a number of experiences, and that first impression was never betrayed.

After he was placed in the Hiroshima Detention Center, Mr. Okuzaki wrote to his wife almost daily. The small catchphrase he would add at the end of each letter was always so unique. For example:

> February 21: I am trailblazing the path of the unpatriotic. I may lose, but I, Kenzō, remain a simple soldier in the emperor's army. To Shizumi, who is still proud of her husband with four priors.
>
> March 31: From Kenzō, a lousy actor in the play called life. To Shizumi, behind the scenes in the play called life.
>
> April 25: From Kenzō, a close associate of God's with time on his side. To Shizumi, the wife of the true Messiah.
>
> May 14: From Kenzō, servant and tool of the emperor's army. To the easily beguiled Shizumi.

> June 16: From the true Messiah, Kenzō. To Shizumi, the wife of the true Messiah.
>
> June 18: From the true messenger boy, Kenzō. To the true messenger girl, Shizumi.
>
> June 23: From heaven's loyal subject, Kenzō. To the candidate for heaven's loyal subject, Shizumi.

The one that particularly struck me was,"*From Kenzō who loves himself more than anybody else. To Kobe's Goddess and my wife, Shizumi.*" His wife was so bashful, but clearly flattered.

Each page of Okuzaki's letters was densely covered with his writing. Twenty, thirty pages were the norm. A hundred and twenty-five, two-hundred and sixty, three-hundred and twenty pages would be delivered in bulk. His wife would then copy each page and mail them to the dozen or so people he wished to communicate with, but the labor involved was intensive. The tips of her fingers were always irritated from handling leaking batteries, so copying hundreds of pages with those fingers was no easy task. Mr. Okuzaki would constantly give pep talks to his wife, while being primarily concerned with her health.

> *Please live with your health as your first, second and third priority. Close shop early. I'm fine as long as you're healthy. Do not sacrifice your health for money. I would rather you be healthy in Kobe than come to Hiroshima sick.*

Every month, there was a court proceeding at the Hiroshima District Court. I would, on occasion, ask to spend the night at Mrs. Okuzaki's on my way home. Perhaps it was the comfort of being in another woman's company, but on those nights, we would eagerly talk until dawn with our pillows inched close together. Her childhood growing up on Kurahashi Island; the siblings she was close to; how she met Okuzaki; memories of the silent and kind Mr. Okuzaki; and the numerous checkered incidents up until now... No matter what, not once did I hear her say anything accusatory about Okuzaki. In fact, it seemed that she was trying to maintain unwavering faith in him. As I dozed off, she would softly repeat ever so matter-of-factly—"I think that one day, the world will be as he says. I think in a hundred or two hundred years, the world will realize that he was right."

From around the end of 1985, she increasingly began to insist that she was in poor health, and it was becoming more difficult for her to make the trip to Hiroshima for the court proceedings.

> *Make sure you keep warm, get plenty of nutrition, and take care of yourself in all other aspects.*
>
> *Under no circumstances should you come to the nineteenth court proceeding on December 16th. Please direct your efforts so you can spend the New Year at home. There will be many great things in our future if you live a long life. That is what we've worked for. I pray for your safety and happiness.*

Mrs. Okuzaki would not visit Hiroshima again after receiving this letter.

On the day of Mrs. Okuzaki's funeral, Okuzaki's request to attend the ceremony was denied. The autumn wind blew coldly that day. The expression on Mrs. Okuzaki's face as she lay in a bed of white chrysanthemums was surprisingly gentle and peaceful. I could not help but think of Mr. Okuzaki's words, "Kobe's Goddess, my wife Shizumi."

I don't doubt that Mrs. Okuzaki steadfastly believed that we would finish the film. If we had completed the film just three months, no two months earlier, she may have been able to see it... However, the final work we put into the film was the addition of a note to a still shot of her smiling face that read, "Okuzaki Shizumi (68), deceased."

I cannot help but think that scenes that were only a few minutes long in *The Emperor's Naked Army Marches On* were built on a culmination of decades worth of each character's life.

I am full of appreciation and respect for each of them.[1]

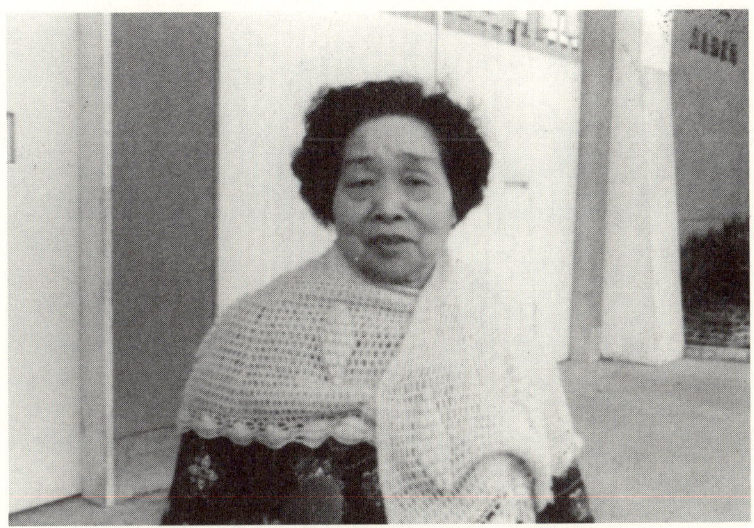

Okuzaki Shizumi

1 I would like to thank Yazaki Yasuhisa from *Hanashi no Tokushu* who took on the task of producing the Japanese edition of this book, and Nakajima Nobuo from the editing department, who patiently dealt with the laborious process of completing this manuscript.

HARA KAZUO
PERSONAL CHRONOLOGY

1945: June 8. Born illegitimately to Suetomi Asa in Yamaguchi City. His mother marries a miner, and he spends his childhood in the mine at Nishiokinoyama in Nagato-Nagasawa in Ube.

1952: Age 7. April. Enters Ube City Hara Elementary School

1956: Age 11. Moves to Yamaguchi City. Transfers to Yamaguchi City Ōdono Elementary School.

1958: Age 13. Graduates from Yamaguchi City Ōdono Elementary School. Enters Yamaguchi City Ōdono Middle School in April.

1961: Age 16. March. Graduates from Yamaguchi City Ōdono Middle School. Enters Yamaguchi Prefectural High School part-time in April.

1964: Age 19. April. Works part-time for the Yamaguchi branch of the *Asahi Shimbun* (2 years).

1965: Age 20. March. Graduates from Yamaguchi Prefectural High School.

1966: Age 21. April. Moves to Tokyo. Enters Tokyo General School of Photography, but drops out after 6 months. Meets severely handicapped children. Is drawn to the world of the disabled.

1967–1968: Age 23. Works as hired assistant at the Tokyo Kōmyō School for Handicapped Children (1 year, 2 months). Begins living with and marries Takeda Miyuki.

1969: Age 24. July 15–20. Has a solo exhibition, "Don't Mock Them," at the Ginza Nikon Salon. Meets Kobayashi Sachiko.

1970: Age 25. June 19. Takeda Miyuki appears on Tahara Sōichirō's television show, "Fuji Keiko Sings Scenes of June," on Tokyo Channel 12. February 13. Their son Rei is born.

1971: Age 26. Winter. Hara, Miyuki, and Rei appear as a family on Tahara Sōichirō's television show, "Japanese Brides," on Tokyo Channel 12. June. Begins filming *Goodbye CP*.

1972: Age 27. February. Finishes *Goodbye CP*. Establishes Shissō Productions with Kobayashi Sachiko. March. Begins filming *Extreme Private Eros: Love Song 1974*.

1973: Age 28. Divorces Takeda Miyuki. May 14. First daughter with Kobayashi Sachiko, Kazami, is born. Marries Kobayashi Sachiko.

1974: Age 29. March. Finishes *Extreme Private Eros: Love Song 1974*.

1975: Age 30. *Extreme Private Eros Love Song 1974* wins the Grand Prix prize at the Thonon-les-Bains International Independent Film Festival. Directs *History Starts Here "Women now..."* for Tokyo Broadcasting Station. August 20. Eldest son Tōno is born.

1980: Age 35. Works as an assistant director on Urayama Kiriro's film, *Children of the Sun*.

1981: Age 36. December. Meets Okuzaki Kenzō for the first time.

1982: Age 37. Starts filming *The Emperor's Naked Army Marches On*.

1983: Age 38. Goes to New Guinea with Okuzaki Kenzō to film on location.

1986: Age 41. Winter. Works as co-director on Kumai Kei's *The Sea and Poison*.

1987: Age 42. January. Finishes *The Emperor's Naked Army Marches On*. February, wins the Japanese Film Directors' Guild, New Director Award. March, invited to screen the film at the Berlin International Film Festival. Wins the Caligari Prize at the Berlin International Film Festival. August 15. Begins screening the film at Shibuya Eurospace. December. Wins the Hochi Film Award for Excellence in Directing.

1988: Age 43. January. Wins the Mainichi Eiga Director Award and the Blue Ribbon Award for best director. Wins Grand Prize at Cinema du Réel (Paris International Documentary Film Festival).

1989: Age 44. Winter. Works as co-director on Kumai Kei's *Death of a Tea Master*. March. Begins filming *A Dedicated Life*.

1990: Age 45. Spring. Works as co-director on Kumai Kei's *Mt. Aso's Passions*.

1991: Age 46. April–July. Goes to New York on an Asian Cultural Council Fellowship. December. Receives the Agency for Cultural Affairs Award for Artists to Train Overseas to study in New York (one year).

1992: Age 47. Directs *Yellow Cab* for the Tokyo Broadcasting Station.

1994: Age 49. April. Finishes *A Dedicated Life*. Autumn. works as co-director on Kumai Kei's *Deep River*. September 23, begins screening *A Dedicated Life* at Shibuya Eurospace. December. Wins the Hochi Film Award for Excellence in Directing.

1995: Age 50. January. Wins the 1994 Mainichi Eiga Director Award. Wins First Place for 1994 Kinema Junpō. Best Ten Japanese Directors Award.

1998: Age 53. Directs television documentary entitled *The Portrait of Urayama Kiriro, Film Director*. Visiting professor at Waseda University.

2000. Age 55. Directs video documentary entitled *Learning and Passion: Takamure Itsue*.

2004: Age 59. Directs first narrative feature film, *The Many Faces of Chika*.

2006: Age 61. Professor at the Osaka University of the Arts.